Food Is Love

Food Is Love

Food Advertising and Gender Roles in Modern America

KATHERINE J. PARKIN

PENN

University of Pennsylvania Press

Philadelphia

10   9   8   7   6   5   4   3   2   1

Published by
University of Pennsylvania Press
Philadelphia, Pennsylvania 19104-4122

Library of Congress Cataloging-in-Publication Data

Parkin, Katherine J.
    Food is love : food advertising and gender roles in modern America / Katherine J.
Parkin.
        p.   cm.
    ISBN-13: 978-0-8122-3929-4 (alk. paper)
    ISBN-10: 0-8122-3929-6
    Includes bibliographical references and index.
    1. Sex role in advertising—United States—History.   2. Advertising—Food—United
States—History.   3. Women consumers—United States—History.   4. Women in
advertising—United States—History.   5. Men in advertising—United States—History.
I. Title.
HF5827.85.P37   2006
659.19'66400973—dc22   2006042227

For Chris

Contents

Introduction

My great-grandmother, Mary Morris, was born in 1906 and stopped school in the third grade, working first in domestic service, then at Jenkins's glass factory, and finally retiring as head of Kroger's dairy department. Living until 1997, she witnessed many remarkable changes in American society. Certainly one of the most notable transformations took place in her kitchen and in kitchens across the country. Convenience foods sped up the cooking that had previously taken long, labor-intensive hours. Yet even as the cooking got easier, she, and not her husband, was responsible for it. This was true even though all of the other housework responsibilities fell to her and she worked outside the home for wages. However, she did not always *make* the food and often used the supermarket and the bakery to supply her feasts. Mary wanted to show her love with food, but she demonstrated her love by procuring and preparing food, not necessarily making it at home from scratch. Indeed, as she was able, Mary Morris bought more and made less, reflecting a growing trend, as more Americans bought prepared foods for their convenience.

Still, throughout the twentieth century, the ideology that identified women as homemakers and men as breadwinners held strong, even as a different reality strained the ideal. Mary Morris's role was not unique; cultures around the world and across time have bound women, food, and love together. American society and advertising in particular have envisioned the preparation and consumption of food in distinctly gendered terms. While everyone eats food, women have had sole responsibility for its purchase and preparation. By commodifying these attitudes and beliefs, women's magazines and food advertisers have promoted the belief that food preparation is a gender-specific activity and that women should shop and cook for others in order to express their love.

Many scholars have considered the role of advertising in American society, but few have considered the centrality of food advertising in shaping twentieth-century gender roles. Big-ticket items like automobiles and appliances have attracted many analysts of advertising, while others have examined what seemed to be more explicitly gendered ads for beauty products and cleaning supplies.[1] Food ads offer a unique opportunity to explore the cultural discourse about American gender roles because of the centrality of food to the human experience. Unlike most other advertised products, food at its core is not a luxury. While advertisers peddled items that some might have wanted, food was something that people needed. This study focuses on the broad category of food, generally ignoring non-essential items like beverages (coffee, liquor) and candy (gum, chocolate). People of all classes have always had to buy food, as opposed to items more easily borrowed, put off, or done without. Moreover, people consumed food on a daily basis, usually several times a day.

When national advertising began in earnest at the turn of the century, food manufacturers quickly dominated in spending. What food lacked in ticket price, it compensated for in tremendous sales volume. While food advertising accounted for only one percent of the fledgling advertising agency N. W. Ayer's revenues in 1877, 24 years later the nation's largest advertising firm took in "15 percent of the revenues from food advertising, the largest of any category." In 1920, the food industry's outlay of well over $14 million for advertising far outstripped its closest rival, toilet goods, which spent just over nine million dollars. In the *Ladies' Home Journal,* food ads in the early 1920s comprised about 20 percent of total ad revenues. While spending in other categories grew over the century, particularly health and beauty products; cigarettes; liquor; and automobiles, food companies remained into the next century one of the preeminent advertising categories in the country. Indeed, many early food-advertising leaders, such as Campbell's soup, Kellogg's, Aunt Jemima, and Quaker Oats, continued to retain a strong presence. A 1993 assessment of the industry found that food advertisers spent about $7.6 billion in the mass media in 1990, with spending rising 13 percent between 1980 and 1990 and 4.5 cents of every food dollar poured back into advertising.[2]

Food advertisers had reason to believe that their investment might pay off. Historian Stanley Lebergott found that at the outset of the century, "Americans typically spent more on food than citizens of almost any other nation." While some thought that it would be impossible to maintain such consumption patterns, American spending on food continued to grow. As one advertising firm proclaimed in 1958, "millions of families now can afford to place quality, style and convenience ahead of price." The increase appears to have stemmed primarily from changes in foods purchased, including more food bought and eaten away from home, and greater reliance on more expensive items, such as meat and bakery products.[3]

During the second half of the century, consumers increasingly spent food dollars on meals outside the home. Periodic studies and articles called attention to the renewal of the "family meal," but their presence belied the growing tenuousness of home cooked meals, particularly those made from scratch.[4] Not only were growing numbers of women working outside the home, but most Americans led lives not conducive to regular family meal times. Food manufacturers' success in creating consumer demand for fast meal preparation eventually became their undoing when Americans started to purchase "no preparation" meals outside the home.[5]

The development of new machinery in the late nineteenth and early twentieth centuries changed the food preparation process. With the subsequent introduction and increased availability of new foods and products, conceptions of cooking changed. The most significant change in American eating habits was the widespread adoption of canned goods. Between 1909 and 1929, spending on canned goods consumption rose nearly six times, from $162 million to $930 million.[6] Over the course of the century, these products, with advertisers' help, contributed to a more ambiguous definition of cooking. Historian Maureen Greenwald, drawing on a 1991 survey, found that, "When asked whether certain tasks were considered 'cooking,' most respondents placed scrambling eggs, preparing a salad, boiling pasta and microwaving a vegetable in that category." She also found that most of the respondents felt "cooking from scratch could include prepared ingredients. In answer to the question, can heating something be considered cooking dinner, forty-nine percent of the respondents said yes and another twenty-two percent said maybe."[7] While cooking used to involve multiple procedures and a variety of utensils and ingredients, according to Greenwald, the definition of cooking expanded to include the assembly of prepared elements.

Some observers resisted this new conceptualization of cooking and used terminology like "traditionalist or contemporary" as they assessed the trends. For example, in a 1998 study, the Canned Food Alliance asked female respondents to characterize themselves as "Suzy Homemakers" or "Prepared Food Paulas." A slight majority of respondents between ages 25 and 39 claimed they "still make almost every evening meal at home, from scratch," although forcing women to consider and verbalize whether or not they were homemakers undoubtedly skewed the results. When asked to "define 'homemade,' consumer opinions varied, but the majority (68 percent) believed that homemade still means 'made at home from scratch.' About a quarter defined homemade as 'anything made at home,' including prepared, frozen or microwavable foods."[8]

Food advertisers helped blur the line defining homemade cooking. Throughout the century, copywriters created ads assuring women that interacting with products sufficed as cooking, even if the action was as simple as removing it from a box, heating it, or adding water. A 1935 ad proclaimed that women were "Soup Wise" if they bought Campbell's vegetable soup instead of making vegetable soup from scratch. The ad campaign dismissed the preparation process, asking, "Why should she spend precious hours washing, cleaning, paring vegetables . . . Today's best recipe for vegetable soup is simply—open a can of Campbell's—add an equal quantity of water—simmer and serve." Fifteen years later, an ad for "Brown 'n' Serve" rolls told readers, "Lady, these 'hot-from-*your*-oven' rolls are made by your Baker" and assured women that they could "make" the rolls by browning them. This line of reasoning reached its apogee with the headline for a 1971 Chef Boy-ar-Dee ad encouraging consumers, "Cook a perfect main dish . . . complete with meat . . . without really cooking at all." The body of the ad reminded women, "If you had to make one yourself, it might take hours. But with these dinners, everything you need comes right out of a box."[9]

Advertisers used language and imagery to persuade women that the foods they served were "home made" and that they were still responsible for providing for their families. A 1937 Campbell's vegetable soup ad assured readers, "Skillful experts have learned how to bring out that real home-made flavor everyone loves. . . ." Nor had much changed at the end of the century. In 1996, the word "home" transformed Betty Crocker's new cereals, Dutch Apple and Cinnamon Streusel, from just another new cereal to one with "home-baked taste." A 1998 ad in *People* magazine announced, "Nothing brings the family together like a home-cooked meal." As the mother removed a Stouffer's "Family Style Favorites" lasagna from the oven and the father put the plates on the table, their three children assumed stereotyped positions in the kitchen: the bespectacled young girl did her homework; the boy wore a backwards baseball cap and a football jersey, while clutching a basketball; and the teenage girl talked on the phone. Even for a product that required only heating a frozen food in the oven, the mother was the one to serve the main dish. The company motto assured consumers, "Nothing comes closer to home."[10]

To expand their market, food manufacturers created products that demanded less time and effort from women. Advertisers did not content themselves with touting ease of preparation; nor did they claim that anyone could make these convenience foods. Instead, advertisers embraced an umbrella of themes to insure that women remained responsible for purchasing and preparing food. Copywriters throughout the century embraced a fundamental theme: regardless of the actual work involved, women should serve food to demonstrate their love for their families. Countless ads reminded women that food conveyed their affections and fulfillment of duty to their families. In the hands of women, *food is love*.

Scholars have long debated the role of advertising, with some speculating that it reflected the culture and others charging that it shaped it.[11] Fundamentally, advertising seeks to shape. That it might at times have reflected reality was coincidental, but not its purpose. While it is tempting to use advertisements as a historical record of the past, they cannot serve as windows into the reality of people's lives. Instead, they can only reveal the ideologies and messages that advertisers hoped would sell products. Of course, underlying all advertisements is a desire to sell the displayed product. In the case of food advertising, however, advertisers used images and text not only to influence consumers' purchases, but also to sell gender roles. As historian Daniel Horowitz makes clear, there is ample evidence of the power of advertising. He notes, "The fact that the nation spent more on advertising than on primary and secondary education, the way advertising was transforming the mass media for its own purpose, its pressure to accentuate the lowest common denominator, and its avoidance of the controversial" are all factors putting advertising in a position of some significant influence.[12]

It could be argued that analyzing advertisers' actions and attitudes denies the agency of individuals or groups, who mitigated the industry's power to impose ideas upon society. It is certainly true that the ads were not simply one-way messages, but instead offered recipients the opportunity to interact with and interpret complex ideas. Arguing for dialogue between individuals and institutions is an important analytical approach.[13] While acknowledging the power of individuals, this study seeks to reveal what advertisers spent billions of dollars to communicate, as well as how and why they communicated it.

While advertisers may have been conscious only of trying to do their jobs and to sell products, collectively they played an important role in shaping American society. Advertisers themselves have even acknowledged that they needed to sell more than their products per se. David Ogilvy, president of a large advertising agency, was reported to have said, "There really isn't any significant difference between the various brands of whisky or the various brands of beer. They are all about the same. And so are the cake mixes and the detergents and the automobiles." If the products were basically the same, then, advertisers had to find another way to sell their products. According to Pierre Martineau, a researcher trying to understand consumer behavior, "what you are trying to do is create an illogical situation. You want the customer to fall in love with your product and have a profound brand loyalty when actually content may be very similar in hundreds of competing brands."[14]

One way that food advertisers sought to sell their products was to encourage women to identify with the role of homemaker. Arguing that magazines or advertisers conspired to assign women a particular role suggests a level of organization not evident in the historical record, but it is clear that the industry believed they stood to gain from promoting a traditional gender role paradigm. To reach women, food advertisers moved beyond trumpeting the merits of particular products and suggested that their products would help a woman fulfill her gender role. Despite the fact that over the course of the century, women gained greater social and legal parity in American society in the arenas of politics, education, marriage, and employment, food advertisers continually urged men and women to embrace static gender roles in the kitchen and dining room.[15]

Concurrent with gender role transformations, the country also experienced revolutionary changes in transportation, mass production, migration, immigration, and technology. These changes all contributed to dramatic new patterns in American food culture, including markedly different menus and eating patterns. One thing, however, remained constant: Food advertisers wanted to attract loyal female consumers who cared about pleasing others.[16]

This study examines how advertisers tried to convince women to plan, purchase, and prepare meals for their households. To advertisers, this responsibility may have seemed inevitable and appropriate, but many women did this work while also sharing with their partners the burden of working for wages outside the home. Why did advertisers want women, specifically, to buy food? How did they try to persuade Americans of the virtue of a food preparation paradigm in which women were solely responsible? This study grapples with these questions by exploring the ways in which advertisers consistently sought to convince women of their accountability in the kitchen.

No consumer good was as essential as food and even with small prices overall (as compared to cars and stoves, for example), the need for every person to eat meant tremendous sales. Yet, unlike most other industries that welcomed male and female consumers to increase profits, food advertisers limited themselves to just half of the population. Exploring why advertisers adopted this strategy is one of the goals of this study.

To assess food advertisers' motives and actions, this study considers a range of sources. Food industries consistently ranked as one of the largest advertisers in mass circulation women's magazines, which played a significant role in forming women's lives. The advertising savvy home economics leader Christine Frederick, writing in 1929, considered magazines to be "consumer colleges" that helped women learn about different products, techniques, and ideas.[17] Therefore, at this study's core is an examination of food advertisements appearing in the *Ladies' Home Journal*, one of the most important women's magazines of the twentieth century. To observe advertising patterns, I considered well over 3000 ads in 150 issues of the *Journal*.[18]

In addition, this book analyzes a wealth of advertisements in other magazines, including *American, Ebony, Good Housekeeping, Life, Reader's Digest, Saturday Evening Post,* and *Seventeen*. Magazines generally carried high ratios of advertising pages to reading pages, with women's magazines at the highest end of the spectrum. As an example of the proliferation, the trade publication *Printers' Ink* reported that in April 1931 more than six of the seven women's magazines had more than two pages of ads to every page of reading text. At that time, advertisements comprised nearly sixty percent of the *Ladies' Home Journal*, the highest of any women's magazine. Magazines continued to carry large numbers of advertisements throughout the century.[19]

This study also investigates the records of one of the premiere advertising agencies of the century. The J. Walter Thompson Company (JWT) archive contains memos, studies, advertisements, and campaign proposals, and offers unique perspectives into some of the strategies advertisers used to help companies position their products. Historian Jennifer Scanlon found that the J. Walter Thompson Company stood out as the most successful of the many prominent advertising agencies with which the *Ladies' Home Journal* worked from the 1920s into the 1970s. One of the reasons for their tremendous advantage over other companies was their early commitment to market research. Starting in 1911, the company organized a department of marketing research that collected and analyzed information about goods and consumers. According to Scanlon, "This department was a first in the magazine industry, and its sophistication and effectiveness provided lessons in marketing research not only to other magazines but also to many advertising agencies."[20] Analysis of several industry publications, including *Advertising Age* and *Printers' Ink*, also helps reveal what the advertisers knew (or thought they knew) about their own work and the public.

Moreover, studies conducted by Ernest Dichter, considered by many to be the founder of motivational research, afford insights into what researchers and advertisers understood about consumers and their motivations during the 1950s and 1960s. Certainly not the first to introduce advertisers to psychological methods, Dichter benefited from the pioneering efforts of behaviorist John B. Watson, dating back to the 1920s. Dichter's Freudian training (he was a Viennese born and trained doctor of psychology) informed his work and led him to believe that it was possible to determine the underlying motivations of consumer behavior, and hence, how advertisers could manipulate that behavior. The archives of Dichter's Institute for Motivational Research contain hundreds of studies undertaken for major industries and advertising agencies around the world. In her 1963 revolutionary book *The Feminine Mystique*, Betty Friedan offered Dichter's studies as evidence of advertisers' complicity in perpetuating women's empty lives.[21]

Lastly, analysis of advertisements themselves informs this study. This analysis is modeled on the approach taken by historians such as Leila Rupp, Maureen Honey, and Jeffrey Steele, all of whom analyzed advertisements for the broader messages that they conveyed. It does not argue for a one-dimensional reading of the ads, but instead acknowledges that ads are rich texts, with multifarious meanings. Though advertising as a visual medium lends itself to multiple interpretations, this work considers advertisements cumulatively, as evidence of institutional directives to target women as consumers. The intention of this study is not to dissect a handful of ads, but instead to see how, taken together almost as a photo mosaic, hundreds of ads created mental images for the reader and sought to shape their vision.[22]

Much of history is concerned with change over time, exploring the ways in which people, institutions, nations, and events evolved, and this focus richly informs our understanding of the past. Many fine historians and cultural analysts have explored the different ways advertising has changed, including attention to stylistic concerns (density of text, introduction of photographs and later color photographs, placement within magazines, etc.); analysis germane to particular periods in U.S. history (modernism, patriotism during times of war, etc.); and the development of the industry itself. This study, however, makes an argument for the surprising sameness that marked American food advertising. In spite of the countless changes that shaped food, the advertising industries, and American society generally, food advertisers demonstrated a remarkable continuity in their approaches. The most fundamental of these commitments was their decision to market food almost exclusively to women.

How, precisely, advertisers did so is central to this study, which identifies six themes that food advertisers employed. While some themes waxed and waned, advertisers relied on several as constants throughout the period. One of the most enduring advertising messages was that women should show their love for their families through food. This underlying current was not always explicit, but instead manifested itself in ads clearly signifying women's roles. While early ads subtly focused on a product's ability to show love, later ads grew even more forthright in asserting this message.[23] Advertisers consistently used the "food is love" dictum to sanctify the connection between women and food, and to reinforce the idea that women should prepare food for their families.

Another significant way in which advertisers sought to maintain their base was to prey on women's insecurities and lavish them with false praise.

Determined to preserve the status quo and grow their consumer base, advertisers also adapted to evolving social trends, including encouraging a belief in an entitlement to free time, to necessitate convenience foods. Latching on to new categories of women, including those who worked for wages outside the home and those who believed in equality between the sexes, advertisers incorporated these groups' identities into ads and portrayed food shopping and preparation as part of their raison d'être.

The third appeal advertisers used was to suggest that through their cooking women had a powerful tool within their home. According to advertisers, women's power lay not only in their ability to please family members, but also to help assimilate their family into American life, to improve its status, and to maintain its ethnic, religious, or racial identity. Advertisers also made connections between food and national identity, suggesting that a woman could demonstrate her family's national loyalty by buying ostensibly patriotic foods. Similarly, they suggested a woman could help improve her family's social status by adopting foods that the upper classes purportedly ate. Thorstein Veblen suggested in *The Theory of the Leisure Class* that women's "conspicuous consumption" served as a visual marker of their family's status.[24] Advertisers hoped to extend this notion and tried to convince women that their family's status depended on their cooking. Advertisements suggested that men's work determined the family income, but that women's work in the supermarket and the kitchen shaped the family's status.

The fourth strategy that food advertisers commonly employed was to use representations of men to suggest that women were subservient to men and should cater to their needs. Men appeared as authority figures and in situations where they demanded food from women. Ads suggested that men were entitled to be angry and disappointed with the food they received from women. Moreover, despite having evidence that men shopped and cooked, advertisers rarely showed them doing so.

Advertisements placed responsibility for their family's health in the hands of women. This fifth theme suggested it was a woman's cooking that jeopardized or ensured her family's health. Ads tried to persuade women that they needed to serve certain foods to ensure their families' well being. Incorporating both scientific and pseudoscientific findings that highlighted relationships between the composition of foods (fiber, calories, vitamins, etc.) and diseases, advertisers claimed that consumption of particular food products would cure or prevent various conditions, including constipation, high blood pressure, and cancer. Although adult men presumably possessed the independence to make their own food choices, in food advertisements accountability for their dietary habits fell to their wives. Advertisers denied men's agency in making choices and placed full responsibility for their transgressions on women.

Food advertisers also commonly used beauty and sexuality to appeal to women. In addition to positive portrayals, the ads also directed a barrage of criticism at women about their appearance, most especially about their weight. The ads encouraged feelings of bodily shame and promised that their products would offer salvation. Moreover, food advertisements created and reflected strong cultural associations between sex and food, including women's use of it as an aphrodisiac.[25] Historians and sociologists have examined the use of sensuality and sexuality in advertisements for cosmetics, automobiles, and clothing, but none have analyzed how food advertisers used these same tactics.

Finally, advertisers also charged women with sole responsibility for their children's health, happiness, and performance. The advertisers claimed that a child's success depended on what foods their mother provided. The size of a child, skinny or plump, suggested that mothers were either failures or heroes in their effort to provide healthy foods. Advertisers' threats could be quite shocking, extending from poor report cards to startling references to children dying. While fathers did occasionally appear in ads as concerned onlookers, advertisers dictated that children's well-being lay exclusively in the hands of mothers. Moreover, it was not enough to provide healthy foods; advertisers also chastised women if they fed children unpopular foods. Women had to satisfy their children's tastes as well.

Food advertisers did not sit back and hope that girls grew into the roles they conceived for them. Instead, advertisers actively sought to exploit girls' feelings of insecurity. In particular, food advertisers wanted to socialize teenage girls into gender roles that rewarded consumerism and caregiving. By encouraging girls to care about shopping and pleasing others (especially potential suitors), advertisers hoped to assure customer loyalty for years to come. Ads showed girls primarily concerned with the happiness of others and their own appearance, while depicting boys engaged in active, physical activity.

While gender roles, advertising styles, and eating patterns did change over the course of the twentieth century, food advertising remained consistent in its quest to convince Americans that women should be solely responsible for cooking. Admittedly these continuities carried different meanings as the historical context evolved, but it is striking, nonetheless, that advertisers' strategies, themes, and targets remained as constant as they did. Entering the twenty-first century, advertisers continued to market almost exclusively to women, in spite of the fact that most women, including those with small children, worked outside the home for wages. Many Americans believed that the women's movement of the late twentieth century ended the disparities that had existed between women and men. However, food advertising reflected a different reality and contributed to a continuing inequality in gender roles, exclusively targeting women to do the unpaid work of planning meals, food shopping, cooking meals, and serving meals to their families. In spite of periodic nods toward other strategies, there were no signs at the beginning of the new century that advertisers' target or tactics were going to change. Food advertising continued to hold women responsible for their family's health, status, and satisfaction because they claimed that, in the hands of women, food is love.

Chapter 1
Advertisers and Their Paradigm: Women as Consumers

The consumer isn't a moron. She is your wife.
—*David Ogilvy,* Confessions of an Advertising Man

White, elite men have always controlled the advertising industry. Many historians, cultural critics, and industry insiders have argued that their power not only led advertisers to be out of touch with their markets, but also to be disdainful and elitist in their approach. One key aspect of this argument was that advertisements did not reflect the broader society because of advertisers' limited range of viewpoints. Critiques came mainly on three issues: the exclusion of African Americans from the industry; the nonexistent or limited role women had within agencies; and the distorting perspective of class that ad executives brought to their work. Historian Pamela Walker Laird wrote of twentieth century advertisers, "they observed their targets through their own experiences—biased and distanced by class and gender; moreover, they were writing, in effect, for another audience altogether—their peers." She could also have noted their race, as largely the same kind of people shaped advertising messages, particularly at the highest decision-making level. Perhaps heterosexuality could also be added to the list of factors shaping their vision of American consumers.[1]

Women as Consumers: The Advertising Paradigm

When national food advertising exploded in the early 1900s, advertisers believed that women were the major consumers of household goods. They tried to insure that white middle- and upper-class women would be their customers by directing their financial resources toward the growing number of women's magazines. Thereafter, food ads appeared throughout the country in magazines and newspapers, as well as on billboards and public transportation. As radio, television, and the Internet developed, they too became prime media for advertisers. Even as the kinds of ads and the types of media expanded, the focus on white female consumers remained constant.

Research demonstrated the appeal of convenience foods to the poor and working classes, but whether through their own socioeconomic bias or the preferences of their clients, advertisers remained reluctant to include them in their target audience. One factor shaping the decision was that throughout the century the middle class sought to maintain the distinctions that separated them from the working class. Seeking to position their products as status symbols in that class struggle, advertisers kept a clear eye on salaries as a key determinant as to whom they wanted to attract. Indeed, many hoped that the loss of outside help would force middle-class women to turn to their products to facilitate housework. Even as evidence poured in that other groups consumed their products, food advertisers ignored the potential of other markets. They wanted white middle- and upper-class women as consumers.[2]

Food advertisers in particular remained hesitant to associate their products with African Americans and resisted including their images in mainstream advertisements. One of the largest publishers in the country, the Curtis Publishing Company, excluded blacks from its famed market research and discouraged circulation agents from promoting its periodicals in neighborhoods and towns inhabited by African Americans. Even at the end of the century, African Americans commonly appeared in promotions for a wide range of products, including automobiles, fashion, and household goods, but food advertisers continued to be uniquely uninterested in reaching African American consumers.[3]

The rare exception was companies like Kellogg's, which initiated an aggressive campaign to promote Corn Flakes cereal to black consumers as early as the mid-1930s. These efforts were notable because Kellogg's advertised widely in the black press, but in keeping with the broader industry trend did not include African Americans in appeals in mainstream periodicals. It was not until the late twentieth century, largely due to lawsuits and social pressures, that a few large corporations broke this pattern. Perhaps able to withstand an anticipated racial fallout from whites because of the near universality of their base products, Kraft and Campbell began to run ads featuring African Americans. These companies largely remain the exception to the rule, which is that food advertisers did not want African American consumers, especially at what they believed would be the expense of white consumers.[4]

In the archives of the J. Walter Thompson Company (JWT), there are only rare references to nonwhite consumers and no indication that they sought them out. Even when they considered African Americans, it was usually in relation to how it would affect white consumers. A 1933 study of "Magazine Coverage of Native White Families" was unusual for its use of the qualifier "white." Likewise, a 1941 study on the "Frequency of Visiting a Grocery Store" was unusual for its categorization, "New York and Chicago white non-relief families." These exceptions are telling in both their racial and class explicitness, but most surveys did not delineate race, taking whiteness as a given in their vision of their market.[5] Corporate files, covering the period from 1887 to the 1990s, reflect that the agency began to monitor industry articles about African Americans as a market in the 1960s, but there is little evidence that food advertisers acted on this data. In fact, the JWT case files reveal that time and again, they targeted white, middle-class women.

Food advertisers kept this focus over the course of the twentieth century, even as the United States faced many dramatic experiences: devastating economic crises and resounding prosperity; racial polarization and attempts at reconciliation; fluctuating immigration, with new groups gaining admittance in the first and last quarters, but many stymied at mid-century; two world wars and several other international conflicts; and changing gender roles. Nevertheless, while other types of advertising changed dramatically in response to changing media and events, food companies continually sought white middle- and upper-class women as consumers and remained remarkably consistent in their messages.[6]

Food advertisers had a unique relationship with women. Unlike other industries, such as automobile and credit card companies, that sought out women as new consumers or imagined new roles for women, food companies wanted to maintain the status quo and rarely considered men as consumers. The one change they did embrace more fully was women who worked outside the home, hoping to position their products to capitalize on their desire for balance as they sought to maintain their home and work outside the home. In so doing, they reinforced traditional gender roles and entrenched the work of food preparation firmly in the hands of women.

"Vats of Frothy Pink Irrationality"

At the outset of the twentieth century, researchers and advertisers developed the general perceptions that would occupy them into the next century. While it was difficult, especially early on, to determine who was consuming, the question of why people bought the things they did remained particularly elusive. Perceptions of consumers, therefore, often proved to be contradictory. That they did not fully understand consumers or know how to reach them did not deter advertisers from their efforts to appeal to women. Indeed, starting with the premise that women were the primary consumers for the home, advertisers, from about 1910 on, undertook countless studies to determine why women bought what they did.

While most observers assumed that women were the country's primary consumers for most goods, market researchers did evaluate men's buying habits. As was true for women, advertisers' understanding of male consumers also continually vacillated. While they hungered for their potential payoff, most food advertisers shied away from male consumers because they dismissed them as unpredictable. Most studies did not result in follow-up efforts to find ways to steady the male market and make it more accessible or reliable. Instead, most researchers and food advertisers appear to have thrown up their hands in resignation and focused all of their energy on women.

Occasionally newspapers or men's magazines touted the importance of their male audience as a consumer base. For example, the *Standard Farm Papers* advertised in the trade journal *Printers' Ink* in 1908, claiming that, "Men Are the Buyers," buying "not only men's goods, household goods and farm tools, but actually women's clothes." Their argument centered on the premise that "Every Home Centres Round a Man," where a wife's "thought is always to please him . . . no new thing or new line of goods is ever bought without it first receives his approval."[7]

Advertiser Albert Leffingwell, an early proponent of advertising to men, also maintained that men made good consumers, arguing that they were more irrational and hence easier to manipulate. His article, "The Practical Appeal in Advertising to Men," appeared in a 1922 JWT newsletter and observed that advertisements geared toward women were "concrete, practical, informative—while a surprising amount of advertising to men still relies chiefly on staccato enthusiasm." He wondered, "Are men natural-born spenders . . . Or is it rather that women, as purchasers for the whole household, have got to count the pennies more carefully than men?" If others shared Leffingwell's beliefs, advertisers might have focused on men. Instead, food advertisers decided to forgo the male market and focus instead on women, whom they presumably thought they could better persuade.[8]

Still, even though they decided to target women nearly exclusively for food advertising, researchers and advertisers struggled throughout the century to understand the female psyche. For example, many believed that women were completely emotional and irrational. Historian T. J. Jackson Lears found that early advertisers held the "tacit assumption that women's minds were vats of frothy pink irrationality." This perception of women as easily manipulable falls at one end of the research and advertising spectrum. On the other end was the belief that women were tough, competent, and rational consumers. While a range of ideas vied for dominance, women remained the focus. Regardless of the swirling debates in the advertising industry and its periodicals, advertisers rarely took their eyes off "that enigmatic and glittering prize, the female consumer."[9]

Some saw the advertising industry as possessing more savvy and control than female consumers, but advertisers simultaneously feared women's power as consumers. Debates about women's nature raged in the pages of company organs and industry publications. In a 1922 company newsletter, Frances Maule of JWT's Women's Department encouraged her colleagues to respect women and their power. She predicated her formula for success on a central insight: "Woman is the practical animal." She suggested that it was better to give women "substantial reasons" to buy their products and listed practical ones: "price, quantity, quality, and service," rather than relying on emotional factors to sell them.[10]

In 1924, in the heady period when women had been empowered by their suffrage victory and other social and political advances during the Progressive era, Maule suggested that advertisers should remember, "the fact—so well expressed in the old suffrage slogan—that 'Women Are People.'" She cautioned that in their efforts to reach women, advertisers tended to "over-feminize" their appeal, relying too heavily on the "angel-idiot" stereotype of women. She disagreed with Leffingwell's assessment of advertisements directed at women as "informative" and wanted advertisers to adopt a hard-sell approach to reach women on the merits of their products. She believed that "Practically every normal woman has an innate instinctive sympathy with the needs of the home and of children that cause them to think more deeply on these subjects than do most men."[11]

Still, the belief that women were not rational fueled the industry. According to historian Michael Schudson, the transformation in the first half of the century from informative to emotional ads came about not because of a changed conception of human nature but because of whom advertisers perceived their consumers to be. Early in the century advertisers shifted away from men, whom they viewed as rational, to women, whom they considered emotional and irrational.[12]

Advertisers commonly believed that women and men spoke "different languages," that their minds worked differently, and that women relied on intuition while men thought things through to their logical conclusions. In an essay on how to handle written inquiries from women, businessman Charles R. Wiers suggested that "the language used in letters and advertisements for women should be common and sensible instead of technical or of the kind that is ordinarily used to influence men." He believed that "A woman is also a combination of whims and peculiarities. She doesn't like our methods of reasoning; she has methods of her own," and speculated that, "their more delicate natures make them keenly sensitive about the little things."[13]

Marian Hertha Clarke tried to enlighten her mostly male advertising colleagues in a 1926 *Printers' Ink* article. Predicated on difference, as so many findings were throughout the century, Clarke posited that while women may not be technically minded, they were careful shoppers, with a highly developed sense of values. She encouraged advertisers to respond to women's "instinctive and creative demand for atmosphere" and to sell a woman on the ability of a product to make her life "easier and happier—if it will add anything to the health and well-being of herself or her family—she will find a way to afford it."[14] Like the industry itself, women in advertising, such as Maule and Clarke, found themselves conflicted as to how best to approach the female consumer. Generally, women writers, while they still attributed to women gendered homemaking traits, took the female consumer seriously and remained respectful of her work in the home.

Most men writing on this subject, however, were dismissive of the female consumer, noting as marketer Tom Masson did in 1928, "With the female, buying is a passion; all of her faculties and emotions are bound up in it. It is closely allied with the hunting instinct of the male." He claimed, "Under the hypnosis of the bargain complex they yield to a widely advertised idea like sheep."[15] Depending on the sex of the researcher, gender impressions of consumers, then, could be wildly different.

What remained the same regardless of their perceptions was that food advertisers wanted women as their consumers. Whatever the attributes with which they credited (or discredited) women, food advertisers remained convinced that women should be their targets. Because they believed they were the principal purchasers, advertisers resolved themselves to coping with female consumers, regardless of their psychological make-up. Solidifying their own perceptions, and those of others, advertisers advertised women's supposed dominance in food consumption. A 1916 advertisement claimed, "It has been estimated that women influence the purchase of . . . 90% of food products." Likewise, the JWT sought to capitalize on its professed prowess in advertising to women when arguing in 1918 that women comprised 89.1 percent of grocery store sales.[16] In no instance did a researcher or commentator suggest abandoning women as a market because they were too fickle or difficult to categorize.

Many women's groups and industry critics charged that advertisers portrayed women poorly. In the 1920s, home economists and domestic scientists, perhaps emboldened by the changes made during the Progressive Era and the suffrage triumph, called for changes on behalf of the common woman. Anna E. Richardson, writing for the American

Home Economics Association, was critical of advertising, claiming that it compounded the confusion perpetuated by modern methods of production. She argued that advertising "displays goods so attractively, that she [the homemaker] is sometimes tempted to buy unwisely, without sufficient study of needs and how they can be met best. The psychology of clever advertising is frequently pitted against the common sense of the homemaker, with the result that she is worsted in the struggle." Paternalistically, Richardson doubted women's strength against the influence of advertising, charging that they were helpless to resist its sway. Other researchers, such as Benjamin R. Andrews, Professor of Household Economics at Teachers College at Columbia University, counseled that each woman "must realize that, to her family, she is the guardian of the treasury, and that her watch over expenditures makes, or mars, the quality of life which they achieve."[17] Researchers such as Richardson and Andrews recognized the agency of women as consumers, but feared their vulnerability in the face of advertisers' power.

Others objected to the food advertisements' condescension and felt exasperated by unrealistic representations of both women's form and function. Several found the artistic renderings particularly infuriating, protesting, "And I do wish that artists wouldn't show us a housekeeper cooking a husky, staggering meal while, immaculate and seemingly just home from the hairdresser's, she smiles dreamily into the distance."[18] Objections to advertisements often came from women who simply wanted to be respected and represented realistically.

More than mere miscommunication or misrepresentation, however, by the 1930s advertisers believed they faced a real crisis of confidence in the public eye. Starting in the late nineteenth century, with growing numbers of women going to college, the evolution of home economics as a profession, and the emergence of politically active women, the burgeoning field of advertising found itself subject to growing criticism. Questions about quality, cost, and truthfulness plagued the industry, and some of the loudest voices drawing attention to these issues were women's. While Upton Sinclair is rightfully credited with stirring dramatic changes in laws related to the meat industry, it was largely the work of anonymous women who forced the hands of politicians, manufacturers, and advertisers, and tried to compel them to provide good, honest products and advertisements.[19]

Women organized themselves in women's clubs and fostered a growing consumer movement. Building on their success with suffrage, women continued to try to bring about social and political changes in their role as consumers. However, the economic crises of the 1930s raised the stakes for both parties. Advertisers, beleaguered after extended and severe economic pressures, felt themselves unfairly targeted and threatened by women. While many wanted to dismiss women as tempests in teapots, many businesses found themselves awakened to women's power as they staged boycotts, pushed for stronger laws, and exposed fraud.[20]

Detailing the movement's growing influence and trying to prod the industry to meet the challenges posed, Mabel Crews Ringland, president of the Women's Advertising Club of Toronto, warned that the consumer movement could break the industry if it did not respond, and pointed to the influence of other groups who fought for changes in advertising and industry. She may have been referring to efforts by groups like the General Federation of Women's Clubs, which "cleaned up" movies with the introduction of the 1930 Hays Code (that sought limits on movie violence and nudity). She argued that if smaller groups were successful, then surely the cumulative force of women could bring the advertising industry to its knees. Better to act preemptively than to antagonize "Gullible Gertie," as she termed the everyday woman, whose numbers reached several tens of millions and were comprised of "the most educated and influential in the country."[21]

Ringland was also frustrated by the many misapprehensions about female consumers, particularly those put forward by men, and did not pull any punches when she described advertiser John Erskine's

insidious half-truths in "The Influence of Woman and Its Cure," which belittles woman's intelligence and character even more than do most male critics. Indeed he interprets us as vain, grasping, possessive persons, gloating in our power over man, dominating him with our fads and notions, our desires and sentimentalism and strangling his manly qualities.[22]

Women writers often wrote articles to castigate the men who thought that they knew the "opposite sex." In a pointed article, "Fear the Facts and Fool the Women," for *Atlantic Monthly*, Margaret Dana wrote,

It has always been a matter of amazement to me that so many mild, amiable men of no more than average experience with women, presumably, can become between breakfast table and office desk pompous oracles on the subject; the most ubiquitous character; indeed, in the retailing world to-day is The Man Who Knows All About Women—and none of it true.[23]

In turn, advertisers also dismissed the assertions and motives of consumer advocates. Mrs. Bert W. Henderson offered an analysis of female consumers that argued that, in addition to the "reformer type, usually as militant as Carrie Nation with her hatchet," and the "philanthropic type," advertisers would have to contend with "the selfish type, interested solely and often secretly in her own profits." Occasionally writers such as Dana thought consumer dissatisfaction was justified. She wrote, "The rebellion of buyers is not against merchandise but against the manner of presentation." In other words, advertisers' arrogant assumptions about women could hurt their sales. Much more common were the refrains of authors like Henderson who expressed antagonism toward female consumers themselves.[24]

Not surprisingly, the Great Depression proved to be a tense time between advertisers and consumers. Women, struggling to feed their families on less, or nothing at all, considered advertising wasteful. Deep into the depression, Ringland reported that it was estimated that businesses spent about two billion dollars on advertising. While advertisers argued that companies had to spend money to increase their sales, thereby bringing down costs, some consumers found this expenditure galling. They believed consumers were paying for the advertising through higher costs for the merchandise, and that if they eliminated advertising, prices would come down. Even more damning, for many women, was dishonest advertising. With so little to spend, consumers needed to make the most of their purchases. More than usual, an untrustworthy advertisement was not just an abstract betrayal, it literally jeopardized women's ability to care for their families.[25]

Advertisers, too, faced ruin if they could not sell goods. Anger at consumers moved beyond charges of egotism and self-promotion to charges of communism. Some advertisers cautioned that, despite the fact that some communists joined the consumer movement, "It should be pretty obvious that a witch hunt is not going to solve the advertiser's or the consumer's problem." One chided his peers, "Apparently it does not occur to some influential advertisers that a very simple way of eliminating a lot of the discontent among consumers is to use thoroughly honest, thoroughly informative copy." In the face of organized consumer opposition, advertisers in 1940 appeared to have resigned themselves to their new reality. In a survey of the *Printers' Ink* "Jury of Marketing Opinion," 172 advertising men across the country who weighed in on questionnaires, fully 166 of them believed that "The advertiser should recognize the 'consumer movement' as a legitimate effort on the part of consumers and cooperate in the solution of the problems it has given rise to." No one thought the consumer movement should be ignored, and by this time only three people thought it should "be opposed and defeated, if possible." The most popular measure to resolve the problems, as they understood them, was that "Advertising should be more informative than at present and less emotional," with 140 ad men either "Mildly in favor" or "Wholeheartedly in favor." Having the government create a "Department of the Consumer" met with vehement opposition, however, with 117 "Wholeheartedly opposed."[26]

Still, recognizing the problem and considering solutions did not amount to resolving the problem. Most advertisers resisted the demands of the consumer movement. Ironically, given the accusations of profligate spending, in July 1941 L. D. H. Weld, director of research at McCann-Erickson, Inc., proposed a $5 million campaign "to educate [the] public about advertising." The editor's note for the article summarized what Weld believed was the reason "advertising has not been advancing as much as national income and other elements," namely, "public indifference toward, or actual enmity for, advertising." He proposed a program to "try to checkmate some of the poison injected by hotheads in the consumer movement."[27]

While a great relief, the end of the economic crisis did not fully resolve the tensions between consumers and the advertising industry. Advertisers' efforts to understand and attract middle-class women as their consumers also did not dissipate. Amidst the chaos and flux of the Second World War, Henry Dorff theorized about "The Woman's Market after the War." He predicted that the postwar consumer "will want advertising copy to speak to her in straightforward, friendly words that meet with her new position. There will be less of the gushy, so-called 'woman's copy' because that was for the woman of 1940 and very few of them will any longer exist." Few knew what to make of the changes wrought by World War II. As Maureen Honey and others have observed, in spite of the radical changes that took place in homes across the country, the rhetoric in the popular discourse remained located in traditional values and expectations about gender.[28]

Like Maule and Clarke earlier, for example, Dorff believed that "the hand that rocks the cradle will certainly rule the market place." He cautioned, however, "It will be a new hand fused in the fires of terrible tempest, emotional forces, and world upheaval. It will be a hand of steel in a velvet glove." While their wartime work had put women "commercially on an equal footing with men," advertisers did not believe this new breadwinner task would change women's primary role. Women would continue to be the family's consumer. Whatever the changes wrought by the war, Dorff encouraged advertisers to believe that "women will insist on remaining feminine and lovable . . . she will want the emphasis on the fact that her choice will sway the man's feelings toward her."[29]

"What Makes Women Buy?"

Food advertisers, in particular, were interested in women's homemaking role, and often seemed uncertain if they should address the growing proportion of wage-earning women, which escalated for all groups dramatically during the Second World War. Researchers and advertisers who struggled to understand women's actions in the past were even less prepared to anticipate the future. Clouded by their paradigm of women as homemakers and primary shoppers, even when they saw deviant patterns, advertisers counseled each other to stay the course. In spite of significant changes in women's lives in the second half of the century, food advertisers focused almost exclusively on women's traditional gender roles.[30]

Asking the all-important question "What Makes Women Buy?" in 1956, researcher Gilbert Burck discovered that "There is no industry that cherishes and ponders the female consumer more deeply than the food industry. Food manufacturers and processors have been leaders in market research, and they have done a shrewder job of selling women than most other industries." He found many business leaders who successfully freed themselves from "the common assumption that women are impulsive buyers, with an almost neurotic compulsion to squander their household money on any bauble that chances to catch their fancy." While he did find that "most merchandisers" still believed "that women as a rule are more intuitive than men," Burck concluded that they found, "women as buyers are behaving more and more as only men were supposed to behave not so long ago." While the answer to the question of "What makes women buy?" eluded Burck, his assessments of women's tremendous spending power in 1956 explain why it was such an important question throughout the century.[31]

To understand women's lives in the second third of the century, researchers often looked to the first third to make comparisons. Tracing women's lives historically, Burck described women at the turn of the century as "home-tied," and those during the "roaring 1920's and the bitter 1930's" as "self-consciously 'liberated.'" Ernest Dichter concurred in his 1956 examination of "Today's Woman as a Consumer," and suggested that after the "forever housewife," the 1920s and 1930s "witnessed the emergence of the career woman, the woman who clamored for identity in every sphere of life, the woman who reacted to 'domestic slavery' with something close to indignation and vehemence."[32]

Generally skipping over any analysis of World War II, perhaps presuming it was an anomaly, Burck and Dichter also came to similar conclusions about women in the postwar era, suggesting that women assimilated their public roles into the standard help-mate model. Even their paid outside work was considered supplemental and temporary, rather than competing with their traditional housewife role. Burck believed that postwar women made a peaceful, permanent transition into the homemaking role, possibly combined with some limited form of paid labor, although he acknowledged that during her

postwar evolution . . . the American woman has not returned to the restricted world of childbearing and household drudgery. She is more active than her

counterpart of thirty years ago in politics, schools, churches, and other organized community activities . . . she is also successful as a working woman. The 21
million women in the U.S. labor force today comprise a third of all women
above fourteen, and 30 per cent of all married women.[33]

Dichter also praised women for moving beyond the embrace of the "forever housewife" role and for their resistance to "domestic slavery," and
opined that in the mid-1950s "the ambitions of the worldly career woman
are in turn being supplanted by the philosophy of a newer, more mature
woman who balances within herself the positive qualities of both her pre-
decessors." He argued that "Though not as sophisticated as the career
woman, she has an intelligent realistic attitude toward her own role as a
female, with none of the self-sacrificing relationship to home-making of
her pre-World War I predecessor."[34]

More than just recording his perceptions, Dichter wanted women to
have this kind of commitment to both home and work. Food advertisers
in particular believed that it was to their best advantage if women valued
her role as homemaker and worked outside the home, because they
hoped it would mean that she would need assistance to fulfill her homemaking responsibilities. As Richard Pollay argued, advertising " 'induces
people to keep productive in order to keep consuming, to work in order
to buy.' "[35] By focusing entirely on women and their roles, advertisers
helped undermine any notion that women might share or reduce their
responsibility for shopping and cooking. Advertisers provided these balanced women the means with which they could do it all, and their messages suggested that they should.

It is clear, too, that there was some advantage for advertisers to speak
to and perhaps exacerbate angst that women felt about their ability to
be "superwomen." If women were " 'uncertain, anxious, and insecure,' "
as the woman playing Betty Crocker claimed they were, then advertisers
had an opportunity to sell on those points, rather than assuage her
fears.[36] Far from ending their angst about their homemaking role, food
advertisers suggested ways in which working outside the home could
heighten women's feelings of inadequacy. Instead of seeing women's
paid work as a threat to their paradigm, researchers pointed to the potential it offered advertisers.

Researchers were well aware of the changes in women's lives and
openly suggested embracing women's "balanced" role as potentially
lucrative. The *JWT News* continuously reported research findings about
women's work and consumption trends. In 1948, for example, the
newsletter reported that, "The 'working wife' is becoming increasingly
prominent in American family life, according to a study just released by
the Census Bureau . . . twice the figure for 1940."[37] At the end of the

1950s, the president of Campbell's Soup Company also recognized that women had changed, claiming

> The average housewife isn't interested in making a slave of herself. When you do it day after day after day, it tends to get a little tiresome, and the young housewife is really less interested in her reputation as a home cook today. She used to feel it was her duty to do all this homework, and she's lost some of that. . . . She doesn't regard slaving in the kitchen as an essential of a good wife and mother.[38]

Whatever women's attitudes toward housework may have been, food advertisers continued to focus on them exclusively, reminding themselves, as Stouffer's did in the late 1950s that, "Our present customers and future customers are and will be primarily women. Women carry the responsibility for feeding the families of America."[39] When confronted with working women, food advertisers evolved a new can-do woman as help-mate to diffuse the threatening challenge to traditional gender roles. Although they wanted to sell their products on the premise that women would not have to slave in the kitchen, advertisers never relinquished their assumption that women would be the ones to buy and prepare food. Even when advertisements shifted their messages about the amount of time and energy it took to prepare foods, they never abandoned their focus on women.

Although many consumers found themselves economically better off in the postwar era, they still put pressure on advertisers and manufacturers regarding consumer protection. Consumer assessments of the industry continued to be fairly negative. According to J. A. C. Brown, "A Gallup poll in 1958 found that the majority of shoppers thought that too much money was being wasted on advertising; an American survey during the same year found that 50 per cent of women associated advertising with exaggeration whilst 86 per cent thought it positively dishonest." The government periodically got involved at the behest of consumer groups. Perhaps reflecting consumer distrust and dissatisfaction in 1961, the Senate Antitrust and Monopoly subcommittee held an investigation of packaging disclosures. Ernest Dichter argued to the subcommittee that better labels would be ineffective because "consumers, despite their growing sophistication, invariably succumbed to human emotional weaknesses no matter what they purchased. 'What people actually spend their money on in most instances,' he said, 'are psychological differences, illusory brand images.' "[40]

In 1966, advertisers continued to see the consumers as problems. John Chrichton, president of the American Association of Advertising Agencies, in a speech read into the Congressional Record and published in *Printers' Ink*, answered his own question, "Consumer Protection: Do

Women Want It?" with an emphatic "No." Beyond citing one survey of consumers in Seattle, where 63 percent reported that they "did not want more protective legislation," Chrichton chalked up consumers' problems to their own weaknesses. He claimed, "people who want information get it" and charged that "people ignore information." This alleged obtuseness carried over to consumers' purchasing habits, he argued, claiming, "People change more slowly than products." In an example concerning instant mashed potatoes, he concluded, "The product failed because housewives failed, and the product was withdrawn from the market." Still, in spite of his frustrations, he returned to the same conclusions advertisers touted nearly twenty-five years earlier, in the early 1940s: "If it is a matter of getting the sizes and weights clearly printed on packages, let's do it. If it is a matter of clear and simple instruction, let's see if we can improve our language . . . well-developed information will probably be far more useful to Johanna than legislation." Of course, clear information was exactly what the consumers sought all along.[41]

To hold onto their target audience, some advertisements in the last third of the century reflected women doing paid work outside the home. Industry studies analyzed all kinds of ads appearing in general, men's, and women's magazines during this period to determine if there was indeed a watershed. However, most studies found limited changes in advertisements' portrayal of women's roles. Moreover, the perception of women as stupid and irrational continued, as in a 1969 ad in *Progressive Grocer*, which assured grocers of women's interest in a game requiring multiple product purchases, claiming, "you know how housewives love to stick things onto things" and "you know how housewives love to win." In advertisements directed toward women, the number of ads featuring women as sex objects declined somewhat, although women's concern with their appearance and presumed dependence on men remained strong features. M. Venkatesan and Jean Losco noted further in their 1975 study that most of the changes they observed were in women's magazines, while general and men's magazines tended to continue to portray women in the roles in which were most frequently represented: woman as sexual object, woman as physically beautiful, and woman as dependent on man.[42]

Even though advertisers were well aware by the mid-1970s that there were more working women than full-time housewives, they continued to lag behind in implementing changes requested, and increasingly demanded, by women who did not see themselves portrayed in magazine and television advertisements. By 1980, advertisers knew that only about one-third of U.S. women were full-time homemakers, according to Rena Bartos, a senior vice-president and director of communications development at JWT, and one of advertising's best-known experts on the women's market. She also claimed, "many homemakers within that 36 percent consider themselves atypical, and they plan later to work outside the home." Tina Santi, a corporate vice president at Colgate-Palmolive, concluded, "Most women are still frying the bacon but the rest of their life and life style is no longer the same."[43] In a rare examination of African American consumers, a 1980 *Progressive Grocer* article reminded readers that "black working women customers are also purchasers of convenience items. Surrogate shoppers are important in black households with the father, aunt or older children picking up the extra milk, eggs or bread for the employed mother." Some advertisers even concluded that "Families with working wives tend to spend more on everything—20% more on food."[44]

In spite of these changes, advertisers wanted women to continue doing the cooking. Even nonfood products drove home the message that cooking was feminine work that made men feel masculine, such as the 1970s pseudofeminist advertisement for Enjoli perfume that had a young woman dressed in a business suit promising that she could "bring home the bacon, fry it up in a pan, and never, ever let you forget you're a man."[45]

Perhaps emboldened because women were still doing most, if not all, of the unpaid work in their homes, the advertising industry made only occasional attempts to create more respectful, representative ads. Critics of the industry, including internal organizations, repeatedly found what they claimed were errant returns to bad behavior. Others were less generous and charged the industry with long-standing negligence. In 1975, the National Advertising Review Board (NARB), fearing intervention by the Federal Trade Commission, formed a panel to determine ways in which advertisers could improve their portrayal of women. Creating the panel in itself suggested an awareness of potential missteps and its findings of impropriety bore this out. The panel concluded, "Advertising must be regarded as one of the forces molding society. . . . Those who protest that advertising merely reflects society must reckon with the criticism that much of the current reflection of women in advertising is out of date."[46] Bartos observed that it "may be a mirror of society but somehow the image in that mirror is a little out of focus. It plays back a 1950's reflection in a 1970's world."[47] This time-warp theme was prevalent in assessments of the industry. Lois Ernst, president of Advertising to Women, commenting on the recalcitrance of the profession, said, " 'It took seven to eight years for them to figure out that women aren't home polishing their floors anymore. It took a while for them to realize that flowered checkbooks and scented bank statements are not the guts of the matter."

She offered, with scant optimism, "In the 1980s, if we're lucky, advertisers will catch up to 1960."[48]

Advertisers generally understood their own chronic shortcomings. Proctor & Gamble spokespeople were surprisingly candid about their campaigns. As late as 1970, an account executive with "a P&G cleansing product reported: 'There's no evidence from the talk around here that they regard the role of women as changing.' " He reflected,

Look, when I came on to this account I felt embarrassed selling to women this way. But when you look at it objectively, it makes sense. I'm insulted, but what critics of this type of advertising have to face up to is that it works . . . Our target consumer just isn't that bright.[49]

Bill Free, who created the infamous "Fly Me" campaign for National Airlines, concluded in 1971 that "the ad community continues to demean women, far more subtly than in our campaign." The NARB reported, "In the advertising of household products, women too often are portrayed as stupid—too dumb to cope with familiar everyday chores unless instructed by children or a man, or assisted by a supernatural male symbol."[50] In spite of growing evidence that women resented their depictions in advertisements, advertisers stuck with seemingly retrograde strategies.[51]

Indeed, a 1977 critique of advertising found that advertisers continued to have a limited vision of women and their potential. An analysis of Procter & Gamble Company, then "the recognized leader and arbiter of format and content in household product commercials," revealed that "the creative people have two formulae they use for 'concepting' a commercial: regular slice-of-life (problem in the home, solution with the wonderful product) or what the agency guys call '2 C's in a K.' The 'K' stands for kitchen; the 'C' is a four-letter word."[52]

Food advertising, particularly as compared to ads for other products, lagged behind in improving their portrayals of consumers. While some advertisers struggled to keep their ads current with the changes taking place in society, the traditional beliefs of the industry appeared immutable. Largely because of their insistence on women as the sole consumers and their prioritization of the homemaker role, copywriters had a fairly limited conception of women's roles. While some products depicted women in more varied roles, food advertisers located their products and consumers almost exclusively within the home. With little or no balance, the homemaking role predominated in food ads.

However, women and their roles underwent dramatic changes during the tumultuous last third of the century. Beyond a desire for self-realization, inspired in part by articles and books such as Betty Friedan's

The Feminine Mystique, economic pressures led many women to seek work outside their homes. As more women moved into the paid labor force, ideas about women's place in society changed. In a 1982 interview, Elizabeth Nickles, senior vice president of D'Arcy-MacManus & Masius, noted that in 1967, 60 percent of women had agreed that "a woman's place was in the home," but by 1977, that percentage dropped to just 25 percent. Undoubtedly, as even greater numbers of women sought employment, the percentage of women who believed that woman's place was limited to the home declined as well.[53]

To cope with these broad changes, some food advertisers tried to eliminate potentially problematic aspects of ads, but often did not truly alter their messages. Perhaps to avoid further criticism, food ads in the last quarter century reduced their use of individuals and the text generally made no mention of gender. However, the continued presence of female hands, with their long, manicured nails and requisite wedding ring, left little question as to who was serving meals. Many advertisers removed this telltale sign at the end of the century, but quickly integrated other gendered messages into their ads, explicitly telling women that food choices fell to them, with slogans like "Picky Mom's choose Jif." Of course, the placement of the food ads almost exclusively in women's magazines further revealed their continued efforts to keep women as their primary consumers.[54]

Advertisers' portrayal of women continued to be a contentious topic at the end of the century. While critics acknowledged that some advertisers made strides in occasionally showing women in varied roles, most noted the slow pace of attitudinal change in the industry. They questioned when advertising would ever stop being a "fun house mirror" and truly reflect the values and realities of Americans. As Barbara Lippert, a critic for the industry journal *Adweek,* asked, "Are reality and women's advertising mutually exclusive?"[55]

Consumers themselves remained disappointed in advertising, and may have grown even more so at the end of the century. In 1992, the editor of *Family Circle,* Valerie Salembier, cautioned "women are paying more attention. . . . Sexism in advertising has turned out to be a very big mistake . . . sales can and will go down." In 1995, Grey Advertising found that the vast majority of women surveyed said, "advertising is more unrealistic than it was even two years ago." More than not reflecting the reality of their lives, "About 70% of women said advertising insults their intelligence," up five percent from two years earlier.[56]

Food advertisers' success in responding to consumer criticism at century's end appeared to be tenuous. Marketing and advertising studies continually demonstrated the economic benefits of creating advertising that embraced women's busy lives outside the home, with some concluding that "any modern female role portrayal is more effective than a traditional portrayal."[57] However, advertisers struggled to create nuanced ads that did not rely on caricatures of women. The only thing food advertisers knew with certainty was that they wanted women to be their consumers, and throughout the century they relied on what they believed were tried and true methods to secure their loyalty.

Chapter 2
Love, Fear, and Freedom:
Selling Traditional Gender Roles

The popularity of the queen of the kitchen depends largely upon her ability to surprise and please her subjects. If she will invoke the aid of Shredded Whole Wheat Biscuit her task will be simplified and the loyalty of her subjects unquestioned.

—*Triscuit ad,* Ladies' Home Journal, *1905*

Advertisers' most fundamental message to women, and one that underscored all others, was that *food is love.* In addition to more expected appeals to taste and quality, advertisers touted their products' love value. They encouraged women to show their love for others with food and promised that women could earn their family's love by serving certain foods. Finally, copywriters honed in on consumers' nostalgia for the love and taste of times past, or imagined.

These positive ideals and the potential for creating pleasure were balanced, however, by advertisers' efforts to create and exacerbate women's anxieties. The homemaker role, with its association of selfless devotion to others, posed some difficulty for advertisers who wanted to promote the convenience of their foods. Walking a fine line, they tried to equate their products with selfishness and free time in a way that did not undermine the necessity or sentimental importance of women's role in the home. Over the course of the century, ads incorporated women's expanded roles and reflected some of their diverse interests and activities, but remained focused on their responsibility for caring for others. In addition to these more positive portrayals of women's lives, advertisements also included a number of warnings that ranged from never marrying to disappointing ones' husband to contributing to the breakdown of the marriage. The message was always the same: through the advertised food product, women could express their love to their families.

Beyond holding on to homemakers, food companies also wanted to expand their consumer base. One way they did so was to reach out occasionally to unconventional customers. Starting early in the century, and sporadically throughout it, advertisers created ads that recognized that women were paid laborers outside the home, but also insisted that they be the primary shoppers and cooks. Advertisers did not suggest that working outside the home eclipsed women's true role as homemaker, but instead assured women that their products would enable them to fulfill both roles. Ultimately, advertisers even tried to enlist feminism in the 1920s and 1970s to cultivate women's exclusive responsibility for unpaid household work.

While it might seem logical, given that food was prepared in the home, that advertisers portrayed all women as homemakers, it was not an inevitable decision. The purchasing of food took place outside the home, and for many working women, the planning of meals also took place outside the confines of their kitchen walls. Moreover, although the amount of time and skill necessary for food preparation diminished dramatically over the course of the century, advertisers continued to emphasize women's homemaking role. Advertisers focused on women's centrality to domesticity and made little creative effort to expand their consumer base by imagining new roles for women and men. Isolating women in the kitchen, they suggested that preparing food for the families was not work, but an act of love.

"Food Is Love"

While food advertisers did not create the connection between women, food, and love, they exploited it thoroughly to win women to their brands. Food ads infused with messages of love and caring appeared as early as 1902. Already by 1920, an article in *Printers' Ink* noted that the "emotional appeal appears to be in high favor." The author correctly predicted the course of the century's food advertising: "There will be no need of changing for we have struck the well of human feeling which never runs dry." Indeed, in the postwar period, as more women entered the paid workforce, these kinds of food ads only exploded in both number and explicitness.[1]

Advertisers suggested that the purported connection between food and love was factual, historical, and inevitable. However, their own history reveals their role in fostering this association. Psychological researchers encouraged the use of love appeals. Particularly significant were two men, JWT's John B. Watson and Ernest Dichter with his Institute for Motivational Research (IMR). Watson, a behaviorist and one of the most influential psychologists of the twentieth century, went to work for the advertising industry in the 1920s. He assured advertisers that they could benefit from basic techniques of predicting and manipulating human actions. He believed that advertising, informed by behaviorism, could harness the primal human drives of love, fear, and rage."[2]

Dichter, in his studies for advertisers, also argued for the importance of love in food advertising. In a 1957 issue of the IMR newsletter *Motivations*, for example, he explored "The Psychology of Appetite." The article counseled copywriters:

> In appealing to appetite, perhaps more than any other area of advertising, it is imperative to avoid the cold, straight pitch, to keep away from the sharp attention-getting devices which jangle the emotions. Appetite flourishes in an atmosphere of love, warmth, trust, and security. Like a loving mother, food advertising must neither demand, nor insist, but rather gently offer its wares.[3]

A few years later, Dichter reiterated this point in a speech entitled "Frosted Foods Need Emotional Defrosting" to the Eastern Frosted Foods Association Meeting. He suggested that one of the problems with advertising the product was its "unfortunate name of frozen or frosted food. Food is full of emotional associations, it is warm, flavorful, it is active and alive and you have surrounded it with a dead name." He encouraged manufacturers to "Bring Back Romance" and "to find ways by which the frozen products can be thawed out and emotions brought back into the picture."[4] The industry appears to have fully embraced Dichter's suggestions and moved their products away from cold connections, highlighting taste and quality, as well as its love value.

Ads that overtly appealed to love in the first half of the century tended to use saccharine symbols and allegories to allude to foods' heartwarming qualities. Some advertisers, for example, suggested food as a symbol of romantic love and loyalty in courtship. Campbell's soup ads in the 1910s and '20s often featured the Campbell Kids finding love with a can of soup. A 1947 cereal ad featured a young loving couple; as the woman served the man "Muffets for Breakfast!" he touched her arm and hearts surrounded them. The adjoining text stated, "Made for Each Other," alluding to both the man and woman and the cereal and the man. Ten years later, the messages remained restrained, as in a 1957 Green Giant ad that featured a cupid shooting a love arrow into peas, while a woman fed peas to a grown man. The ad sold the vegetable as a "lovin' touch for any meal" and encouraged women to "Fuss over 'em like a hen over her only chick."[5]

During the 1960s, however, more sexually suggestive and emphatic love ads appeared. Pillsbury adopted the tag, "Nothin' says lovin' like something from the oven and Pillsbury says it best!" Quaker Oats placed ads that encouraged women to serve "Good hot Quaker Oats for breakfast—because you love them so much!" A 1964 Fleischmann's

Figure 1. This 1957 Green Giant ad used romantic imagery to associate its foods with love.

Yeast ad used the threat of marital strife to promote its product. The photo featured a woman offering a plate of baked treats to a smiling man reading the newspaper. The text of the ad claimed, "Maybe home-baked butterscotch buns never saved a marriage—but they never did one any harm. You bake them *yourself.* Right from scratch. You just add everything. Especially lots of love . . . and Fleischmann's Yeast."[6]

At the end of the decade, a Parks Sausages ad, featured in such magazines as *Look* and *Reader's Digest,* proclaimed—with sausages formed into letters—"FOOD IS LOVE." In the 1970s, the message remained the same, with the California Avocado Advisory Board proclaiming the avocado the "love food from California" and suggesting that the meeting of avocado and Kraft mayonnaise was a "Love Story." The Food Council of America encouraged Americans to eat the four basic food groups every day with a 1971 ad that featured a photo of an African American family as they enjoyed a candle-lit dinner. The header declared, "Food is love."[7]

Allusions to love were especially prevalent in fast food advertising. Burger King adopted the "America loves . . ." campaign in the 1970s. Its creators, JWT, "set out to convey the message of leadership in the industry and concern for customers" and in case it was not self-evident, they explained, "in other words, LOVE." Burger King's group vice president of marketing explained that, "The scenes of laughing, playing, caring and sharing show our customers that we understand their feelings . . . that we care about them." At the ad agency, Burt Manning, executive vice president and executive creative director, made it clear that "We do not choose the word 'love' loosely. Visiting a Burger King restaurant is more than just eating to your customers. It's a feeling, it's an experience and it's an attitude that they bring with them when they enter the restaurant and remember when they decide to come back."[8]

Perhaps occurrences of love were common in fast food advertising because it was as far from the kitchen as you could get. To sell no-preparation, ready-to-eat foods, bought primarily by young men, advertisers still likened it to the paradigm of emotional sustenance. James Helmer's study of McDonald's advertising revealed that in the 1980s the industry giant, like its rival Burger King, "moved its primary marketing emphasis off the food it sells and turned instead to marketing love, a sense of community and good feelings." Helmer argued that based on a perception of family life as "an increasingly frenzied and fragmented experience," the company tried to "paint itself as many things that answered people's basic and powerful need for someone to mend the fragments with caring." McDonald's commercials suggested that their restaurants were "the glue that holds friends and families together" and "reassuring of stability, security and love."[9] The approach contributed to a growing market share (19 percent), more than twice that of its nearest competitor, Burger King. By deemphasizing its menu of prepared foods, McDonald's subsumed them in images of love and family, wholly alien to their creation.

Beyond the fast food category, two of the most common foods put forth as love-filled were soups and baked goods. In a "Creative Memorandum on the Psychology of Soup," Ernest Dichter reported to the Young & Rubicam advertising agency that "soup is one of the most emotion-charged foods. Effective soup advertising must, therefore, take into consideration all the sources of that emotionality, all the meanings soup has consciously and unconsciously to today's consumers." He went on to argue that "Soup is magic" and that "People often tend to feel about soup as the product of some mysterious alchemy, as a symbol of a kind of love that arises from the profoundest depth of inner man. Soup represents gratification of personal longing that cannot be named."[10] That it was mass-produced and bought in a can did not diminish Dichter's firm belief that advertisers should market the emotional power of soup; indeed, it made it more imperative.

Late twentieth-century advertisers rarely contented themselves with subtle allusions. Manipulative ads, bearing the mark of what ad critic Bob Garfield calls "emotional dishonesty," attempted to yoke people's most intimate emotions to convenience foods. While advertisers have always sought to shape consumer behavior, some ads exceeded previously set norms in their effort play upon their targets' emotions. One example, a 1998 television ad for Campbell's soup, depicted an orphaned child meeting her foster mother for the first time. To coax the emotionally vulnerable child, the foster mother brought her a bowl of chicken noodle soup. Garfield described the encounter:

But as the woman reaches the door, the little girl has uncurled from the fetal position and tasted the soup. "My mommy used to fix me this soup," says the vulnerable angelic, idealized child—which naturally touches the caring, understanding, stable, idealized foster parent. "My mother used to make it for me, too," she smiles. "Why don't I tell you about my mom and you can tell me about yours?"[11]

Campbell and other companies used this type of advertising to extend their claims beyond their products' appeal to suggest that their foods would generate such powerful love that it could help people overcome their worst disappointments or tragedies. Moreover, copywriters continually cultivated a product's nostalgic potential to ensure later sales.[12]

Researchers and advertisers for baked goods adopted a similar approach. In his 1957 memo "What Motivates Housewives to Buy Bakery Products Other Than Bread," Dichter claimed that baked goods represented "the love, fertility, and reward that mother has for her family and children." Just over ten years later, in another study on "The Psychology of Identification: A Creative Memorandum on 'Grandma Keebler,' " he again pushed for the invisible souls of baked goods when he claimed, "Cookies are morsels of love." Dichter asserted that while people might rationally read the list of ingredients, advertisers also could persuade them that foods had an emotional content as well. In his analysis of the company, Grandma Keebler, and the cookie itself, Dichter theorized, "Cookies have content. Cookies are mysterious and magic. They always have something in them. They are mixed like a love potion." In the postwar era, baked goods advertisers like Betty Crocker and Swans Down adhered to his recommendations and continued to identify food as love. One Swans Down ad asserted, "A gift you bake is a gift from the heart" and "Remember, men love Swans Down cakes (and the girls who bake them!)." Even at the end of the century, a 1999 Nestlé Toll House ad featured a young boy about to take a bite out of a cookie. The text scrolled down the page, flowing over the reader: "Each cookie, a feeling of love, a desire to eat one more. One more." While food writer Laura Shapiro optimistically argued in the early twenty-first century that, "Although most women still prepare most of the family meals, cooking has become the first domestic chore to float free of sex roles," it is not clear from food advertising that this was the case.[13] Domestic chores like vacuuming and doing the laundry had much more potential to be gender neutral, perhaps because they were less demanding; required less skill; and were less essential. Not free from these restraints, food advertisements remained enmeshed in emotional rhetoric.

Anthropologist Daniel Miller's 1998 study of consumption in North London provides some insights into why the relationship between American women and food shopping retained such poignancy. Miller believed that shopping could best be understood as an expression of a "relationship between the shopper and a particular other individual such as a child or partner." He considered love to be the "main force which carries provisioning." Miller resisted a narrow definition of love or one limited to courtship, and instead characterized it as "much more to do with obligation, duty and a set of predispositions which exist prior to the relationship which manifests them. It is situated largely within the expectations of kinship and pattern of interdependence." Acknowledging that men had been "constantly reintroduced" to shopping, he found that "shopping as a category was overwhelmingly associated with women. Furthermore, it was women who were predominantly represented by themselves and others as the natural gender of love."[14] Miller's understanding of love and shopping is helpful in discerning what advertisers tried to communicate to consumers. Advertisers hoped that the mantra "food is love" would forever tie up their targeted consumers in an arrangement of women shopping and cooking to express their emotional commitment to their families.

"Bake a Loaf of Love for Your Family Soon"

A woman showing her love for her family through food purchases was one of the enduring advertising images of the twentieth century. Advertisers and researchers remained convinced that women should care about pleasing others. Dichter, for example, claimed that that the "womanly symbol of soup" was strongly directed toward men, "And accordingly, soup is for father, for son much more than for daughter."[15] Moreover, advertisers held no expectations that men should care about pleasing others with food. This emphasis on women giving to others, particularly men, was so complete that ads rarely portrayed women finding gratification in eating.

The IMR studies in the 1950s reinforced this notion as they continually recounted interviews in which women "would state that they bake desserts to please their husbands, children, etc. . . . It is morally wrong to indulge oneself, but it is quite noble to exert one's efforts to indulge others." According to researchers, just procuring the food was evidence of women's love. In a 1955 report on "The Psychology of a Woman on Food Shopping Day," Dichter argued that

Partly consciously and partly subconsciously she is aware that she is keeping her family alive, that she is protecting and encouraging life and growth, that her deepest instincts are at play. In a sense, next to bearing children, shopping for food is the most important action in which a woman may engage.[16]

It also claimed that a woman shops "for recognition of herself in her various roles and functions. It is this psychic charge which surrounds shopping with such a dense emotional atmosphere." In both cooking and shopping, advertisers expected women to deny their own preferences and indulge their families' desires.

Magazine editors and publishers also encouraged this trend, with some going so far as to create gendered versions of their magazines. According to magazine analyst Ellen McCracken, in the early 1980s *Newsweek* mailed unwitting female subscribers a different version of the national weekly news magazine, with advertisements targeted to their supposed female needs and sensibilities. In 1987, advertising director Jerry Firestone admitted that *Psychology Today* published gendered editions so that food and beverage companies could market certain products that they hoped would appeal more to one gender than the other. Bev Hood, editor of *New Woman*, a magazine targeted to working women, defended its embrace of the differentiated food ads, claiming, "Food preparation and presentation are a form of self-expression. It makes our readers feel good about themselves. It's another way for a woman to express her love for her family and friends." With the support of magazine editors, advertisers tried to persuade women that baking and cooking with such products as Fleischmann's Yeast was a "wonderfully warm way to express yourself and to express your love for family and friends."[17]

Copywriters suggested that women historically had put a lot of love into the food they served, a level of caring unmatched until the advertised corporation started manufacturing the food. Dinty Moore, for example, claimed in a 1966 ad, "No one but you and Dinty Moore makes beef stew with such loving care." In some ads, adding love and care to the ingredients purportedly helped transform foods from institutional products to "home-made" ones. Others argued that buying foods from a company that took care in choosing the ingredients showed a woman's love. For example, after detailing the quality products the company used, a series of 1970s ads proclaimed, "For the people you love, Stouffer's plays it straight." These reminders continued to the end of the century. Bisquick ran a campaign in *Ebony* in 2000 that reminded women, "Bisquick makes it good. You make it *special.*"[18]

Ads designed to pull at consumer heart strings proliferated in the 1970s. Advertisers for convenience foods competed with those for ingredients like yeast to assert their ability to convey love. A 1970 ad for Red Star yeast in *Farm Journal* tried to lure women into making bread from scratch with a header that boldly proclaimed, "Baking Bread Is Making Love." It encouraged women to "Bake a loaf of love for your family soon."[19] In addition to familiar baking ads, manufacturers also proposed that women demonstrate their devotion with luncheon meats and frozen dinners. The following 1972 Stouffer's ad appeared in *Sunset*: "Today your youngest picked a flower for you on his way home from school. Your husband finally fixed the kitchen faucet. And, somehow, you wish the plain dinner you've planned were a little less plain. It's a good day for Stouffer's."[20] A few years later Oscar Mayer used a picture of a towheaded boy waving good-bye as he headed off to school, with his schoolbooks and lunch box. The only text read, "This is why we make bologna the way we do."

Nor did things change during the 1980s and 1990s. A 1986 ad encouraged women to "Put a little love in lunch with Skippy" and featured a smiling little girl clutching a piece of bread covered with peanut butter, a prominent heart carved into it. Quaker Oats ran an ad in 1992 that used a collage of images of a mother getting her daughter ready for school, and confided that its cereal was perfect, "For moms who have a lot of love, *but not a lot of time.*" In 1995, Post claimed that its Bran Flakes were a "Care Package" and reminded women, "Hey, he's not just any guy. So don't just give him any bran flakes. Post Premium Bran Flakes. Another Way to Show You Care."[21] Advertisers across the century hoped to manipulate women's love for their families into a purchase of their products by arguing that they needed it to show their love.

At the end of the century, advertisers still drew explicit connections between food and love. A Kraft ad appearing in April 2000 asked, "How long does it take to say I love you?" Below the picture of a woman looking adoringly at her daughter and husband, she answered,

How long does it take to say I love you?

In just no time, I show my family exactly how I feel about them when I come home from work and prepare our favorite: KRAFT Deluxe Macaroni & Cheese! After they taste that rich creamy cheese sauce that reminds them of homemade, I always hear them say, MORE PLEASE ... which really means, I love you too, Mom!

Figure 2. While featuring a familiar focus on love, this ad was unusual for its inclusion of African Americans, who rarely appeared in general audience magazines, with most, like this April 2000 ad, found in *Ebony* and other targeted media.

In just no time, I show my family exactly the way I feel about them when I come home from work and prepare our favorite: KRAFT Deluxe Macaroni & Cheese! After they taste that rich creamy cheese sauce that reminds them of homemade, I always hear them say, "MORE PLEASE" . . . which really means, "I love you too, Mom!"[22]

Advertisers used the "food is love" dictum to forge a connection between women and food, and to strengthen their argument that women should prepare food for their families. Advertisements featured women generating feelings of love, even from foods they did not cook from scratch, and appealed to women's desire for credit when they promised that serving particular foods would earn them love from their families.

Figure 3. Promising more than good health and taste attributes, food ads tried to sell food as love.

"I Don't Hear 'I love you' When I Do the Wash, But When I Take Out the Domino . . ."

Food advertisers also exploited the connection between food preparation and love toward women, enlisting mild allusions, floating hearts, and pecks on the cheek to demonstrate how her food selection accorded her affection. The message was clear: when she chose such a high quality, tasty product she was entitled to receive love and credit for her pains.

One of the earliest and most prominent advertisers to promote its product as a love potion was Jell-O. Starting in the late nineteenth century, ads assured women, "Even if you can't cook, you can make a Jell-O dessert." With frequent references to new brides' debacles in the kitchen, the copy promised that Jell-O would not fail to please men. The opening line of a Jell-O promotional giveaway book zeroed in on their market, "Every day a host of brides become housekeepers, each with a man to feed and keep happy." A promotional card that featured a bride with a young flower girl, suggested that "Jell-O: America's most famous dessert" contributed to women's matrimonial status and well-being. An ad headed "Their First Dinner at Home," described her accomplishment, noting, "And now, proudly successful, she holds up to *his* delighted gaze the beautiful dish of Strawberry Jell-O which she has prepared with her own hands."[23]

Twenty-five years later the promise of love and devotion remained. A 1941 ad for Jell-O Puddings asked women, "What do you want most in a chocolate dessert? Rich flavor, of course—a luscious, deep, old-time chocolate taste. *That's* what gets you kisses and compliments." The drawing featured a man bussing a woman's cheek, while a heart sprang up from the encounter. A few years later, a Crisco ad featured a woman walking by her family carrying an Apple Crunch Pie. The smell of the pie wafted over the husband, son, and daughter, and sparked hearts. Assuring women of baking success, copywriters also wanted women to believe that their products guaranteed love with everything they made. A 1950 Pillsbury ad claimed, "Men Love Lemon Pie" and tried to persuade women to "Get a fresh grip on his heartstrings with a wonderful, homemade pie like this."[24]

Advertisers thought women might fear that using convenience foods would deprive her of "credit for preparing a tasty dish" and its attendant emotional payoff, so they designed ads to establish a reciprocal relationship between love and even the most readily prepared foods. Ernest Dichter argued, "Not only does appetite respond to an atmosphere of love, but appetite itself can be an act of love. Eating and enjoying the food of a beloved person is a way of showing one's love or respect."[25] Advertisers put that notion into action. A very direct 1954 Pillsbury ad featured a little girl, about seven years old, holding a huge piece of cake in both hands, her fingers covered with frosting, and the statement, "Mother, I love you." To drive home that it was easy to make and guaranteed to bring love, the text assured women,

You've never turned on the lights in a pair of eyes quite so easily. With Pillsbury Cake Mixes, big, beautiful, tender cakes almost pop out of the package. Pillsbury, the leading cake mixes, the ones with choice, country-fresh eggs right in the mix. Milk is *all* you add.[26]

The notion that food not only had the power to show women's love but could also generate love was a powerful message.

Competing against convenience foods, advertisers of primary ingredients struggled to make their products a necessity. They acknowledged that it could be faster to use convenience products, but would not concede that it was easier, and certainly not that it was better. Moreover, advertisers gave value to the authentic, home-baked goods made from scratch and defined them as real. Ads equated real foods with real love and affection.

In the 1960s and 1970s, the feminist movement awakened many women to the reality that housework was unappreciated work. While advertisers' messages in this period continued to hold women responsible for the work, they also began to promise not just love but also respect for their labors. Fleischmann's Yeast ads, for example, generally had two consistent features: a photo of husbands smiling or eating and the recipe that would guarantee success. One 1964 ad asked, "What's so special about Christmas this year? *You* are . . . when you bake them a Christmas stollen. What do you put into it? Well . . . time. And love. And Fleischmann's Yeast. What do you get out of it? Well . . . love. Smiles. Even thanks."[27]

The ad admitted that women's work was often thankless. By 1971, the message was even more blunt. Appearing in the staid *Farm Journal*, one ad encouraged women, "Take the time. Then take the credit." In the photo, the husband had just brought the wife roses and he and their little girl looked at her adoringly. The text contended, "Baking from scratch is as easy as baking someone else's pre-packaged ingredients. It's just not as quick. But what you bake in that little extra time is a very special kind of gift—the real thing. And only you can bake it this good, so only you can take the credit."[28] Male approval of women's cooking in ads lent credence to both the foods' quality and their success in winning their spouses' love. Ads encouraged women to "Make your husband glad he's yours" and "Let him brag about you."[29] The image of men's enthusiastic approval of the food held out the promise that a woman could reach her husband's heart through his stomach.

Ads throughout the century used wedding dresses and wedding bands to establish that women's choices in the kitchen determined her marital fate. These ads generally did not refer to the betrothed couples featured in their ads, confident that women would get the message: serving this product will bring you a happy marriage. Rather than just demonstrating positive outcomes, some ads sought to uncover women's anxieties. One 1969 Hunt's ad featured in *Seventeen* explicitly tried to generate and exploit women's (and girls') fear of not marrying. Titled "Hunt's guide for single girls (who don't plan to stay that way)," it featured a young woman standing behind a set candle-lit table for two and recipes for meals that promised romantic success, such as one entitled "The Clincher (or is that a ring in hand?)."[30]

Even at the end of the century, advertisers continued to rely on the hope that women craved not food, but love and acknowledgement for their labors in the kitchen. A 1992 ad for Domino Sugar spilled over two pages. The first page claimed, "I don't hear 'I love you' when I do the wash," and the second explained, "but when I take out the Domino . . . I'm Mother of the Year. Call me superstitious but I only bake with Domino Sugar. It's pure, so I know what I bake is a sure thing. And if I care enough to bake in the first place, I'm going to do it right."[31] In 1997, an ad for Kraft's Shake 'N Bake encouraged women to serve "Italy night" and alluded to the potential payoff when they claimed, "And don't be surprised if they shower you with amore." Advertisers wanted women to care what others thought about the food they provided.

Their wishes were borne out in Daniel Miller's above-mentioned study of late twentieth-century shopping in London. when he concluded, "What the shopper desires above all is for others to want and to appreciate what she brings." In the world of food, all of women's hard work, frustration, and investment became evidence of her love. To challenge the connection between women and food was to challenge the connection between women and love.[32]

"Like Mother Used to Make"

Advertisers made both a short- and long-term investment when their copy involved nostalgia. From the earliest food ads and into the next century, advertisers wove women, food, love, and the past into a tapestry of emotional warmth. In scores of pages, ads invited women to fuse products into their family traditions and raise children with the brand-name products embedded in their food—and love—memories. Ads promised a lasting emotional payoff if women prepared foods that created and triggered feelings of love and loyalty in their loved ones.[33]

Ernest Dichter encouraged companies to consider the importance of nostalgia to consumers. In a study for the convenience product Crustquick, he discovered that

In this age of efficiency, electrical equipment and harried living, people look back with nostalgia at the days when things were done for you with thoughtfulness and care. The long hours that our mothers used to spend in the kitchen signified to us how much she loved us. The greater the amount of personal effort she used to exert, the greater we felt her love for us was.[34]

It was irrelevant to advertisers that appeals to nostalgia harkened back to the earliest food ads. In one 1902 ad entitled "Like Mother Used to Make" the writer reminisced,

It makes my mouth water to think of it—most cooks won't bother now-a-days as they did then to get things "just right," and so we make None Such Mince Meat to save the labor and expense and give the husbands and boys plenty of mince pies "like mother used to make."[35]

Advertisers wanted consumers to believe that their food products had the ability to create connections and continuity between the perceived constancy of the past and the chaos of the present. Moreover, they wanted women to assume responsibility for creating traditions in their family's history.

Another way manufacturers promoted their products was to plant the idea that it would help create special memories, essentially future nostalgia. Campbell's soup specialized in this manufacture of nostalgia. A 1923 ad positioned Campbell as "A soup no home kitchen could produce. A soup that lingers in your memory." Fifteen years later, ads claimed that chicken noodle soup was a

cherished food of our pioneer ancestors. . . . There, in their time, our foremothers simmered the chicken broth long and slow, and kneaded, rolled and cut the noodles. . . . So, for Auld Lang Syne and for your family's pleasure, won't you serve it to them tomorrow?[36]

Creating a false connection between foods made in the eighteenth and nineteenth centuries and those manufactured in the twentieth century enabled advertisers to profit from consumer desire for an idealized past.

Other soup makers also helped promulgate the idea that soup and love had a historic, and therefore inevitable, relationship. Companies sought to connect their instant food products with emotional weight. To sell Lipton's "Just add mix to boiling water" soups, a 1957 ad reminded women, "Soup tastes best when it's fresh home-cooked" and assured them that "In minutes you're dishing up rich chicken broth and golden noodles fragrant and delicious as the old-time slow-simmered kind."[37]

Lipton did not let up over time. A 1971 ad encouraged women to make "Chicken soup for your loved ones" and featured a picture of a mother serving her son a bowl of soup. All she had to do was add water, but ad designers put the woman in her kitchen work clothes—an apron—to suggest that women were still working and could therefore generate feelings of love. More than immediate emotional gain, Lipton also promised that women had the potential to "Make a memory for your kids." They suggested a slew of opportunities, prompting, "Remember fresh, hot chicken soup for the sniffles? For cold, frosty days? For little sadnesses?"[38]

In its nostalgia campaign, Lipton may have been building on findings in the previous decade. Dichter, for example, conducted a 1960 survey

Figure 4. In this 1992 ad, Hunt's used nostalgic imagery to suggest that its spaghetti sauces were authentic.

on the psychology of soup and found that 98 per cent of respondents associated soup with mothers. He concluded,

The deepest psychological meaning of soup is found in images of home and mother. It is a matter of clear and certain knowledge that when people are sick, soup becomes an especially craved food. Sickness is usually accompanied by tendencies to infantile regression. When we are ill, we become children again and we want mother-love. Soup is the perfect symbol of that mother-love.[39]

Campbell's longevity in the marketplace allowed it to promote itself as a long-time favorite. A 1974 ad for Campbell's tomato soup informed consumers, "You know it's always going to taste as good as you remember." In just one sentence, copywriters conveyed quality, taste, continuity, and nostalgia. The rest of the ad confirmed that the soup had been "America's favorite for generations" and encouraged women to "Stir up some happy memories."[40]

One of the most successful companies to market nostalgia was bread manufacturer Pepperidge Farm (bought by the Campbell Company in 1961). As a staple of American cuisine, bread products were a central part of many diets. Ads for the bread company took that centrality and extended it backward, suggesting that they were an "old-fashioned" company. Margaret Rudkin did start the company in her kitchen in 1935 when she created bread with no additives to help her son's asthma. It was not until 1947, however, that she built her first modern bakery, which allowed the business to expand. A company that did not take off until mid-century became renowned for their nostalgic slogan, "Pepperidge Farm Remembers."[41]

Dichter would surely have approved of Pepperidge Farm's tactics. In a mid-century study, he encouraged white bread manufacturers to appeal to emotional, homemade associations, demand for variety, and the importance of bread as a "family-centered" food. Pepperidge Farm was often successful in making all of these appeals in one ad. Their ads usually started as questions like, "Remember when the only thing you liked better than your Mom's homemade jam was your Mom's home-baked white bread?" and "Remember the golden streudel, packed with apples, hazelnuts and raisins, that made a visit to Grandma worthwhile?" The response, of course, was that "Peppridge Farm Remembers" and went on to detail their quality ingredients and the amount of care they put into their products.[42]

To compete against companies like Pepperidge Farm, manufacturers that supplied the ingredients for baking had to fight nostalgia for bread with nostalgia for process. Gold Medal flour, for example, suggested numerous scenarios in which women could "Bake a Gold Medal Memory." Teaching girls to bake, thereby creating a new generation of consumers as well, was a favorite theme. Boys in those ads invariably appeared as appreciative eaters, rather than as bakers. Another ingredient company, Fleischmann's Yeast, encouraged women to "Bake Someone Happy." A 1973 ad featured photos of bread—the caption simply read, "Home."[43]

Soup and bread ads also made frequent references to aroma. The Fleischmann ad above asked, "Remember the rich, warm feeling you got in your home every time she baked? The smell? The taste? It seemed to tell you just how much she cared." Ernest Dichter and other researchers had long understood the importance of aroma to the human psyche. In his research on soup, Dichter reported that

It is well known that scents, odors, smells are a very powerful stimulus in starting a chain of associations and in evoking memories. Small wonder then if over 30% of our respondents related their childhood soup associations in terms of the aroma. In general, aroma is one of the most important factors in connection with soups.[44]

One of Dichter's successors in speculating on *why* people want what they want is Clotaire Rapaille, a French-born medical anthropologist. Rapaille argued that "sublimated emotional memories occupied a place between each individual's unconscious (Freud) and the collective unconscious of the entire human race (Jung)." In his research into how cultures acculturate individuals, he learned that people create "mental highways" that associate words with emotional resonance. For example, in America, coffee brewing in the kitchen coincided with the childhood experience of warmth, feeding, and love. He told Procter & Gamble, "Don't care about the taste. You have to own the aroma." They created ads for Folgers focused on aromas wafting throughout the house, symbolizing love.[45] Food advertisers also took advantage of the romance of aroma and its historic (or promised) resonance in the psyche to persuade women to buy their products.

Advertisers granted mothers and grandmothers a central role in creating meaningful, historic associations with food. Some ads merged mothers and the product so completely that they did not even mention the brand name. A 1944 ad for Chicken of the Sea, for example, featured two American GIs in their fatigues reminiscing about home while they fought in the Second World War. One soldier dreamily asked, "You know what I'd like best right now? . . . One of Mom's nice cold tuna salads." The ad reminded readers, " 'Home' and 'Mom's cooking' are the two things that millions of Service men want most. And, high on the culinary list are dishes, either hot or cold, made (as only Mom can make them!) of these famous brands of tuna." A 1973 ad campaign for B&M baked beans encouraged women to "Help him remember his mother's baked beans" by purchasing theirs.[46] Even the simplest food preparation took on heroic proportions in food ads, which suggested that mothers and wives held the key to offering quality food and unlocking deep emotions and memories for their loved ones.

Older women, however, continued to grip the imagination of ad executives and the images they embraced of grandmotherly women remained static throughout the century. Ads usually depicted grandmothers with glasses, white hair up or under a hat, and an apron. Adoring adult children or grandchildren often appeared at her side, reflecting their love and devotion to her and her food expertise.

Occasionally ad creators, not content with just the grandmother connection, situated her in the kitchen or dining room setting to provoke

Don't you wish mornings were just like they used to be?

Pancakes and orange juice on the table.

A school bus rumbling in the distance.

Bright eyes and matched socks.

Get Real

Now more than ever, the best start under the sun.
Florida Orange Juice.

Figure 5. Past or present, food advertisers' idealized home featured women feeding their families, catering to men's needs.

nostalgia. A 1975 ad for Mary Kitchen roast beef hash featured a grandmother serving hash to her grandson. It presented a romantic turn-of-the-century kitchen with a Hoosier cabinet, open sink, and wood-burning stove. A couple of years later, an ad for Mrs. Paul's frozen candied sweet potatoes showcased Norman Rockwell's painting *Freedom from Want* from his Four Freedoms series. The grandmother's role in preparing and presenting the Thanksgiving meal is central, and the company offered women seeking to replicate this "Holiday spirit in the American tradition" their frozen side dish.[47]

Grandmothers exceeded mothers' power because they had taught the mothers. Very often, ads suggested, mothers just followed their own mothers' recipes or bought the same brand she did. Ads also promised consumers that their products most closely approximated the buyers' mothers' or grandmothers' cooking and would therefore generate the same memories. Historian Karal Ann Marling's description of Betty Crocker's changing appearance, for example, noted that with her 1995 makeover, which included graying temples, "this was an older and a wiser Betty Crocker, a woman fully capable of giving the kind of household advice that mothers used to give." One 1970 ad had a grandmotherly woman proclaiming that Burry's Best were "Cookies like Mother used to make." The text juxtaposed the past, "when nobody ever skimped on the baking ingredients," with the present; the only guarantee of love and nostalgia was to buy Burry's.[48]

At the end of the century, "Grandma" remained powerful. Kraft's Stove Top Oven Classics used a print and television campaign featuring two grandmothers to sell their prepared foods. These irate women scowled at consumers and clerks, demanding to know, "What's next, Thanksgiving in a box." The text explained that the advertised food was "like Sunday dinner at Grandma's. No wonder they're miffed." The grandmother stand-ins were concerned that the food was so good and so easy to make ("Sunday taste, Tuesday effort"), that their skills would be obsolete and they would become unnecessary to their families.[49] While gender roles, advertising styles, and eating patterns did change over the course of the twentieth century, food advertising maintained its quest to convince Americans that food is love, and that women were the most capable of creating both.

"Follow Directions—And You'll Never Be Disappointed!"

At the same time, food advertisers preyed on women's anxieties and insecurities to compel them to consume. While some copywriters may have believed women were already afraid, that they helped to encourage this concern is conclusive. Advertisers acted as though women should fear a multitude of failings, including being a bad wife, mother, hostess, and cook. Women throughout the century were vulnerable to these threats because of their financial dependence on men. With many marriages, particularly in the first two-thirds of the century, predicated on men fulfilling their role as provider and women caring for their families as homemakers, women's livelihood often depended on their ability to please their husbands.[50]

While some ads were subtle, many were explicit in their efforts to rattle women's confidence. Ads for baking products such as flour and sugar tended to be particularly threatening throughout the century. Preying on fears that cakes would not rise and cookies would not taste good, ads repeatedly asked women, sometimes literally as in a 1929 ad for Swan's Down Cake Flour, "Afraid of failure?" Seventy years later, the message remained the same. With a picture of a middle-aged woman jumping out of an airplane, a 1999 ad claimed that this woman "Dares to be different. Drinks milk without checking expiration date. Encourages her kids to take chances." However, the ad's bold headline warned, she "Never takes chances when it comes to her brown sugar pinwheels. Baking is no time to start living on the edge." Advertisers conceded that women could have interests outside the kitchen and even be adventurous, but continually reminded them that cooking for their families should be a primary concern and be an area where they played it safe. Advertising messages consistently told women, "Follow directions—and you'll never be disappointed!"[51]

Insecurity is a prevalent theme throughout food advertisements. The advertising business, according to historian James D. Norris, "Tapped a very deep American insecurity and deadly pressure to conform by equating consumption of an article with social status and approval." Regardless of an ad's tone—cajoling or foreboding—it always carried the same implied threat: not using the advertised product would result in some type of failure. Advertisers tried to make women feel vulnerable and uncertain, so that they would pay attention to their messages. A 1905 ad for Triscuits warned women, "The popularity of the queen of the kitchen depends largely upon her ability to surprise and please her subjects. If she will invoke the aid of Shredded Whole Wheat Biscuit her task will be simplified and the loyalty of her subjects unquestioned."[52] Even as they granted women a royal role in their households, advertisers still warned them that to earn their family's approval they had to purchase convenience foods.

Ads also suggested and exploited the dread of being passé. Food manufacturers wanted women to believe that their products could transform their lives and appealed to their desires to be modern and progressive. A 1926 ad sang the praises of "ambitious" women who used Campbell's soups:

These women do not neglect their housekeeping. Far from it. They do it more efficiently every day. But they accomplish better results with less drudgery. They serve better food with less time in the kitchen. They raise the standard of their family's health and their own—with less expense and effort. All praiseworthy steps in the onward march of their social ambition.[53]

Modernity's blessings had limits, evidently, because the advertisements never once in this period suggested that a man or child could heat up a can of soup. Advertisers tried to persuade women that only they possessed the skill to cook in the modern world.

Researchers and advertisers found that in addition to encouraging women to be what Dichter called "obsessed by feelings of guilt," they could further prey on and fan women's insecurities by using false praise. Shapiro recounted the history of the Pillsbury Bake-Off, which rewarded women for their baking skills if they used Pillsbury flour. The company believed from surveys that what women needed most to make "homemaking a full and satisfying career" was appreciation.[54] With their baking contest, the company backed up their rhetorical praise with money and national attention. Other advertisers adopted this strategy in different forms, but the premise of these ads and promotions was that women were strong, capable, and competent *if* they used the advertised product.

Advertisers suggested that women were "clever," "ambitious," "creative," and "smart," and applauded their ability to complete cooking feats. For example, a 1960 ad for Softasilk Cake Flour featured a photograph of a middle-aged woman. The header proclaimed, "Picture of THE SMARTEST WOMAN IN THE WORLD! She's just made a homemade cake that's 'out of this world' . . . naturally made better with soft, soft Softasilk Cake Flour." Betty Crocker's image appeared below the caption; the text next to her head assured the reader, "Here's a cake that will show everyone how smart you are" and provided the complete recipe.[55]

Ads praised women's intelligence for remembering to buy their products and tried to persuade them to express their originality through cooking. A Libby's ad that appeared during World War II provided women with a recipe "custom-made for these days of shortages." It encouraged women to bake with Libby's products and "Call it your Ingenuity Cake."[56] Encouraging vapid creativity ensured the consumption of the promoted food and women's participation in a never-ending kitchen culture of food preparation.

Ernest Dichter strongly encouraged postwar advertisers to provide women with opportunities to be creative, claiming that it would mitigate the drudgery of housework. He went so far as to suggest, "She has a great need for 'doctoring up' the can and thus prove her personal participation and her concern for giving satisfaction to her family." Moreover, he claimed, "It permits her to use at home all the faculties that she would display in an outside career." Shapiro's astute analysis of this phenomenon in the 1950s captures the ways advertisers transformed the idea of "cooking" and made creativity "the personal touch that would turn an ordinary dish into an epicurean one . . . (it) was the fairy dust that would transform opening boxes into real cooking." Even though their praise of women was essentially self-congratulatory, researchers encouraged advertisers to give women "credit" for buying the right products and embracing the role of consumer and home-maker.[57]

Ads encouraged women to be creative with food in two primary ways: modifying its appearance and altering its taste. Advertisers suggested that the appearance of food was critical to cooking success. At mid-century in particular, ads included an emphasis on color. One 1946 ad claimed obtusely, "More color—better eating" and suggested, "See how such a simple change as adding the golden cheer of Niblets Brand whole kernel corn brightens up a meal." In 1949 food critic M. F. K. Fisher ridiculed "the spate of recent recipes concocted for their visual appeal alone, without any consideration for the palate," or "the on-slaught of marshmallow-vegetable-gelatin salads and such which smile at me in Kodachrome from current magazine advertisements." One exam-ple of this emphasis on appearance as an indicator of quality and taste was a 1960 ad which featured a photograph of a woman in a formal dress in the background and a piece of cake in the foreground. The headline made the connection, declaring "Butter Yellow: Fashion's freshest color news for Spring!"[58] The ad, part of a full fashion-themed campaign, wanted women to consider food part of the fashion world, with the cap-tion listing who had made the dress, the jewelry, and the cake (Betty Crocker). Food advertisers may also have wanted to embroil women in a belief system that had dishes going in and out of style, holding them hostage to changing preparation trends the way the couture world did.

Some advertisers encouraged women to design foods with molds, ironically claiming that the outcome would be unique and different. One of the more dubious projects proposed was the "Oscar Mayer Holi-day Hostess Tree." This concoction set women to task creating tree or-naments from Oscar Mayer products, including bacon, Little Wieners, Cotto Salami, Little Smokies, and Liver Sausage. It promised that the tree was "fun to make and the ornaments *taste* so good!" Sometimes ads told women that these projects would demonstrate their love, creativity, and talent; others just asked questions like "Why settle for plain rye when you can have rye rolls baked in the shape of turtles?"[59]

Advertisers did focus on taste, although not always tastefully. One 1965 ad taught women the "Gay new way to be saladventurous: Mix two Kraft Dressings to make your own special blend!" It told women the "delicious new blend" would be their "own special concoction." Not content to let women truly "experiment," they offered a "few combinations to start you off." "Be bold. Be daring. Be creative," charged a 1967 Hellmann's ad. It proposed sauces for burgers, such as Burger Foo Yum, a blend of mayon-naise and soy sauce, and Pink Panther, mayonnaise, catsup, and relish. However, this ad, like so many others, provided recipes, negating the necessity for inventing original combinations of convenience foods. The most simplistic were ads that asked women to cook at all. A 1986 Uncle Ben's ad implored, "Some people cook. You create. . . . Let 'em think you're a genius." To achieve this, all women had to do was cook up the rice, sauce, and vegetables "in just 5 minutes." The placement and content of ads suggest a desire to keep women as the only family member who could open a can. Advertisers wanted to convince readers that convenience foods needed women to turn them into meals.[60]

Researchers and advertisers realized that by placing full responsibility for feeding families on women, they could exploit women's legitimate frustration and desperation to provide palatable, approved foods to their loved ones. Ernest Dichter, in particular, may have understood before Betty Friedan and others that women were not finding fulfillment in the home. His response, however, was decidedly different from theirs. Instead of taking the quest outside, he strategized that advertisers could try to satisfy women's need for creativity and self-expression inside the home with food projects. Advertisers forestalled women's efforts to change or challenge gender roles by besieging them with ideas for new and improved ways to occupy their minds in the kitchen.[61]

One strategy was to make shopping and cooking appear to be more complex by introducing products and uses that women needed to know in order to appear competent housewives. For example, the apple industry realized that they could promote their produce by marketing their apples' attributes and uses under the headline, " 'Know Your Apples.' " Posing questions about what apples should be used for bobbing and which kind made the best pie, advertisers gave answers like " 'Cortland. Best for salads—stays white longer when sliced or diced. Also a fine eating apple and a quick cooking and baking apple.' "[62] By introducing these "rules," advertisers suggested that women could demonstrate their culinary expertise by mastering foods and their uses, and avoid the social faux pas of serving up the wrong food or brand at the wrong time.

Granting female authority was another aspect of the false praise strategy. Advertisers granted women influence in food matters when it served to promote their products, but also undermined women's valid skills and expertise. Ads cautioned that making foods from scratch at home was "now distinctly passé" and challenged those who belonged to the "fast diminishing list of women who go to all the trouble of making their own" to try the advertised products.[63] Advertisers praised women for being smart enough to buy convenience foods, rather than encouraging any culinary skills they might have possessed or sought.

Food advertisers derived the most common female authority from the "everywoman"; be it wife to wife, mother to mother, mother-in-law to new wife, mother to daughter, or neighbor to neighbor, the authority of her gender sufficed. A 1938 ad epitomized the kind of parable advertisers offered women throughout the century. Six photos illustrated the story of a woman who served a luncheon to several other women, but worried

My salad had definitely been a flop. Why, some of the girls hardly touched it. . . . So after they'd gone, I asked my friend Marjorie to tell me the bitter truth. I admitted that even Dick didn't seem to have much enthusiasm for my salads lately. . . . Marjorie said, "They just seem to be a wee bit flat. The trouble may be that you don't use the right kind of dressing." . . . "I believe you've got the answer," I said. "Let's phone Judy and get the recipe for that marvelous dressing she served last Sunday night." "Recipe, my eye," said Judy, . . . "that was Miracle Whip." . . . I had a buffet supper a week or so later, and the salad was the hit of the party. Even the men praised it, and kept coming back for more. Am I glad I found out about Miracle Whip in time![64]

Advertisers wanted women to be worried about their cooking performance and suggested that other homemakers and the advertisements could help them navigate the uncharted, uncertain waters of consuming convenience foods. The ultimate goal of pleasing men was an integral part of women's strategies.

More than factual information, the advertisements gave women the opportunity to "listen in" to women giving each other advice on how to succeed in their kitchens. Advertisers believed that word of mouth endorsements were more important than any kind of advertisement they could create. To circumvent their lack of control over this phenomenon, advertisers created scenarios, such as the Miracle Whip ad described above, in which women made buying suggestions and demonstrated product approval to "eavesdropping" readers.

Women frequently asserted the merits of products, including their delicious taste, sound economic value, and triumphant role in pleasing a man. A 1942 ad in *Good Housekeeping* claimed, "Farm women had voted on what brand of ham they prefer. Swift's Premium won decisively!" A nameless woman, whose smiling face was featured in a 1947 ad for A&P Super Markets, claimed, "I find pin money at my A&P Super Market!" The ad assured readers, "Let your food dollars provide really good meals for your family . . . and more pin money for other things you want to buy." The Cream of Wheat Company used the L'il Abner cartoon extensively in the 1950s. In 1952, the voluptuous, scantily clad Daisy Mae told *Saturday Evening Post* readers, "Ah got mah man wif dee-lishus 'Cream of Wheat'! So kin you!!" L'il Abner, finally caught by Daisy Mae in this installment, offered women male approval of the cereal when he affirmed, "Hit's th' world's bes' mate-bait! Ah knows fum experi-unce."[65] These mid-century examples were not unique. Ads throughout the century granted female consumers the authority to endorse products, but only in the context of using their expertise to reinforce traditional gender roles.[66] Unlike male authority figures, most female figures were not scientists, government officials, or trained professionals. Their authority in those roles would have undermined the power dichotomy advertisers claimed should dictate women's behavior.

The most fundamental concern female characters addressed was male approval of the food product. Sometimes ads explored the multiple benefits to women who successfully satisfied men and their hunger. A 1941 Stokely's ad for peas used four frames to reveal how "Edith finds way to get new Easter outfit by helping hubby land an order." First, he told her, "Honey, you can have a new Easter outfit if I land Brown's order—An extra-nice dinner tonight ought to help." Next Edith and Jane discussed what to serve. Jane offered, "Men like Stokely's Honey Pod Peas . . . They taste so fresh . . . And there's a grand recipe on the back of the label." Edith replied, "Thanks, Jane. I'll try it. I do want this dinner to be a success." At dinner Mr. Brown praised Edith, "Say, that's a slick idea, Mrs. Green—Fixing peas like that. They taste so fresh, too! You're a lucky fellow, Bill." Demurely she replied, "I'm lucky, too. To have a man like Bill to cook for." Finally, in the last frame, Bill rushed toward Edith, announcing, "Well, Sweet, I got the order—and you get the Easter outfit! You certainly deserve it, too!"[67] More than just creating fears, these kinds of ads often spoke to legitimate concerns women had. For example, this ad illustrates the significance of women's work, not only in the immediate sense of pleasing her husband and securing her marriage, but also in a broader sense of impressing her husband's employer, thereby solidifying his position as breadwinner and the security of her dependence.

Ads frequently featured women who claimed to hold expertise on a number of other issues, including cost and quality. Suggesting that women were credible authorities, one 1935 ad featured a woman who claimed " 'I allow myself only a dollar a day for food—so I can't afford to risk a failure when I bake—that's why I stick to dependable Royal Baking Powder." Granting this housewife tremendous respect for her ability to "feed three on $7 a week" in the midst of the Great Depression, the ad predicated her success and that of her "growing boy and a hard-working husband" on her use of Royal Baking Powder. A woman in a 1947 ad testified in a courtroom before a judge, "Honest, Crisco makes everything I cook taste better." Merging fantasy and reality, a 1955 General Foods Corporation advertisement used the children's story of the "Old woman who lived in a shoe, Who had so many children" to declare that, "she *knew* what to do! She lined them all up for a penny-wise feast—A huge bowl of Jell-O and one spoon apiece."[68] For many during the postwar baby boom, a story about a woman who faced the economic struggle of feeding and satisfying a lot of children may well have resonated with their concerns.

The home, the kitchen in particular, was one of the few places women had authority in American culture prior to the 1970s, so there was a logical reliance on female authority figures who located their expertise there. However, as women found greater influence throughout society, it is striking the extent to which advertisers maintained this approach, frequently tying it to nostalgia and the influence of grandmothers. A 1982 ad, for example, presented two friends, Martha and Harriet, who appeared as old-fashioned as their names, with pearls and aprons, sitting at the table with tea, writing letters, and proclaiming themselves as the authorities on mayonnaise. Entitled "Spreading the Word," the ad shared that "For years, Martha and Harriet told everyone they knew to use Hellmann's . . . now they know better. They've discovered . . . Kraft, and now they have to tell Susan, and Linda, and."[69] Even at the end of the century, advertisers only granted women authority within their circumscribed role as homemakers.

Food corporations often informed consumers that they employed women, which they hoped would lend credibility to their quality claims. Sometimes ads used testimonials from self-proclaimed "experts," such as a 1926 testimonial ad for Borden's Milk. As was typical of ads during the period, dense text filled the ad. Written by Mildred Maddocks Bentley, the former director of the Good Housekeeping Institute, the ad offered women information and advice about using canned milk. Bentley encouraged women to send away for the free book she had written, but also offered, "after you have read the book, if you have any questions or comments to make, I shall be delighted to hear from you and to give any advice I can." An August 1958 memo to the Stouffer Company Review Board Members affirmed the importance of women as corporate advisors, noting that Stouffer's offered consumers "quality food created on the basis of a tremendous amount of experience in feeding people, with the advice and counsel of women experts all the way along the line." Advertisers always touted the approval of supposedly influential women, such as a 1972 ad for Morton's that assured women that "Virginia Watjen, Inventor of the Frozen Chicken Pot Pie, hasn't quit checking on us for 25 years."[70]

Using celebrities to endorse products was another long-standing practice of food advertisers. While most celebrities who appeared in ads were men, some ads granted some renowned or quasi-famous women authority. These testimonials usually claimed that products enabled their achievements or that because of their position, be it wealth, status, or beauty, they were in a position to know best which products to choose. Marguerite Jordan, the third place finalist from Atlantic City's 1927 National Bathing Beauty Contest (later the Miss America Contest) credited Fleischmann's Yeast with her success. She recounted that she used to be "run down and underweight. My digestion was bad and I was very nervous."[71] The ad claimed that she was cured two weeks after her doctor suggested yeast, went on to win the title of Miss Kansas City, and competed successfully in the national beauty competition.

To offset any trepidation women might have in taking advice from women with unusual professions, advertisers took special care to tout women's femininity and emphasize their focus on pleasing men. In 1941, Esther Williams appeared as a "professional swimmer and housewife" hawking Kellogg's Corn Flakes; the ad assured women that she was now Mrs. Leonard Kovner. In a 1999 *Ebony* ad, Lawry's Seasoned Salt tempered the WNBA's Lisa Leslie's sports authority by featuring her in a long red evening gown and text that assured, "And she cooks too. Not only does superstar Lisa Leslie have all the right moves on the runway and the basketball court, she has a string of victories in the kitchen."[72]

In addition to actual women, advertisers also relied on female icons and symbols to gain the audience's trust. Reflecting on the "The Current State of Live Trademarks," a 1957 *Tide* article asserted that "One of the great stereotypes of this century is the big corporation—cold, impersonal, frightening. For companies which sell cake flour, or canned ham, or colorful desserts to small, warm human beings, such an image can be damaging." Fundamentally, then, women needed to be sold by some*one* instead of some*thing*. According to the *Tide* analysis, "Ideally, the corporate character is a woman, between the ages of 32 and 40, attractive, but not competitively so, mature but youthful looking, competent yet warm, understanding but not sentimental, interested in the consumer but not involved with her."[73] Countless food companies and industries followed this model and created female characters like "Aunt Jemima," "Aunt Jenny," "Elsie the Cow," "Carolyn Campbell," "Miss Fluffy Rice," and "Ann Pillsbury." These characters gave companies a female voice to offer advice, judgment, and ideas. Sometimes these characters had fairly small parts, such as signing responses to consumer mail, and limited campaigns, but occasionally characters seemed to take on a life of their own, literally and figuratively.

Across time, across generations, and across the country, consumers embraced characters, some assuming nearly mythological status, and many believed to be real. Most famously, the public embraced Betty Crocker. In a 1953 research study on the "Effectiveness of Betty Crocker in Promoting General Mills Products," Dichter discovered that "Women find in Betty Crocker, whether a person or a role, the satisfaction of many important psychological needs." Virtually every respondent described her as "the externalized image of the ideal American woman." Betty Crocker addressed women's feelings of self-doubt by providing "a vindication of the value, dignity and importance of the role of the homemaker and cook." Researchers found the "greatest acceptance of a *real* Betty Crocker on the part of the home-body type of woman, the least sophisticated and the least intellectual type." These women often thought they had elaborate details about her life, including her age, and marital and maternal status.[74]

Ironically, while she validated women's role in the home, Betty Crocker also, for some women, loomed as a secret that could undermine their reputation. Some wives, for example, kept their husbands in the dark about "her" existence. One woman responded, "He thinks I'm a good cook and that's all he should know about the whole matter. Do I ask him who helps him fix the car?" Dichter also warned that even though women generally felt encouraged and approved by Betty Crocker, many still worried that she was a competitor. Unlike Elsie the Cow, who "cannot make a perfect cake or bake a perfect pie," Betty Crocker loomed as a "perfect woman, a woman without failures, who makes no errors." They therefore counseled General Mills to make her more accessible, "more natural and prone to error as is every woman."[75]

The use of female authority figures evolved over time. When research studies found women responding favorably to particular types of women, advertisers modified their time-tested icons to reflect new values. Betty Crocker and Aunt Jemima both underwent considerable changes over the course of the century, with each receiving "make-overs" that distanced them from past ideals and made them more attractive to modern day consumers. By the end of the century, advertisers had transformed Aunt Jemima from a heavy-set woman with a head wrap to a thin, stylish, graying woman with lace and pearls. Betty Crocker underwent a dozen such changes over the century, morphing from a staid Anglo-grandmother type with graying hair to a much younger, non-Anglo looking woman with a casual air. General Mills revealed the last twentieth century incarnation in 1996, after asking American women to submit essays on the "spirit" of Betty Crocker. According to journalist Steven Roberts, "With help from the latest computer technology, pictures of the 75 winners were combined into one image. The result clearly reflects the changes in a nation that is one-quarter nonwhite and shifting rapidly."[76] This effort to reflect a changing America, however, was unusual.

A 1999 study found that, while spokescharacter ad styles changed over time, "no increase in female or nonwhite characters seems to have occurred since the 1950s." Of the hundred identifiable spokescharacters that appeared, only seven were nonwhite and all of those represented food products. In their fifty-year analysis of *Sports Illustrated* and *Good Housekeeping*, they found that, while "The single largest product category associated with spokescharacters was food (54.6%)," there were no food advertisements, no female spokescharacters, and no nonwhite spokescharacters in *Sports Illustrated*, with an audience estimated to be about 77.7 percent male.[77] Women's authority as spokescharacters in advertising historically has been limited to advertisements directed at women.

In addition to appeals to women about their vulnerabilities and efforts to ply them with false praise about their accomplishments and authority, advertisers also suggested that women were entitled to be a little bit selfish. Ads still laid out the expectation that women should be exclusively responsible for caring for the home, providing variety, and knowing good products. Some ads, however, also suggested that women should make time just for themselves. The apparent incongruity of these expectations is constant throughout the century.

Early food sellers hesitated to show women enjoying leisure activities. A 1919 ad for Campbell's soups featured five female Campbell Kids, each at work washing clothes, ironing, cooking, drying dishes, and sewing. The ad promised that "It is like extra help on your busy days to have Campbell's Tomato Soup at hand on your pantry shelf."[78] Food advertisers did not seem confident portraying women outside the home, perhaps for fear that they would leave it. This apprehension certainly reflected the ideology of one early *Ladies' Home Journal* editor, Edward Bok, who thought that shopping was the only reason a woman should leave the home. [79]

As the century wore on, food ads did start to reflect women's activities outside the home, particularly in promoting convenience foods. While aiding housework continued to be an important theme, some advertisers began to suggest that women did not want to spend as much time cooking. Some analysts have found that women's magazines and advertisements encouraged women to use store-bought products to free them to direct their energy toward sexual companionship. In addition to pleasing men, ads explicitly featured women engaged in a variety of activities outside the home. Advertisers' ethnic, racial, and class biases tended to limit what they imagined women doing in their "free time," although by the end of the century ads generally portrayed a more diverse range of interests.

Early ads focused on upper-class activities. A 1923 ad featured a drawing of a woman arriving home at 5 P.M. with a set of golf clubs. It reassured women, "R&R Boned Chicken Solves the Problem of the Impromptu Meal. A late return from an outing or a shopping expedition—the dinner hour approaching! No need to worry." Until the 1950s, advertisers used their own upper-class entertainment activities to sell products and seemed oblivious to any disparity between their lives and those of their consumers. From the 1930s to the 1950s, for example, playing bridge was a common vehicle to suggest products to use as party nourishment and as the solution to women not having prepared the evening meal. For those who feared their husbands' disapproval, advertisers advised limited freedoms and products that would measure up to women's cooking standards.[80]

In the postwar era, Ernest Dichter observed changes taking place in women's lives and attitudes. He found that "Today's woman increasingly thinks life is here to be enjoyed. Her concepts, however, are very far from the frenzies of the twenties, or from bridge and dance madness. She just wants to make life pleasanter and more enjoyable whenever an opportunity arises." In order to reach these consumers, Dichter suggested that advertisers "Appeal to this thirst for greater fun, usually family fun, is a potent advertising device. Tell her that you are adding more zest, more enjoyment to her life, that it is within her reach now to taste new experiences and that she is entitled to taste these experiences."[81]

Advertisements eventually became less specific about women's activities. This enabled advertisers to reach both homemakers and career women, and gave women the ability to imagine their "extra time" in whatever way they wanted. Studying Duncan Hines Cake Mixes in 1955, Dichter found that "Even the 'serious' home-maker has many outside interests, and she appreciates the fact that cake mixes permit her to use the 'extra-time' she saved from baking to spend more time with her children, to visit her local PTA, etc." Advertisers continued to address homemakers, but also expanded to include women who worked outside the home. Both, according to the ads, could benefit from using convenience foods. Sometimes ads would ask, "Racing the clock all morning?" Regardless of women's role, the answer was the same, "Time for a Campbell lunch!" A 1972 ad featured women at the beauty parlor, buying vegetables, at the zoo with her family, playing tennis, as mother-daughter taking up a dress, and on the telephone using a typewriter, and proclaimed, "Because you've got plenty to do, Mrs. Paul's makes Onion Rings." Readers could imagine themselves in each of these positions, or only one, but regardless, advertisers hoped she would see herself as a Mrs. Paul's consumer. The underlying message found by researchers who analyzed ads from 1970 and 1974 was that women in the ads "rarely venture from the home by themselves or with other women. They do smoke, drink, travel, drive in cars, and use banks, but primarily in the company of men." Moreover, they pointed to what was missing as well, noting that professional women were "conspicuously absent . . . although there are over 20 million working wives in this country, few ads showed a woman in a working situation or were geared to appeal to this market segment."[82]

The one exception was frozen foods, first popular in the 1950s. Advertisers often targeted busy women, hoping to capture a market of consumers that they believed needed convenience foods to balance their lives. According to Ellen McCracken, Stouffer's began to promote their foods in the 1980s "by using the persona of an implied working woman: 'For me, freedom comes in a bright red package.' . . . Next to the product is a set of car keys; within the rhetorical system of the ad, the two images are symbols of freedom for the successful working woman."[83] By the 1990s, advertisers generally moved away from explicit feminism to vaguer "feel good" campaigns, such as a 1993 Stouffer's Lean Cuisine ad that had two women walking in the park, with the header "Do something good for yourself." Advertisers believed that appealing to women who were a little selfish and aspired to some limited freedoms would encourage sales of convenience products.

"These Days, You Have to Do It All"

Since the advent of the industrial revolution, with men seeking paid employment outside of the home, domestic work was considered the sole province of women. While some young, white native-born, and later immigrant women found work in early factories, such as the Lowell Mills, there was still a tremendous demand for women to assist in the work done within other people's homes. The scarcity of domestic help long plagued those who could afford it in North America.

In a comprehensive examination of the national picture in 1917, an anonymous *Printers' Ink* author considered the factors contributing to the shortage of domestic workers. They noted, for example,

On the Pacific Coast and in the Southwest where the Mexicans, Chinese, and Japanese once leavened the situation, every year finds the supply less adequate to the demand, and even in the South, which, thanks to its colored population has heretofore been immune from shortages of domestic help, the northward migration of the past two years has left housewives shorthanded in addition to elevating wage scales to undreamed of levels.[84]

Moreover, they argued that this was not a temporary problem brought on by the Great War. According to the labor experts they cited, "it has been gradually taking shape" and was just accelerated by the war efforts. In trying to assess whether future immigrants from Europe might offer some salve, they concluded that it was unlikely, and suggested that, according to the "best qualified government specialists," "the women of America must, in vastly increasing numbers prepare to do their own work." In 1933, a *Printers' Ink Monthly* article reminded those trying to reach women, "Less than 5 per cent of American families have servants." In spite of their own evidence, ads with servants continued to appear in the 1930s.[85]

Though early twentieth-century copywriters continued in the Victorian vein by suggesting that women were dainty, weak, and helpless, as the century wore on, the stereotype had limited usefulness. Housework was a dominant aspect of most women's lives, demanding long hours to complete monotonous, physically demanding tasks and, particularly in the first half of the century, a lot of heavy lifting. Advertisers had to reconcile the Victorian myth of women as frail and delicate with the reality that women's work could be physically exhausting. Occasionally ads made reference to women's housework, noting as Campbell did in 1914, that their foods could help women "whenever tired or hurried." A 1915 Campbell's ad played on the Declaration of Sentiments, written for the 1848 Senecca Falls Convention for Women's Rights by Elizabeth Cady Stanton and Lucretia Mott. While early feminists rewrote the Declaration of Independence to address women's equality and rights, Campbell used a Revolutionary male figure to proclaim women's "Declaration." With quill pen, he wrote, "When in the course of household events it becomes necessary to dissolve the bonds of needless drudgery and care, the problem requires an immediate solution. Campbell Kids." The advertisement encouraged women to "Send for a dozen and declare *your* independence *today*."[86]

Trying to sell women on using new appliances, in 1920 the Western Electric Company created a booklet entitled, "The Eight Hour Day in the Home," which adopted the rallying cry of the labor movement and drew a direct parallel between the goal of paid workers and that of unpaid housewives. Food advertisers generally did not make those connections. While offering to help lighten their load within it, advertisers still maintained that women should remain within the home. Their work load was indeed a heavy one with studies showing that the "amount of time middle-class urban housewives spent on food preparation actually increased slightly from 1931 to 1965." In the 1940s, for example, Del Monte acknowledged, "1095 meals a year—to plan, prepare and serve. It's a big job. And we suspect most men are apt to regard it rather lightly. But a woman never can. Nor can we."[87] In the second half of the century, this attention to women's work within the home often was tempered by the growing realization that women worked outside the home as well.

Women's waged work outside the home further complicated advertisers' efforts because it was hard to square the notion of women as weak and dependent with the actuality of women as strong and independent actors. Food advertisers generally avoided portraying women who worked outside the home. Advertisers certainly knew women were working outside the home. Still, in spite of the evidence that the number of women working for wages rose throughout the century, food advertisers did not create many ads that took focus away from women's role as the primary caregiver for their families. When ads did feature working women, such as those appearing during World War II or late in the century, they still usually highlighted their homemaking role.[88]

Advertisers for products like breakfast foods and soups promised women working outside the home that these products could fit their needs. In keeping with the trend toward bureaucratization, ads emphasized the importance of productivity for women employed outside the homes as artists, novelists, reporters, factory workers, nurses, war workers, secretaries, and businesswomen. A 1911 ad for Steero Bouillon Cubes asked *Ladies' Home Journal* readers, "Are you a Business Woman or a Teacher?" and tried to sell them on the ease and speed of preparing its product. Advertisers acknowledged, "millions today must spend the sunny hours in cave-like offices and factories" and positioned convenience foods as inexpensive options for working women, who had consistently low wages. A 1912 ad for Shredded Wheat was surprising in its acknowledgement that working women faced "The Strain and Stress of Life." The solution for the young, tired-looking switchboard operator and all "workers of the world who do things with hand or brain must live simply and serenely in order to reach the highest efficiency," was to eat Shredded Wheat Biscuits. Still, ads featuring women working outside the home were rare, even as the number of women entering the workforce increased, sped along by growing industrialization, the increasing number of offices and department stores, the First World War, and the economic distress of the 1930s.[89]

It was not until the Second World War that a spate of ads with working women appeared commonly. They depicted women in a large variety of occupations, particularly as compared to peacetime ads. Women appeared in traditional roles as nurses and food industry workers, as well as appearing as "Rosie the Riveter" welders and WACs. During this time period, copywriters evidently felt comfortable enough with the temporary nature of women's work outside the home to use it in their ads. While it took time for advertisers to appreciate that the war demanded increased labor participation by women, including their coveted white, middle-class consumers, food advertisers immediately encouraged a return to traditional domestic roles after the war. They did so in spite of their own research. A 1948 J. Walter Thompson newsletter, for example, noted, "The 'working wife' is becoming increasingly prominent in American family life."[90]

Food advertisers generally resisted depicting women's desire and need to work outside the home in the second half of the century and feared women's growing dissatisfaction with homemaking as a career. In 1954, the Institute for Motivational Research suggested that because women participated in almost all of the same activities as men (business, education, politics, sports), "the few remaining differences in activities between men and women, are highly valued as a means for each sex to elaborate the basic sex differences." While their acknowledgment that women and men could and did participate in the same activities would perhaps suggest there were not any sex differences, in their study for Fischer Flour they suggested "Baking and cooking have remained essentially feminine pursuits" and encouraged the company to "subtly challenge her to be a better woman by becoming a better baker."[91]

This strategy was consistent with the overall industry response, which was to develop a flexible strategy that accommodated women's desires and needs in the postwar era. For example, one of the most popular themes was "'luxury convenience'—distinctly pleasant dishes which can be prepared with minimal time and 'mess.'" Analyzing even easier meals, those prepared by someone else, historian Andrew Hurley found that, according to a 1959 study, "wives were twice as likely as their husbands to suggest that the family eat a meal away from home." It concluded that a "marketing strategy that targeted women without challenging conventional domestic roles made good sense."[92] Advertisers hoped that by promoting the work as less onerous they could continue to compel women to take sole responsibility for it.

In the postwar period, advertisers for new products began to make some concessions in how they targeted their products. Frozen food manufacturers, in particular, tried to craft a market for their products. Advertisers faced an uphill battle because initially the industry was "so young that relatively few grocers even owned a frozen food display cabinet." Even as they overcame that problem, "The very people whom the industry had identified as the likeliest consumers of frozen food, namely working couples and small families in cities and towns, had no place to keep frozen food." As was so often the case, frozen food advertisers ignored the research data that clearly demonstrated that "it was the extra activities that wealthier women engaged in that differentiated" the classes, and it was the "better-off families . . . that purchased more convenience foods." Even their expectation that working women would make better consumers was not born out by the research, which "consistently indicated that working women bought convenience foods at pretty much the same rate that full-time homemakers did." Moreover, even though they thought working women would be their consumer base, "images of working women rarely showed up in ads for frozen foods. . . . An industry convinced that its very future depended on a steady increase in the number of working women still couldn't bring itself to target them directly." In spite of the dramatic changes in women's working patterns and consumerism in the postwar era, "So obvious did this cause and effect seem to the experts that the first major study of working women and convenience foods wasn't published until 1968."[93]

Advertisers also stayed focused on women in spite of research that reflected fluid gender roles in society. Ina Torton of Baeder/Torton Newtim, an agency founded on a 9:30–3:15 schedule, warned, "With the woman going to work, she won't have time to worry about the millions of fabricated product differences." She suggested that with growing independence, women "alone just won't be able to make all the consumer decisions." Nor were women just going to be limited to domestic decisions. The Ford advertisers also noted that women were "increasingly having an effect on brand choices," with women purchasing 42 percent of the first million Mustangs sold. They also reported on a significant component of women's new freedom: "'A greater number of women have driver's licenses than ever before (about 50%)'."[94] Increasingly, women realized that they did not necessarily need to depend on men or be tied to their homes.

In the last thirty years of the century, advertisers grew concerned about "less loyalty to the home unit" and a 1971 report by the J. Walter Thompson Company found they had reason to be worried. It found that the "traditional division of household responsibilities for the woman and income-earning job for the man is breaking down . . . the woman is very likely to be employed as well—and not give up employment with the arrival of children—and the couple share household tasks in common." While the report did not conclude that this revolution would dissolve traditional households in the short term, it cautioned that it was this "general rootlessness which would have a distinct impact on the kinds of products and services that could be marketed to such an audience of buyers." According to a *Better Homes & Gardens* study cited by the report, "as the homemaker's sense of rational, significant responsibility for consumed food declines, there is most likely going to be an increase in her vehemence about not working strenuously and arduously."[95] Advertisers struggled to hold on to women and their sense of responsibility for feeding their families.

The Campbell Soup Company conducted a 1985 study on "The Food World of Working Women and Dual-Earning Households" and found that targeting working women not only held tremendous promise, but also was increasingly a necessity. They found that working women were the majority of their female customers, were growing faster than the population at large, and as affluent dual-earners, were the largest subgroup. This is not to say that advertisers anticipated an easy sell. Reporting on the challenges of reaching this group, they noted that it was difficult to reach women "whose main energies and attention are not focused on the traditional household roles that provided themes for our past appeals." This was especially true for unmarried working women, whom Campbell found spent overall less on groceries than nonworking and working wives, in part at least because they ate meals away from home more often. The study concluded that it therefore behooved the company to pursue working women as a market, which they increasingly did at the end of the century. Statistics demonstrated that Americans ate one out of four meals on the go, and food companies accelerated plans to make their products competitive.[96]

In 2002, for example, the Ragu Company found that its new microwavable product, Ragu Express, ready in three minutes, was already behind the times, with other products ready even sooner. To introduce its new single-serve microwaveable soups, Campbell slightly altered its popular slogan to read, " 'M'm! M'm! Good! To Go.' " Competing against Uncle Ben's Lunch Bowls, Campbell tried to claim "active women who have previously skipped lunch" as their target market.[97]

By the end of the century, advertisers had truly embraced Dichter's earlier admonition to target the "balanced-woman." An ad for the National Cattleman's Beef Association appeared in 2000 with hands pulling a female doll from each of her limbs, suggesting their product for "The bendable-stretchable-pulled-in-all-directions modern mom." It assured readers, "Go to the game. Go to the client. These days, you have to do it all."[98] Food manufacturers adapted to women working outside the home and eventually came to see them as an ideal market. However, food advertisers generally did not reflect images of women's paid work, perhaps because it was ultimately incompatible with their ideology of housework, marriage, and motherhood.

"The Women's Vote"

Historically, cultural analysts have placed cooking at the heart of women's identity. In the mid-nineteenth century, domestic reformer Catharine Beecher advocated cooking efficiency to increase women's productivity in the home. Her distant relative, late nineteenth-century feminist theorist Charlotte Perkins Gilman, wanted to move food preparation out of the home to free women. With minimal fanfare, technological innovations in the late nineteenth and early twentieth centuries created the potential to realize Gilman's vision with the development of convenience foods prepared by others that made home cooking faster and easier. Americans began purchasing these goods and incorporating once radical ideas about food preparation and consumption into their daily lives. This revolution in cooking and eating patterns was not the result of an organized movement to improve women's lives or liberate women from kitchen drudgery and, indeed, these changes did not truly liberate women. For many women, convenience foods changed the work they did, but did not challenge their exclusive responsibility for food shopping and preparation. As cultural analyst Laura Scott Holliday observed, "Kitchens of Tomorrow, in other words, sold conservative gender roles disguised as an escape from them."[99]

At the end of the century, grocery shopping began to go full circle, as Internet users turned to grocery stores that delivered. An *Advertising Age* article found that these e-grocers were conscious of the gender implications of their business. " 'We're asking people to change the way they shop and to forgo a very human experience,' said one e-grocer marketing executive. Female consumers . . . told researchers the moment of delivery of groceries causes great discomfort. Stay-at-home mothers are concerned neighbors will say, 'She doesn't work and doesn't even go to the store.' For working women, the perceived criticism is: 'She can't even do one womanly thing' "[100]

In their efforts to promote conservative gender roles, advertisers appropriated feminist themes and deftly turned them into marketing tools. Advertisers' manipulation of themes such as freedom, judgment, and skill enabled them to appeal to women's sense of themselves as independent actors. Throughout the century, ads subverted women's assertiveness and freedom. Some ads, such as one in 1911, suggested that women demonstrate their autonomy by choosing which Campbell's soup to have. The ad assured women who had no time to prepare a hearty meal:

Just think how independent you are when provided with Campbell's Soups. You can pick out exactly the "kind" that appeals to you at the moment—the Tomato Soup, . . . the "Ox Tail", . . . the Beef Soup, hearty and substantial, almost a meal in itself; or whatever you choose from the whole varied list.[101]

Similar ads in the late 1910s and the early 1920s reduced political aims into support for consumer products. Proclaiming "Votes for Women," a 1914 ad featured a dozen little girls parading with boxes of Kellogg's Corn Flakes, suggesting that women should "vote" for their product when they chose from the available cereal candidates. A 1922 ad used a female Campbell Kid marching in a parade holding a placard with the header "OUR CANDIDATE." The candidate was a can of Tomato Soup and below the picture of the can it read: "Stands for health and happy homes." All of these suffrage themed ads clearly wanted women to link the legal right to vote in elections with choosing their products, but few made their claim explicitly.[102]

One exception was a Shredded Wheat ad that moved beyond symbolism and announced, "Two million women will have a right to vote in the next Presidential election." The ad immediately connected this revolutionary, hard-fought, democratic political action with consumer action and diminished its significance by claiming, "Twenty million women have voted for the emancipation of American womanhood by

GREAT FOR BREAKFAST—GOOD, HOT SOUP

We're the ladies' aid in a big parade
'Mid the shouting crowds and the din,
The issue, we state, is the full dinner plate
And Campbell's is sure to win!

OUR CANDIDATE

STANDS FOR HEALTH AND HAPPY HOMES

The Women's Vote

Stand in any grocery store for a few minutes and hear the other customers give their orders for soup. "Campbell's" is the name you'll hear practically every time—any day, anywhere. Order some Campbell's yourself and enjoy a delicious hot plateful of

Campbell's Tomato Soup

Campbell's famous chefs in the spotless Campbell's kitchens make this soup from their own exclusive recipe, with vine-ripened tomatoes, luscious and tempting. Golden butter is blended in the rich puree and delicate spices add their zest. "Real tomato soup," you will say, "and it will get my vote every time!"

21 kinds   **12 cents a can**

Figure 6. This 1922 ad for Campbell's soups appealed to progressive era interest in suffrage and legislation for better living.

serving Shredded Wheat in their homes." Moreover, they claimed, "Every biscuit is a vote for health, happiness and domestic freedom—a vote for pure food, for clean living and clean thinking." Advertisers took the progressive ideals of the period and suggested that one purchase would guarantee these ideals in women's homes. Some historians writing on this phenomenon have claimed that as the suffrage cause grew in strength, businesses wanted to associate their products with it. While this interpretation could suggest that advertisers wanted to get on the bandwagon of suffrage support, food ads did not truly embrace the cause of suffrage. Instead, they co-opted suffrage messages, diluting the power and significance of women's political goals to further their own profit margin.[103]

Advertisers used women's political participation as a backdrop for promoting their food products throughout the century. One example comes from the upscale *New Yorker* in 1940. Focused on what appear to be the only two women at a national political convention, the reader found them nervously discussing whether they had remembered to chill the Campbell's consommé. A 1960 ad followed a woman into a voting booth. As she stood there, curtain open, hand to her mouth, and one knee bent uncertainly, a box of Kellogg's Corn Flakes prominently protruded from her grocery bag. The ad suggested that her selection of the cereal was a "vote" for the best cereal, when it encouraged the reader to "Remember to vote for the best *man*, too." Their damning assessment of women as political citizens prioritized their role as consumer citizens over their interest in and aptitude for democratic participation.[104]

Food advertisers also exploited the appeal of political freedom to endorse a narrow, limited role for women in society. For example, a 1912 ad proudly noted that the time and energy women would save using their product meant, "She has just that much more freedom to make her home and herself attractive." Food advertisers wanted women to gain freedom, but then encouraged them to channel the time and energy they gained from convenience foods into traditional pursuits, usually focused on pleasing men. Ernest Dichter wanted advertisers to adapt their products to women's changing lives by merging modern and traditional notions. In a study for Duncan Hines instant cake mix, he reflected that the "emancipated" woman "is receptive to the kind of cake mix that will permit her to express her femininity and at the same time shield her from the limitations of the ordinary house-wife role of drudgery and dull, prosaic sacrifice."[105]

Occasionally ads suggested that women participate in fun activities, but never strayed far from the expectation that women use their "free" time to concentrate on housework and beauty. A 1927 Campbell's soup ad touted "modern women" who had discovered its products' benefits. Stretching their notion of what women could do, they assured women,

Don't be misled into thinking that the woman who knows how to have a good time must be neglecting her home. Along with other outworn ideas that have been thrown into the discard in recent years has gone the old notion that a woman cannot have a splendidly kept home and still find ample time for relaxations and recreations she deserves—for the books she wants to read, the music she wants to hear, the movies she wants to see.[106]

Women's primary responsibility for feeding their family always came first but, when it served their ends, advertisers also suggested carefully circumscribed freedom outside the home as an ideal. Food advertisers suggested a variety of scenarios when women's efforts to satisfy their own desires might rankle their husbands. The solution for women was to appease men with the right food, often a dessert. A woman in a 1951 ad for Minute Tapioca was trying on a hat in a store. The header, "Got an urge to splurge?" encouraged women to spend, noting, "An occasional shopping spree can be good for your soul! Just remember this—feed your husband his favorite dessert and *then* break the news. He'll be meek as a lamb if you've given him creamy-smooth, super-luscious Minute Tapioca." Consumption, then, took on spiritual benefits for women. Nor had much changed twenty years later, when a 1970 ad featured a woman in a $950 fur coat holding a plate of Jell-O Pudding Boston Cream Pie, with the header claiming it was "The 'notice anything different about me tonight dear?' Pudding." The Jell-O campaign, however, also included an interesting twist on women's desires. Clearly reflecting the cultural conflicts of the 1970s, another ad featured a woman holding a Jell-O dessert and asking, "Dear, don't you think I'd be a more interesting person if I went to work?"[107]

Ads with a freedom theme often appeared in the summer months when the heat of the kitchen made it especially uncomfortable to cook. Food ads appeared with reminders of the liberty convenience foods could provide, including the assertion that "The Campbell label (red-and-white) stands for women's rights to carefree summers." Many ads focused on the idea of escaping housework, like the 1939 ad that declared, "Wise ladies are closing up their kitchens, and faring forth to freedom. There's worlds of good in a half-day off; you'll find it's so, if you try it. And it's easy—far easier than you may think." A 1945 ad dramatically asked, "Why be a galley slave when you can make chow-time an easy time with ready-to-serve Derby Foods?" Ads in the second half of the century tended to be more blasé and downplayed the difficulty of women's housework when they casually suggested "freedom from muss and work."[108]

Advertisements throughout the century suggested that the goal of the women's rights movement was to achieve the right to leisure rather than political equality. Capitalizing on the rhetoric of the second wave women's movement a 1982 Stouffer's ad for Beef Stroganoff declared, "For me, freedom comes in a bright red package." The reader eavesdropped on a person who concluded about the frozen entree, "I know it'll be as good as if I'd made it myself. Without the work. Freedom. It's delicious." The ad encouraged the reader, "Set yourself free. With Stouffer's." In her analysis of Stouffer's "freedom" campaign, Ellen McCracken argued that, "Just as readers are asked to imagine that freedom has an identifiable taste, so too are they to believe that freedom can be obtained through purchase of a commodity." With words like "independence," "freedom," and "change," food advertisers hoped to diffuse the threat of women's aspirations into more traditional pursuits.[109]

In her analysis of women's magazines in the postwar period, Joanne Meyerowitz challenged Betty Friedan's assertion that a conservative promotion of domesticity was the only ideology of the postwar era. Meyerowitz examined nonfiction articles in a variety of women's magazines to assess if indeed the magazines "represented a repressive force, imposing damage on vulnerable women." She clearly included herself when she argued instead, "Many historians today adopt a different approach in which mass culture is neither monolithic nor unrelentingly repressive. In this view, mass culture is rife with contradictions, ambivalence, and competing voices."[110] While Meyerowitz's analysis provides a nuanced reconsideration of women's magazines during this period, her findings only tell part of the story. Examining only nonfiction stories, Meyerowitz ignores the largest category of the magazines' content: advertisements, which overwhelmingly did limit messages to a conservative promotion of domesticity.

The food advertisements contained in women's magazines unequivocally gave women the same traditional messages, not only in the postwar period, but throughout the century. Moreover, food advertising's almost exclusive presence in women's magazines, targeting women for the responsibility of feeding their family, betrayed their consistent purpose. Regardless of the overt message, advertisers sought to ensure that women had sole responsibility for shopping and preparing food in their homes.

There was one period in history, however, when food advertisers blinked. Even if they had been impervious to the dramatic changes swirling around them during the 1960s, during the 1970s advertisers began to read increasing numbers of research reports and essays indicating that growing freedom in the broader society had led girls and women to begin to imagine a different kind of world. Tellingly, some writers, even as they argued for change, found themselves circling right back to the beginning. Writing about "Women's new role," one for example, argued that, "As much as they want the power and independence that comes with their new freedom, they want to retain their distinctiveness, as well. . . . One of the ways in which women express this need is their absorption in fashion." Even though the writer considered serious issues, like women's pay only averaging "60 per cent of men's for comparable jobs requiring comparable skills and experience" and the resulting Equal Pay Act of 1963, the analysis of women concluded that achieving equality would push women "to convey their femininity with more concentration than they have in the past couple of decades. Cultivation of feminine wiles will be high on the list; and it's a good guess that the weaker sex will allow themselves a little more luxurious self indulgence. Bath oils. Curls. And, of course, topless bathing suits."[111]

A 1970 article about the "new" American woman argued that "With her new freedoms, affluence, assurance and self-assertiveness, she'll be an ever-increasing challenge to advertisers." Taking stock of the plentiful changes, marketer Ralph Leezenbaum reflected,

With the advent of the pill, more liberal abortion and divorce laws, more universal higher education, more women and business and all the ramifications for changing values these phenomena bring with them, advertisers . . . are having to reevaluate the traditional concepts on which they base their communications with women.[112]

He noted with surprise that advertisers had so far been unwilling to take notice of the 29 million women in the workforce, pointing out that "More than 41% of all women work . . . nearly three-fifths of them are married." Citing others, such as *Woman's Day* editor Geraldine Rhoads, who warned advertisers that women were not going to "routinely tolerate such stereotyping anymore" and *McCall's* editor Shana Alexander, who believed that "Advertising can no longer address the ladies as lovable drudges, or as witless, cuddly beings who exist solely to please men," Leezenbaum tried to drive home the message that the times had changed and advertisers could be more successful if they changed with them.

Even from within came the rare call for change on the basis of pragmatism. Anne Tolstoi Foster, named vice president at J. Walter Thompson after twelve years with the agency, used her clout and New York base to write an article for the Madison Avenue feature of the *New York Times* in 1971. With a classic marketing technique, she suggested ignoring Women's Liberation for a more important goal: "Ad Lib," which called for an end to "the slurs and slams and putdowns given to women in today's advertising." She argued that while women's lib found such advertising "immoral," proponents of Ad Lib found them "impractical," if they were going to take the "female audience seriously." If, she theorized, the object of a commercial was to "sell something," then advertisers could not afford to "think of women as easy to fool, so slow they must be shouted at, so unalert they won't get your messages unless you repeat it endlessly, or so bored they accept anything as entertainment."

Touting the litany of statistics, she also made an insightful observation to her colleagues about a prevalent "reality gap." She challenged them to recognize that their "life may be vastly different from the lives of your audiences. . . . Take a simple example like the game of bridge . . . only about 15 per cent of Americans even know how to play bridge, and some must be men . . . shouldn't you find some other way to get women in a commercial together . . . ?"[113]

A 1976 research report on teen trends for *Seventeen* magazine also spelled potential trouble for advertisers, as they reported that 15 percent of teens surveyed considered "Women's Rights" one of the top five major problems facing the United States. While admittedly this was nowhere near as grave an issue for the girls who ranked "Crime" and "Unemployment" as some of the most serious issues, when questioned on some particular "issues pertaining to women in society," the girls reported some startling opinions. More than 75 percent of the teens suggested that they were "somewhat" or "very interested" in "Ending of stereotyped portrayals of women & girls in all media & encourage efforts to portray them in positive & realistic roles." In what must have been another unsettling finding, researchers asked the respondents about some "statements concerning marriage and morality." In the midst of questions about abortion and premarital sex, they asked the girls to respond to the statement, "Marriage, home & children are still the primary female goals." Fewer than 10 percent "strongly approve," and even when merged with those who marked "approve," their numbers fell just shy of 30 percent. Meanwhile, those who indicated they "disapprove" or "strongly disapprove" reached nearly 45 percent. Tellingly, nearly a quarter of the respondents were "neutral or not sure." The 1970s were a turbulent time for gender roles, and young and old alike were not sure what was going to happen next.[114] Advertisers faced a dilemma. They could continue on, not only in their "woman only" approach, but also with the same traditional messages, or they could consider the evidence before them and adapt to it.

Anticipating that new future, JWT's Research and Planning Department prepared a report in September 1979 concerning "Middle America in the 1980s." They noted that the "Traditional role of housewife is diminishing" and cautioned that those who reported themselves to be traditional housewives had a median age of fifty-five. Each piece of data was more jarring than the next. "Homecare was not central to women's role definition, to her self concept, motherhood concept, or love concept"; "Neither marriage nor childbirth interrupts a working woman's career"; "52% of women with children work"; "⅔ of the women in our most important target market aren't homemakers!" Advertisers had gotten bad news before, but this information had the potential to radically alter their target audience. The report went on to consider some possibilities to address the situation, none of which included new or modified messages for women. Instead, they believed that "Results will include blurring of sex roles—males will increasingly be performing 'female' household tasks and vice-versa." Even more dramatically, they suggested "appealing to men and children to establish 'family' brand loyalty (beyond classic female-oriented media vehicles)," and noted that there was an "opportunity for more products that any family member can prepare" because "more males and children doing it themselves."[115]

While the content and focus of the ads generally do not reflect it, advertisers did have evidence of more men helping around the house and more women working. Articles and reports produced about the rights movements of the 1960s and 1970s briefly scared the industry into thinking that they might need to adapt to a new world. They occasionally speculated that they might need to change their approach. Ultimately, however, the women's movement did not alter food advertising's focus on women nor their encouragement of women's traditional behavior.

Advertisers just as consistently avoided targeting blacks as consumers. Just as happened with the women's rights movement, articles forebodingly predicted doom and gloom if advertisers did not respond to the demands of civil rights groups. One mid-1960s article, for example, threatened that blacks "could mobilize $12-billion worth of purchasing power against manufacturers who discriminate against Negroes in employment of selling practices," warning that "If asked to by their leaders, 63 per cent of Negroes interviewed by Harris [Louis Harris & Associates, public opinion analysts], said they would stop patronizing stores or buying products represented by discrimination." African Americans had reason for dismay; "In the fall of 1962 a page-by-page check of four national magazines over a full year had shown only two companies had placed ads showing representatives of minority groups." Only a few companies, including department stores and clothing stores, as well as personal care products, decided to include African Americans, while most decided to "avoid putting Negroes in ads and commercials, arguing that it is not realistic."[116]

Food advertisers in particular appear to have been reluctant to focus on African American consumers. Black executives contended that "advertisers are neglecting black advertising because they don't want their products identified as black products. Jack Johnson, vice president of marketing and advertising at *Black Enterprise* magazine, says he believes such attitudes are behind some of the refusals he's had from advertisers." The one exception was the fast food industry, which aggressively targeted African Americans in all types of media. Only about 12 percent of the population, African Americans comprised about 25 percent of fast food consumers. A 1984 *Wall Street Journal* article noted that the rare positive roles for African Americans in television commercials largely came from the big three: McDonald's, Burger King, and Wendy's.[117]

In a striking omission, the JWT archives contain almost no references to African Americans as consumers, except as to how they might shape the consumer patterns of whites. Agency files created in the 1970s and '80s were filled with reports on class issues focused almost entirely on the affluent, wealthy, yuppies, and so on. Hardly any attention was paid to the middle class and virtually none to the working class and poor. Moreover, in the collection of criticism directed at advertising from the 1950s to the 1980s, there was no mention of racism, sexism, or classism. Along with articles defending against critiques by Vance Packard and others, they considered issues that might bring them legal and financial troubles, such as ethics and trust, but not the social movements pounding on their door, demanding to be heard.

Nowhere in the records, for example, is evidence of monitoring some of the broader cultural changes inspired by and reflected in such phenomena as Betty Friedan's 1963 publication of *The Feminine Mystique* or the 1970 feminist protest at the offices of the *Ladies' Home Journal*.[118] A rare reflection in the *Printers' Ink* "A Woman's View" column challenged advertisers: "If your wife has a copy of Mrs. Friedan's book, borrow it. If you hear the women in your circle talking about it, listen in." Her recommendations, in fact, echo Dichter's suggestion that advertisers should embrace women who "run active households and who also have jobs and serious pursuits outside the home . . . [as they] have a more crying need for ready-made products, more crucial requirement for convenience and speed." The columnist, Sara Welles, astutely assessed the unfolding cultural phenomenon, noting "An upheaval, a turning point may be taking place in our thinking about the role of women and this book can speed changes impossible to outline now—but vast and deep."[119]

Reflecting on her advertising experience between 1949 and the 1970s, Anne Toltsoi Wallach (formerly Foster) said of advertisers' attitudes toward women, "They had statistics and facts on behavior and ignored their own eyes." Making reference to David Ogilvy's famous quotation, "The consumer isn't a moron. She is your wife," Wallach remarked that he "and others like Dichter who, at least, assumed people had inner lives and were not just statistics or what they said out loud in surveys, had an uphill battle." Fundamentally, Wallach thought advertisers regarded women as "dumber than men, but few consumers were given the respect of intelligent, thoughtful creative work."[120]

Advertisers largely chose to ride out the storm and push aside the evidence, clearly hoping that these women (and men) were a minority and not powerful. In a scathing review of *Born Female* in *Marketing/Communication*, Franchellie Cadwell, president of Cadwell-Davis Company, dismissed author Caroline Bird's assertion that in 1968 "the working woman's predicament is equaled only by the plight of the Negro," claiming, "Granted some remnants of prejudice against women in business remain, but how serious can it be." Ticking off the few prominent, successful marketing women (Mary Wells, Helen Gurley Brown, and Geraldine Stutz), she suggested that there was no handicap. She conceded that the book did make some good points about the "the middle stratum job market," but concluded, "the plight of working women is hard to get worked up about."[121]

Still, even Cadwell later joined other women to try to threaten, cajole, and encourage advertisers to effect change. In 1971, Midge Kovacs, advertising manager of E-Lite-Co., Inc. and member of the Image Committee of the National Organization for Women, proposed a list of "Do's and Don'ts for Ad Men." Starting with the premise that they were "probably already aware of the burgeoning women's movement,'" Kovak encouraged advertisers to hear the message, and warned that if they did not they would "be hearing it at ever-increasing decibels." Claiming that "sexist stereotypes are out!" and reminding them that "Almost half of all working-age women are out working," she suggested that they "Talk to her, not down to her." Kovak concluded her entreaties with a plea made by Frances Maule nearly fifty years earlier, to remember that "Women are people!"[122]

In keeping with that line of reasoning, Carol Taber, publisher of *Working Women*, argued in 1992 that advertisers had ignored the dramatic changes in the women's market, and claimed, "The majority of women are offended by how they're portrayed in advertising." Taber urged companies to spend their advertising dollars in *Working Women* and ran ads for their ad space that said things like, "'I'm not a feminist . . . but . . . I believe in equal opportunity, equal pay and the right to run my own life.'" Their campaign to peg women as "New feminists" stemmed from Yankelovich Clancy Shulman findings that only "33% of women identify themselves as feminists, but 77% think the women's movement has made life better." Joanne Lipman, a journalist for the *Wall Street Journal*, reported that the marketing and media industries characterized women as "Supermoms who had it all" (1980s), "New traditionalists" as "they went back into the kitchen" (1990s), and "New feminists" (1990s). Leslie Savan commented on the political and commercial implications of these new titles, noting that advertisers tried to capitalize on George H. W. Bush's use of the term 'new traditionalism' when he campaigned for and won the presidency in 1988 with a campaign predicated on family values.[123] These new categorizations left intact the traditional expectation that women's identity as cook for their family was still paramount. Under the guise of responsiveness to change, food advertisers used new language to coopt societal changes and reinforce the status quo.

Lipman's assessment of advertising at the end of the century was bleak, evident in her title, "Finally, Some Marketers Seem Ready to Give Bimbo Ads a Rest." She believed that Anita Hill's sexual harassment charges against Supreme Court nominee Clarence Thomas riled women up and was hopeful that men in the industry were listening. Still, she was cautious when she quoted a female advertising executive who opined that "many advertisers will shy away from showing women in the kitchen or women at work—for fear of riling either group." While Fitzgibbon pointed to Levi Strauss & Co.'s positive self-esteem imagery in their print campaigns targeted at women, Lipman acknowledged that "advertisers still have a long way to go. Most ads still cling to stereotypes of women as sex toys or career women or moms."[124]

Sometimes the absence of foods ads can be telling; a study of *Ms.* magazine in its first fifteen full years of publication (1973–1987) reveals that food ads made up a negligible portion of the copy it carried. Gloria Steinem explained that the magazine sought advertising from traditionally male categories, such as cars, stereos, and financial services, but did not seek more traditionally 'feminine' categories because it "'didn't want to have to supply complementary copy and traditional female products wouldn't come without it." Unwilling to have a "home and food" section or a food columnist who promoted recipes with brand name products, *Ms.* found that it could not attract business in that category, traditionally one of the largest, even though its base readership was women.[125] Food advertisers were seemingly unwilling to create ads to reach out to feminists in *Ms.* because they had little experience approaching shopping and cooking outside of a framework of traditional gender ideals.

Indeed, throughout the century, food advertisers operated on a set of assumptions about their consumers. Foremost was a belief that women comprised their primary market. Even though advertisers commissioned countless research studies to evaluate female consumers, food advertisers frequently neglected their findings and almost exclusively marketed their foods to women using a traditional guise. In order to maintain and stimulate their base, advertisers preyed on women's insecurities, lavished them with false praise, and encouraged an entitlement to free time to necessitate convenience foods. Determined to maintain the status quo and grow their market share, advertisers did adapt to evolving social trends. Latching on to new categories of women, including those who worked for wages and women who believed in gender equality, advertisers coopted these groups' identities and tried to make food consumption part of their raison d'être. "Women, women, women" was the mantra of the advertisers.

Chapter 3

Women's Power to Make Us: Cooking Up a Family's Identity

"What will people say?"... Of course women are sensitive to every criticism or comment, however slight and trivial, about their homes. Why shouldn't they be? The home is their special responsibility and delight. It is the sign and proof of the kind of people who live there. It is the woman's ideal to see that the home shall reflect the culture, refinement, and good taste of the whole family ... She knows that the daily service of soup is expected. .... One of the things that help to "place" a family.

—*Campbell's Soup ad,* Ladies' Home Journal, *1927*

Food advertisers throughout the twentieth century wanted white women to believe that they had the power to influence their families' identity through their cooking. They targeted these women with patriotic, religious, class-based, racial, and ethnic appeals that suggested that women should see their purchasing decisions as opportunities to ensure their families' stability and mobility. Even as ads adapted to changing social norms regarding ethnic, racial, and religious acceptance, they revealed a remarkable consistency in their promotion of traditional gender roles in food preparation and consumption. Advertisers maintained that only women could access the power that came from shopping and cooking.

White women customarily received these messages about the power of food to shape their families, while African American and Hispanic families generally did not. Ironically, the evidence suggests that racism might have made African Americans especially vulnerable to advertising appeals that linked food consumption and status, but marketers did not even begin to consider whether to target them in earnest until about 1970. Even at the end of the century, as advertisers continually rediscovered that blacks and Hispanics existed, they continued to question whether or not it was worthwhile to spend money on them. Their focus on whites belies the extent to which food advertisers retained conservatism in their approach, unwilling to challenge racial categorization or gender roles.[1]

Food advertisers suggested that white women possessed the influence to shape their families through food. Ads promised that by serving certain foods women could demonstrate and enhance their family's religiosity, social status, or national identity. As early as the 1920s, advertisements also claimed that eating Chinese, Mexican, and Italian foods might enable women to help their families become more debonair, modern, and paradoxically American by leaving behind customary eating patterns.[2] Still, even as they constructed new rationales that allowed women to venture into the unknown and consider new foods and products, advertisers held strong to the notion that women should influence their family's status—from the kitchen.

Like American culture generally, food consumption over the course of the century expanded to assimilate different customs and tastes. Advertisers sold new foods by fitting them into an established model of American gender and food arrangements. Mass-produced ethnic foods, in particular, gained in popularity over the course of the twentieth century. Their entrance into the homes of Americans was not always a smooth one, plagued as they were by deep-rooted suspicions of foods that were foreign or different. Immigration patterns, the nation's economy, the world wars, and technological developments, however, all contributed to the growing availability and acceptance of foods previously not found locally, or even nationally. Aided by these broad changes, food advertisers successfully standardized many ethnic foods as "American foods." By the century's end, in homes across the country, people ate chow mein, pre-packaged taco seasoning and shells, and spaghetti with ready-made sauce, not as exotic adventures but as accepted staples of the American diet.[3]

Through their purchase of these convenience foods, women helped expand societal expectations of what constituted American eating patterns. As consumers, women played an important role in defining their family's position in society, as well as shaping the society in general. More than just cooking, women's economic power translated into powerful social and cultural messages about what foods and styles would be welcomed onto America's tables and integrated into the menus of families across the country. Moreover, it was not just the white, middle-class women, targeted by advertisers, who sought to influence their family's standing. African American, immigrant, and poor women who faced racism and discrimination in American society sought to do the same and could have been courted by advertisers with this approach, but throughout the twentieth century advertisers ignored the potential of this status-conscious market.

"Do Advertisers Face a Negro Boycott?"

Food advertisers generally did not consider African Americans as consumers. The evidence does not suggest that the industry made a decision to exclude them, as much as it reflects a denial of their existence and potential as a market. Beyond articles about icons like Aunt Jemima, trade journals and company files at J. Walter Thompson (JWT) contain virtually no attention to blacks before 1960. There were exceptions, as when Raymond A. Bauer and Scott M. Cunningham in their 1970s assessment of "The Negro Market," laid out an unusually thoughtful history of marketing to African Americans. While focused on the post-World War II developments, it detailed the ways companies in the early 1900s had marketed such diverse items as gas stoves (1916) and paint brushes (1922) to African Americans. It also established that early advertisers believed that African Americans had distinctive food preferences (1930) and that by 1931, they had determined several key factors in marketing to blacks: use African Americans in ads, demonstrate concern for them, consider differential product usage and media preferences, and do not ignore their spending power.[4] Marketers did not listen to their own data in the 1930s and struggled to learn from these lessons throughout the rest of the century. Indeed, some evidence suggests that they did not need to do so.

Robert E. Weems, Jr., described a 1936 study which found that African American women across the country bought brand name products, even if companies did not tailor advertising to them. It was possible then that specialized advertising was not necessary. For most of the century, however, advertisers did not have much information available to make that determination. A 1966 research report, for example, characterized those marketing to blacks as being in a "state of confusion," uncertain how to proceed, relying on scarce systematic market studies, and dependent on research done by the black media.[5]

Industry analysts generally chalked up past exclusion of blacks to expectations based on their socioeconomic class. They argued that blacks could not afford the advertised items or did not spend enough on them to justify the advertising expenditure. Moreover, they claimed they risked alienating whites by including blacks in mainstream advertisements or even by placing advertisements in black magazines and newspapers.[6]

Ironically, much of the evidence available in trade journals and the JWT archive suggests that African American consumers would have made an excellent target group. In 1949, the *New York Times* reported a study that compared food consumption between 1936 and 1948 and found an increase in African American use of spaghetti and macaroni, pancake mix, and canned peaches. A 1962 Special Report on "The Changing Face of the Urban Markets" for *Food Business* suggested the power of the black market, finding that blacks offered "a largely untapped market for many specialty foods" and bought a lot of convenience foods, which generally meant higher profits for retailers.[7]

Trying to assess the significance of the urban black population, the article summarized the dramatic changes of the early 1960s, noting that, "what has occurred is that urban white populations have moved in droves to the suburbs and Negroes are taking up the void in the cities." The report was critical of the fact that "Food marketers still approach the big cities with sales appeals that are almost entirely directed, as least subconsciously, to a white population." As an example of a business sector that got it right, the article pointed to downtown department stores which had earlier seen the profit in African American consumers. Questioning how food advertisers could ignore such a lucrative base, the author put forth population statistics and data on annual spending. For example, a 1960s study claimed, "The Negro's annual dollar spending is currently pegged at about $20 billion—roughly equal to the entire purchasing power of Canada. Of this Negroes spend nearly 20% ($3.75 billion) in food stores."[8]

A 1960s study on "Negro Food and Entertainment Habits," supported those findings, concluding, "Negro Consumers Excellent Prospects for Planters Peanut Sales." Beyond peanuts, they found that African Americans spent more than comparable-income white families at the grocery store. The old arguments about economic determinants also fell away when, citing the Survey of Consumer Expenditures put out by the Bureau of Labor Statistics in 1960, which reported that, percentage-wise, blacks outspent whites in food purchases. Reflecting on these findings, some researchers attributed the greater expenditure by blacks as "unquestionably" a reflection of Engel's law, that is, the lower a family's income, the greater is the proportion of it spent on food.[9]

More than just the cold data, however, the Planters Peanuts study also included evidence from the Market Research Corporation of America (1960) that found that, "'The fear of possible embarrassment limits Negro visits to restaurants, night clubs and other similar sources of outside entertainment." The study argued, "Consequently the rapidly expanding Negro populations of large cities are finding their social outlet through home entertainment."[10] One researcher contended that in marketing to African Americans, "sellers would do well to emphasize the body-building power of a food product, especially as it relates to keeping the individual physically fit." He suggested that this kind of approach would exploit fears about physical incapacitation and the consequent economic anxieties if people had to miss work due to illness, or died and could not support their families. A proponent of integrated advertising, he also thought advertisers would do well to join this health theme with white consumer concern about entertaining, and create ads that said, in the words of an upper-class black housewife, "She is a good hostess who serves nutritional foods." Also taking note of the experiences of blacks in shaping their shopping patterns, a *Food Business* article found that blacks tended to have more people in their families (4.4 versus 3.6 for whites), wives were 50 percent more likely to work than in white families, and "social barriers prevent the Negro from spending much at restaurants, on homes, in travel, etc., where whites can and do spend freely." Of particular interest to food advertisers, the Planters study noted that "The Negro woman's desire to achieve status is often revealed in the elaborate display with which she serves her gourmet foods. . . . This is an outgrowth of her traditional interest in food." Even more ironic, given advertisers' dismissal of the black market, is the concluding reminder, "Remember, the urban Negro family is extremely brand conscious, and once sold, is very hard to shake from a preference." A 1973 study supported this notion, finding that of the 26 food products they surveyed, the "leading brand purchased was the same in 1971 as in 1966 for 19 products," suggesting that black households were extremely loyal. Given their more tenuous social and economic circumstances, African Americans sought out the security of known brands as an assurance that they would be protected.[11]

This loyalty stemmed from centuries of betrayal by American society. As early as 1936, researchers found that "Constant and humiliating subordination has done something to the Negro. It has had a profound psychological effect upon him. It has affected his consumption characteristics—in fact his whole mode of living." Not surprisingly, therefore, some found that "African American consumption patterns continue to be based on an attempt to 'buy' respect and dignity."[12]

Part of the assessment by the author of the *Food Business* article and other ad analysts in the 1960s and 1970s, however, included a read of the broader social climate for advertisers with regard to African Americans. They analyzed the kinds of products that might benefit from targeting blacks, and found that blacks consumed considerably more rice, corn meal, cooked cereals, canned and powdered milk and cream, pork and poultry, and spaghetti than did whites. The authors also considered strategies for reaching black readers. The standard advice of using black media, such as the radio, *Ebony* magazine, and the *Chicago Defender* newspaper, and black models was prevalent.[13]

Not content to wait, some civil rights and consumer advocates noted that African Americans could wield incredible economic power and considered some ways to use it effectively to advance change, including the threat of boycotts. Beyond just demanding advertising in the black media, for example, some critics charged that companies needed to do more to demonstrate, "how sincere the recognition of the Negro market is." For example, one author cited the experience of the Pepsi-Cola company in Philadelphia. Even though Pepsi employed some African Americans, a group of ministers successfully organized a boycott to force the company to hire more African American white-collar workers and truck drivers. Increasingly in the 1960s, it appeared as if companies that wanted to benefit financially from black consumers would have to move beyond lip service and demonstrate a true commitment to the civil rights movement sweeping the nation.[14]

In a 1963 talk before the New York Chapter of the Public Relations Society of America, John H. Johnson, president of the Johnson Publishing Company, which published *Ebony, Jet, Tan,* and *Negro Digest,* reiterated this point, arguing, "The new Negro consumer judges you and your client by what you do, not by what you say. It is no longer possible to buy Negroes off with token appointments; it is no longer possible to buy them off with rhetoric. A deed is required." He characterized the "Negro revolt" as "a crucial turning point in the relations between Negro and white Americans" and warned that "If PR people are not telling their clients the truth about this revolution, their clients are going to end up with a net loss of sales." He argued that the "peaceful, non-violent social revolution" was for all Americans and that "The American business community has a personal, a selfish interest, if you will, in this struggle. The Negro public already has an annual spendable income of $23.5 billion. . . . By understanding and supporting the aspirations of Negroes, you understand and support yourself."[15]

Johnson had reason to believe that advertisers should heed his warnings. Civil rights groups had wrought tremendous changes by 1963, and articles like "Do Advertisers Face a Negro Boycott?" began to take notice of boycotts and "selective buying" campaigns. Organizations such as the Congress for Racial Equality (CORE) and the National Association for the Advancement of Colored People (NAACP) began to threaten "direct action" to encourage corporations to integrate their advertising in a meaningful way. The 1966 Long Range Planning study acknowledged that the market concentration of black consumers in the 50 largest US cities made it easier for advertisers to reach them, but cautioned that it also meant "the danger of an effective boycott action." As late as 1973, there were still rumblings that "Blacks are extremely race conscious and will switch brands if it can be demonstrated that it is in the interest of the black community to do so." To demonstrate the power of that threat, Rev. Jesse Jackson, then president of People United to Save Humanity (PUSH) organized a 1974 consumer preference survey among Chicago blacks, and planned one nationally. Knowing that Kellogg's was the brand favorite of 62 percent of black Chicagoans, over twice as high as any of the other cereals, was the kind of information which Jackson and other civil rights leaders intended to wield to effect change.[16]

Some businesses did sign statements of agreement to place more blacks in advertisements not aimed specifically at blacks. However, in spite of their efforts, by 1969 industry analysts noted that "there appeared to be no great tendency to use integrated advertising." Even more significantly, there were no reprisals and African American organizations did not make new demands. Some questioned "whether Negroes feel it is really important and worthwhile to see members of their own race appearing in ads in general media." A brief analysis of NAACP member responses concluded that advertisements that focused on social interaction met the still-valued ideal of integration, which it was hoped would contribute to reduced racial stereotypes and racial prejudices. However, they warned, "Ads showing Negroes segregated from whites, or standing near but not interacting with whites, or engaging in implausible situations of interaction, may be worse than ads showing no Negroes at all."[17]

Rather than risk it, many businesses decided to avoid potential conflicts by removing all people from their advertising and their packages. A 1970 *Marketing/Communications* article (successor of the late *Printers' Ink*), argued, "The plain fact is that today when advertising moves into integration of whites and Negroes, the risks of offense prove to be greater than when no people at all are shown." Already for African Americans, "group integration scenes, while becoming more common, are often considered worn and trite—a sure candidate for rejection if something is slightly amiss in portrayal of Negroes."[18]

It was also in the 1970s that some analysts began to express optimism about the changes that had been effected. In his research on "Mass Media and Social Change," Walter Weiss theorized that over time, advertising directed toward African Americans would change to reflect new attitudes of black dignity and pride, as well as their improved social status. Vernon E. Jordan, then president of the National Urban League, commented that

The increasing use of blacks in general market advertising says something about the changing nature of race relations in America, paralleling how American society has moved from almost total exclusion of blacks to a degree of integration within the mainstream that while still not satisfactory, is far better today than it has ever been.[19]

Even with this positive look to the recent past, he cautioned that "it would be folly for the advertising industry to sit back and applaud itself . . . much there remains to be achieved." And the reality was sobering. Looking back at the advertising record, researchers in 1980 found that only two percent of magazine ads contained black models, the same percentage as appeared in 1968. Even taking into account two major black publications, *Ebony* and *Essence*, the percentage was still only about five percent. The corporate response was sometimes surprisingly candid. Marketing expert Alphonzia Wellington recalled a conversation with executives at Quaker Oats in which they acknowledged that blacks comprised a large part of their business, but conceded, "'Oh, we don't do any promotions . . . on most of our products because they're products that black people are going to buy anyway.'" African Americans' trumpeted brand loyalty meant that instead of being catered to as valued customers, companies were free to ignore them.[20]

Just as feminism was unable to persuade the industry to end its most egregious behaviors, so too did the civil rights movement find itself thwarted in its efforts to get more realistic images of African Americans into magazines and onto television. Certainly there were some changes and advances in more realistic representations, but it was particularly significant in the last quarter of the century that most media failed to be integrated. A 1981 study of commercials, for example, found that blacks and whites were found to interact only 1.7 percent of the time people were on screen, and concluded, "Gone with the sixties is the movement to better depict blacks on television commercials." A 1991 study had similarly bleak findings when an analysis of 21,007 people in magazine and catalog advertising found that only 3.2 percent of them were African American.[21]

Advertisers were certainly aware of this disparity and its significance. In the wake of the Los Angeles riots in 1992, advertisers reflected on their industry's role in shaping modern society. An *Advertising Age* "survey of 470 marketing and media executives found more than half of all respondents believed advertising has played a role in the country's current racial problems." Slightly more than half the respondents said that television and print ads did not include enough black people and nearly half thought they did not portray black consumers accurately. Surely, respondents suggested, if more African Americans were employed in the industry things would improve, but Valerie Graves, a senior VP-creative director at UniWorld Group in New York characterized advertising's record of minority hiring and involvement as "horrifying."[22]

Curious about the amount of advertising money directed at African Americans, economic analyst John W. Templeton tried to determine its significance. While the industry proudly claimed they spent a landmark $1 billion advertising to African Americans in 1997, Templeton concluded this was not impressive and continued to reflect the undervaluing of the African American market, given that advertisers overall spent $115 billion in 1997. He concluded that if advertisers had strived for real parity, based on the "African American percentage of national income, 3%, the figure should be $3.45 billion." He also noted that there was not "a single major national advertiser who devotes at least 3% of its ad budget to the black market." Many researchers noted the propensity of advertisers to do a " 'Super Bowl' blitz of minority ads" on Martin Luther King's birthday, and particularly during Black History Month, and criticized their inclination to ignore African Americans the other ten months of the year. Clifford Franklin, for example, questioned, "How committed can a corporation be in placing a few pennies in these targeted publications in only the first quarter?"[23] Journalists and scholars turned the question over in their minds: what should be done? Some, such as Marjorie Whigham-Desir, thought that boycotts constituted "Punishing negative behavior" and that "To be taken more seriously by American business, an increasing number of public policy, business and community leaders believe, black Americans must begin to forge a 'conscious' consumer agenda."[24] In spite of this rhetoric and some small localized efforts to organize the purchases of African Americans, the advertising industry and corporations were largely left to their own devices.

Simultaneously, not only did food advertisers generally not make direct advertisements to African Americans, but food retailers also largely avoided serving large African American populations in cities. As one reporter observed, "Generally, major supermarket chains steer clear of African American communities because they underestimate the community's potential spending power and overestimate the risks." There were exceptions; she cited the president of Restoration Supermarket Corporation, Roderick Mitchell, who noted that his Pathmark grocery store in Brooklyn's Bedford Stuyvesant neighborhood was one of the highest sales generators in the 144-store chain and suggested, " 'Other merchants use the misperception as a justification for charging higher prices or not entering the neighborhood at all.' " They did so in spite of evidence, such as that provided by Market Segment Research & Consulting, which found that in 1996 "African Americans spent approximately $23 more than other ethnic groups during each trip to the grocery store. If the major food chains chose their locations based on the facts, supermarkets would be popping up all over black neighborhoods."[25]

At the end of the century, in spite of research demonstrating their spending power, advertisers' distrust of African American consumers continued. An article for *Black Enterprise* titled "The Madison Ave. Initiative" examined the effects of "an inflammatory memo" from the Katz Radio Group in 1998 that stated, in part, "When it comes to delivering prospects not suspects, the urban [-formatted] stations deliver the largest amount of listeners who turn out to be the least likely to purchase. The median age is 23. Very young, and very, very poor qualitative profile."

It also considered the findings of a Federal Communication Commission report initiated by the memo that found that, "for many years many advertising companies have exercised policies that denied advertising to urban- or Spanish-formatted media, or forced minority media to accept less compensation than white-owned media delivering an audience of comparable size." Scott also found that this distrust of consumers extended to advertisers' use of magazines and newspapers. Tom Ficklin, CEO of *Inner-City Newspaper*, a weekly based in New Haven, Connecticut, with a statewide circulation of 35,000 was told by an ad agency in 1998, " 'black folks do not read.' "[26] In spite of the evidence, food advertisers did not think it was worthwhile to target ads to black people in any media, fundamentally not seeing them as consumers.

"In Five Years, They'll Be the Biggest Minority in the U.S."

Even though it was largely unheeded advice, as early as 1963, sporadic articles in industry magazines called on advertisers to consider not just the black but also the Hispanic market for their goods. From the outset, there was an awareness of the heterogeneity of the market, taking note of the many different subgroups that could be categorized as such, including, but not limited to, Puerto Ricans, Mexicans, Cubans, Columbians, and Dominicans.[27]

As with their analysis of African American consumers, some of the early articles were surprisingly astute, identifying issues that would continue to resonate with Hispanic market researchers into the twenty-first century. For example, Richard P. Jones, vice president and director of media of JWT, remarked in 1967 on the "surprising degree" to which the Spanish-speaking community "defied the 'Melting Pot' " and clung "to its own language and customs." While he considered their pride "an ingrained trait," he did accurately capture the extent to which Latinos held on to their language and the advisability, therefore, for advertisers to speak to them in Spanish. Indeed, researchers cited startlingly high statistics about how many families spoke Spanish at home, with some estimating as high as 90 percent. Jones held that, like African Americans, Hispanics were also extremely brand loyal and enthusiastic consumers of staples, such as dry cereals, cooking oils, evaporated milk, and tomato sauce and paste.[28]

Reinforcing Jones's findings, a 1971 report laid out the parameters of the Spanish-American market. It held out the carrot to food companies, noting "Experience has shown that advertisers who have communicated their messages in Spanish have been amply rewarded," and then threatened the stick, "while those who have relied on spill-over from English media have suffered." It drew on a strong example, comparing pre-migration consumption habits in Puerto Rico to behavior in New York City, noting that "Beech-Nut, an extensive user of Spanish media, has 60% of the Hispano market, while Heinz, which has relied on general media, has only 4%." Researchers commonly found that Hispanics considered themselves Hispanic first and American second, and had a strong desire to be addressed in their own language.[29]

Beyond reaching out, and doing so in Spanish, the other important suggestion was that the advertising "be based on the life style of Spanish Americans." In particular, many researchers interpreted that to mean family centered and suggested ads highlighting family scenes. Many expressed optimism that by adopting these tactics American food advertisers would be successful in breaking into the market, as "The Spanish-Americans have adopted several of the eating habits of the Anglos, while retaining some of their native practices . . . Many American food items are gradually accepted, when promoted properly."[30]

As they had concerning African Americans, researchers pounded home the many reasons to appeal to Hispanics, including their growing size, loyalty, and spending power. In 1977, for example, one study suggested that the Latino market was the "fastest-growing one in the U.S.— up 23% since 1970 vs. 4% for the total population as a whole—and Latino households tout more than $31 billion in buying power." It estimated that "in five years, they'll be the 'biggest minority' in the U.S." It also touted Hispanic spending, comparing Spanish and non-Spanish home spending on food purchases and finding that Spanish homes spent 24 percent more. While acknowledging that Latino-owned and -operated *bodegas* did capture a great deal of the market share ("$600 million of the $1.6 billion spent by Latinos on grocery purchases"), it assured advertisers that the balance was being spent in traditional supermarkets. Later researchers would crow that by reaching out to Hispanics with Spanish advertising, employing Spanish speaking employees, and carrying Spanish products, supermarkets had garnered even greater shares of food purchases. Moreover, to a greater extent than African Americans, Hispanics lived in urban areas, with estimates overall in 1977 at about 84 percent, and those for specific groups such as Puerto Ricans at 97 percent and Cubans reaching 98 percent.[31]

Another similarity between black and Hispanic consumers was their aversion to coupons. For Hispanics, as with blacks, many attributed this stigma up to the association with food stamps, noting that in Spanish a coupon was called *cupón*, while a food stamp was known as *cupón de comida*, which perhaps was "too close for comfort in the Hispanic mind." Traditionally, according to researchers, "The use of coupons has been perceived as a lack of self-sufficiency that would be embarrassing for the Hispanic family." In 1980, however, in the midst of the national economic crisis, Hispanics found themselves increasingly more willing to use a *cupón* to enable them to offer their families what they perceived as the best, and to purchase brand name goods. While previously fewer than 10 percent of Hispanics admitted to coupon use, in 1980 between 40 and 50 percent did so. By 1982, a study of two million Hispanic households showed that 87 percent used coupons when shopping in supermarkets, drug and discount stores. Interestingly for advertisers, coupons allowed them to do something unusual with Hispanics: "target in on an increasingly affluent national audience," and indeed "Higher income Hispanic households were more likely to use 'cents-off' coupons than lower income Hispanics."[32] For many Hispanic women, then, coupons enabled them to demonstrate their skills as shoppers and to improve their family's status by purchasing more or better foods within their budgets. Perhaps, too, their better class position meant they were not directly competing and defining themselves against poorer consumers and were thus freed to use coupons to fill their carts.

In seeking to reach Hispanics in Spanish, some advertisers blundered terribly. For example, Frank Perdue's slogan, "It takes a tough man to make a tender chicken," was translated as "It takes a sexually stimulated man to make a chick affectionate."[33] Fear of these mishaps and the difficulty in communicating to such a diverse group, with many different sub-ethnicities, may have deterred even more advertisers from pursuing the market.

While food companies were credited with being some of the leaders in reaching Hispanics with national advertising, for some companies it was not until the early twenty-first century that they yielded to the call to target the Hispanic market. KFC, previously known as Kentucky Fried Chicken, announced on their website in 2002 that it was launching its "first-ever national Spanish-language advertising and community outreach campaign." In one of its first Spanish-language ads, "Meet the parents," KFC used a popular Spanish-language TV host, Fernando Arau, and a classic advertising tableau:

The Hispanic boyfriend, Jorge, has been invited to meet his girlfriend's parents, and the mom hopes to impress their new "ethnic" guest with the quintessential all American meal—hamburgers. Mom asks Jorge politely, in broken Spanish, if he liked the hamburgers, and he hesitates to answer because bland hamburgers are not his idea of a great meal. Suddenly, Fernando Arau appears in the dining room next to Jorge with a bucket of KFC chicken. He persuades Jorge to fess up and tell the family that he would have preferred KFC's Original Recipe chicken. The family is convinced, decides to serve KFC for dinner instead and Arau's mission is accomplished.[34]

The family-focused ad zeroed in on the cultural authority that Hispanics granted KFC products, while simultaneously granting and reflecting their ethnic hipness. Advertisers also played to the tendency to defer to male authority, especially prevalent in Hispanic culture. Not only Fernando Arau but also the teenage boy were able to trump the mother's authority in her own kitchen, making clear that women should listen to men.

"Like a Brave Man's Cheek Should Be."

Americans with other racial backgrounds appeared in ads occasionally, but almost never as consumers. Native Americans, for example, virtually never appeared during the century as consumers. Even local appeals were infrequent because "Indian tribal newspapers are not widely considered worthwhile media buys."

Native Americans did appear as trademark logos, however. Advertisements often featured Native Americans as symbols of purity and honor, to convince women of a product's quality. Appealing to a belief that Native Americans lived clean, wholesome lives, advertisers hoped to associate those characteristics with their foods. In 1920, the Indian Packing Corporation touted its Council Beans as "Fresh from sunshine and pure air." The label featured men in large tribal headdresses, seated in a circle around an open fire. The image suggested purity and simplicity, as did the header, which screamed "Real—." Yet, a glance at the other products featured by the company revealed Vienna Style Sausage, Ol' Mammy Hash, and Chile Con Carne, all of which were clearly not Native American dishes.[35]

The 1920s was unusual for the plethora of Native American imagery in advertisements. During this short-lived period, advertisers used language and drawings to create the sense that Native Americans endorsed or created their products. A Quaker Oats ad featured a large painting of three Native American men standing in a cornfield, and consumers were encouraged to write away for it, for 10¢ and a box top. Designed to appeal to mothers and their children, the copy entreated,

Dear boys and girls:—Here are the Three Good Spirits of Beautiful Youth—the Spirit of Strength, the Spirit of Courage, and the Spirit of Truth. They come now to greet you, as they came long, long ago to the Indians, and to the little Quaker boys and girls whom the Indians taught to see them . . . called them to enter a fairy box of corn flakes . . . named Quaker Quakies. And if you have eyes that see such things the Three Good Spirits will greet you as soon as ever you see these flakes.[36]

As the ad went on to describe the qualities of the spirits and how they affected the cereal, it made an interesting claim. In its accounting of the Spirit of Courage, it noted that the Spirit had "colored them [the cereal flakes] a ruddy brown, like a brave man's cheek should be." This ad,

Figure 7. Native Americans never appeared as consumers in food ads; instead they usually represented a comic foil or the embodiment of the product's natural purity and quality, as in this 1920 ad.

then, was unusual in its admission of a positive, enviable quality held by a nonwhite American. Most ads just used Native Americans to suggest a wholesome, natural lifestyle.[37]

Largely absent during the 1930 and 1940s, Native Americans who appeared in ads in the 1950s and 1960s tended to be comic foils. The baby boom following the Second World War found tremendous numbers of children living in more spacious, suburban environments and playing outdoor games like Cowboys and Indians. Depicting Native Americans gave advertisers several useful devices. The Native American language and imagery advertisers used was unusual and different, yet customary and familiar. When Post Toasties cereal was marketed as "Heap Good Corn Flakes," no one thought it was a typo; people knew from the imagery that the ad was "speaking Indian." Adding "um" to words transformed them into "Indian speak," like an Indian baby saying, "Me wantum stayum-fresh Post Toasties . . . no mush up in milk!" or, trying to chase two boys, a dog proclaimed, "No can catchum—they eatum Post Toasties—Heap full of energy!" Ads tried to persuade mothers to buy these products to win their children's approval and to ensure their health and fitness.[38]

Even as Native Americans pushed for recognition, respect, and rights in the 1960s and 1970s, advertisers continued to create ads with offensive stereotypes that tried to make playful use of Native American culture. A 1962 ad in *Life* featured a tight-lipped, serious-looking, middle-aged Native American man with long braided hair and a broad-brimmed hat with a colorful band and a feather. He held a box of Corn Flakes and the tag line had him claim, "No trade 'em for Manhattan." Serious or playful, advertisers throughout the century hoped that white women would accept the authority of Native Americans on issues of purity, quality, and goodness.[39]

"Backbone of a Mighty Nation"

Food companies also sought to reach women by embracing American patriotism in their advertising, particularly during times of war. This type of appeal called on women to recognize the national importance of serving particular foods to their family. Ads asked women to make purchases to demonstrate their devotion to the United States. This type of advertising could resonate with those who already identified themselves as Americans and wanted to affirm their loyalty, as well as newcomers who sought to identify as Americans.

Many companies sought to position their products as quintessentially American, asserting that their foods dated to the Colonial period and blurring the relationship between foods made in the eighteenth century and their twentieth-century inventions. Several different advertisers laid claim to national authenticity. One of the most assertive was Van Camp's, who claimed, "From the time of the Pilgrims, pork and beans have been our racial food" and, indeed, that it was our "National Dish."[40]

Not pulling any punches, a 1905 ad for Uneeda Biscuit tried to suggest a direct link between consuming their product and the well-being of the country. Like the name of the company that made it, the National Biscuit Company (later Nabisco), the ad alluded to the cracker as a national food. The advertisement claimed that Uneeda Biscuit "will soon be on every table at every meal, giving life, health, and strength to the American people, thus in very truth becoming the backbone of the nation." During the 1920s, Campbell's advertisements suggested that its soups were internationally known and that finding them abroad was a comforting reminder of home. One ad's hyperbole concluded, "To the foreigner, soup of such high quality and such fresh garden flavor, made thousands of miles away, yet ready for her table in a few minutes, is a revelation of progressive, inventive America."[41] Ads frequently suggested that women serve their families foods that would not only uplift the individual, but the country as well.

Patriotic advertising was especially prevalent during times of war. Wartime provided the ideal opportunity for companies to tout their contributions and loyalty to the country. As Americans faced the crisis of war, advertisers called on women's pride of country as they made purchasing decisions. One of the most common tactics was to advertise that the company was providing soldiers with food, thus identifying their products as patriotic and American. As Daniel Boorstin observed about Borden's condensed milk during the Civil War, companies providing provisions to soldiers hoped to gain those men as advertising vehicles, because when they returned home they brought "a familiarity with the product."[42]

As always, advertisers did not limit their appeals to words alone. A striking example of the power of pictures was a 1917 ad for Kellogg's Corn Flakes. A picture of a young boy, perhaps six years old, filled three-quarters of a full-page ad. He stood at attention, saluting with his right hand, while his left clutched a gun and a box of Kellogg's Corn Flakes. He wore a scouting uniform, gave a scout salute, and the gun was undoubtedly a toy, but the symbolism of the earnest youngster was real. The header, "Ask the American Boy Why He Prefers Kellogg's," reinforced the notion of the cereal as patriotic and beloved by its boys, that is, its soldiers.[43]

Advertisers sometimes directly linked their products to national aims. During wartime, the government often tried to encourage Americans to eat more frugally and more healthfully. While ads made broad references to Uncle Sam and the government, some ads were explicit. In 1917, a Campbell's ad claimed that at the company, "We all are doing our bit, To help Uncle Sam make a hit. With food from our farms we strengthen his arms, By Making the nation more fit." It reminded readers, "you also serve when you practice wise economy. As President Wilson says, you thereby 'put yourself in the ranks of those who serve the nation.'" A 1918 ad took a similar tack, using the United States Food Administrations (USFA) Home Card and its admonition to "Use soups more freely," to encourage consumption of Campbell's soups. It explained, "You are in line with the urgent food requirements of our Government, and at the same time you meet an essential health requirement of your family." Advertisers wanted to ensure that women interpreted the government's message as an endorsement of their products.[44]

This direct approach was particularly evident in advertising during the Second World War. Advertisers promoted their products as healthy, economical, and patriotic. Meat was one of the most prevalent foods advertised, perhaps in response to the shortage or scarcity of meat. Meat companies, and the meat industry in general, placed ads assuring women that their products were critical to their family's well being. A 1944 ad placed by the American Meat Institute emphasized the idea of "Meat and the American Family." The Institute drew on nostalgia to convince women to rely on meat in their cooking. Beneath a large drawing of a wholesome family, a script caption wistfully suggested, "Since it cut this country out of the wilderness, the American family has always reached for the true, the genuine, and the virile—We were never a bland people—Our wives and mothers plan our meals around flavor— by native preference, the flavor of meat."[45]

In addition to asserting a historical connection to meat, ads also highlighted alleged medical prescriptions to consume meat. Similarly, the Armour Company wanted women to know the benefits of their products. They bragged that because they were supplying meat and dairy products to the U.S. Army, "the average soldier gains 7 pounds during his first month in the Army." By selling their products' health and patriotic associations, advertisers hoped women would buy their rationale and their products, in spite of the rationing present during the war.[46]

Companies also employed patriotic advertising to encourage women to maintain brand loyalties in spite of shortages. They feared that if consumers could not find their products on the shelves they would switch to another brand and forget about the previous one. To remind consumers that the shortages were a direct consequence of their effort to feed the American and Allied troops, advertisers ran numerous ads during the Second World War touting their contributions. For example, the Kraft Cheese Company ran an ad campaign in 1944 that meshed self-praise with a tribute to the work of America's farmers. Large Norman Rockwell-esque portraits of gritty, hard working white men dominated the full-page ads. "While son Jim helped capture Hill 205," headlined an especially striking ad, accompanied by the image of Jim's father astride a large tractor, the expansive farm laid out behind him, his face strong and earnest, and his hands gnarled. The main text detailed a recent crop crisis, and reminded readers,

You hear about the brilliant actions of our boys on the battle fronts, including the sons of our dairymen. None of us at home can match what they do for victory. But none of us here works more days, more hours, more valiantly than the people left on America's dairy farms. They're in the front line of the battle for food . . . and they know it.

Off to the right, in an italicized sidebar, Kraft put its advertising message: "Because of the tremendous demand, both military and civilian, you may not be able to get as much Kraft Cheese as you would like, or get your favorite varieties."[47]

While many ads during the Second World War acknowledged women's participation in the war effort work force, food advertisers throughout the century wanted women's primary role in shaping the national identity to be as a consumer, not as a paid worker. Company ads invited women to stand strong for their country by purchasing their products; for women, consumerism defined patriotism. For example, Armour and Company ran a series of 1944 ads touting the "American Way." They claimed that, more than providing citizens with more and better goods, our competitive economy offered

Freedom of choice, which is the essence of Americanism, exalts the individual, recognizes that he is created in the image of God and gives spiritual tone to the American system. Recognition of the human personality as a sovereign being for whose happiness and welfare all institutions, including government itself, are created tends to make us more considerate of each other, tends to break down class distinction and to build toward the brotherhood of man.[48]

Women's decisions in the supermarket, then, took on enormous significance. Not only were they choosing a good cut of beef, they were fully participating citizens in a capitalist democracy. Advertisers blurred the line between promoting their products and propagandizing for their country to convince women to buy the complete ideological package: name-brand foods, strict gender roles, and democracy.

Beyond particular foods, advertisers were part of a broader movement, "feeding Americans properly." At the start of American involvement in the war, in a 2 January 1942 *Printers' Ink* article entitled, "'Food for Freedom,'" T. Swann Harding tried to persuade advertisers that this program, along with postwar planning, represented the "most stupendous and important social and economic undertaking ever attempted in the United States." Castigating advertisers for their poor past efforts, he hoped that advertisers would "understand its implications" and realize that an advertiser could "at the same time help the nation and help himself."[49]

Chef Boy-Ar-dee and other companies took up the challenge and placed the homemaker in the epicenter. In a 1943 ad headlined, "She, too, is making History!" they argued "Not just in overalls or a uniform— but even more in an apron—the American woman is serving her country today as never before. Planning good meals is still a woman's biggest job. Our nation's families must all be strong and well nourished to build for Victory." To further cloak her work in militaristic terms—against a backdrop of Abraham Lincoln delivering a speech and George Washington crossing the Delaware—it said, "Every day, ammunition for the 'Food Front' is passed from farmers to food workers to grocers to you. Just as surely as any soldier or war worker, you are in the fight to win this war. To you is entrusted the most powerful of weapons—the one that helps build all other weapons—the world's best food. No one knows better than you how to use it."[50] Advertisers felt comfortable suggesting that citizenship was gendered, with men fighting on the front lines, while women's fight centered on their grocery store purchases and the foods they whipped up in their kitchens.

The postwar era saw an increase in another kind of patriotic appeal, one wholly vested in a nostalgia for an idealized past. Using characters dressed in colonial garb speaking "Ye olde English," advertisers suggested continuity between historic American cooking and their modern products. The Campbell Soup Company, for example, was not created until the end of the nineteenth century, but ads for their chicken noodle soup made frequent references to its role in pleasing men "From 'way back in Colonial times." Claiming they had a "Truly American" product, advertisers made ready use of words like "homey," "homespun," and "tradition" to affirm their claims that their foods enabled women to please their families, particularly their husbands, throughout American history. Advertisers' use of historical references gave weight to claims of quality, value, and tradition.[51]

Advertisers occasionally targeted immigrants and their children with appeals for Americanization. Companies believed Jewish women, in particular, were willing to try new products and ran advertisements in the Yiddish press to attract their attention. In addition to prominent health assurances, the ads promised that the food readers bought would offer social success in American society for their children. Leaving no question was a Borden's Eagle Brand canned milk ad placed in a popular Jewish women's magazine, *Di Froyen Velt* (Women's World), that declared, "Every President of the United States Can Claim Immigrant Origins."[52]

Starting in the 1970s, researchers also pointed to the possibility of targeting Hispanics with Americanization appeals because it was believed that they too craved economic and social security. For this largely blue-collar class of people, heavily advertised products "represent a sort of status symbol, something they can talk about or show off." "Because most Hispanics come to the U.S. from poorer countries seeking a better life, the status symbols of that better life are what turns them on—specifically the things they can buy to demonstrate that they've 'arrived.'" While many Hispanics still shopped in *bodegas* in 1983; the director of Goya's advertising, Joe Franklin, suggested that "the ability to do more shopping in a single stop is perceived by many Hispanics as a 'step up.' "⁵³ By offering products that symbolized both higher class status and a distancing from traditional shopping patterns, then, advertisers could appeal to women's desire to improve their family's standing through their purchases.

Ironically, given these claims, Hispanics were also considered exceedingly difficult to reach on mainstream Americanization appeals. One researcher explained, "total Americanization has not proved effective in all ethnic areas. This is especially true in Hispanic communities in the nation where total assimilation is far from being a reality. When referring to the Hispanic assimilation process, the 'salad bowl' theory is more applicable. All the ingredients are there, but one does not become an integrated part of the other."⁵⁴ So while it was possible to appeal to the desire of Hispanics to be Americanized, marketers viewed ethnic pride as having more potential as an incentive to buy.

Advertisers also long believed that African Americans consumed products to demonstrate their adherence to a modern American lifestyle, although as already demonstrated they made less effort to reach them directly on this basis. For example, a study of "Negro Attitudes Toward Food," found that "the women in the present study display patterns of food preparation and consumption which are distinctly American and which minimize traces of minority or cultural status." The 75 women interviewed in Chicago, Detroit, and St. Louis reported their ideal meal was one "completely removed from southern and slavery origins or from the status of sharecropper. By serving and eating this kind of meal, the Negro housewife and her family demonstrate how far they have assimilated modern American ways."⁵⁵

"If Lenten Meals Seem Hard to Plan; (We Mean the Kind That Please a Man)"

Unlike the prideful assertions of a food's patriotic qualities, food advertisers only cautiously tied their foods to consumers' religious beliefs. To do so, they created ads predicated on the idea that women played a fundamental role in keeping the faith for their families; women made the decisions that allowed their families to adhere to religious strictures. By preparing foods in accordance with set guidelines, women could enable their families to uphold the ideals of their faith. Moreover, in so doing, women allowed their families to maintain their status as a "religious family" within their communities.

Food has always played a critical role in helping groups define themselves. Religions have used eating habits to involve their followers in their faith, through both prescription and denial of certain foodstuffs. Food has long been a means by which religious adherents bonded according to their particular practices, while serving to isolate those with different dietary habits. The food served in their homes enabled women to mark their families as belonging to a particular faith.[56]

National food advertisers focused their appeals on Christian women. While some companies made localized appeals to Jewish, Islamic, and Mormon communities, food advertisers rarely made broad national appeals to adherents of these religions. Advertisers may have been unwilling to risk alienating Christian consumers, who comprised the vast majority of consumers throughout the century. The small size of these other markets, a lack of awareness of product appeal to other religious groups, or even blindness to the existence of these potential markets may have influenced advertisers to target Christians exclusively.[57]

Religious ads generally did not claim that foods had religious qualities, in contrast to patriotic ones. Ads never claimed, for example, that eating a particular food made you a better Christian. Instead, ads focused on women's desire to observe their faith and serve delicious, nutritious meals. Religious ads almost exclusively focused on Christian women's observance of Lent, Easter, and Christmas.[58]

While they had long advertised locally, food advertisers realized in the 1930s that they could profit from national advertising to Christians, particularly Catholics, whose faith stipulated that they abstain from eating meat on Fridays and during Lent. The ads often suggested in large headlines the food's usefulness for Lent, although occasionally it was just mentioned in the text of a generally nonreligious ad. The most common argument put forth in the ads was that preparing meatless meals was a problem, but that the company's product could help. Campbell Soup Company, for example, offered its soups as the perfect helpmate for religiously observant women. More than merely presenting an option, it intimated that without Campbell's soups women would have difficulty providing delicious, nourishing meals because of the exclusion of meat. A 1930 ad presented Campbell's soups as women's savior, reassuring them, "At such times when your choice seems more than ever limited and when your daily problem of serving fresh and attractive meals is intensified, how comforting and helpful to have these splendid soups at your command." Fish and seafood advertisers took full advantage of the admonition by religious authorities not to eat meat. Companies such as the Canned Salmon Institute, Birds Eye Frozen Foods, and Star-Kist Tuna all advertised their products as the perfect answer to the meatless dilemma women faced. Religious ads promised women that they could give their families variety, and that doing so was essential to satisfying their appetites and earning their praise.[59]

Even though the ads focused on a religious purpose, pleasing men was never a separate concern. A 1941 ad by the Canned Salmon Institute assured women, "If Lenten Meals seem hard to plan; (We mean the kind that please a man); Then try a dish that never misses; And win yourself a flock of kisses!"[60] Advertisers repeatedly told women that it was not enough to cook dishes that upheld religious doctrines; they had to ensure that their families would eat them. Adhering to religious dietary guidelines was only permissible if the alternatives were acceptable to men.

Beyond the need to provide variety and please men, advertisers also wanted women to be concerned that the meals were healthy enough. Suggesting that a meatless diet would deprive a menu of essential nutrients, several companies, including Planters Peanuts and Kraft Cheese, advertised their foods as tasty, healthy snacks during Lent. Anticipating the hunger that comes with fasting, these ads reminded women that they should stock snacks that would revitalize their pious families. Again, it fell to the homemaker to ensure that their family kept its religious status by catering to their fancies within the guidelines put forth.[61]

"And Only One Maid! How Do You Manage So Nicely?"

In addition to convincing women that through food they had the power to identify their families as patriotic and to demonstrate religious piety, advertisers also suggested that women had the power to improve their families' socioeconomic status. America's fluid class system held out the possibility that, by acquiring economic wealth and adopting the lifestyle of the upper class, one could move up the social ladder. It was primarily the work of men in the twentieth century to be self-made and rise above humble origins. Women occasionally did so independently, but more often it fell to the housewife to help her family adjust culturally to a new socioeconomic status by decorating the home, wearing appropriate clothes, and cooking foods that would mark the family's arrival in the higher stratum.[62]

Early food advertisers made three presumptions when they designed and placed advertisements. First, as explored in Chapter 1, they assumed that women made the majority of food purchases and they never let go of that conception. Second, they believed consumers had a great deal of discretionary money to spend. Third, they primarily wanted to appeal to the wealthy. Historically, advertising agencies divided the population into two categories: class (educated and wealthy people—their desired customers) and mass (those with lower income and education). Initially companies believed it was futile to target those perceived to be part of the vast mass of Americans. However, new research and trial campaigns targeting the working class did lead advertisers to reconsider their belief that only the upper classes could afford their products. Still, even when they did target the working class, most food advertisers adhered to adman David Ogilvy's suggestion that they appeal to "snobbery: 'It pays to give your brand a first-class ticket throughout life. People don't like to be seen consuming products which their friends regard as third-class.' "[63]

In the 1910s, the Curtis Publishing Company, which published *Ladies' Home Journal* and *Saturday Evening Post*, wanted to convince the Campbell Soup Company and other food manufacturers of the importance of advertising in its magazines. To do so, Curtis researcher Charles Coolidge Parlin conducted a study which found that, "Campbell's soups knew no class. Everyone regardless of income ate one or more of the twenty-one varieties." In the first decade of the century, Campbell's executives had thought, because of the prices they charged, that only the wealthy bought their soups. Therefore, they suspected that *Post* readers, primarily working people, could not afford their soups. Historian Roland Marchand found that advertisers even considered a certain percentage of the population 'non-citizens,' meaning that their income was too low to buy goods. Parlin's study, however, revealed Campbell's broad appeal to all economic classes and, surprisingly, especially to the working class. He found that wealthy families had servants who could make soup from scratch, whereas working-class families could not afford servants or the time it took to make soup from scratch.[64]

By 1917, a study conducted by the Commercial Research Department of the Curtis Publishing Company found that soup had solidified itself as "a necessary staple article of diet" in both lower- and upper-class communities. Its use increased around World War I, and the great majority of housewives reported that "canned soup saves time and labor, it is an emergency ration, it is often cheaper, it is an article of convenience." For women on both ends of the economic spectrum, canned soup was important to their ability to feed their families. In the late 1910s, working-class women realized that convenience foods made it possible for them to work for wages in the war industries, while wealthy women turned to canned soup as they lost servants to industry work or left home to volunteer for the cause.[65]

Campbell and other convenience food companies realized that people of all classes were eating convenience foods, so advertising started to reflect that reality. Therefore, while ads continued to display foods in elegant settings, starting in the 1920s more food ads openly recognized that women of all classes were buying canned and packaged goods. Advertisers still wanted to persuade wealthier women to buy their foods because they believed those women spent a higher percentage of their income on food, but some companies began to realize that reaching out to working- and middle-class women made good economic sense.

One of the earliest and most consistent advertisers in women's magazines, Campbell Soup shifted its ads from an elite focus to a more diverse pattern of advertising. Its early advertisements made frequent visual and verbal references to paid help. For example, one 1912 ad typified the kind of scenario Campbell executives presumed led women to buy its soups. Three women dressed in their finery and plumed hats were gathered for lunch, and one exclaimed, "And only one maid! How do you manage so nicely?" The text that followed generalized the question, asking,

How does any woman with only one maid—or sometimes with no help at all—manage dainty little luncheons and other company affairs with perfect smoothness and ease? She takes advantage of modern ideas. She avoids needless and useless labor. For one thing, the modern house-wife uses Campbell's Soups.[66]

Advertisers wanted women to think about how efficiently they operated their houses, and argued in advertisements that a well-run home reflected on the quality of women's lives. Even in this early ad, the copywriters created an appeal that could resonate with a range of women. The possibility of having limited help, or even no help, suggested that all women could take advantage of the convenience of Campbell's soups. The affluence of those in the advertising industry in the early century blinded them to most people's struggles to maintain their homes without assistance. By the end of the 1930s, perhaps chastened by the difficulties of the Great Depression, food advertisers began to reflect the economic reality of most Americans by eliminating most references to paid, outside help.[67]

All aspects of the ad described above—the women's appearance, the table presentation, and the event (the luncheon)—alluded to wealth. Advertisers often left it to images and descriptions of "Snowy linen, delicate china, shining silver and glassware correctly placed" to drive home the idea that the food was elegant, high-class, and refined. In addition to table accoutrements, advertisers also included important, wealthy individuals to suggest the high quality of both the product and its consumers. A 1910 ad that claimed, "you will be surprised to know that a certain Washington hostess accustomed for years to entertain the most important personages in the 'diplomatic set,' provides her table regularly with Campbell's Soups." Another Campbell's soup ad that appeared in 1926 addressed "The March of Social Ambition!" It claimed that, "It has been said that every American woman is a social queen in the making. By this is meant that at no other time in the history of the world and in no other country has every woman had the chance she has in America today to gratify her desire to shine socially among her friends and neighbors." By stating their aspiration as self evident, the ad encouraged women to aspire "to take her place among 'the best people'

Figure 8. This 1912 ad for Campbell's soups appealed to women across class lines to be modern and efficient.

in her community" by using their soups. They claimed that women's purchasing decisions were all "praiseworthy steps in the onward march of their social ambition!"[68] Advertisers claimed that the food women bought was the determining factor in their family's community identity.

Advertisers have always strategized that by highlighting their products as high-end they could attract both wealthy consumers and the rest of the society who strove to emulate the rich and become wealthy themselves, pursuing what Roland Marchand called the "democracy of goods." As historian Susan Matt argued in her history of envy, in the early twentieth century, "Bourgeois women were acutely aware of the social significance of possessions and often were convinced that they might elevate their status, and that of their household, by duplicating the spending habits of the wealthy women they envied." One might not be able to afford a maid, a tuxedo, or caviar, but advertisements promised that name-brand products available in the local market would enable all women to provide their families the same foods that the social elite of supposedly ate.[69]

Nor did researchers' and advertisers' perceptions of women as consumers change as the century wore on. In the 1950s, Ernest Dichter found that most consumers considered white bread a low status food that did "not 'keep up with the Joneses.' " Tellingly, 81 percent of the respondents reported that they "would be embarrassed if it were served to guests." The report suggested that advertisers stop accepting the low status of white bread and strive to raise it by featuring men eating it at exclusive clubs, women eating it at luncheons, and people eating it in distinguished restaurant settings. By combining visual signifiers and coded language, advertisers hoped to convince consumers that their products were imported, opulent, and in exceedingly good taste.[70]

Maximizing a European connection, in either name or appearance, was a common method to achieve this effect. Cultural critic Susan Williams found that during the Victorian period, "Foods from distant areas were generally held in high esteem. Northern European foods, especially French and English, were particularly impressive and would have placed an aura of refinement and 'good taste' about any hostess who served them."[71] Early in the twentieth century, these imported foods continued to be accessible only to those with discretionary income. However, over the course of the century, the infatuation with European foods persisted, prices fell, and it was increasingly possible for mainstream America to buy European-style foods already prepared and boxed, canned, or frozen.[72]

Advertisers wanted American consumers to believe there was an upper-class association between European culture and their products. Advertisers put forth this association with authentically European foods like Lea & Perrins, a British Worcestershire sauce, as well as with those endorsed by or named after Europeans, such as "Old English" Process Cheddar Cheese. A 1940 ad featured a rotund, monacled man in a formal coat and full cravat who proclaimed, "Definitely, I say. Definitely, it has the sharp flavour of fine, aged Cheddar." His appearance, his speaking pattern, and the British spelling of "flavor" all alluded to the product's supposed upper-class English connection, even though it was a Kraft food, made in the United States.[73]

Starting in the 1950s, and perhaps reflecting both the new world order and the new era of airline travel that developed in the postwar era, advertisers began to expand their upper-class, high quality European associations beyond England and France. With the United States firmly aligned with Western Europe, advertisements featuring such recipes and imports as Danish cheese, Polish ham, German cheesecake, and Viennese beef stew all appeared in women's magazines. These ads often took on the responsibility of informing readers how to pronounce product names, using phonetic spelling and assuring them of familiar parallels. Advertisers suggested that women's familiarity with these European style foods and serving them in their homes would demonstrate discerning upper-class taste, even if the foods themselves came in a box.[74]

It was also in the postwar era that consumers began to allocate more of their income for food, with one *Fortune* magazine study finding that food expenditures had tripled between 1941 and 1953. This surprised many economists who had predicted a "*decline*—to perhaps 20 per cent." It was also surprising because

poundage figures cannot fluctuate very much . . . in *The Wealth of Nations* Adam Smith stated it clearly: "The rich man consumes no more food than his poor neighbour. In quality it may be very different, and to select and prepare it may require more labour and art; but in quantity it is very nearly the same . . . The desire of food is limited in every man by the narrow capacity of the human stomach."

Trying to make sense of the new patterns of consumption, Dik Warren Twedt of Oscar Mayer & Company observed in his 1964 study, "The ability of the majority of families to buy what they 'want' rather than what they 'need' has resulted in profound changes in selling approaches."[75] Americans were spending more to demonstrate their status and refined taste; spending more on less was a clear message that a family had arrived.

While most class concerns focused on whites, industry journals in the 1960s and 1970s began to reflect the angst of African Americans and their concerns about their status as second-class citizens. Some researchers concluded that whites wanted to obtain exclusivity with their purchases, while the goal of blacks was to become part of mainstream America. Pointing to the opportunities for the industry, one article about black consumers' brand loyalty argued, "Ironically, the conclusion to be drawn is that the injustices that make Negroes feel they are second-class citizens tend to make them first-class consumers." In assessing how blacks rated a grocery store, they found that low prices were the least of their concerns (15%), with convenience (92%), friendliness (85%), and neatness (54%) all much more important. A 1970 study by the *Progressive Grocer* also deduced that black housewives cared deeply about quality and heavily used nationally advertised brands. They concluded about black women, "By purchasing well-known brands rather than house labels or secondary labels, she is purchasing a status symbol." However, some researchers argued that blacks were more likely to spend money on socially visible items, such as clothing, personal care, alcohol, tobacco, and home furnishings, and suggested that items like food were not critical to the desire to express one's status. Indeed, some argued that many blacks "interpret eating more as a biological than a social activity," whereas for whites "food is relatively a socially prominent product"[76]

At the end of the century, despite these naysayers, many researchers believed that food advertisers could still capitalize on the African American desire for status. In 1981, advertiser Alphonzia Wellington credited advertising with facilitating the desire of consumers "who want to improve their station in life regardless of cost." She noted that the brand-name label was a "guarantee of a higher level of quality, and therefore, thanks to advertising, the promise of a better life in general."[77]

One interesting shift in African American consumer behavior developed in their use of coupons, a traditional way food companies have advertised their products. According to B. G. Yovovich, black consumers, like Hispanics, had a reputation for low coupon redemption rates, and he speculated that some marketers thought this was due to their association with food stamps and welfare. He quoted one director of marketing who theorized, "Blacks saw coupon redemption as another situation in which they could be looked down upon and get resistance at the checkout counter," but argued that in the early 1980s attitudes were changing. While lower than the rate of whites (79 percent) and Hispanics (69 percent), an A. C. Nielsen Co. survey found that 57 percent of black households used coupons, which according to a Nielsen executive was "a lot higher than a lot of people thought they'd be." Trying to capitalize on this trend, some companies put together "The Black Shoppers Guide," which contained coupons and "helpful hints." Distributed through 430 New York City churches, the booklets appropriated the motto of the Negro College Fund and informed recipients that "coupons are 'a terrible thing to waste.' " Still, even with appeals to racial pride and uplift, African American fear that coupons were associated with lower status often led to lower redemption rates. They wanted to use food to demonstrate their status, a desire they seem to have perceived to be at odds with coupon usage.[78]

Advertisers made new efforts to reach old consumer bases like African Americans and also began to recognize new opportunities for market growth. Breaking onto the scene in the late 1970s, by the 1980s newspapers and industry journals articles began to focus on a new subset of Americans: Yuppies. These Young Urban Professionals, also known as DINKS (Double Income No Kids), made an especially attractive target for advertisers. With larger incomes on average, these households also made an ideal consumer group for many companies because without children they had more discretionary income to spend. Caught up in the excesses of the period and its focus on individual satisfaction, these wealthy Americans made ideal consumers of foods advertisers positioned as upscale.[79]

"Black-Eyed Peas, Collard Greens and Tempura Shrimp?"

National food advertising did not encourage the broad based consumption of traditional, southern, African American dietary staples, such as black-eyed peas and collard greens. Before the early twentieth century, most foods prepared and consumed by Americans who lived outside the Northeastern, urban, white milieu did not enter the mainstream national market. Over the course of the twentieth century, however, manufacturers and advertisers gradually embraced some foods previously locked out by virtue of their geographical origins or their too close association with ethnic Americans. Improved transportation and manufacturing made it possible to bring people and goods from across the country into close proximity.[80]

Still, given that the southern African American diet evolved in part from African traditions and the severe want that typified the diet of slaves and poor whites, advertisers of these foods may have found themselves limited by its less than glamorous past.[81] Moreover, a pervasive racism and classism against African Americans and their culture throughout the century undoubtedly affected advertisers' ability to market traditionally African American foods to whites. One scholar has noted, "Southern is a code word for White, while 'soul food' is decoded as Black." While there was a limited embrace of "soul food" in the last quarter century, its arrival was generally restricted in its availability. Even in African American magazines like *Ebony* and *Essence*, African Americans only rarely found ads integrating these traditional dishes into modern incarnations. Headlined, "Black-Eyed Peas, Collard Greens and Tempura Shrimp?" a 1999 Lawry's Seasoning Salt ad asked optimistically, "What's this world coming to?" Unlike ethnic foods that eventually found their way into supermarket aisles and frozen food bins across the country, African American products (even those broadly constituted as southern foods) generally did not find a national audience in the twentieth century.[82]

In addition to not advertising African American foods, advertisers also rarely placed African American consumers in mainstream food advertisements. Particularly in the first half of the century, African Americans appeared as servants preparing and serving food, but never as consumers.

Although African Americans generally were not portrayed in subservient positions in the postwar era, they continued to appear throughout the century as trademark logos. Advertisers often used a character in a dual fashion, with the icon doubling as a cook and as a product trademark.[83]

While African Americans have historically protested the racist, stereo-typed imagery in food advertising, corporations that built their fortunes with these kinds of images took the position that brand names and sym-bol familiarity were valuable commodities. Aunt Jemima, for example, was the namesake of her product line and her image appeared on every box. Food ads from her "birth" in 1899 to the mid-1950s detail Aunt Jemima's famed history as a cook "before the Civil War." With no direct mention of slavery per se, they preferred the euphemisms like "the South that never shall be again." There were, however, consistent references to the plantation, the Civil War, and her role as a cook and mammy, and as G. A. Nichols observed in 1920 in "Aunt Jemima Comes to Life," adver-tisers infused their product with "an element of pleasing romance that ordinarily never would be associated with such matter-of-fact thinking. Pancakes and romance, pancakes and history are surely strange partners when viewed from the usual standard."[84]

Epitomizing the gist of the appeals, one 1940 ad featured a conversa-tion with a white woman saying to an African American woman playing the role of Aunt Jemima, "With a box of your ready-mix in my kitchen, it's like having you there in person, Aunt Jemima!" Aunt Jemima replied, "You see, my secret recipe is already mixed fo' you in dis box, so when yo' pops 'em on de griddle it's like me doin' it myself." A woman inter-viewed in a 1953 research study by Ernest Dichter reported, "That Negro image stands for quality. The quality of the old South. . . . I don't quite know why, but I too would enjoy being cared for by a Southern mammy and to live the gracious life in a white pillared house." Advertisers offered white women the promise of "domestic help" in their kitchens for just "a few pennies."[85]

Even though many African Americans openly objected to the racist, oppressive image of Aunt Jemima, particularly as the century wore on, the company did not give up her name or image. One opponent was Raymond A. League, the first black man to head an integrated national advertising agency, Zebra Associates. He argued that the images of Aunt Jemima and the Cream of Wheat chef were "prime examples of undesir-able role aspirations," and encouraged the use of more realistic imagery. Still, the Quaker Oats Company, which produced the brand, claimed "that research indicates that not only do black consumers find the pack-age inoffensive, but that the brand is even more popular with Negroes than with others." In a 1970 article, a company spokesperson claimed that they had repeatedly surveyed consumers on the Aunt Jemima brand and that, "The extensive research overwhelmingly affirms that the 'Aunt Jemima' brand enjoys a reputation for excellence in quality that is extremely high—higher than virtually any other 'personality' food trademark—both in the black and white communities, in both the North and South." A 1982 study on black and Hispanic consumers confirmed the old finding that blacks consume twice as much cornmeal as whites or Hispanics. However, it noted,

What's more interesting is that blacks give more than 50 percent of the business to the Aunt Jemima brand while whites and Hispanics give nearly 50 percent of their business to the Quaker brand. It is also interesting to note that Quaker Oats Company . . . produces both the brands. Inside sources claim both brands to be similar in make-up . . . The major difference is the model used on the package.[86]

Emboldened by the evidence that African Americans bought their product in tremendous quantities, in spite of its similarity to the Quaker brand product, the company held on to their trademark.

While they gave her periodic makeovers to appease critics and attract consumers, a 1986 ad featured Aunt Jemima rising like the sun over five houses. Claiming "Nothing could be finer than the taste of Aunt Jemima in the morning," the ad assured women that "She spent a whole lot of time beating and blending and baking so you don't have to."[87] In spite of the pressure to remove the loaded, problematic image, advertisers continued to use racial imagery to assure women that they could buy "help" by purchasing convenience foods. The return on their recognizable icon outweighed the loss of business of a disgruntled few.

Uncle Ben attracted less critical attention, at least in part because, unlike Aunt Jemima, slavery was not the basis of his alleged history. As the company told it, Uncle Ben was an African American "rice farmer renowned throughout Houston, Texas, for the quality of rice he delivered to local millers." While his bowtied image certainly suggested a worker, the company did not present him as subservient as Aunt Jemima or the Cream of Wheat figurehead, Rastus. Even though there were protests, these products still attracted African American consumers. Uncle Ben's Rice proved to be very popular. Indeed, in 1981 African Americans consumed "between 25% and 35% of the total rice sold" and Uncle Ben's had the predominant share of that market.[88]

Rarely referred to by name, the Cream of Wheat symbol, Rastus, was a constant part of twentieth-century food advertising. Heavy advertisers, and avid promoters of their cereal with promotions, the Cream of Wheat chef appeared on a wide variety of items, including posters, bowls, and children's wood blocks. In response to an inquiry on his origins, Nabisco Foods Company, which bought the Cream of Wheat Company in 1961, explained, "In the early compositions the benevolent chef cleverly appears, sometimes in a subtle, soft-selling guise, other times taking center stage. The message is the same: like the hot cereal which brightens a cold, blustery morning, these paintings make the viewer feel warm inside."[89]

Historian Charlie McGovern confirms the complexity of this symbol, an "image that we find palpably racist and offensive today, yet for many people who remember Cream of Wheat fondly, there's an association of comfort and nurturance, with the illustrated figure of an African American man." The always smiling image of Rastus sought to reassure white women that his cereal would enable them easily to serve and please their families. After the 2002 sale to Kraft, spokesperson Mary Jane Kinkaid said that "the image of the black chef will stay on Cream of Wheat boxes because he remains a symbol of quality goodness, and because he is beloved by fans of the cereal."[90]

Beyond these kinds of caricatures, food advertisers rarely made use of African Americans. When African Americans did appear in ads in the first half of the century, it was exclusively as workers, never as consumers. Even as the century wore on, advertisers resisted placing African American consumers in their ads. Many Americans believed that images of African Americans would improve, in both quantity and type, across the century. However, studies by sociologists found that progress was slow or negligible, even in the last quarter of the century. These findings hold particularly true for food advertising, with African Americans rarely appearing in food ads. The most common exceptions were athletes and entertainers who appeared as spokespeople for products. Michael Jordan, one of the most popular athletes of the twentieth century, signed countless lucrative endorsement deals, including one for Ball Park Franks. Likewise, Bill Cosby stood out as a spokesperson for Jell-O. However, African Americans as typical, nameless consumers rarely appeared in food ads in the mainstream media at any time in the century.

Only toward the very end of the century did advertisers even start, slowly and sporadically, to suggest African Americans as consumers. Advertisers continually rediscovered the African American and Hispanic markets in the last quarter of the century (similar to the continual rediscovery of male consumers discussed in Chapter 4), but made only periodic efforts to target them as consumers. Advertisers greeted each study that pointed to the economic opportunities these markets afforded with cautious enthusiasm and continued uncertainty about their existence and viability. The most common placement of ads featuring African Americans was within media targeted to them, rather than presenting them as consumers in mainstream publications, where they remained largely invisible in food advertising.

"A New Mood in Food"

Unlike African Americans, some ethnic spokespeople did appear with growing frequency in food ads, but only because of the growing number of ethnic foods they promoted; they were not integrated into mainstream ads. While advertisers did make use of Asian and Italian imagery, even to the end of the century they generally avoided using Hispanic symbols to represent their products. In particular, ethnic food advertisers hoped to encourage women's desire to be modern and American with messages promoting foods they claimed were unusual and exotic. To persuade women to serve these ethnic meals, however, advertisers had to offer assurances that men liked these foods. Advertisers also served as guides, helping women navigate unfamiliar tastes, ingredients, and names.

As a nation of immigrants, it is not surprising that the food consumed in the United States reflected the diversity of its occupants. What is astonishing, upon reflection, is the extent to which the American people and their foods became one by the end of the century, even as they retained varying degrees of individuality. Some twentieth-century cultural critics questioned the accuracy of describing America as a "melting pot," charging that the country would be better represented by "salad bowl" imagery. These critics disliked the idea that groups of people lost their contribution to the whole when they "melted." They claimed that being part of a salad allowed a group to contribute a unique "taste" without undermining its essence. Perhaps, as we shall see in examining ethnic food advertising, a better analogy would be America as a "stew": a stew with many different components, distinct, contributing taste to the whole sauce, and retaining their own texture even as they absorbed the sauce, but clearly losing the hard, defined aspects they held prior to inclusion. Of course, local communities held on to ethnic and regional traditions throughout the century, but increasingly the national market affected and was shaped by people's different eating traditions, particularly as supermarkets grew in size and popularity, and as Americans became more mobile.[91]

Ironically, one of the earliest foods welcomed into the stew pot was Chinese food. The irony lies in the extreme difficulty Chinese immigrants found in gaining admittance to and acceptance in America. A series of harsh, restrictive immigration laws left the United States in the early twentieth century without a large Chinese population, except in the largest cities on the West and East coasts. Most immigrants who arrived in the United States were men. As in many cultures, venerated cooking was a male domain, but male Chinese immigrants to the United States did all of the day-to-day cooking as well, because there were so few

Chinese women. Moreover, they soon found they could profit from feeding a large male population of miners, railroad workers, and cowboys who worked the West.[92]

By the late 1920s, food producers were able to take advantage of white upper-class fascination with "Oriental" culture to expand their consumer base. Fascination with all things "Oriental" flourished in the late nineteenth and early twentieth centuries and merchants helped encourage this interest by promoting artifacts and clothing. Women's magazines helped introduce American women to some foreign possibilities, with articles like "Entertaining in Japanese Style" and "Foreign Menus for College Entertaining," both of which appeared in the *Ladies' Home Journal* in September 1929. The first article clearly delineated the difference between Chinese and Japanese cuisines, explored (and impressed upon the reader) the formality of the meal, and finally offered some "typical recipes." From the outset, the author alerts the reader,

There have been purposely omitted from this discussion any recipes using the delicate and choice raw tuna fish . . . thinking that eels and rice, and octopus, and the inevitable sweet breakfast soup made of fermented beans might not sound so entirely delicious as they are in reality, no mention of them is made in the recipes.[93]

This article anticipated the tendency of American food manufacturers to dilute authentic menus and products, paring down foods to what they hoped would be the most profitable faux-exotica.

Embracing a common advertising tactic, a La Choy chop suey ad appeared next to the "Foreign Menus" article. Conveniently, the Chinese Supper menu called for Chop Suey or Chicken Chow Mein and the Japanese Dinner referred the reader to the "Entertaining" article, just three pages back. The menus suggested for "College Entertaining" and the La Choy ad, which recommended its chop suey "After Bridge or Theatre," both clearly sought to attract elite consumers or, at the very least, suggest themselves as sophisticated foods. While women attended college in growing numbers in the 1920s and sought out new horizons, college curricula and society still impressed the importance of domestic skills.[94]

Even though the food was markedly different from what most Americans ate at the time, advertisements for Chinese food took a remarkably similar approach in their efforts to convince women to buy their products. The copy of a 1929 Chinese food ad could have appeared in almost any food ad:

At very little cost and in just a few minutes, you can prepare genuine Chop Suey or Chow Mein and serve piping hot from your own kitchen. No other one-dish serving combines such a variety of wholesome ingredients. To surprise your guests or family and win their praise.[95]

The themes of affordability, speed and ease of preparation, variety, and the constant need for women to win approval from others all make this a familiar ad. The recipe and the promotion for an "assortment package" were also recognizable, as manufacturers searched for ways to convince consumers to buy their advertised products and to pressure grocers to carry them. Benefiting from these efforts and contributing to them, "Buwei Yang Chao's *How to Cook and Eat in Chinese*, first published in 1945, had gone back to press five times by 1950."[96]

While their early efforts were more sporadic, by 1950 La Choy advertising became steady. It adopted several additional components to reassure readers. First, to guide women in their exploration of this new and different food world, La Choy created Beatrice Cooke, a white spokeswoman for their company. Second, to assuage fears that the food was unclean or too foreign, ads proclaimed "La Choy American Cooked Chinese Foods." And finally, to remind readers of its exotic qualities, La Choy ads featured a caricature of a Chinese man, with a chef's hat, long hair braided and tied with a ribbon, and wearing a Chinese shirt with a high neck and big sleeves.[97]

The acceptance of prepared foods accelerated during the 1950s and it was "no longer thought odd to make a meal of a precooked item such as fish sticks, chicken or meat pies, chow mein, ravioli, and similar items." Chinese food found itself listed as one more prepared food, rather than standing out as an ethnic food. With no pretense of being a Chinese company, Swanson introduced a Chinese dinner in the 1950s.[98]

Starting in 1956, Chun King also started to advertise nationally with ads designed by JWT that claimed that there was "a new mood in food!" To expand the market for Asian foods, Chun King promoted itself with educational campaigns associating "the Oriental and exotic 'good eating' of Chun King dishes," as well as competitive campaigns to endorse the "advantages of Chun King as a brand." Its ads asked consumers to consider Chun King a "breath of fresh air" in their kitchens and promised that the products would enable women to create "a new mood." The words "change" and "variety" spiced Chun King advertisements, as they entreated women to try "The change-of-pace meal with glamour appeal."[99]

By the early 1960s, the approach had grown more descriptive, assertive, and personal. Moving beyond abstract moods, Chun King tried to reach women with the personal statements of individuals. Ads in the 1960s were more sophisticated than a decade earlier, appealing to readers on a multitude of levels. The header was a familiar "Just like Grandma

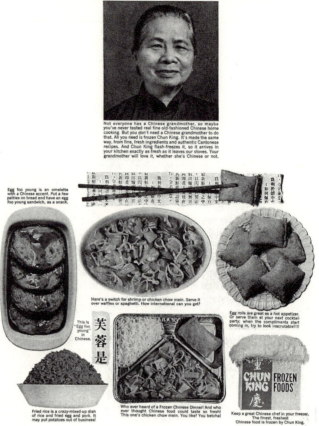

Figure 9. Chun King characterized its foods as modern and authentic in this 1963 ad.

used to make," except that the featured grandma was Chinese. This served to remind readers that Chinese food was a long-standing family tradition and that women held the key to its history. The copy reassuringly introduced something new when it claimed,

Not everyone has a Chinese grandmother, so maybe you've never tasted real fine old-fashioned Chinese home cooking. But you don't need a Chinese grandmother to do that. All you need is frozen Chun King. It's made the same way, from fine, fresh ingredients and authentic Cantonese recipes. And Chun King flash-freezes it, so it arrives in your kitchen exactly as fresh as it leaves our stoves. Your grandmother will love it, whether she's Chinese or not.[100]

The ads also played the role of tour guide, introducing women to a variety of dishes, like egg foo young, fried rice, and egg rolls. Each dish offered the opportunity to make it familiar, as in the description of chow mein that read, "Here's a switch for shrimp or chicken chow mein. Serve it over waffles or spaghetti. How international can you get?" The backdrop of the ad also highlighted for women the exotic quality of Chinese writing and utensils.

To help guide the way and approximate the friendly face epitomized by Betty Crocker, Chun King introduced an Asian woman, "Aunt Jenny." She served to verify that their food "tastes the same as her good, old-fashioned, home-made dishes." Ads also introduced white women peering out from their refrigerator's freezer door, and proclaimed each one "a great Chinese cook," because all that women needed to cook Chinese was "a freezer full of Chun King and a stove."[101]

In addition to the fact that it was easy to make, advertisers wanted to convince women that men would like Chun King. A 1966 ad featured a white, male police officer proclaiming, "We Flannerys grew up on corned beef 'n'cabbage, but faith, Chinese is a glorious change." Using a male police officer told readers that even the most masculine men with traditional (and ethnic) habits would like it. The copy assured readers, "Chun King is not out to change your lifetime eating habits. But as Officer Flannery discovered, a Chun King dinner does add spice to your life . . . Tomorrow, you'll go back to regular fare with renewed taste buds."[102]

In the late 1960s and early 1970s, sales of Chinese foods escalated and JWT targeted ads to women whom they believed were the audience for its canned and frozen food lines. Specifically, the ad designers characterized their ideal consumer as an adult woman with older children, residing in a major metro area, probably on the East or West coast, or a major Midwestern market. They also thought that a woman with an above average family income and a high school (or better) education would increase the likelihood that they and their families would be "adventurous and interested in new foods." According to the JWT Review Board Records, there was concern with promoting authenticity in the advertising and they considered two approaches in 1972. The first was to use footage of Hong Kong in Chun King Skillet Dinner commercials. The other idea was to use Victor Sun Yung, who played Hop Sing on the popular television show *Bonanza*, in the commercials. These different but familiar images would have helped advertisers persuade women that Chun King foods would be exotic and different, but still be embraced by their families.[103]

Increasingly in the late 1960s and through to the end of the century, advertisers without Asian-based names tried to convince women to use their products to make Chinese food. The Campbell Soup Company, for example, put forth recipes for "Chop Soupy," using copy mimicking the words and speaking style of Chinese people. As a 1969 ad put it, "Ah so new! Ah so good! Ah so easy! . . . (Very clever, these Campbell's)." Nor had much changed in a 1977 ad for "Souper Tuna Crunch," which bore even less resemblance to a Chinese dish. The ad, which called for a can of Campbell's Chicken Noodle, a can of Campbell's Cream of Mushroom, and a can of Chicken of the Sea Tuna, claimed a "touch of the Orient" by including a can of Chinese noodles and serving it with soy sauce. "Ah'h! So! Good!" exclaimed the ad, thereby granting the banal American dish Chinese approval. Planter's Oil claimed in a series of 1970s ads that its product would make the food taste authentic, with headlines like "Chinese cooking without a wok isn't authentic. And wok cooking without Planter's Oil isn't Chinese."[104] While peanut oil was common in Chinese cooking, that it come from an American-based company was not essential, nor, one could argue, authentic. Advertisers wanted women to believe they were creating ethnic meals and suggested that this pursuit lent their families some degree of panache.

While the use of non-Chinese foods and products to create Chinese meals continued unabated, this style of ad, with its Sino language and imagery associations, diminished somewhat as Americans grew more sophisticated in their appreciation of Chinese culture and cuisine. Increasingly, the ads for Chinese foods and recipes, even those by companies like La Choy, focused on speed and ease of preparation, taste, and quality. In 1980, for example, Chun King "scrapped their 'change of pace' theme and talked instead about 'you and your beautiful body' nurtured by these all-natural, no-preservative foods, those 'good things from the good earth.'" Still, chopsticks continued to be a commonplace feature until the end of the century. A 1983 ad for Karo syrup and Kikkoman soy sauce assured readers that their products would ensure "Authentic Chinese taste, and the only hard part is the chopsticks." In their continual effort to guide women as they coaxed their families down this new path, they concluded their ad with a three-part demonstration on how to use chopsticks.[105]

By the 1990s, advertisers had moved beyond just suggesting using their products to make Chinese foods, or even combining their products to make traditional American fare, to recommending them to enhance the flavor of fettuccine alfredo and buffalo chicken wings. Chinese food ads no longer presented themselves as solely Asian; they envisioned their products as staple parts of menus around the country, serving to "complement rather than conceal the personality" of the dishes. While invariably based in San Francisco, Chinese food companies positioned themselves as familiar, sophisticated, and integrally American, hoping to convince women of the value of serving or cooking with their products. To do so, the ads implied, would demonstrate their family's modern sensibility.[106]

"¡Sí! How Easy Enchiladas Can Be"

Advertisements for Mexican food followed a similar pattern in the United States, first appearing consistently in the late 1940s and growing in acceptance, particularly during the last twenty years of the century. Unlike Chinese foods, which started by advertising complete meals, Mexican food advertisements started out promoting general products that could accompany familiar dishes. Over time, as new manufacturers entered the fray, advertisers developed campaigns featuring main courses. Eventually processed Mexican food grew in ethnic authenticity. Even at the end of the century, however, like all ethnic foods, it remained tempered for American tastes.[107]

The exception to the overall pattern for Mexican food was Chili con Carne. Ads for this dish date back to at least 1914, and a Van Camp's ad from that year proclaimed it an internationally renowned Mexican dish. It claimed that a "Mexican chef gained international fame by a zestful Chili Con Carne. We brought him here. He is now in our kitchens making Chili Con Carne for you." A few years later, Libby's promoted it as one of its "New Spring Dishes." The ad focused on men's satisfaction, assuring women,

He will want it often. Your "tired business man," who is so dependent on you for every variation in his meals, will welcome this new dish, with its meat, beans and rich, tangy sauce. Heat a package of Libby's Chili Con Carne in hot water. Mix with one-half pound of boiled spaghetti or macaroni. Serve piping hot. Not only is this dish a refreshing change—it is so delicious he will want it very often.[108]

Suggestions of spiciness, such as a "zesty" sauce and a strong "tangy" taste, however, were short-lived, as was the proud advertising of Mexican food generally. This change may have stemmed in part from the hostility directed at Mexicans during the Great Depression, when they competed with Americans for work. Whatever its origins, ads throughout the century, even those that employed Mexican themes and icons, generally avoided the suggestion that Mexicans cooked it or that Mexico produced it.[109]

Safer was a foray into ethnicity, with the familiarity of traditional foods and assurances of an American identity. One of the earliest such products to advertise nationally was Niblets Mexicorn. What made it "Mexicorn" was that the corn also contained sweet red and green pepper. In 1947, the Green Giant Company advertised it with a Mexican theme and featured the Green Giant strumming his guitar, singing a Spanish song, and wearing a sombrero and a colorful serape over his shoulder. These cultural symbols served as identifiers in the ads. Women also appeared in national costumes, as in a 1953 ad that had the Green Giant posed as

Figure 10. Traditional costumes, landscapes, and foreign languages often appeared in food ads to suggest authenticity, as in this 1953 Niblets ad.

a bullfighter, while three adoring women in traditional dresses looked on. The ad used these symbols to send a message about familiarity and difference. The company assured women, "Don't let the bullfighter get-up fool you. It's your old friend, the jolly Green Giant." The colorful additions to the Green Giant's costume, then, paralleled the addition of the vibrant peppers to the corn. Using a familiar, beloved icon, the company affirmed that the product remained good and trustworthy; it had just been dressed up for variety. The familiar icon helped make "ethnic" food acceptable to women and their families.[110]

Some Mexican icons did create controversies for the companies they represented. In 1968, for example, the Frito-Lay company introduced Frito Bandito, one of the most infamous stereotypes in food advertising history. The company was criticized because the campaign had the Mexican Bandit stealing tortilla chips from honest customers. The company eventually removed the character from campaigns after pressure from those who protested its offensiveness.[111]

While a variety of visual indicators continued to appear throughout the latter part of the century, companies generally did not rely on them heavily to advertise their products. Advertisers, such as Taco Bell in the 1980s, believed that it was more effective to promote a sanitized, Americanized version of their foods without visible reminders of a potentially negative association with Mexico or Mexicans. There were exceptions, as in a 1980 Spam ad that featured a Hispanic woman wearing a modern Mexican dress. In the case of this ad, however, the effort to sell processed meat as Spam Enchilada probably demanded that they use cultural signifiers.[112]

The largest exception was the use of the Spanish language as a cultural signifier. Mexicorn ads used Spanish to encourage "Señora" not to "put off till Mañana" serving the corn, assuring her that everyone loved Niblets corn "Muy mucho." This use of Spanish in some ways paralleled advertisers' use of Chinese language and customs. Advertisers provided women with the opportunity not only to expand their menus, but also to pick up a few words of Spanish and become more cultured and worldly. As with the Chinese food ads, advertisers for Mexican food did not limit themselves to reserved, tasteful uses. Instead, ads sometimes tried to joke with Spanish, as in a 1980 Old El Paso ad that featured a recipe for " 'Sí Food Tostada,' " made with tuna (sea food), and a 1986 Mexican Velveeta ad claiming, "¡Sí! how easy enchiladas can be." While the catch phrase "Yo quiero" was pretty straightforward, Taco Bell's controversial use of Dinky the Chihuahua led some Hispanic critics to charge that the ad campaign "reinforced negative stereotypes." The executive vice president of the San Antonio Taco Bell franchise dismissed criticism of the controversial dog and its catch phrase, when he said, "It's a catchy phrase and to say that it's racism or immigrant bashing, it's just silly."[113]

While these examples draw on national brands that expanded their menus to include Mexican-style foods or flavors, starting in the late 1970s, the Hispanic company Goya Foods began to target foods to the Anglo market. According to a 1979 special feature article in *Advertising Age*, however, "some Hispanic media execs complained that Goya—ranked by *Nuestro* as the No. 1 Hispanic company in sales, by a wide margin— has not yet begun anything similar in its advertising to the approaches taken by Ronzoni and other Italian food marketers, in terms of promoting the Hispanic heritage to the general public." This held true to the end of the century. While the romance and beauty of Italy and its foods was a common theme in advertisements, particularly the promise that it was imported or modeled on authentic foods from Italy, Mexican food ads reinforced the idea that it was a fun, safe food to eat, and rarely included Hispanic people or scenery that might suggest it was produced in Mexico.[114]

By the last decade of the century, Mexican food had made such inroads into American kitchens that companies like Amy's and Healthy Choice were making frozen burritos, enchiladas, and tacos without any Mexican associations, and almost anything that could be was put into tortillas and wrapped, to be eaten on the go. Taco Bell had become so popular that they could market their foods as "Home Originals" and sell them at the grocery store. By 1991, salsa had even surpassed ketchup in top condiment sales in the country. Women across the country adopted what had been exotic and different into their menus, redefining American food and their families in the process.[115]

"Neapolitan Spaghetti Will Disappoint You When You Know Van Camp's"

Even more than Chinese or Mexican food, Italian food, over the course of the twentieth century, overcame the prejudices against it to become completely American. Italian food advertisers made overt emotional appeals to women. They suggested that serving Italian foods would not only help preserve or create a sense of cultural and family identity, but, increasingly and seeming paradoxically, would also demonstrate their American identity.

Italian immigrants who came to the United States in the late nineteenth and early twentieth centuries brought with them various pasta, sauce, and bread recipes. However, most Italian foods mass-produced and consumed in the United States throughout the century would have been unrecognizable to native Italians. Indeed, in contrast to ads for ethnic Chinese and Mexican foods, most early ads for Italian foods did not rely on cultural symbols to identify them as Italian. However, as the century wore on and acceptance grew, advertisers were more likely to associate their products with Italy by using Italians and Italian Americans (identified as such by name) in their ads. These individuals granted cultural authority to the products and verified their authenticity. Beyond the endorsement of the advertised product by someone Italian, ads often included the assurance that the product was as good as the authentic article. The assertion that products exceeded native Italian foods in quality was admittedly rare, but a 1920 ad for Van Camp's Spaghetti argued for its superiority, ingredient by ingredient. It explained that, "In Italy, spaghetti is dried in the open. The atmospheric changes affect it. The Van Camp Spaghetti is dried in sanitary rooms, under studied and fixed humidity." Declaring each ingredient superior, the ad trumped the competition in totality, claiming, "Neapolitan spaghetti will disappoint you when you know Van Camp's." Advertisers made these claims to convince women that they were buying something superior to the Old World. Much more common were ads that did not aggrandize canned, mass-produced American Italian foods, but instead assured women that the foods were authentic, delicious, high quality, and convenient.[116]

In the first two decades of the century, the popularity of pasta-based meals, particularly spaghetti and macaroni, grew. This entry of Italian foods into American homes was facilitated by the Great War. Pasta proved to be a good response to meat shortages and the national embrace of Italy as an ally in the war. Ads during this time period suggested canned spaghetti as a high-class food, featuring it in elegant dishes in upscale settings. A 1926 Heinz ad, for example, featured a man lifting the lid from a tureen and proclaiming "Good!" Consistent with all other food ads, Italian food ads used male approval to assure women that they would like this exotic food.[117]

During the Great Depression, Italian foods became an integral part of the American diet for many because they offered women the means to provide a healthy, filling, and affordable meal for their families. The economic crisis led advertisers to take the otherwise unusual step of promoting affordability. Ads not only mentioned the economy of pasta, but also featured the price of the product. The popularity of these dishes continued during the Second World War, as women sought out quick, easy to make, healthy meals. While attention to the economy of pasta did occur periodically, it did not occur on the same scale until the economic pressures of the 1970s, when ads again noted the cost per serving. During that period of economic struggle, it was common to see ads like one in 1979 that featured a woman giving a victory sign because she had successfully won "the battle of the budget with a Victory Garden Skillet Dinner."[118]

In the 1950s, however, the Italian government sought to promote Italian foods in the United States, but found their promotions overshadowed by U.S. firms like Chef Boy-Ar-Dee that sold their foods as Italian. Even with the popularity of Italian-style foods, researchers found that the Italian symbols employed in advertising, such as the flag and the language, created "great confusion in the minds of U.S. consumers between genuine Italian food products and products of domestic or non-Italian foreign origin." They also discovered that Italian manufacturers could not count on Italian Americans alone to form their market, discerning that pasta was "nearly as popular with the general public as with Italian-Americans."[119]

Ernest Dichter found that American women in the 1950s had begun to question the value of Italian convenience foods, or more precisely, had begun to worry that these foods undermined their own value to their families and their peers. Over the course of the century, some of the strongest selling points for inexpensive foods like spaghetti turned into weaknesses. The convenience and affordability of canned and pre-packaged spaghetti dinners came to suggest laziness and poverty. Dichter reported in a 1953 study that canned spaghetti elicited several negative stereotypes, including the assumption that it was "More filling than nutritious" and "An economical, poverty-associated food."[120]

Even more problematic was a belief that the Franco-American Spaghetti ads addressed "the lazy housewife kind of woman, not the thoughtful, considerate wife and mother that they picture themselves being." One of the survey respondents revealed,

I'd really feel like a lazy slob to serve *canned* spaghetti. The kind of woman that uses it lays around in a housecoat all day, or the kind of person that doesn't care about their home at all, or someone who knows or cares nothing about food. . . . The woman who serves canned spaghetti for lunch to her kids I get the feeling that the kids aren't the least bit important to her. There's no feeling of family.[121]

Addressing these concerns and attitudes, Dichter had several suggestions for the company. In order to redirect these feelings, he told Franco-American to create ads that focused on "fun" and women's "ego-satisfaction." One 1955 ad appears to have heeded his advice. A woman appeared before a plate of spaghetti with a fork poised before her smiling face, and the header proclaimed, "*Everybody* enjoys it—even the cook!" The rest of the ad assured her, "You'll get an extra kick out of the way your family goes for Franco-American Spaghetti."[122]

Ultimately, it appears as if the problems women faced with the product had nothing to do with it being ethnic or Italian, but lay instead with the fact that it was canned and already prepared. The things that made it attractive to use (ease and efficiency) also made it difficult for women to use it. It posed a risk. They might still make spaghetti, heating up boxed pasta and making a sauce, but many claimed they would not heat up a can of spaghetti because they did not truly feel they were making it. One woman shared her feelings about cooking for her grandson,

I like to cook something special for him and then I like to hear him say, "Um, Granny, this is good!" But if I open a can for him, what can he say? "Um, Campbell's is good." . . . That wouldn't give me any special pleasure and I wouldn't feel I had accomplished anything.[123]

Advertisers quickly moved to encourage women to feel as though they were creating a meal. A 1960 Kraft ad told "the modern mother who wants to be a little old-fashioned about food" that their Spaghetti Dinner offered them a solution. It assured them,

This way, *you* cook the sauce. It takes 15 minutes—but no heat 'n' eat sauce compares for flavor. You add tomato paste. You add the ground beef. Kraft gives you the rest: fragrant Herb-Spice Mix, grated Parmesan Cheese, thin spaghetti. You get 4 servings of homemade-tasting spaghetti with oceans of sauce. And you get the smiles of a happy family.[124]

Ads by other companies and for other Italian-style products followed suit, portraying women as bonafide cooks, making something homemade, not just heating up a mass-produced can.

In 1962, JWT created an ad campaign for the Copper Kitchen Sauce Line's Spaghetti Sauce Mix predicated on the idea that itpromised "no fear of failure." Research led the company to believe that the consumers most likely to use its products were "younger housewives in upper income families." With this ideal consumer in mind, ads were created that sought to "assure even the novice cook a success" and "give her the wanted opportunity to add variety to everyday foods." While subsequent research fine-tuned the consumer profile and found that she was most likely to be a mother and live in urban areas, the company meeting notes concluded that "virtually all households are considered to be potential" and they continued their national advertising on television and in magazines.[125]

Advertisers, including Franco-American, generally moved away from suggesting canned spaghetti as a family dinner. Instead, ads usually suggested it for individual meals, like mom home alone or a boy who wanted something to eat quickly. Even more unusual, the ads began to suggest that canned spaghetti was so easy to prepare that even a man could do it, so it was perfect for a night when mom could not cook. The ads adopted Dichter's suggestion that they use the fun aspect of spaghetti to sell it, particularly the idea that men loved it and found it a treat.[126]

Ads continued to embrace the theme of Italian foods as fun and helped establish pasta and pizza as foods that men could handle in the kitchen. Often played for laughs, these ads set forth the simplicity of making their products. Ads during this decade continued to target women as consumers, but expanded to suggest another role for women. Beyond shopping for their own cooking, women had the power to buy foods men could cook as well. Ads featured frozen and packaged complete dinners that were ambiguous as to whether they were appealing to men, or women, or both in their ads. Headlined "Men's Liberation," a 1978 Stouffer's ad appeared in *Better Homes and Gardens*, asking,

So what if you don't know how to cook? With Stouffer's, you can get along just fine. Because we make more than 30 different single and two-serving entrees, to give you the variety you like. Delicious things, like our Lasagna. Meaty meat sauce, three Italian cheeses, layers of *al dente* noodles, hearty flavor. And all you have to do is heat. And enjoy. Good food. When you want it. Without cooking. That's liberation.[127]

While the headline suggested it was appealing to men, the text of the ad, also used in other ads in the campaign, did not mention men or women. Advertisers wanted to sell their products' versatility to empower women and extended their appeals beyond speed and convenience to suggest that occasionally men might share the cooking (or heating up) burden.

In keeping with general trends in Chinese and Mexican foods, Italian food producers accelerated their advertising appeals in the last quarter century, and suggested integrating their foods with a host of other products to create uniquely American Italian food. A 1971 JWT report assessed the effect of recent social and cultural changes on the market for Standard Brands. Entitled "Women Demand Change," one section explored some of the changes in women's cooking patterns. It observed that the "expansion of the modern housewife's cooking into regional and ethnic dishes, the upsurge of once-spurned cheeses, odd meats, and exotic souces (sic) has done a good deal to remove food choices from publicly honored, unwritten agreements about what flavors go with what." The 1980s and 1990s saw a plethora of foods advertised as Italian, including an ad by the California Avocado industry, which joined with Creamettes Macaroni to promote Avocado Italiano. Their headline screamed, "Bravissimo!," and the text assured women that "Pasta is all the rage," and encouraged them to "cook it up *al dente* (a little firm to the bite) the way the Italians do." Ethnic food advertisers, even at the end of the century, used language and cultural associations to promote their products' cachet.[128]

Whether it was enabling her family to fit into a group, improving her family's status, or holding on to her traditions, a woman's power in the kitchen was critical. The foods women bought and prepared determined societal perceptions of their family, as well as their understanding of self. Eating particular foods enabled people to affirm their identity of themselves. Advertisers encouraged women to believe that their food choices gave them power to shape their family's social standing. Even as they persuaded women to try unusual and exotic foods, advertisers maintained their traditional focus on women as consumers. Whether they appealed on patriotic, religious, class, racial, or ethnic bases, their advertising methods remained remarkably consistent. Advertisers assured women that cooking gave them the ability to control their family's destiny and win their love.

Chapter 4

Authority and Entitlement:
Men in Food Advertising

I don't know what kind of a woman would serve canned spaghetti to her family. Some kind of a sluttish person. . . . It shows an utter disregard for the pleasure of her husband.

—Consumer response, "A Psychological Research Study on the Sales and Advertising Problems of Franco-American Spaghetti," October 1953

Food advertisers directed their messages to women, but they wanted men to be the focal point of women's role as the purchasing agent and cook for their families. Advertisements consistently suggested that women should serve men. They repeatedly emphasized that men's happiness was paramount and suggested countless foods and recipes that would win their approval. While some ads promoted ideals, others played on and created women's insecurities about fulfilling their role as homemaker.

Male figures frequently appeared as authorities on quality, taste, and value to convince women of the merits of the foods. However, their appearance in ads was more significant than just an endorsement of the food product. Advertisers used male authority to complete the gender role paradigm: women were consumers and men sat in judgment. All males, from infants to elderly men, had the authority to critique the food and the women who prepared it. While some male characters did have titles or degrees, the overriding message of all male icons and figures was that their ultimate authority derived from their gender.

Food ads focused on male entitlement, repeatedly suggesting that women should serve husbands and sons what they wanted when they wanted it. Instead of presenting companionate marriages, ads featured women as subservient to men. Women were reminded that pleasing men could bring the rewards of praise, love, and appreciation. Conversely, not fulfilling men's desires for food could make men angry, with dire consequences for women. Advertisers played on women's insecurities and frequently suggested cooking as a stressful and even potentially dangerous endeavor. Ads that reinforced the message that women should please men, and that men were entitled to good food and service in their homes, appeared commonly throughout the century.

When Ernest Dichter and the Institute for Motivational Research undertook a study for Franco-American Spaghetti in 1953, some of the consumers they interviewed feared that using canned spaghetti would make them "appear lazy and inconsiderate." Like these women, many others expressed internalized fears that advertisers both generated and exacerbated with their threatening messages. To assuage women's fears and maintain their focus on pleasing men, the Institute suggested that the company highlight the positive associations they discovered between "spaghetti and fun." Finding that women cooked to please their families and to gain "ego-satisfaction," the study suggested ads employ a "family fun" theme, emphasizing eating spaghetti "as one of the many things which father and son have in common. They might be shown watching a baseball game together, fishing, building a wagon, etc." The report described an advertisement that conveyed the image and feeling the researchers thought would be effective:

Both My Men earned a hearty treat tonight. A possible point of entrance into the theme might be a picture of the young son coming home after an afternoon of football practice at dusk, with Father—seen over Mother's shoulder through the window of the house, capturing some of the sense of a reward and treat that a spaghetti supper represents to son and father coming home on a cold day."[1]

Countless ads like this one appeared in the twentieth century, calling on women to care about pleasing the men in their lives.

Ads that did suggest that men cooked food or shopped for groceries appeared infrequently. Advertisers consistently ignored male consumers and the potential of their market, even though researchers constantly "rediscovered" its potential. Copywriters did use males cooking on rare occasions to promote the ease of preparing convenience foods, but generally preferred to maintain men's role in food ads as the entitled authority figure.

"When a Man Says It's Good . . . It Is Good!"

Food advertisers relied heavily on male authority and used images of males and their pronouncements for validation. From husbands to doctors, chefs to U.S. government officials, ads drew on male authority in a variety of fields and capacities to influence women's attitudes about convenience foods and gender roles. Sometimes the man featured was a generic husband, as in a 1926 Heinz ad that had a man lifting the lid

When a man says it's good...it is good!

21 kinds to choose from..

Asparagus	Mulligatawny
Bean	Mushroom (Cream of)
Beef	Mutton
Bouillon	Noodle with chicken
Celery	Ox Tail
Chicken	Pea
Chicken-Gumbo	Pepper Pot
Clam Chowder	Printanier
Consommé	Tomato
Julienne	Vegetable
Mock Turtle	Vegetable-Beef

LOOK FOR THE
RED-AND-WHITE LABEL

Eating Campbell's
Every day
Sends me smiling
On my way!

TRUST a man to know good soup when he tastes it ... If there's one thing he's frank about, it is the food he eats...Yes, too frank sometimes, to a woman's way of thinking...But there's never any doubt about it, at least...And when he gives his O. K. to the soup, that's all she wants to know...agreed...the soup is good!

Describing Campbell's Vegetable-Beef Soup as a "natural" for men is just another way of saying that it is a soup for hale and hearty appetites...the real old-fashioned vegetable soup with hunger-quelling pieces of meat among its nourishing vegetables...a meal in itself ...one that especially fills the midday need for sustaining food...tempting and delicious to eat...wholesome and easily digested. Enjoy it often!

Double rich! Double strength!

Campbell's Soups are made as in your own home kitchen, except that the broth is double strength. So when you add an equal quantity of water, you obtain twice as much full-flavored soup at no extra cost.

Campbell's Vegetable-Beef Soup

Figure 11. This 1935 Campbell's ad encouraged women to respect and acquiesce to male authority.

and smelling the steaming meal, declaring, "Good!" Gold Medal Flour ran a series of ads in 1932 based on statistics such as, "Men just simply go for Cranberry Roly Poly say 407 out of 409 wives" and "By unanimous vote, 807 husbands elected this [pigs in blankets] their favorite snack." This type of advertising that gave males the power to approve products or prepared dishes did not dissipate over the century. A 1978 ad featured three men enjoying Stove Top Stuffing and the reminder that "over 62% of the husbands polled preferred" it to mashed potatoes with their chicken dinners.[2]

Ads credited men with a great deal of authority for "knowing" good food and good economic practices. Throughout the century, they depicted males definitively knowing what they wanted to eat. For example, a young boy in a 1914 ad pointed his mother to Campbell's tomato soup, and the header assured the reader, "He knows what he wants." In 1920, the manufacturers of Wilbur's Cocoa also introduced a new slogan, predicated on the belief that "the effectiveness of the child appeal to women is unquestioned." In addition to clean charcoal drawings of mother and child that evoked "sentimental" responses, the advertisements featured the reminder, "'The Masters of the House demand it—!'" During the Great Depression, the United Fruit Company ran an ad for bananas that pictured an unhappy baby boy who cried out, "Broke or not we men must have our nourishment!" Advertisers even granted a male infant the power to assert his desires. A 1935 ad put it bluntly, "When a man says it's good . . . it *is* good!" Ads frequently featured men saying things such as "The best macaroni-and-cheese I've ever tasted!" Advertisers assumed that women were constantly trying to satisfy men, while men judged their efforts.[3]

In addition to palate authorities, business and financial experts that appeared in advertisements were invariably male. In a 1912 ad, a husband and wife sat discussing homemade soup, with the headline "Don't tie yourself down to needless drudgery." The husband admonished his wife, "I don't want you to live in the kitchen. Do as I do in business. Take advantage of modern ideas. Don't bother with homemade soup. Use Campbell's Soups." Men brought their outside business world authority to challenge women to be more modern and efficient; they also gave approval to the store-bought product. While advertisers struggled to establish a world in which soup would always be store-bought, they were equally concerned with holding onto rigid gender roles.[4]

Men generally controlled their family's finances in food ads, which lent legitimacy to their critique of women's expenditures. In another 1912 ad, a husband and wife sat at the dining room table, as he puffed on his pipe and wrote out checks. Seeking approval, she remarked about her Campbell's soup purchases, "See how they cut down the bills." He agreed, and then commented, "Good! That's sense. That's business." A 1943 ad took a more critical tone. It had another man with a pipe asking, "Is your wife cooking 30% of your pay check?" His wife's initial response was disbelief, as she stood with her hand on her hip and suggested that the only way to save money was for him to eat less. Using his proclaimed business savvy, he found food savings at the A&P Super Market. As she realized the savings and quality of A&P foods, she remarked, "Well, I'm dumbfounded," and acquiesced to his authority.[5]

Historian Phyllis Palmer finds that "by the 1920s, women's magazines purveyed a picture of sexy, well-educated partners in companionate marriages." However, food advertisements did not reflect this trend. Ads did occasionally ask questions such as, "Partner—or Housekeeper?" or promise, as in a 1938 Franco-American ad, that their convenience foods would leave women with "pep enough to still go to the movies." Still, throughout the century, most food ads depicting female-male relationships did not suggest a shared partnership of leisure activities. Instead of focusing on women as companions, advertisers zeroed in on their role in serving discerning men.[6]

Food advertisers reflected and helped contribute to the reality that most men generally did not engage in consistent domestic work in the twentieth century. Men's archetypal role in American society in the twentieth century was to be the breadwinner for their families, which paralleled women's role as nurturer and homemaker. In the first half of the century, men did become more involved in their family life, but historian Margaret Marsh defined this involvement as separate from any responsibility for its daily upkeep. Even on those rare exceptions when women could not perform their duties, men enlisted their children to do the necessary work.[7]

Nor had much changed by the 1950s. Historian Robert Griswold found that,

Despite bold claims that "today's young husband isn't ashamed to be caught wearing an apron" and that "there is no longer any sharp dividing line between man's work and woman's," systematic analyses suggest otherwise. . . . Men's belief in the sanctity of the division of labor and the ideology of male breadwinning precluded sustained involvement in daily housework.[8]

In his examination of the last third of the century, Griswold found that men's ideological beliefs shifted and that most men publicly held that husbands should do half of the work if their wives worked outside the home. However, he discovered, as did their wives, that men were mostly talk and very little action, doing minimal amounts of childcare and housework. Even as their wives worked outside the home in paid employment in growing numbers, men remained resistant to participating fully in the housework. Food advertising, then, reflected reality and helped to reinforce the norms and ideals of the times.[9]

While women rarely appeared as equal partners, men too only infrequently appeared as a "sexy, well-educated companionate partner." Ads commonly portrayed men as emotionally immature, needing to be appeased or pampered. One Green Giant ad asked women, "Is the man in your life a problem child at mealtime?" It adopted a knowing tone, acknowledging that, "Put a man at the table with a napkin on his lap—and often he's quite a problem." The solution, if women had this trouble, was to serve their corn. Other companies, such as Campbell, also promised that their products would "stamp out grouchiness" or make him "'snap out of it' . . . [until] he becomes an affable companion instead of just somebody at the other end of the table."[10] The ads suggested it was normal for men to act like babies, throwing tantrums and pouting when they did not get their way. These ads contributed to a culture of male entitlement, which one could poke fun at but still must tolerate.

Food ads started to use professional authority to legitimize their products in the early 1900s, coinciding with a time when the mass media was replacing familial authority. Throughout the first half of the century, advertisers used references to and pictures of doctors, nurses, and scientists to suggest that medically trained professionals endorsed their foods. One ad showed a nurse bringing soup to a resting patient with the text, "Every physician knows that such tomatoes are full of elements that promote digestion and purify and enrich the blood." Photographs of doctors from European clinics and hospitals helped to substantiate their claims. For example, a 1929 Fleischmann's Yeast ad featured Dr. Gaston Lyon of France and his declaration that "Yeast regulates the intestine" and explored the value of yeast in treating skin diseases.[11]

Another 1929 ad combined scientific authority with the influence of law enforcement, when it suggested that when you think of Maltine with cod liver oil, "You can visualize the four vitamins as four policemen. They stand guard against disease. They promote healthy growth and development." Advertisers took full advantage of the influence of medical practitioners and their dietary admonitions, urging women to turn to male authority to validate health and safety claims. They could then supply male images and words to buoy their product sales.[12]

Advertisers before the 1950s suggested that most Americans relied on a local grocer to assist and guide their purchases. They used the familiar image of a grocer in his apron to recall the influence that these men wielded over women's food shopping. Their alleged expertise in knowing quality products and helping women find the best bargains gave them a great deal of authority. The grocers generally did not say much in the ads, but sent self-evident messages by pointing to or holding the product as endorsement.[13]

Another source ads cited frequently for expertise and moral authority was the United States government and its representatives. Ads quoting government figureheads appeared fairly consistently throughout the twentieth century, increasing during the First and Second World Wars as the country faced shortages and crises. A 1912 ad pictured a man carrying a piece of meat out of a meat locker and claimed Campbell made its beef soup with "whole quarters of fresh, high-grade beef, certified by the Government inspection stamp." This certification was important because of the negative exposure meat processing received in the early twentieth century, most infamously from Upton Sinclair's sensational novel, *The Jungle*. Ads had to pacify the fears and disgust raised about the health dangers posed by processed meat. Ads also employed national imagery to endorse products, such as a 1914 Van Camp's ad that claimed their Pork & Beans as the "National Dish" with "Uncle Sam" looking on approvingly. During the First World War, the Campbell Company again found itself touting the approval of the U.S. government. For those women eager to do their part at home, ads asserted that by eating Campbell's soup "You are in line with the urgent food requirements of our Government, and at the same time you meet an essential health requirement of your family in a most practical way."[14] Advertisers embraced government proclamations whenever they wanted to make health and safety claims.

Chefs, the ultimate food authorities, also appeared to affirm that foods were of the highest quality. A 1930 ad highlighted Campbell's "Head Chef Emeritus," a Frenchman who had supposedly cooked for Campbell's kitchens for twenty-seven years. The French government gave him an award "for having contributed in distinguished degree to the appreciation of the artistry of French cooking throughout the entire civilized world." Campbell's ads drew on the authority of French cooking and chefs and suggested that women who bought Campbell's soups could serve "the genius and art of the world's most famous chefs!" Even though ads dictated that women should be solely responsible for cooking, women never appeared as chefs.[15]

Some companies even adopted male chefs as their icons, which enabled companies to put forth a unified, thematic message with their product and in every ad. While not always a self-conscious, traceable decision, icons reflected inherent race, gender, and class messages. When the Cream of Wheat Corporation began in 1925, its creators immediately adopted an African-American man as their symbol. They chose the now familiar chef image and named him Rastus. By 1949, the chef had become one of the "best-known trademarks in the country" and remained a recognizable icon at the end of the century. Scholars have argued that Rastus had a great deal of authority, even as a servant with "irregular dialect and broken speech patterns." Such characteristics, however, reassured consumers that Rastus's authority did not extend outside of the kitchen.[16]

Ads throughout much of the century generally focused on Rastus serving young children Cream of Wheat cereal and proclaiming its health benefits. Twisting an old nursery rhyme, another 1902 ad had a parent saying, "Little Miss Muffet, Sat on a tuffet, Winsome, charming and sweet, Our fat darkey spied her and put down beside her a luncheon of good Cream of Wheat." A 1914 ad based on the same premise featured Rastus weighing a baby with a hand-held scale, while his mother looked on approvingly. With a bowl of cereal steaming on the table, Rastus proudly proclaimed, "'Dat Cream of Wheat done shore make him grow, Missy.'" This reliance on the Rastus icon to serve and care for Cream of Wheat consumers continued throughout the century. A 1959 ad featured a young child sledding outside. Rastus only appeared on the cereal box, but his image warned readers, "Guard your family with hot 'Cream of Wheat'!"[17]

Cream of Wheat was not the only brand to use an African-American male as an icon. The Uncle Ben's rice company took its name from an African-American farmer known nationally for his high quality rice. However, he had nothing to do with the product eventually developed and it was not his picture that appeared on the boxes. Still, unlike many company representatives, he was a real person considered an expert rice farmer and advertisers traded on his reputation. As with other icons, Uncle Ben's relied on the male authority of experts to gain the confidence of consumers.[18]

Food writer Carolyn Wyman detailed the history of another male icon: Duncan Hines. In the 1930s, Hines began to gain fame for his restaurant endorsements, and eventually those of hotels as well. As a salesman who did a great deal of traveling, he evaluated the places he ate and shared his rating system with friends, who then shared it with others. As Americans clamored for this type of information with the growth of automobile travel, Hines became a well-known author of travel books. His endorsement of an establishment was supposed to assure consumers of quality. In 1948, he wanted to grow his enterprise and started to put his name on cake mixes. His transition to convenience food promoter was a comparatively slow one. Seven years after he began his new association, 76 percent of respondents to a 1955 survey by the Institute for Motivational Research, "first heard of Duncan Hines as a guide to good eating in restaurants, whereas only 21% first heard of him in connection with cake mixes."[19]

To determine whether or how the company should continue to rely on Duncan Hines to advertise the cake mix, Dichter and his Institute asked people how they perceived Hines. They found that, "Almost 40% of our respondents saw Duncan Hines as an uncle." Significantly, this role as someone who "is able to give sage advice without any disciplinary strings attached . . . (who) does not punish, correct, or criticize" made him a good spokesperson. For most women, his image could not compete with the female images of Betty Crocker and Ann Pillsbury, but Dichter found that those most likely to use Hines's mix (and cake mixes generally) were college-educated women who were more "inclined to reject the 'housewife' association" of those brands. He discovered that

They prefer Duncan Hines because the name has a "sophisticated" and "modern" appeal, and because using the mix does not "threaten" them with being pigeon-holed in the housewife category. . . . College-educated women tend to be more receptive to male authority than their high-school grad sisters or their other sisters who didn't get past the sixth grade.[20]

Thus, their socioeconomic class tied into their trust of Hines. The women who could afford to go to college were more likely to have been able to afford to travel and have patronized "hotels and restaurants endorsed by Duncan Hines." Advertisers relying on this type of research found that male endorsements could be a valuable way to attract consumers.

Male imagery often called on adventuresome, strong, larger-than-life male icons. The Dinty Moore Company used a Paul Bunyan-esque figure as their symbol. They wanted to suggest how satisfying big men found their soup and how eating the soup would make them healthy and strong. Dinty Moore ads tied the icon to the product and the message by reminding consumers, "Look for my thumbprint on every can." While not all stood the test of time, these icons advanced their products by connecting them in the mind of the consumer with the attributes of the male characters who promoted them. Even when individual icons faded, their enduring messages remained.[21]

Advertisers also used sports imagery and metaphors to associate their foods with energy, quality, and American ideals. Starting in the 1920s, the Green Giant proved to be a multifaceted symbol for Niblets. In one 1962 ad he appeared as an aspiring baseball player who never got to play the game. Because he was "Too big and too green," the giant committed himself to "growing the very best peas and corn in the land."[22] Male icons such as the Green Giant enabled companies to use a male voice to assert their products' virtues to women.

Advertisers hoped that male characters would carry greater authority, power, and confidence. In a 1970 excerpt from *The Youth Market*, Melvin Helitzer and Carl Heyel argued that

A child old enough to look at, grasp and respond to a television commercial has reached the age where mommy's voice has on occasion become a tiresome and sometimes even painful sound. He has heard it day in and day out for hours on end. As any mother will testify, her voice is often limited in effectiveness. For this reason, the male voice is far superior in reaching the child. It is authoritative. . . . The associations with the male voice are usually less frequent, and hence command more attention and respect. Female voices are all too reminiscent of the don't and do of mother and teacher.[23]

Beyond the voiceovers, Helitzer and Heyel also advocated using boys in commercials, suggesting that "A good rule of thumb is that when in doubt, leave out the girls." Just by their appearance, advertisers believed males granted foods authority and legitimacy that females could not.

"Mother Never Ran Out of Kellogg's Corn Flakes"

Portrayals of male entitlement were rife throughout food advertisements. Ads consistently suggested that males of all ages could expect females to feed them. Moreover, they were entitled, according to the ads, to foods they approved of, prepared to their tastes. If women did not meet their needs, male reaction could range from hunger to disappointment, and even extend into anger as a legitimate response.[24]

Ads suggested that boys could expect their mothers to cook for them, but rarely depicted girls demanding food. A 1951 Kraft ad had a young "cowboy" holding two pistols on his mother while he told her to "Fork over some grub . . . pronto!" This ad illustrated an underlying message: boys could count on their mothers to "rustle up" some food for them on demand. This is also evident in a 1955 ad that showed a boy sitting on a stool in the kitchen watching his mother prepare Chef Boy-Ar-Dee spaghetti. The ad assured women that "When time is short and appetites big" they should turn to these quick, easy meals. A 1969 ad had a boy standing in the open doorway asking his mother "What's for dinner, mom?" She replied, "Plenty" and was baking Hungry Jack rolls and biscuits because she knows how to "Feed 'em good." While parents were responsible for nourishing their children, these ads suggest that boys had an entitlement to food not shared by girls. Moreover, the expectation that women should provide for boys was a constant and extended to adult males as well.[25]

Kraft had a series of ads in 1951 that featured husbands telling their wives things like, "It's my pals, honey, on the way over to play poker" or "Drop everything, Mom! Let's go on a picnic!" In the picnic ad, the woman held a broom and a feather duster and stood next to a bucket and mop. She was cleaning the house while the man was sitting down reading the paper with their two children next to him. The text asks the reader, "Why not? You can pack the lunch before Father finishes the funnies." Husbands appearing in the ads rarely asked their wives if they could help them; instead, boys and men could expect snacks and meals served on demand. One 1977 ad for Duncan Hines cake mix even illustrated a husband who could not wait for his wife to finish the treat she was making. He had eaten a quarter of one of the cakes that was presumably to be part of a double-layer cake. The note he wrote, "Sorry Hon—But your cake tastes so good I couldn't wait for the frosting," while apologetic, left no question that the cake was his for the taking.[26]

The expectation of timely meals put forward in the ads particularly centered on a husband's arrival home from work. A Kraft Macaroni-and-Cheese Dinner ad that appeared in newspapers in 1939 depicted a businessman coming home from work exclaiming, "Just starting dinner now?

I'm hungry." The ad reassured women, "But he won't grumble long! This clever wife is going to serve Kraft Dinner. From the Kraft dinner package she takes the special macaroni . . . cooks it in boiling water for seven minutes . . . no longer!" The featured woman is smiling and at ease throughout the three panels, knowing that his dissatisfaction will soon evaporate because she knew which convenience food to buy.[27]

Except during times of crisis (economic depressions and wars), ads suggested that leftovers were one of the worst things a woman could serve a man. The purpose was twofold. They wanted to persuade women to buy more food and to buy their products to disguise or improve leftovers. A 1932 Crisco ad promised that, "He'll never guess they're Left Overs!" It told women,

You have my sincere sympathy if your husband looks scornfully at cold meat and warmed-up vegetables. A man's just like that! But you can get around him—if you change your left-overs into dishes that taste brand-new. I've tried out these three left-over dishes on the most finicky men I know.[28]

During tumultuous times, advertisers fully expected women to serve food prepared on previous days, so they introduced the idea that women should be anxious about their husbands' dissatisfaction and turn to their product for guaranteed results. While promoting concern for men's happiness, they also suggested that they were conspiring with women to cope with the potential for men's irrational and unreasonable demands.

Still, advertisers contended that men could expect the foods they wanted. Advertisers encouraged women to avoid ruts, but women then faced the challenge of finding new dishes and persuading their husbands to try them. Advertisers also faced the challenge of trying to convince women to try new products, while trying to secure their brand loyalty. Ultimately, they wanted women to trust their brand, but to experiment within the range of products they offered.

To promote its products, Quaker Oats ran a 1957 ad in the form of a letter with what psychologists might characterize as a passive aggressive tone. It was introduced as, "An open letter to my wife" because the husband, Bob, "figured other husbands might feel the same way" and he could help women around the country better meet their husbands' needs. Writing to "Ellen," he began by praising his wife. However, the rest of the letter was devoted to romanticizing hot breakfasts, "Like (forgive me) Mother used to make." Nostalgically, Bob described how, "On those mornings I used to feel I could lick the world. I think Mom used to feel pretty good, too." He then suggested oatmeal as a quick, inexpensive, healthy option and told his wife, "I love you." Playing to women's guilt over not providing loving food, the ad played up both the physical and emotional feelings men wanted from a warm, loving breakfast.

'Mother *never* ran out of Kellogg's Corn Flakes'

Figure 12. This 1957 Kellogg's ad makes it clear that mothers and wives were responsible for catering to both their children and their husbands, who were entitled to a lifetime of being fed by women.

A "real breakfast," not with "fresh-yesterday sweet rolls. Or the instant coffee that tastes almost as good. . . . Or the box of munchie-wunchies." This ad is an explicit example of the type of advertising that appeared throughout the century, with males decreeing the type, quality, and brand of food they expected. They often couched their right to food served by women in terms of love, nostalgia, and quality, as Quaker Oats did in the "Open Letter."[29]

Even more aggressive was another 1957 ad featuring an older couple. The man stood over the breakfast table, bellowing at his seated wife, "Mother *never* ran out of Kellogg's Corn Flakes." The image and the text both conveyed the message that it was the woman's responsibility to care for the male, be he child or adult. Advertisers frequently presented mothers as infallible in their devotion and success in pleasing their sons, while wives often came up short pleasing men. Ultimately, women learned from ads that if they did not please men, they could certainly expect their wrath.[30]

Advertisers worried that the mid-century development of frozen dinners would prove a hard sell to women and the men they were supposed to please. Ironically, the frozen food companies themselves occasionally suggested that their foods were cold and heartless. Dichter cautioned advertisers about this approach. He wanted advertisers to present their product in an upbeat way, noting that young housewives did not report feeling guilty using frozen foods and that ads could emphasize the freshness, variety, and creativity that these convenience foods allowed.[31]

Frozen food advertisers believed so wholly in a paradigm of gender relations in which women were responsible for preparing food that they seemingly placed their need to maintain it ahead of the sale of their foods. Perhaps reflecting the gender tensions of the 1960s and appearing in the same year as the formation of the National Organization of Women, Schrafft's 1966 frozen dinners ads were unusual for their explicit threats. Ads acknowledged that frozen foods were less than ideal and might not express the love inherent in a meal made from scratch, or even from jars and cans. The ads wanted to present the entrees as the best of a bad set of options. Women forced to rely on frozen dinners for their husbands had best use Schrafft's. With startling headlines like, "How many frozen meals can a man eat before icicles form on his heart?" ads challenged women to think about the unhappiness they might be causing their husbands. The men in the ads were all woeful and sad. The advertisers reminded women that while their product may not win "you looks of love as you set it on the table and waltz out the door, at least it won't get you icy stares."[32]

Headlined "Why husbands leave home," another ad featured in *Woman's Day* presented a scenario with the man coming home "from a typically miserable day at the office." He found no love, no tender hugs and kisses, only a frozen dinner. Ads assured women that because Schrafft's foods "taste like the meals you fix yourself when you have the time to really fuss, . . . He may be angry for a little while, but then he'll taste it, and when you get home the chances are extremely good that he'll still be there."[33] Women who worked outside the home got the message that if they did not use Schrafft's, they could be in danger of their husband walking out the door.

Another Schrafft's ad in the same vein told the story of the Averys. The husband, Phil, ate two frozen meals a week, but the ad assured the reader that the frozen meal was not the problem. "Convenience foods

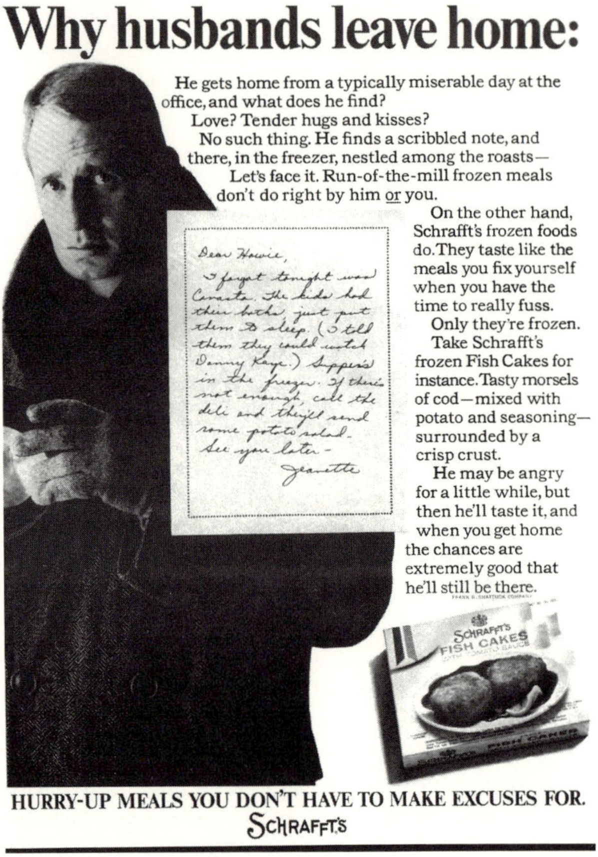

Figure 13. Endorsing men's anger at women's absence in the kitchen, this 1966 Schrafft's ad held out the threat that serving bad food could lead their husbands to abandon them.

play a useful role in the lives of most of us," they recognized, "but most of them are not very good." Magnanimously, they proclaimed that Schrafft's cared enough to make good products: "to save a marriage like the Averys' it's the least we can do."[34]

The ads generally did not focus on what the women were doing instead of cooking for their husbands or attempt to justify the frozen dinners. Instead, they tried to persuade women to worry about making their husbands so angry that they would abandon the marriage. Advertisers suggested that women should be concerned because they were not cooking and worried that the convenience foods they bought might not be a good substitute. Men were entitled to a hot cooked meal when they get home, and even if women could not be there to provide it, they were accountable for ensuring that men were well fed and felt loved.

Another ad assumed that men would be disappointed with their wife's homemaking when she worked outside the home. Appearing in *Time* magazine in 1971, the Stouffer's ad counseled women, "It isn't every girl who can work and run a home; And, luckily, you've got an understanding husband; Tonight, you're going to thank him for all the times; He could've grumped and didn't; It's a good day for Stouffer's."[35] Appearing in the early 1970s, the ad acknowledged that women were working outside the home in growing numbers and wanted them to continue to "run" their homes. Women were encouraged to serve quality frozen foods to show their appreciation to an "understanding husband" whom advertisers claimed had the right to be disgruntled with the quality of care he was receiving at home.

"Meals to Please a Man"

Throughout the twentieth century, ads consistently reminded women to gratify men with their cooking. Beginning with infant boys, and extending to include all males, be they fathers, sons, boyfriends, husbands, or male guests, ads reinforced an ideology of deference to male desires. Food advertisers promoted the belief that food preparation was a gender-specific activity, and suggested that they could help women to do their jobs. They encouraged women to cook for men and children to express their love. The ads subordinated women's own preferences and tastes; the emphasis on giving was so complete that ads almost never portrayed women eating. Instead, ads focused exclusively on men's satisfaction. They highlighted nostalgia for meals cooked by women in the past, threatened that not pleasing males could jeopardize a marriage, and employed a rhetoric by which foods and recipes took on gendered qualities.[36]

Pairing boys and men together as men was a useful technique for advertisers. It allowed advertisers to make blanket claims about male desires and gave all males legitimacy and respect based only on sex. Ads occasionally referred to male children and adults as boys, for example, the 1950 Calumet Baking Powder ad that advertised Chocolate Nut Sundae Cake "For a Boy—Aged 8 to 80." Advertisers referred to males as boys to suggest boyish loves or enthusiasms. More common were ads that considered all males to be men. With this language, advertisers promised women taste, heartiness, and virility for growing boys and discerning husbands. Using pictures of a young boy in 1925 and a man in 1953 playing with train sets, Franco-American promoted its food as "A boy's favorite food that a man still loves." Just as the train sets they played with became more sophisticated and complex, so too did boys grow into men, all the while loving their Franco-American spaghetti.[37]

A Colman's Mustard ad in 1932 promised that its products were "Zestful foods that delight a MAN!" The first paragraph of text focused on male approval, declaring, "How the men, big and little, just love pickles and relishes! And how they brag, among themselves, about those glorious seasoned delights that 'my wife' and 'mother' know so well how to make!" Women, then, were to be confident that young boys and men talked to each other about what good cooks women were when they used Colman's. A 1935 ad for Anglo Corned Beef was titled, "Little Men thrive on Anglo" and featured a young boy enjoying a sandwich. It stated that there was "Nothing so satisfying" to boys and went on to remind women, "And how Father enjoys corned beef hash made with Anglo!" Advertisements bombarded female readers with ways to please their "men." Mooseabec Sardines also linked father and son together in a 1957 ad. It assured readers that their sardines were "secret-seasoned for he-man flavor" and encouraged women to "Treat your men to Mooseabecs today!" Advertisers wanted to define male tastes and preferences, and to ensure that women cared about catering to men's desires.[38]

Advertising frequently intertwined food and affection. Sometimes the message was subtle, as in a 1917 Libby's ad that observed, "Your 'tired business man,' who is so dependent on you for every variation in his meals, will welcome this new dish." A 1944 Stokely's Peas ad offered two recipes to help women keep their "husband in a honeymoon mood," while other ads used pictures of men kissing their wives or men bragging about their wives' cooking skills to suggest the appreciation women would gain by using their products.[39]

Some ads explicitly called on women to gain admiration and love with food. A 1935 Brer Rabbit Molasses ad told the reader, "Mary wasn't always such a popular lass." However, she made gingerbread with their molasses and "Then one of the boys actually asked if he might come again. . . . Something that had never happened to Mary before. . . . Now she's one of the most popular young ladies in town." Even more blatant was a 1943 Derby Foods ad that encouraged women to serve their products to their hungry husbands; it concluded, "He'll love you!"[40]

One of the most common ways advertisers alluded to providing love and caring was to make connections between women in the past and present. As early as 1902, a None Such Mince Meat ad looked back wistfully to the days when cooks went to the trouble to get things just right. It declared, "give the husbands and the boys plenty of mince pies 'like mother used to make.'" Ads encouraged consumers to make comparisons between their mother's or grandmother's cooking, and the meal served. The ads inevitably stated that their products were "just like the homemade kind," or went further and promised that they would be better. A 1932 Bisquick ad, for example, promised that their mix would make "biscuits he will say are better than those his mother made."[41]

Advertisers generally focused on women pleasing men with two meals: breakfast and dinner. Lunch was not usually the focus, particularly as the century progressed, as most men (and children) ate lunch outside the home. The themes adopted for breakfast and dinner ads were the same. They used a dual approach, captured by a 1917 Aunt Jemima pancake ad headlined, "Do you make your husband happy?" The ads wanted women to both aspire to pleasing men and to fear their dissatisfaction. They counseled women to avoid trying other products. One Aunt Jemima ad cautioned, "Don't experiment, don't risk failures that disappoint him— you can so easily start him off every morning humming a little tune of contentment." Ads credited women with making it their "business" to start his day off right, noting he would be "well pleased with the world— and with you." French's Mustard ran a series of ads in 1941 that contrasted two men. The unhappy man scrunched up his face in disgust with his hamburger and his wife. The happy man beamed because French's mustard topped his hamburger and he had a wife who cared enough to buy French's. A 1959 ad for Kellogg's Corn Flakes featured a middle-aged couple and the reminder, "Foresight can be fun. If you want to be taken out in the evening, don't run out in the morning." The husband held an empty box of cereal upside down and frowned at his wife, who stood with a full box behind her back, smiling. She understood the importance of pleasing a man who would reward or punish her homemaking skills.[42]

While ads alluded to male anger, they rarely explicitly illustrated it. A 1947 ad for Herb-Ox was unusual because of its virulent hostility. It contained drawings of a man, dressed in a suit, kneeling on the ground outside of his house and lighting the fuse of a stick of dynamite that filled his house. With the header, "He was going to 'Raise the Roof,'" the ad explained that "My husband walked out on my 'flat' meals, even the children wouldn't finish them!" The next frame had the man standing up from the table, with his wife unhappy and sweating. The two children also looked concerned and fearful of his actions. The ad concluded that, "When food tastes better—it's better for you!" This ad sent a significant, chilling message to its readers: not serving a good meal could jeopardize women's physical safety and happiness.[43]

A 1956 ad used a fairy tale to sell its idea: "The Queen of Hearts, she made some tarts—It took her the whole afternoon. Said the king with a bellow, 'I'd rather have Jell-O; It's grand and it's ready so soon!'" To further assert his authority, the king yelled out and pointed to a picture

HE WAS GOING TO

"Raise the Roof"

My husband walked out on my "flat" meals..even the children wouldn't finish them!

But I found that Herb-Ox flavors up main dishes. For better stew, stir in 2 cubes for 4 portions..

And you have a really grand-tasting dish! (P.S. You can use Herb-Ox in soup and gravy too.)

WHEN FOOD TASTES BETTER —IT'S BETTER FOR YOU!

So "flavor up" your meals with

Write for FREE menu booklet, illustrated in full color!

Herb-Ox

BOUILLON CUBES

The PURE FOOD COMPANY, Inc.
Mamaroneck, N. Y.

Figure 14. An explicit illustration of men's anger over women's cooking, this 1947 Herb-Ox ad made it clear, "When food tastes better—it's better for you!"

The Queen of Hearts, she made some tarts--
It took her the whole afternoon.
Said the king with a bellow,"I'd rather have Jell-O;
It's grand and it's ready so soon!"

Figure 15. A woman's devotion to cooking for her husband was not enough—
she had to make sure to cook the foods that he wanted, or in the case of this
1956 Jell-O ad, angrily demanded.

of a Jell-O mold. The queen was so upset and startled, she dropped the
tray of tarts. Even in the world of fantasy, women had to divine men's
desires to avoid their wrath. Fortunately, the lucky reader could learn
from the queen's mistake. It was best to stick to men's established favorites. Advertisers embraced this message to insure brand loyalty. Moreover, ads such as these suggested that it was acceptable for men to be
angry and disappointed; men had a right to yell at women who displeased
them with their cooking.[44]

J. Walter Thompson Review Board records for French's Potatoes in the
early 1960s reveal efforts to set their products apart from others on the
market. Decision makers for the advertising agency and the company

decided to associate French's with "male taste and flavor satisfaction." They reasoned that "A woman may dress for other women, but her reason for cooking, and her reward, is her man's approval. His approval will put the dish on her regular list. His disapproval will discourage her even if she likes it herself." They went on to decide on a campaign with a "male" look that claimed, "Every French's potato dish is approved by an all-male jury."[45]

Advertisers encouraged women to make men's satisfaction their top priority. They associated men with products and recipes, invariably connecting men to meat and potatoes, alluding to "man-sized" portions, and concocting recipes that promised to please reluctant men. They wanted to ensure that women associated the males in their household with particular convenience foods. Some ads subtly inserted expressions like "A favorite with the men" or "Men like beef and vegetables" to catch women's attention. Others were more assertive, with bold headlines like, "Menus with Manpower" and "Put spice in his life." Food advertisers relied on the expression "he-man" to suggest that their products or recipes offered truly big portions. A 1947 Chicken of the Sea ad showcased a recipe for "He-man tuna cutlets," while a 1962 Swift's Premium ad wanted women to try its "hearty, he-man Thick-Sliced" bacon. Campbell wanted it both ways with its 1944 ad that declared " 'He-Man' is the word for these Hearty Soups! But, Ladies, you'll like 'em, too!"[46]

One of the surest ways to disappoint a man, according to the ads, was by cooking foods that were not manly enough. A 1929 French's Mustard ad provided women with "complete instructions for making Sandwiches to any man's taste" and reminded women, "No man likes a feminine sandwich." A 1951 Nabisco Shredded Wheat ad admonished women to "Give him a breakfast that's a good honest meal, not 'sissy' food!" These products, as well as countless others, sought to portray themselves, as Campbell did in 1968, as able to "handle a hungry man." Campbell even categorized some of its heartier soups as "Manhandlers."[47]

Food companies frequently advertised their products with recipes designed to please men. Ads encouraged readers to write away for recipe books with titles such as, "15 Ways to a Man's Heart" and " 'Man-pleasing' rice recipes." A Birds Eye advertising campaign appearing in the early 1970s headlined the ads "How to cook for a man." The ads featured the Birds Eye package, the finished dish, and directions on how to cook the meal. The ads had other subtle foci, including the importance of variety and the ease of preparing these meals, but their primary focus was on pleasing men. The language in every aspect of the ads sought to remind women that they should be concerned with providing meals men would like.[48]

"Helpless Males, Huh?"

Advertisers generally ignored that men could and did cook. Ads rarely showed men cooking, and especially resisted the idea that men could be responsible for the day-to-day task of cooking for their families. Historian Jessamyn Neuhaus, however, found that while "Cookbook publishers, magazine writers, food processing companies, grocery stores, and kitchen appliances devoted most of their attention—and their recipes—to the married middle-class female consumer . . . during the 1920s and 1930s, popular household magazines also regularly discussed and depicted male culinary adventures." Indeed, as Neuhaus argues, "they portrayed men as naturally skilled in the kitchen, more adventurous and willing to experiment at the stove than the women, and less inclined to slavishly follow a cookbook recipe." Advertisers, however, were reluctant to include men in their ads or to target them directly and during the Second World War, "discussions about male culinary prowess . . . virtually disappeared."[49]

Beginning in the 1950s, however, advertisements occasionally addressed instances in which men might want to, or more likely in their view, *have to* cook. The ads portrayed men cooking in unique circumstances and usually presented their food product as a solution to this potential disaster. Advertisements often suggested that it was so simple to make their foods that even a man could do it. As food became simpler to prepare with the advent of frozen foods and easy-to-make mixes, advertisers also presented their convenience foods as a solution to the problem men faced living alone, without a mother or wife to cook for them.

Still, food ads that presented men cooking usually suggested it was a fluke and wanted their foods to be the emergency remedy. A 1956 ad asked, "Cook for a day?" and had a man scratching his chin as he stood in his wife's apron holding a pan. Wives anticipating this quandary would find a solution in Creamettes frozen dinners. Their "quick, easy, delicious" meals would be the salvation of her husband and home. A 1957 Vita herring advertisement gave more skill and authority to men in the kitchen. The ad alerted the reader that every Sunday Dad wore a chef's cap and a bow tie (instead of the effeminate apron), made brunch, and showed off his discovery, "luscious Vita Imported Herring Fillets."[50] While not an emergency, it was still a rarefied, specialized event.

Ads frequently suggested that Sunday brunch was a meal men could handle because it allowed them to help once a week, gave mom a break, and create a meal to claim as their own. The Institute for Motivational Research, in a newsletter column on "Pancakes & Men," futilely promoted other themes. A staff member reported,

> We have repeatedly stated that the division of labor between the sexes is changing and that men are increasingly interested in cuisine. The other day, in a restaurant, I sat next to a table occupied by three men. They all had ordered pancakes and they were discussing earnestly the best way to prepare pancakes. Each of them had a treasured "special" recipe. Listening to them it occurred to me that if you added three fishing rods to this scene you would have a perfect pancake ad, one which was consistent with the latest trends uncovered by motivational research.[51]

In spite of the changing times, advertisers did not try to cultivate men as consumers. Instead, they placed ads like those for Aunt Jemima that featured dads cooking pancakes as a special treat. A 1962 ad had a father, comfortable in his masculinity wearing his wife's smocked apron, getting a hug and kiss from his towheaded daughter. Ads continued to maintain that a man cooking was a special treat for rare occasions and reassured women, who could then comfort men that their product was not difficult to make.[52]

Advertisers continued to operate in this vein in spite of compelling evidence that contradicted their assumptions. In the late 1950s, Campbell Soup, General Foods, General Mills, and Pillsbury supported a research study of the country's eating habits, investing more than $500,000; they certainly cared a great deal about the findings. One of the most significant discoveries, highlighted in a 1958 *Tide* article, was that "As much as 25% of all home meals are prepared by male members of the family."[53]

Still, as for most of the housework that they did throughout the century, men's efforts to help in the kitchen tended to be sporadic and specialized. Just as their household responsibilities only fell weekly or monthly, mowing the lawn or changing light bulbs, so too did ads highlight men cooking outdoors in the summer or on weekends. Most noticeably, advertisers focused on men and the barbecue. According to Laura Shapiro, "Long popular on the West Coast, barbecuing in the backyard was an idyll that raced across the nation in the years following World War II as millions of families moved into burgeoning suburbs and excitedly took possession of their own small portions of land. . . . 'Possibly it is the closest thing to a natural, national phenomenon since baseball.' " Ads by meat producers and marinating sauce companies usually had images of men standing over their grills. Even though women did work the grill, they were supposed to purchase the supplies and "hand him the bottle"; cooking meat over an open fire was supposed to be the strength of men. Barbecuing was supposed to reflect masculinity in men and cookbooks targeted for men in the 1950s contained recipes for barbecuing or mixing drinks.[54]

Ernest Dichter, acknowledging the general simplicity of barbecuing, realized that it allowed men to cook,

Without any cultural cost to the male ego. . . . The American male need not cook; in emergencies he can pop waffles that are ready-made and frozen into the toaster, pop frozen TV dinners into the oven . . . not only doesn't the American male cook, *he shouldn't!!*"[55]

In his essay on cooking, he wrote that the kitchen was a "woman's place" and, while it was all right for men to embrace cooking meat out of doors, they should leave the rest of the cooking to women. A 1995 Weber GrillWatch Survey conducted by Leo Shapiro Research found that many men were even leaving the grilling to women. While men lit the grill 80 percent of the time, it fell on women to do the vast majority of the actual barbecuing. Men only grilled 64 percent of the time in households with both women and men. Additionally, women were generally responsible for the remainder of the work, including buying the groceries, inviting guests, planning the menu, preparing other foods, washing the dishes, and cleaning the grill.[56]

Another scenario advertisers loved to employ, exemplified in several Franco-American Spaghetti ads, was the dilemma of "Mom's night out." The ad presumed, "Helpless males, huh?" It featured a father and son enjoying their "man-size" feast and reassured women that men could handle the directions. Velveeta cheese took a similar approach, emphasizing "fun" and "happy times" for men who made sandwiches or concocted "Dad's specialty . . . easy Velveeta sauce." Food advertisers wanted to assure women that men could handle these basic products on rare occasions. They never expected men to cook on a daily basis.[57]

Ads did occasionally depict males baking, which again was a specialized, infrequent type of cooking. In their effort to convince rural Americans to continue baking at home, Fleischmann's yeast ran a series of ads targeting farming families in the late 1950s. Unlike ads for baking products appearing in more mainstream, national magazines, these ads targeted to rural, farm-oriented Americans occasionally included boys and men baking. They featured teen-age boys and went to great lengths to assure readers that they were "real" boys, who liked baseball, archery, and the Boy Scouts, and who also won cooking awards at state fairs.[58]

Most of the men who won cooking awards were showcased with their wives. One ad, placed in the *Nebraska Farmer*, highlighted a Lincoln man who had won awards at two different Nebraska state fairs. It tried to shock the reader, announcing "There's a prize-winning cook in the Norman family all right—*Mr.* Robert Norman! Yes, Mr. Norman has been winning cooking contests for three years now." An ad in *California Farmer* feted a man who had won 44 cooking awards. Of course, they assured the reader, "Mr. Bancroft is a restaurant owner as well as a prize-winning cook, so naturally he's an authority on cooking ingredients." Lest the reader think it was the norm for men to cook, the ad shifted immediately, declaring, "Start the New Year right—you women who bake at home—and get a supply of Fleischmann's Active Dry Yeast." Men were able and even encouraged to cook in the context of public competitions, but advertisers expected women to do the unheralded, day-to-day cooking.[59]

The reliance on men as occasional bakers became an acceptable marketing tactic for mainstream audiences by the 1970s. An ad playing on generational differences appeared in *Family Circle* in 1971, and proffered, "One example of what people can accomplish if they just talk to each other." Entitled "The Accidental Exchange," it featured an older man in a plaid shirt and a hard hat debating Betty Crocker Supreme and Traditional Brownies with a long-haired, younger man with a necklace. Having inadvertently eaten a bite of the younger man's Supreme Brownie, the construction worker offered, "try mine. Betty Crocker Traditional Brownies. That word 'traditional' made him edgy, you know? But I got him to try it. . . . But he's sticking to Brownie Supreme. Says he won't touch anything 'traditional.' " This ad was unusually complex in its portrayal of generational tensions, but superceded them with a debate on which style of brownie was best. The ad did not feature the men baking the brownies, but their authority on style and ingredients suggests that they might have prepared the mix.[60]

In the 1970s, advertisers used boys' interest in cooking to advance their products' qualities. A 1976 ad asked, "Who baked those marvelous new Pillsbury Quick Muffins?" The family response spoke volumes. Dad proclaimed his approval, looking at the reader, "Danny baked them for breakfast. I love 'em anytime." Mom, pinching the cheek of her son, assured "Quick Muffins are so easy. And they bake in just 17 minutes." Grandma tilted her head and declared, "I never thought I'd see the day! Muffins that go from the refrigerator right to the oven." She might well have been surprised that her grandson made the muffins. In fact, Danny claimed, "I bake a lot of muffins for this family—apple-cinnamon, corn, and bran. Dad usually eats three or four." These four statements told the reader a wealth of information: men approved of them, they could be eaten for any meal, they could be made quickly, you could keep them in the refrigerator, there were a variety of styles, and finally, they were so easy to make that a ten-year-old boy could make them. The ad used the cook's age and sex to tell the reader how easy it was to make the muffins. As in the earlier yeast ads, the boy's masculinity was affirmed, in his case with a football jersey.[61]

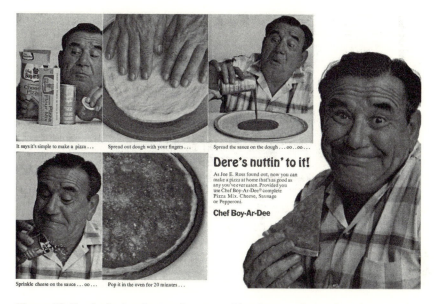

It says it's simple to make a pizza . . .   Spread out dough with your fingers . . .   Spread the sauce on the dough . . . oo . . oo . . .

Dere's nuttin' to it!

As Joe E. Ross found out, now you can make a pizza at home that's as good as any you've ever eaten. Provided you use Chef Boy-Ar-Dee® complete Pizza Mix. Cheese, Sausage or Pepperoni.

Chef Boy-Ar-Dee

Sprinkle cheese on the sauce . . . oo . . .   Pop it in the oven for 20 minutes . . .

Figure 16. Food ads that featured men cooking frequently insulted their abilities, sometimes to make the case that their foods were so easy to make *even* a man could do it, as in this 1967 Chef Boy-Ar-Dee ad.

Some ads had an explicitly insulting attitude toward men's cooking abilities and featured men who helped in the kitchen doing fool-proof tasks. A Campbell's ad suggesting recipes for soup and egg delights had the Campbell Kids cooking. The female had authority over the dish and the stove, while the male had the task of breaking the eggs into a bowl. A Wesson Chef's Salad ad featured a recipe and told women, "You fix it!" and "He'll toss it!" A man appeared in the ad adorned with an apron and a chef's hat to perform his duty. By the end of the century, there was limited progress in the portrayal of men as competent cooks, but generally, the belittlement continued. A 1967 ad for Chef Boy-Ar-Dee featured a regular guy, Joe Ross, claiming about the complete Pizza in a Box, "Dere's nuttin' to it!" The frame-by-frame history of his cooking showed him nervous, wary, and tentative with his efforts, but by the time he sprinkled on the cheese, he was pleased with himself.[62]

Ads often portrayed men as proud of giving their wives a break when they heated up frozen dinners and cans of soup. These ads often featured children, particularly newborns, as justification for why women could not handle their prescribed cooking duties. The ads suggesting that men cook only appeared in women's magazines, appealing to harried women to buy their products as a solution to an anticipated emergency. A 1968

Cheez Whiz ad presented a scenario featuring "The jar that gets you out of a jam." A woman recounted, "The last thing my husband said as they wheeled me into the delivery room was: don't worry about me and the kids. I didn't. I'd loaded the shelves with my favorite little jar." While men might sometimes lighten women's load, as with the barbecue, women were still responsible for buying the products and providing instruction on how to cook the meals.[63]

One tremendous development in men's participation in meal preparation was the American embrace of the sandwich. Advertisers for processed meats, condiments, and bread all encouraged the popularity of this item as a meal in itself. Sandwiches were not a common meal in the first half of the century, but by 1952, according to a Wheat Flour Institute study, Americans ate about 27 million sandwiches a day. By 1956, the number had grown to nearly 90 million. Researchers determined that Americans ate sandwiches at home for lunch and dinner, packed them in their lunch sacks, and ordered them in restaurants. They realized that this type of meal "was being served in 97% of American homes at least once a day!"[64]

Advertisers realized that the ease of preparation made sandwiches the ideal meal to target for unusual circumstances in which men might cook. The 1963 J. Walter Thompson Review Board Meeting Records for French's mustard reflect their intention to rely on situations with "natural, emotional appeal," such as "The night the baby comes home from the hospital" or it is "Mother's night off, with Dad and children fending for themselves." Another typical scenario they suggested was "Father and son on a fishing and camping expedition—with sandwiches brought along in case the fish didn't cooperate." This type of advertising was common. A 1977 ad featured a father and son laughing and enjoying a sandwich in a boat, with their fishing gear. The header pulled at the heartstrings, sighing, "This is why we make cold cuts the way we do." As with the barbecue, it was all right for men to cook, as long as it was easy and done in a rugged, outdoor, sporting, and all-male environment.[65]

Recognizing the growing number of men who were doing more in the kitchen, advertisers began to address ads to couples in the last third of the century. General Mills placed an ad in 1970 written by "Betty Crocker." Titled, "Love and Marriage and a job!," the ad reflected on the current trends whereby

Today's couples with a marriage and two jobs are on a tight schedule. Happily, the old-fashioned labels "man's work" and "woman's work" are relaxing—to make life easier for husband and wife. By working together, planning ahead and taking advantage of shortcuts, the working couple makes a loving partnership of marriage. Here are a few ideas that'll keep your kitchen a smooth-running part of your busy lives.[66]

Moving away from gendered advice, the ad offered generic tips about preparing foods the night before or over the weekend for the busy week featuring General Mills products. The ad was not suggesting parity in kitchen responsibilities, however. In its consideration of both women and men working outside the home, it noted, "A girl can have a hard day at the office, too. So why not teach your husband a few 'masculine specialties' he can fix on those—hopefully—rare occasions!" They encouraged women to write away for a recipe book for "That man in your kitchen," expecting women to help encourage and prepare men to cook. In spite of their grudging recognition of women's place in the workforce, advertisers still only wanted men in the kitchen on "hopefully rare" occasions, rather than with any regularity as the primary or even equal cook in the home.[67]

A 1991 feature in *Family Circle* called "What's for Dinner" provided women with recipes for Macho Meals. It asked, "His night to cook? Not to worry. Turn him on to these 'man-plan' dinners . . . prep is easy; taste, fabulous." The recipes for things like honey-mustard chicken and meatloaf were given names like, Jeff's Choice and Earl's Loaf, presumably to make them more masculine (and acceptable) fare. These scenarios also avoid any mention of children, which suggested that men were only cooking for two and had more freedom to try fun and exotic (spicy) recipes.[68] Moreover, it still fell on women to plan the meals, look for recipes, and otherwise supervise men's cooking.

When ads featured men as cooks it was an unusual and unique occurrence. Early on in the century, this was the only extent to which ads represented men cooking. Even by the end of the century, ads rarely showed men's cooking skills to be demonstrably better than pouring cereal and milk into a bowl. While they did occasionally focus on the growing numbers of men who did not always have women to cook for them, advertisers suggested that if women were unable to cook for men, they still should provide them with frozen meals, sandwich fixings, or canned soups.

"Gee. We're Walking Down the Aisle Again!"

Food advertisers believed that women were their primary consumers and marketed to them almost exclusively. Research over the course of the century, however, continuously revealed that men did shop for food, and significantly, that their numbers could and did grow. Food advertisers still generally ignored the potential and actual market of male consumers, even when research continually demonstrated their existence. Their belief that women should be responsible for food shopping blinded advertisers to the potential of male shoppers throughout the century, with only a slight increase in attention toward the end of the century, when they could no longer ignore men's food dollars. Advertisers have continually acted to promote strict gender roles, in spite of evidence that they could tap into a new market of consumers. While their actions seem to go against the evidence they held, advertisers evidently believed that maintaining women as consumers trumped the potential of male consumers. Ultimately, advertisers' cultural values thwarted what could have been a rational choice—to maximize profits by expanding their market.

One exception to this trend illustrates the potential of the male market. Appearing in 1912, when men and women still rode in separate street cars, advertising cards for Dunlevy's Young Pig Sausage featured businessmen riding the trolley and would probably have been placed in the cars themselves. Analyzing the campaign, the *Printers' Ink* author captioned the ad, "Copy Written to Be a Hunger Maker," and the copy itself encouraged men, "Don't Go Home Without a Pound." Tracey Deutsch found that, even in the years surrounding World War I, trade journals occasionally urged grocers to make men more comfortable in their stores, and she uncovered evidence that grocery stores could sometimes be male spaces. Still, advertisers tended not to believe in a male market and did not generally create advertisements for them. Instead, they remained focused on women. JWT, in particular, touted their knowledge of the female consumer. A 1918 advertisement for its services stated that "Eighty-five percent of all retail purchases are made by women," and claimed that the staff of college-educated, trained-in-advertising women were best suited to, "establish facts which cannot be even approximated by men working alone." The claim of "eighty-five percent of all retail purchases" was asterisked, and the footnote explained that "The most reliable figures available show that sales made to women are as follows: department stores, 80%; drug stores, 68.3%; grocery stores, 89.1%; automobiles, 50.9%." Believing that women purchased nearly 90 percent of all food for their homes, advertisers felt confident of where to direct their messages.[69]

The same self-evident logic did not apply to other products. Advertisers generally did not limit their sales efforts for other items to only one sex. However, the reason for this disparity was that advertisers saw food preparation as a female responsibility in which women were best suited to make purchasing decisions. Their desire to hold on to this market may have influenced their findings and those they put forth to the public.

Nevertheless, by 1950, the *JWT News* was reporting,

The old contention that women make as much as 80% of family purchases is not true today. Instead, women actually buy 55% of all consumer goods, and men buy 30%. Husbands and wives shopping together make 11% of the family's purchases.

Children buy the other 4%. . . . Men are now doing more of the family buying than they did in the early 1940's, presumably because of the shorter work week, plus the fact that a larger proportion of wives now work outside the home.[70]

Another study on supermarkets done that same year found even more dramatic evidence for food companies. The percent of women solely responsible for grocery shopping had dropped to under half (49.7), while men walking the aisles alone made up nearly 20 percent of the customers (18.8), and men and women shopping together made up 17.9 percent. Men, alone or with their families, were shopping in extraordinary numbers, approaching forty percent of grocery consumers. By 1952, the JWT newsletter was reporting that, according to the U.S. Chamber of Commerce Committee on Advertising, while women bought 80 percent of all consumer goods, men alone were buying 25 percent of groceries.[71]

In her *Printers' Ink* column, "A Woman's View," Sara Welles suggested in 1964 that supermarkets "offer a limited delivery service." She argued, "It's heavy, exhausting work and women hate it. That's why so many save shopping for weekends when husbands can help." Beyond the difficulty in carrying groceries, food experts did not think supermarket shopping demanded very much skill of men (or women). Whereas it had once required experience to avoid being duped, "The quality of prepared and convenience foods has been raised and the risk taken out of meat selection. Once the household meat buyer had to know the different cuts and watch the butcher's thumb on the scale. Today the shopper reaches into a freezer bin and takes out a plastic-wrapped package that's been stamped, weighed and priced in an assembly-line fashion."[72] It went without saying that the process for selecting other foods, previously sold in bulk in barrels and at specialty stores, had also been streamlined.

Beyond being capable, there was even the possibility that men might be preferable to women. "Supermarket managers," for example, "report that they prefer men as customers because they work the aisles methodically and don't get together to gossip with their friends in mid-aisle as women sometimes do. Also, the male weekend shopper usually buys luxury items his wife didn't have on the grocery list." Minimally, the author proposed, "The presence of men in supermarkets in substantial numbers should cause food advertisers to consider directing more than their 'outdoor barbecue' messages at the male."[73]

In 1968, Dichter rediscovered a new trend: "Men are getting more involved in the actual shopping situation. An increasing number of married men are now being asked by their working (or busy) wives to 'help out and do the shopping.' " He broke down male shoppers into three groups: the extremists, the economy-conscious, and "those who get involved in the excitement of the fantasy world of foods." His study found the first group, the extremists, to be those men likely to purchase products with luxury appeal. The second group, those who watch their pennies, revealed that they wanted to "prove to their wives that they can get a lot for a little (generally without regard to quality)." The last group of shoppers are men who

select items which appeal to them regardless of price. This last group of male shoppers are psychologically very much like children—they are amazed and awed by the availability of products from which to choose, and more importantly, they appear to really enjoy the shopping experience.[74]

According to Dichter, then, males made no rational shopping decisions and bought without regard to price, quality, or necessity. Moreover, advertisers read men's shopping patterns as unpredictable, unreliable, and unmanipulable, so they kept their attention on women, whom they hoped they could persuade to buy their products. While many held on to this perception of male shoppers as unknowable and the myth that women controlled 85 percent of the nation's spending power, over the next fifty years advertising agencies and researchers documented and commented on the number and type of men shopping for groceries.

A 1972 JWT researcher, for example, after acknowledging that men were contributing more to house and child care, suggested that male grocery shoppers spent more than the average woman shopper. In a 1978 letter to the *Harvard Business Review*, T. J. Wolfe, senior vice president of sales and marketing for Welch Foods, asserted that

We are living with the cliché of the shopping list dominated male, who is highly susceptible to impulse buying. Marketers should begin to concern themselves more with challenging this cliché, and understanding how deeply the 50% of American men who are participating in marketing chores, are also calling the shots on what goes into the basket.[75]

The late 1970s were filled with articles in trade journals like *Progressive Grocer* and *Magazine Age*, which called attention to "The Men Who Man the Shopping Carts." One 1979 article, entitled "Men Buy Food and Men Cook, But Most Food Advertisers Are Ignoring Them," openly criticized the ad industry, noting "It's hard to believe—after all you're talking about some of the most sophisticated consumer advertisers in the world—but the evidence shows that food companies haven't caught on that men cook."[76]

Evidence of a growing number of male grocery shoppers coincided with strong growth in the Hispanic market, with one 1983 article noting the tendency of Hispanics to shop together as a family, what one

Southern California retailer called "a real family event." In 1987, the Food Processing Fifth Annual Teenage Food Survey found that young men were shopping alone in extraordinary numbers; "of the 35% of teens shopping one or more times a week, the boys are shopping 8% more than the girls."[77]

Even with this evidence, advertisers remained unconvinced that advertising food products to men and women would be more profitable than advertising to just women. While food columns occasionally appeared in a range of publications, from *Playboy* to *Good Housekeeping*, food advertisers evidently believed male cooking to be sporadic and specialized, and perhaps suspected that even if men did cook, women were still likely doing the shopping. Although by the 1980s advertisers began to market to men in some men's magazines, in instances where they did target men, they did not appeal to those who were shopping for their families. Instead, they targeted bachelors with "masculine foods" and products' ease of preparation.[78]

A major study in 1990 caught the attention of a few companies, such as *Sports Illustrated* and Campbell, but it did not report new findings. Instead it rediscovered that 40 percent of supermarket shoppers were male. Advertisers' faith in this "new" market was tempered by a belief that women were still dictating brand choices and making most purchasing decisions. It did, however, inspire more food companies to place gender-neutral ads, and ads targeting men in men's magazines, as well as general-interest media, such as *People* and *Reader's Digest*. Perhaps the most significant change was in a subtle move away from completely gendered ads, with some ads showing families cooking or eating, with no indication of who shopped or made the meal. For example, the Proctor Company aired an ad for Jif peanut butter in which the father did the shopping, yet clung to their slogan, "Choosy Moms choose Jif." As one advertising executive opined, "Mr. Mom isn't going to replace Mrs. Mom."[79]

Instead, advertisers frequently presumed that women were their only market, with little or no evidence for their beliefs. Historically, just as with claims about how much money women controlled, advertisers advanced beliefs with little or no substantiation. The JWT 1959–1960 "Review of Objectives for Stouffer's Frozen Food—Cooked Foods" claimed "Whether they are single or married, workers or housewives, young or old—women are our primary target." It went on to acknowledge that, "This will be true always, we believe. It is an area, however, in which we have practically no factual information." This frank admission of their limited understanding of the market was rare but insightful. Most food companies continued to ignore male shoppers, even though their share of the grocery market grew, and toward the end of the century, they controlled upward of $96 billion dollars in sales, about a quarter of the grocery store market.[80]

Ads almost exclusively targeted women, but men did appear shopping in some food ads. Most notably, ads for A&P in the post–World War Two era subtly included women and men shopping in their grocery stores. A 1947 ad had nineteen adults crammed into the produce section: three

"Gee, We're Walking Down The Aisle Again!"

June, the traditional month of brides, is a happy time at A&P. For, thanks to countless brides of many Junes, A&P has become a tradition, too. Seeing newlyweds in the aisles of A&P Super Markets always makes us proud of our part in helping make America's dreams come true.

Each generation of new homemakers wants more of the better things of life . . . and they

look to A&P to do its share in providing them. Often this calls for new ideas, new and better items, more efficient storekeeping. And in providing more and better food for more people *for less money*, your A&P has prospered and grown, also.

Have *you* visited your A&P Super Market lately? You'll enjoy the new free-wheeling

baskets that are roomier . . . the more convenient arrangement of food stocks . . . the ever improving check-out system. Best of all, you'll like the "Right-in-Sight" pricing of every item, *right on the package* as well as on the shelf! And you'll surely notice that all prices are mighty reasonable, too. Not just for June brides, either . . . but for *everyone!*

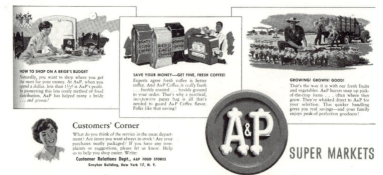

HOW TO SHOP ON A BRIDE'S BUDGET
Naturally, you want to shop where you get the most for your money. At A&P, when you spend a dollar, less than 1½¢ is A&P's profit. In pioneering this less costly method of food distribution, A&P has helped many a bride . . . *and groom!*

SAVE YOUR MONEY—GET FINE, FRESH COFFEE!
Experts agree fresh coffee is better coffee. And A&P Coffee is *really* fresh . . . freshly roasted . . . freshly ground to your order. That's why a practical, *inexpensive* paper bag is all that's needed to guard A&P Coffee flavor. Folks like that saving!

GROWING! GROWN! GOOD!
That's the way it is with our fresh fruits and vegetables. A&P buyers snap up pick-of-the-crop items . . . often where they grow. They're whisked direct to A&P for your selection. This quicker handling gives you real savings—and your family enjoys peak-of-perfection goodness!

Customers' Corner
What do you think of the service in the meat department? Are items you want always in stock? Are your purchases neatly packaged? If you have any complaints or suggestions, please let us know. Help us to help you shop easier. Write:
Customer Relations Dept., A&P FOOD STORES
Graybar Building, New York 17, N. Y.

A&P SUPER MARKETS

Figure 17. Although advertisers were well aware that men did shop in considerable numbers, A&P was unusual for a series of ads depicting men shopping.

male grocers, and twelve women and four men shopping. Another A&P ad, appearing in 1950, featured a storefront with glass windows. The six baby carriages parked outside symbolized the baby boom the country was experiencing. The illustration also betrayed another trend—a significant number of male shoppers—six of the twenty-five shoppers inside were men. One ad featured a young couple shopping together, cooing, "Gee. We're Walking Down the Aisle Again!" The supermarket used this play on words because they wanted to attract young women as shoppers, hoping that a "June bride," living on a shoestring budget would soon have more mouths to feed and become more economically comfortable in the years to come. Even in this ad focused on a newlywed couple, of the three background shoppers, one was a man. Two of the five shoppers in the ad, therefore, were men, a fairly accurate and therefore unusual representation of who was doing the shopping.[81]

To assuage reader's concerns that these were *real* men, men featured shopping in ads often smoked pipes. This symbol of virility and masculinity served to define these men in the context of the supposedly female space they occupied. Advertisers also frequently included couples shopping, perhaps thinking it was more acceptable for men to shop with their wives, who had presumably hoodwinked them into making the trip.[82]

One exception appeared in 1962, where the sole man participating in the Del Monte Round-Up, "one shopping spree your husband won't want you to miss," was a cowboy; replete with checked shirt, jeans, bandana, and the requisite hat, his masculinity again reinforced by his appearance. When Del Monte used the same "Round-Up" theme the next year, thirteen of the fourteen adults and the five children were male. A young boy shopping with his mother was dressed in cowboy garb and watched as men loaded up their wagons (station and horse-drawn) with Del Monte products. The bulk nature of the shopping necessitated male participation to help carry the goods and the narrowed focus on Del Monte enabled men to make purchases independently.[83]

Ads often suggested that the men who did appear shopping in ads were not making the purchasing decisions themselves. Occasionally men shopped with their daughters, who presumably assisted in the decision making, based on their knowledge of brands and necessity. Another signifier of men's limited role was the grocery list they carried. A 1957 ad for Post-Tens cereal featured an incompetent man, with a string tied around his finger, and encouraged women to "let Pop shop." The shopping list he held, however, was chaotic, suggesting that his wife had a coded system. The ads suggested that advertisers did not believe that men were making independent decisions on what to buy and suspected they were merely footmen for their wives.[84]

An examination of the portrayal of male shoppers, or the startling lack thereof given their numbers, reveals that advertising was not merely reflecting society. Advertisers wanted to perpetuate traditional gender roles to hold onto women as consumers. They hoped that their hundred years of experience and finely tuned messages of an idealized strictly gendered world would enable them to continue manipulating women's purchases. Embracing the male market, even on a small scale, would sacrifice all their hard work and leave advertisers facing the unknown. Would men be brand loyal? Would they try the products? Would they spend as much money? Rather than facing their fears and catering to this market, advertisers buried their collective heads in the sand, dismissing the research that kept reminding them of men's arrival at the checkout line. They hoped that men were just doing their wives' bidding and buying their mothers' brands, but did nothing to ensure their loyalty. The ads created reflected advertisers' dreams, not the reality of America.

Advertisers perpetuated women's role as subservient to men, consistently presenting men as authority figures, entitled to service and pleasure. While the broader media may have started to suggest marriages as companionate in the 1920s, food advertisers held on to traditional notions of gender roles in the kitchen. While women's historians have traditionally considered the domestic sphere to be a place of strength and authority for women, food advertising consistently denied women's authority in the kitchen. It prioritized men's expertise and preferences over women's knowledge and experience. To strengthen their threats and to encourage competition between women, advertisers frequently fostered a sense of insecurity in women. They even suggested that poor cooking could make marriage an anxious, even a potentially dangerous endeavor for women.

To further their goal of keeping women as consumers, advertisers also held women responsible for the health of their families. The next chapter explores the ways in which ads charged women with the well-being of their husbands. They implored women to use their cooking as a preventative measure to keep men and children healthy, as well as a curative to fix whatever ailed family members.

Chapter 5

Health, Beauty, and Sexuality: A Woman's Responsibility

Catching his eye is one thing; keeping it's another. Be a little sneaky. Remember, boys love to eat . . . What a subtle, feline way to show you care.

—*Wonder Bread ad,* Life, *28 October 1966*

Throughout the twentieth century, food advertisers tried to persuade women that they were accountable for their family's health, which enabled advertisers to exploit concerns about treating or preventing a whole host of ailments, both real and imagined. This strategy also reflected a continued desire to keep women as consumers, by suggesting that if they did not accept this responsibility, their families would suffer from neglect. In particular, advertisers sought to keep women accountable for the health of their husbands. Like most other advertisers, food advertisers also tried to use sexuality, as well as health and beauty ideals, to persuade women to view the advertised foods as inextricably tied to their own physical and marital well-being. Of course, to achieve this aim, they also used ploys to exacerbate women's fears about being overweight and unattractive.

"How One Mother Met Her Family's Most Troublesome 'Health Problem'"

Food ads throughout the twentieth century placed the health of men and children in women's hands. Predicated on the premise that women had full liability for their family's health, health-themed food ads made arguments in two veins. They claimed that in addition to diagnosing and treating their family's ailments, women should also anticipate health problems and prevent them from occurring.

In the late nineteenth century, most ads for curatives were for patent medicines. These unregulated potions promised to be cure-alls for diseases. The growing distrust and resultant regulation of these remedies coincided with the emergence of the packaged food industries. As patent medicines came under increasing scrutiny and regulation and lost their ability to advertise in popular periodicals in the early twentieth century, food advertisers adroitly positioned their products as the best solution to the illnesses they claimed were plaguing Americans. Ads suggested that women should determine the root cause of health problems and were frequently depicted detecting hidden health problems. For example, ads featured women determining whether a family member's grumpiness or lack of appetite stemmed from unappealing food or a health ailment. Women were then supposed to heal their patients with convenience foods.[1]

Relief from constipation was one of the most consistently advertised food benefits. Even in a society publicly reticent about bodies and their functions, constipation problems were evidently perceived as serious (or lucrative) enough to make advertising a promised cure with scientific vocabulary acceptable. Cereals, in particular, emerged as a health food in the late nineteenth century; advertisers suggested their products as beneficial to those who suffered from irregularity. In the early years of the century, ads used suggestive wording to refer to food's "tonic-digestive properties." However, the food's alleged scientific benefits made it acceptable for advertisers to break down unspoken rules governing acceptable discourse and by the 1930s ads were much more explicit, assuring consumers that "Cases of recurrent constipation, due to too little bulk in the diet, should yield to Whole Bran." In fact, Kellogg's All-Bran had "Relieves Constipation" printed on the front of the boxes that appeared in their ads.[2]

Cereal manufacturers had reason to take on this delicate subject. They faced a variety of obstacles in their effort to infiltrate or maintain their position in women's kitchens. First, they needed Americans to learn to eat cereal, not only at breakfast, but also in a variety of forms and throughout the day. Second, cereal had to be something that everyone ate throughout their lifetime, not just as children. Third, because cereal was easy to make, it had to overcome its image as a "lazy" meal. And finally, particularly for those companies who produced "healthy" cereals, such as bran, it had to taste good.

Advertisements, then, often suggested scenarios incorporating these themes, as well as highlighting the cereals' benefits to health problems, such as constipation. A 1942 ad for Nabisco 100% Bran, for example, described, "How one Mother met her family's most troublesome 'health problem.'" The ad depicted the woman, her husband, her son, and grandpa at breakfast time, and she shared with the reader that, "We're a pretty healthy family . . . but frequently some of us were bothered by constipation. Dr. Jones suggested that perhaps our diet lacked sufficient bulk." The family loved the taste and "its mild, gentle action." Another ad for Nabisco 100% Bran was even more explicit, emphasizing the double-milling process that "Makes the bran fibers smaller—less likely to be irritating." It encouraged women to try their recipe for muffins, "If you want a real thrill!"[3]

An ad for Uncle Sam's Laxative Breakfast Food was as subtle as the product's name. The older man featured in this 1955 *Los Angeles Times* ad cried out in the headline, "Constipated since 1911 . . . cereal gives welcome help." The man's picture appeared alongside his purported testimonial, which told readers, "I have been constipated since 1911 when my back was broken in a coal mine accident. Several months ago I tried Uncle Sam's Breakfast Food. After several servings—I've had no trouble since." The ad then assumed an authoritative tone, assuring readers of the food's flavor. For the woman facing the task of curing a constipated loved one, this man's detailed story held out hope.[4]

A Kellogg's All-Bran campaign that ran from the late 1950s to the mid-1960s and appeared in *Reader's Digest* epitomized the themes on which many ads in this period focused. Some seemed to suggest that there was nothing individuals could do, given that it was "the bane of the middle years" that caused irregularity. Others seemed to give false praise when they reassured the reader that "constipation is particularly common among sensitive and intelligent people." The constant theme throughout the years, however, was that improper eating caused constipation and that the advertiser's food could remedy the problem. Advertisers moved away from the forthrightness of the past by the 1970s and embraced the coded language of "food fiber" and "regularity" during the last quarter of the century.[5]

Cereal manufacturers were not the only ones that sought to expand their utility to housewives through curative appeals. In the 1920s, Fleischmann's Yeast faced a declining market because Americans increasingly purchased packaged bread, forgoing the work of baking at home. To counter this loss, the J. Walter Thompson advertising agency devised an ad campaign called "Yeast for Health." The campaign promised that eating three cakes of Fleischmann's yeast every day would cure constipation. They cited scientists, such as Dr. Gudzent of the University of Berlin, who confirmed that, "Constipation is one of the commonest of all ailments. It has a serious effect on health." Moreover, he cautioned, "When food wastes are retained in the body too long, poisons develop which filter into the blood . . . leads to headaches, coated tongue, bad breath, poor appetite, loss of energy." For Fleischmann's to maintain its business, consumers had to need the product for a new purpose. The ad campaign made no mention of the yeast's traditional usefulness in baking and focused solely on its alleged medicinal value in curing bodily disorders. Historian Roland Marchand commented on this remarkable success story, noting that in the 1920s Fleischmann's became one of the ten largest magazine advertisers, in spite of the product's terrible taste and high price.[6]

The discovery of vitamins enabled 1920s advertisers to encourage the concern that Americans were undernourished. The JWT set its sights on encouraging this anxiety in women and hoped Grape Nuts cereal could cash in on what it saw as its "remarkable food value" with a campaign that claimed it had joined the "Popular Crusade Against Malnutrition." A JWT newsletter reported that when soldiers were drafted for the First World War, approximately "one-third of the men called were rejected because they were unfit for service" and that malnutrition was recognized as "a national menace." The newsletter further claimed that "the most common defects were underweight, overweight, bad teeth, constipation." Advertisers magnified these concerns to make their product appear invaluable, not just to women, but also to the nation as a whole. Copywriters occasionally gendered these problems, such as in ads that considered fatigue a particular problem for women, but they generally suggested that illnesses such as "poor circulation" and "nervous organization" could affect everyone. Most important, they claimed women could find the antidote in the kitchen.[7]

In addition to curing family ills, the second theme advertisers adopted was that women had the power to *prevent* potential illnesses with the meals they prepared. As one 1902 ad intoned, "There's Life Assurance in Every Package of Wheatlet." They wanted to ensure that no responsible woman would pass up the opportunity to provide her family with this product, which "cereal analysis" showed to have a "superabundance of life-giving elements."[8]

Bad weather was one of the most common scenarios used to encourage women to take preventative steps to ward off illnesses in family members and was employed particularly by companies selling hot food, such as soups and cereals. Market researcher Ernest Dichter reported in 1960 that over 85 percent of those surveyed closely associated soup with cold weather. He explained that, "Soup is most welcome and wanted when the weather has been trying—whether it has been bad, cold, wet, windy. . . . The warmth of soup gives a feeling of comfort and strength. One respondant (sic) says: 'Give me hot soup on a nasty, cold day and I am happy.' " For soup companies, however, the research only reinforced what they had long surmised. For decades, they had consistently positioned their products as a response to wintry elements. A 1916 Campbell's soup ad featured a female Campbell Kid holding an umbrella in one hand and an enormous can of soup in the other. She told readers, "Campbell's is an inside protection. Umbrellas and overshoes are all right, but what you need most of all to fight the elements is the warm-blooded, vigorous health which comes from good food and good digestion." Campbell sent the same message promoting soup's powerful defense against the cold and wet to women throughout the century. In a television ad airing in the winters of the 1990s and early twenty-first century, a woman let a snowman into her home and he sat down to eat a bowl of hot soup. As he ate the soup, the snow melted away to reveal her son. In addition to providing warm coats, scarves, and mittens, ads expected women to ensure that family members were warm from the inside out by providing them with hot, nutritious food. Here, then, was an opportunity for women to prevent family members' potential illnesses, by insuring their warmth with the fuel that the advertised foods provided.[9]

Advertisements also suggested that women winterize their husbands and children for cold mornings with hot cereal breakfasts. Ads for companies like Quaker Oats and Cream of Wheat focused particular attention on the needs of active little boys playing outdoors and husbands going off to work. In the 1950s, Cream of Wheat ads used the Dennis the Menace comic strip to illustrate the benefits of its hot cereal for Dennis and his dad. Whether they were walking in the rain or building a snowman together, the warm breakfast guarded them against the elements. Keeping the same theme in the next decade, Quaker Oats ads in the 1960s employed an interview format, which paired a picture of the wife or mother with that of her protected loved one. The women were quoted saying things like, "I know I've done my *best* for Bill with good hot Quaker Oats" and "When I fix good hot Quaker Oats on schooldays, I know I've done a better job as a Mother." Using language like "sticks to his ribs," the ads focused on males warmly dressed to suggest women's ability and responsibility to strengthen their family as they faced life's challenges.[10]

Advertisers also appealed to women's general concern about their family's health. In the first half of the century, advertisers frequently employed images of sickly children and then depicted them after they had gained weight and strength from drinking or eating a particular product. In the midst of the Great Depression, Sunkist prepared campaigns to unleash "when cold and flu bugs become active in each territory." Marketers counseled advertisers, "Her family's health is a vital matter to her. Poor health means doctor bills for her children. If her husband is not kept up to par, it may even endanger the family's income." However, in a 1957 analysis of Ovaltine, Dichter found that associations with illness held down sales. He encouraged the company to move away from illustrating illness and appeal to health ideals people held. He counseled, "Almost everyone wants to be healthier and stronger than he is. Almost everyone wants to be well nourished and well fortified against illness.

Everyone wants to sleep well." Thereafter, advertisers adopted this strategy and focused almost exclusively on images of robust, active children in the second half of the century.[11]

As early as the 1920s, the advertising industry reflected critically on the usefulness and appropriateness of using health appeals. Industry journals such as *Printers' Ink Monthly* ran articles in the 1920s and '30s with titles like, "*Must* We Have Meals from the Medicine Chest?" and "The Health Appeal Is Being Overworked." Over the course of the century, while some authors questioned why foods were being sold "not on appetite, but on sex appeal," others noted the pitfalls in claiming too much about foods' healthful qualities and questioned whether those messages resonated with all consumers.[12]

Toward the end of the twentieth century, there was a new development. Advertisers began to grow concerned about women's receptiveness to their messages. Women were the primary targets for these health messages, yet some studies in the 1970s reported that women's changing work patterns affected their attitudes and behavior toward their housework. In "The Seventies: A Marketing View," a report for JWT offered a condensed view of some of the issues facing the industry. A section, "Women Demand Change" provided some insights into how women's work outside the home, as well as their involvement in both the consumer and the women's liberation movements, had affected them. Drawing on a study conducted by *Better Homes and Gardens*, the author warned,

> Homemakers are increasingly less preoccupied and less energetic about getting their families to eat certain kinds of diets. Not only are they more permissive, but they indulge in the "negative permissiveness" of not caring very much. They seem generally less informed about nutrition than housewives were twenty years ago, and the ignorance is combined with indifference rather than curiosity. The over-rising [sic] concern is whether or not the family likes the food and will eat it in a "mood" which is gratifying to the homemaker.[13]

Still, even with this more complete understanding of women's attitudes and actions, advertisers continued to target women through concerns with health.

"You're Not Doing Your Husband Any Favors"

Ads consistently placed responsibility for men's health in the hands of women, suggesting that their food choices either jeopardized or ensured his health. Advertisements commonly depicted women in an uphill battle to convince men to eat healthy and often unusual foods, while simultaneously having to deny them familiar, tasty foods. Women were in a position to be blamed for men's ill health, particularly upon diagnosis of a problem or if an illness did not disappear. Although men were adults and ostensibly able to make their own food choices, accountability for their diet and eating habits fell on their wives. Advertisements suggested that men not only cheated on their diets, but by so doing, also disappointed and betrayed their wives.

Women also got the message that whether in overalls and a plaid work shirt or a suit, tie, and hat, men needed nourishment to do their jobs. A 1903 ad simply told the reader, "Back them with the firm, sure strength of will and brain and body that you get from Quaker Oats." As white-collar jobs came to dominate men's work in the twentieth century, advertisers sent a clear message to women that men needed a good breakfast to give them both physical and mental stamina to do their jobs.[14]

Ads in the first half of the century tended to express a positive attitude toward women's role in shaping men's eating habits. A 1926 ad for Grape Nuts, for example, suggested that accomplished husbands owed their wives a great deal of credit. The illustration of a stately dining room with a beautiful 20-foot tall window, a butler serving breakfast, and a couple eating at an enormous table, suggested that the simple act of planning a breakfast with Grape Nuts had brought this woman's family wealth. The text confirmed the impression, claiming, "Many a wife has helped her husband to success and fame by giving him the right kind of breakfast! . . . Hundreds of brilliantly successful Americans have recently made this statement. All wives, attention!" This ad, like many others, suggested that women made the difference in their husbands' performance by serving the right foods.[15]

There were exceptions, however, to this wholly upbeat tone. An ominous Postum cereal ad explored, "Why men crack." The ad described broken men,

You know them. Strong men, vigorous men—men who have never had a sick day in their lives. They drive. They drive themselves to the limit. They lash themselves over the limit with stimulants. They crack. Often, they crash. . . . So we speak to you—the wife, the mother—because the well-being of your household is largely in your hands. Your finger is close to your family's pulse. You know how the men in your family look rather helplessly to you for a certain amount of "mothering."[16]

The ad offered readers a week's supply of Postum cereal and concluded, "As the guardian of a man who has not cracked—it might be well for you to accept." In 1932 a threatening Fleischmann's Yeast ad featured a "Men Wanted" employment sign, but the headline cautioned women, "Half-Sick Men Need Not Apply!"[17] In the midst of an economic crisis, women were told that it was their responsibility to ensure that men were ready, should an opportunity appear. Women, then, were responsible for caring for the health of their husbands, even though they could only influence, not force, men to eat well.

Also in the midst of the Great Depression, Karo Syrup ran an ad asking, "Want to feel like a 'Fighting Cock'?" It featured an illustration of a man's phallus-like head atop the body of a rooster. The text explained that

The game cock is alert, courageous and aggressive. That's why the expression, "Fighting Cock" so aptly describes the confident, ambitious, up-and-coming individual. But if we intelligently trace the source of unusual energy and alertness, it invariably revealed that the FOOD we eat and drink contributes most to the physical reactions of the body.[18]

As was common in early advertisements, it was not until the fourth paragraph, after extensive scientific detail, that the text revealed the advertised product. Women should cook with Karo Syrup to provide their husbands with a "quick revival of poor circulation, of fatigued nerves, of flagging muscles." For a depression era family with an uncertain future, its livelihood dependent on the ability of its members to work and work hard, the promise of vitality was a serious one.

Paid employment was not the only reason men needed energy. Ads regularly showed, described, or alluded to men engaged in action, ranging from an anonymous man playing cricket in a 1911 ad to one in 1950 featuring Tommy "Ol' Reliable" Henrich of the New York Yankees. Removing the line between play and work, ads argued that regardless of the type of competition, "The healthy, clear-thinking individual is usually the winner." In the Wheaties ad, Henrich shared the billing with his wife. The ad claimed that he was a champion because he ate the cereal, but that she was also a champion because she "loves keeping family happy and healthy" and knew how to prepare his favorite cereal, Wheaties with milk and pineapple. Women benefited not from eating the food, but from buying and preparing it for men.[19]

Cereal advertisements made consistent appeals to women's responsibility for men's health, but they were not the only food to claim health benefits. Vegetables, salads, and dressings all appealed to women to get their husbands to eat more healthily. Women featured in the ads told readers, "He really ought to eat more green things and fruit." They were frequently shown at their wits' end trying to get their husbands to eat salads. One 1938 ad for Miracle Whip used a common device. The perplexed wife phoned her sage mother-in-law, who of course had already been in that difficult position of convincing her son to eat his vegetables. She knew that Miracle Whip salad dressing was the key.[20]

Nor did much change in the second half of the century. Zeroing in on the responsibility of women to feed their families healthily, Birds Eye created an ad campaign in the early 1970s that assured women that their vegetable combinations would eliminate the need for pleading. Some of the ads featured headlines such as, "His mother needed peg-legged pirates. All you need is Birds Eye Combinations." One of the ads summarized the entire campaign when it claimed, "When your man was a little boy, he had to be coaxed to eat his vegetables. Now that you've got Birds Eye Combinations he doesn't."[21]

Ads throughout the century assumed that women prioritized caring for their husbands and their health, and assured women that they faced a difficult task, featuring statements like, "As much as you might spoil and pamper your husband, a lot of husbands still don't get too excited about ordinary vegetables." Men proclaimed their gratitude when women told them what to eat and drink, as in a 1941 ad for Quaker Sparkies, which had a man exclaim, "Am I being taken care of, or am I being taken care of *right*!" Star-Kist tuna featured a "success story" campaign in the late 1960s that explored why men ate the tuna dishes their wives made. One appearing in March 1967 claimed, "Larry used to think tuna was for pantywaists. But he'd eat it just to keep peace in the family." Another featured Dave, who was on a diet and hated fishy salads. The ad concluded with a moral, "a husband on a diet needs sympathy, love and Star-Kist Tuna." Women had to overcome men's resistance to foods to make sure they ate right.[22]

One of the most important responsibilities women had was caring for men during times of war. Ads placed special emphasis on women's patriotic duty to make meals to help win wars. During World War II, an Armour ad proclaimed, "The first concern of any good mother is that her boy gets plenty to eat. And Uncle Sam's Quartermaster Corps is just as solicitous for every man in our fighting forces today." It announced that the meals were so nourishing and well-balanced that the average soldier gained seven pounds. . . . And it's not soft fat." It also provided army menus as models and asked, "How do they compare with those served in your own home?" At times ads asked women to make meals without meat or without sugar, suggesting that rationing enabled soldiers to eat well and kept Americans strong at home. Others asked them to serve products that adhered to U.S. Nutrition Food Rules, ensuring that their families got daily allowances of vitamins, protein, and nutrients to allow them to do war work.[23]

Broad health concerns quickly replaced wartime anxieties in the second half of the century. Food companies always have had a complicated relationship with science. They needed scientific claims about foods' beneficial qualities such as vitamins and fiber to bolster their credibility. However, they also feared scientific pronouncements that decreed some foods, such as those containing cholesterol or fat, to be bad for one's diet. In order to combat those charges, companies created extensive campaigns to reassure consumers of their products' health benefits.

The discovery and growing understanding of cholesterol gave advertisers more ammunition to pressure women to ensure their husband's health was good. Some of the strangest campaigns came from companies producing oils used in cooking. A 1959 ad for Wesson Oil tried to turn around a potentially negative response to its product. It recommended that dieters follow their Miracle Diet for one month, drinking a six-ounce glass of their concoction seven times a day. To make a one-day supply, the recipe called for "3 tablespoons Wesson Oil, ½ cup orange juice, 5 cups skim milk, 3 eggs." It promised that, "With the Miracle Diet you *drink* daily protein equivalent to the protein in four large hamburgers or two large porterhouse steaks." The ad touted the oil's unsaturated fat and its benefits to one's health, attempting to overcome the negative associations created by scientists.[24]

Mazola Corn Oil ads in the 1960s and 1970s suggested that women could manage their husband's diet, watching calories and total fats, and make an important change, by replacing saturated animal fats with polyunsaturated vegetable oil. Their ads suggested that life could go on as usual, with tailgating parties and midnight raids on the refrigerator, and that the fried chicken would be better because their oil was the highest in polyunsaturates on the market.[25]

Advertisers in the last quarter of the century also jumped at the opportunity to influence women's meat buying habits, a staple of the American diet. As scientists investigated the source and consequences of fat and cholesterol, companies began to develop meat alternatives, made with "textured vegetable protein." They chastised women,

You're not doing your husband any favors when you serve him hamburger. Because next to eggs, ground beef is the largest source of cholesterol in the American diet. And high blood cholesterol is a major risk factor in heart disease. . . . Get your husband on a low cholesterol diet and keep him there. With Morningstar Farms. It may be one of the nicest things you'll ever do for him.[26]

The ad placed responsibility for what men ate squarely in the hands of women. The food women bought and prepared, advertisers warned, could jeopardize their husband's well-being. Most ads with health themes reflected concern for family members, and men in particular, except those directed at women as consumers of food, in which case the ads focused on appearance over health.

"When She Grows Up, Will Your Little Girl Have Lovely Legs?"

Throughout the twentieth century, ads encouraged women to fear aging and its effect on their appearance. Ads held up a youthful ideal and promised that their products would serve as a fountain of youth, or at least slow down the aging process. As early as 1902, Quaker Oats ran an ad with an attractive young woman holding aloft the facial mask of a much older person. The headline confirmed that their cereal "Puts Off Old Age." More than a half century later the message remained the same. An ad for milk featured a middle-aged woman looking at her tired, wrinkled face in a hand-held mirror. The ad warned the reader that without enough calcium bodies slowly degenerate and shorten their "period of prime." While the text did discuss the biological consequences of depleted calcium, such as brittle bones, the ad focused on appearance as a primary reason for action.[27]

Throughout the century, food advertising assumed that women cared a great deal about being attractive and posited that eating their products would give women external, physical beauty. They predicated this assumption, at least in part, on the economic dependence of women on men. Given the preference that men typically exhibited for younger partners, women faced pressure to be pretty and youthful. Advertisers therefore believed interest in the appearance of skin, hair, and nails to be an exclusive focus of women and designed their messages accordingly, tying the promise of beauty to each bite. For example, the face of a striking woman dominated a 1908 ad for Kellogg's Corn Flakes. The ad suggested that her beauty came from the cereal and that there was no substitute for its effect. A 1933 ad for Kellogg's All-Bran forthrightly promised that with the cereal on the shelf, "There's a beauty-parlor in your kitchen." This type of simple, directed advertising continued throughout the century, as with a 1961 ad of a smiling, thin, blonde-haired woman walking in the rain with a big umbrella, holding a box of Kellogg's Corn Flakes. The caption provided the only text and told the reader that this attractive young woman had a "corn-fed appetite."[28]

In addition to showcasing the beauty benefits of their foods, advertisers also used women to attract the reader's attention. The positioning of a woman's face or body often served to invite the reader to the text. For example, a 1941 ad for Campbell's soups had a woman turning back coyly to the viewer with a smile, as she told them, "Company's Coming for Dinner!" Although that situation might have worried another woman, she was confident and self-assured because she had Campbell's soup. The principal purpose of this woman, then, was to attract readers and tell them that she was able to look calm and beautiful because Campbell meant she did not have to fret.[29]

Advertisers wanted readers to connect their product with a woman's appearance. Many adopted a direct approach that left nothing to chance. Illustrations and later photographs usually accompanied text that reinforced the promises held out by the images. For example, headlined, "Why Women Look Younger Now," a 1911 Van Camp's Pork and Beans ad was headed by two contrasting illustrations. The first featured a dour, older looking woman displaying the beans she presumably made herself in 1850, the second a smiling, younger looking woman holding out Van Camp's beans in 1911. The ad did not leave it to the reader to infer that buying the beans would make women look younger. Instead, it asked, "Dear Madam, Have you ever thought how the past sixty years have lessened women's drudgery? And how women today, on account of that fact, look younger at fifty than they used to at thirty?" The ad went on to detail some of the technological advances that had lessened women's work in the home, focusing especially on the sixteen long hours it used to take women to make homemade beans.[30]

Others were even more explicitly focused on beauty. A 1926 Grape Nuts ad featured an attractive woman draped in a nightgown and robe sitting slumped in an armchair. Her body posture suggested she was listless and the caption explained that indeed, she was, and why. The ad read like a newspaper notice, "LOST . . . at the breakfast table this year—a beautiful complexion. Information leading to the recovery of same will be greatly appreciated by the owner." The ad made broad promises about the food's properties and its ability "to protect health and beauty by properly nourishing the body." This focus on beauty continued throughout the century. A 1978 ad for Kretschmer's Wheat Germ, for example, told women, "If you take care of the inside, the inside will take care of the outside." It promised that Kretschmer's would provide proteins and minerals that would not only help a woman's skin, hair, and nails, but would help stave off feelings of tiredness and irritability.[31]

The emphasis on beauty did not start with adult or even young women; it extended to small children. The consistent message was that the food girls ate would help them to become attractive women. As Joan Jacobs Brumberg has documented in *The Body Project*, American girls increasingly focused on their outward appearance in the twentieth century. Many parents were willing to invest time and money ensuring that their daughters would be attractive. Food advertisers, not surprisingly, wanted to cash in on that market. A small girl, perhaps five or six years old, appeared in an ad for milk in 1941 proclaiming, "My beauty treatment is Golden Guernsey." The ad was an "interview" with the little girl, who reported that, "Mother says I have to drink just lots and lots of Golden Guernsey if I want to be as cute as I am now. . . . It helps make nice straight legs and pretty teeth."[32]

Cocomalt built a whole campaign on the value placed on women's legs. Appearing in 1947, the ads captured the connection between the present and future of a little girl. The first frame showed a cute, young girl and asked, "When she grows up, will your little girl have lovely legs?"

The second frame showed her as a young adult, flirting with a man, her long, thin legs exposed to the reader, and the reminder that "no girl can have lovely straight legs like these without strong bones." The final frame returned the reader to their opportunity to take action and make this dream come true, with a young girl drinking a tall glass of Cocomalt and the reminder that it "gives your child extra calcium so vital for strong bones." The ads did show the girl and the woman engaged in physical activities, such as playing tennis or ice skating, but it was clear that the objective was not those leisurely pursuits, but the men who were pursuing them.[33]

In addition to all the laxative properties explored earlier, advertisers also marketed their bran products as a "tempting 'beauty treatment.'" In 1933, the Kellogg Company produced a booklet, "Keep on the Sunny Side of Life: A New Way of Living," devoted to convincing women to eat more bran, particularly their cereal, Kellogg's All-Bran. It alerted women,

There's a beauty-parlor in your kitchen. Powders and creams are delightful aids to beauty. They will do wonders—if you start with a healthy body. For health, itself, is the source of sparkling eyes, of a smooth, lovely skin and an engaging personality. Bran helps.[34]

Along with several recipes and a scientific exploration of the dietary benefits of bran, the 33-page booklet also provided menus and other beauty tips.

The Fleischmann's Yeast Company also expanded its promised effectiveness beyond the alleviation of constipation and positioned its product as a cure for acne. Assessing the ad campaign, one writer noted that it "was aimed directly at feminine readers and was based principally upon the beauty appeal." In one ad, a girl with a visible skin problem, asked the man examining her, "'Doctor—will these pimples scar my face?'" The caption read, "Adolescent pimples . . . wise mothers realize . . . may affect a girl's whole future happiness." Beginning in the 1920s, medical treatment for acne was a popular recourse for those who could afford it. As with so many other biological problems, it is interesting that food advertisers were able to isolate the problem, refocus it as not just a health issue but a beauty problem, and suggest a cure. The scientific aspects of these otherwise unspeakable problems made it acceptable for women to get involved in their cure. Moreover, particularly with their daughters' acne, it was imperative that mothers do so. According to Fleischmann's Yeast this was important, "not only because of the risk to the youngster's skin, but also because a pimply, repulsive skin can give young people a permanent sense of inferiority." The ad concluded with a photo of the same girl with a clear complexion, happily surrounded by two attractive boys, and a final reminder that "Friends . . . parties . . . youthful happiness . . . depend so much on the clear, smooth skin that is your youngster's rightful heritage." Far from an isolated effort, in the midst of declining marriage rates during the 1930s because of the Great Depression, Fleischmann's continued to remind women of the importance of consuming their product, with menacing tales headlined with "Nobody ever asks her out!" and "Men Just Can't Stand Bad Skin!"[35]

By the 1940s, cosmetic use had become an integral aspect of women's appearance. Kathy Peiss has shown that by 1948, 80 to 90 percent of adult American women used lipstick, about two-thirds used rouge, and one in four used eye makeup. As more American girls and women began to use cosmetics, food advertisers embraced the opportunity to present their products as an alternative, natural way to achieve an attractive appearance. For example, knowing that consumers faced shortages during the Second World War, Jell-O advertised its pudding mixes as a healthy beauty aid. With a picture of a thin, young, blond woman sitting at a counter talking with a man in uniform, the caption revealed that, "Sis has stopped living all day on the ends of her nerves—she drinks milk with her lunch and cleans up her plate at dinner. If she forgets her rouge these days, nobody notices." Presumably she was working to support the war effort and her hard work and Jell-O pudding combined to make her glow from within.[36]

With the premise that beauty was happiness, Postum created an ad in 1947 headlined, "Help Yourself to Happiness." The ad utilized "before and after" shots of a woman who had consumed Postum. In the first, she held a tissue and her face in angst. After drinking Postum she was adored by men and women. The ad warned, "No special cosmetics—no extra-fancy hair-do—no merely artificial aids could ever duplicate the complete and utter transformation of this girl into the poised, beautiful, radiantly healthy person you see."[37] This juxtaposition of women's appearance before and after they consumed foods began to fall out of favor as an advertising style around mid-century. As with associations with sickliness, advertisers undoubtedly feared that negative images would tarnish their products. Thereafter, ads relied almost exclusively on the ideal of young, attractive women. These women, usually smiling seductively, served as the promise of things to come for those who consumed the product.

Ads consistently used women's images to sell their products, although the portrayal of their bodies varied over time. Starting in the 1940s, women's bodies became more visible, as loosening cultural norms allowed artists to reveal more of the female body, starting with a peek at the ankles, moving up to the knees, and even expanding to include thighs. Most advertisers relied on illustrations, which provided them with the necessary flexibility to convey ideals and outcomes from eating the advertised foods. Illustrations of absurdly disproportionate women with distorted waists appeared as the pervasive norm throughout the century, but were especially common in the 1940s and 1950s. The icon for Colman's Mustard was Connie Colman, a Barbie-doll-like figure who appeared in ads wearing a tall chef's hat and high heels that exaggerated her long look. Incredibly thin, her legs dominated her body, and she had an apron with a heart pocket tied at her virtually nonexistent waist. This type of imagery was common during this period, with products such as Crisco, Velveeta, and Shefford Cheese embracing it in their ads.[38]

One 1947 Heinz ad stands out because the featured woman was not only incredibly thin but unusually busty. Instead of the slight protrusions common in most depictions, the woman had full, round breasts. Even later ads that were more sensual or sexual tended not to focus on women's breasts. This was true even in the 1950s, which Brumberg characterized as "an era distinguished by its worship of full-breasted women," epitomized by movie stars such as Marilyn Monroe and Jayne Mansfield.[39] This is not to say that ads did not employ sensual or sexual messages, but rather that long legs and thin waists, not large breasts, were the critical feminine features in food advertising.

While appearing much less frequently than male icons, female characters did represent several products. Foods associated with the ocean, particularly tuna fish, often prompted advertisements with mermaids. Chicken of the Sea tuna ads in the 1970s featured a blonde mermaid. This type of image skirted feminist criticism because instead of using a scantily clad, attractive real woman to sell the product, advertisers used an illustration of one. Still a familiar icon at the end of the century, the Chiquita Banana Company dressed up a banana as an attractive woman. In print ads, she appeared replete with thick eyelashes and full lips (but no breasts). On the radio, advertisers used the voice of Latina film star Carmen Miranda as Miss Chiquita in 1944 to sell their brand-name bananas. While banana advertisers have frequently played with fire, blatantly alluding to the phallic shape of their product, they grounded their campaigns with an emphasis on the product's health value. They alluded, as did so many ads for food products, to its ability to help women "have a more beautiful appearance and complexion; A daily dose of bananas will help you look per-fec-tion."[40] Whether they also intended to suggest that women would also benefit from daily sex, they coyly left open to reader interpretation.

In the late twentieth century, food advertisers began to zero in on women's health and beauty concerns with a series of products marketed exclusively to women. While advertisements historically focused on the products' usefulness in protecting men's health or in helping women lose weight, these food advertisements and the branding of the products made it clear that women should be concerned about their own well-being. Companies like General Mills and Quaker produced cereals that they hyped as the answer to women's unique physical needs. General Mills advertised their cereal Harmony as "Made just for a woman's body," while Quaker was even more explicit, naming their cereal Quaker Oatmeal Nutrition for Women.[41]

"Fated Not to Be Mated? . . . Better Reduce the Ry-Krisp Way!"

The ideal female body went through many transformations. At the turn of the century, the model figure shrank from corseted curves to the athletic Gibson Girl, surpassed in the 1920s by the even thinner flapper. Even in the midst of the Great Depression, when carrying more weight might have indicated the wealth to procure food, middle- and upper-class women continued to regard eating less and losing weight as a goal.[42]

Food advertisers promoted an intricate relationship between food, health, and body image. These connections fascinated researchers throughout the twentieth century. The J. Walter Thompson Research Department found, for example, that in 1947, "Most people—6 out of 10—say their health is good." They also found, however, that, "One-third of the adults are either dieting or avoiding certain foods." Food advertisers wanted to capture this market of concerned dieters, which grew throughout the second half of the century. Yet companies that wanted to encourage weight loss faced the irony that all dieters confront. Unlike other substances to which people develop addictions or unhealthy consumption patterns, food is the only one that must be consumed to survive. Decisions to cut back or eliminate foods must be confronted and negotiated on a daily basis, usually several times a day. Some food advertisers, therefore, wanted to position their foods as the ones dieters should turn to when they wanted to lose weight. But they faced potential rejection by those who wanted to cut back even more or by those who stopped dieting. Moreover, advertisers also wanted to reach those people who did not have to reduce and instead just wanted to maintain their figures.[43]

Until the end of the 1930s, food advertisers used sporadic and restrained diet campaigns to target women who sought to improve their body image. The ads generally did not go beyond presenting an image of a slim woman and the recommendation to use the product to lose weight. One 1932 ad for Sun-Maid Raisins used the bold header, "A message for women only!" The ad described how raisins burn up the fat content of other foods and suggested that this quality "will mean much in the lives of modern women who want to remain modern." This coded language suggested that thin women who wanted to stay thin would understand the significance of the information imparted in the ad, and more importantly, the implications of eating raisins.[44]

The Kellogg Company's 1933 "Keep on the Sunny Side of Life" advertising booklet counseled women on "Dieting for Charm and Chic." It recommended weight ideals based on insurance company estimates of the healthiest weights for women (and men) and offered dieting tips. It warned, "Today, there are thousands of girls starving themselves to gain rounded slimness, and many lose the very beauty they are trying to achieve." Kellogg's wanted women to diet, but needed them to continue to eat its cereals. The booklet suggested a focus on eating, but counseled women to eat slowly, check common constipation, and count calories.[45]

Starting in the 1940s, ads became much more direct in their pointed criticism of women's weight, even to the point of being cruel. While the broader culture did not appear to assert a thinness mandate until the 1960s and 1970s, food advertisers started to promote a "fat" obsession at the end of the Great Depression. In the midst of the economic crisis, advertisers ran the risk of suggesting that people were thin due to financial difficulties. However, with the economic recovery of the 1940s, food advertisers enthusiastically embraced the thin ideal. Generally, they only showed women who were thin. They wanted to suggest the ideal outcome of eating their product and did not want to chance what they presumed would be a negative association by using a full-figured woman.

The Ry-Krisp Company was the most flagrant exception to this trend. A campaign created by Beatrice Adams depicted women who, in the company's words, were "fat." Appearing in the late 1930s, the ads took women out of the privacy of their own homes and placed them in humiliating circumstances. Each Ry-Krisp ad contained a full-figured woman and a good-looking man. The message, spelled out explicitly in each ad, whether she was at the theater or at the beach, was that, "Gentlemen prefer a slender youthful figure." One man in a 1940 ad appeared evil, with his eyebrows drawn into a "V." "Someone ought to tell her about Ry-Krisp," he said, as though it was self-evident that men only preferred thin women. The ads provided tips on exercise and eating and encouraged women to write away for their "Eat and Grow Slim" booklet.[46]

Ry-Krisp ads suggested that being full-figured was a woman's greatest nightmare. Ads commonly portrayed women facing ridicule because of their size. In the midst of World War II, the company ran an ad with a header that challenged readers to "Get rid of fat, Pitch in, Help Win! Reduce the Ry-Krisp Way." Set up as a comparative story, the 1943 ad first pictured a woman sitting on a front stoop watching a thin, uniformed woman walk by. The reader could not determine the size of the sitting woman, but the caption informed them, "Mrs. A is fat. She can't pitch in and work like other women—excess fat drains her energy. She

Figure 18. In one of the cruelest ad campaigns of the century, Ry-Krisp tried to shame women to "Eat and Grow Slim," in the case of this 1940 ad explicitly tying women's weight to their ability to gain the financial and sexual attention of men.

should try Ry-Krisp's reducing plan for normally overweight and enjoy Ry-Krisp as bread." Advertisers not only suggested that it was problematic for women to be overweight, but also heightened their criticism by claiming that these women would be unable to help the country fight the war. The next frame presented a stark contrast, with a thin, attractive, uniformed woman and the text, "Mrs. D. is slim. She works all day, is a Nurse's Aide at night. Like many smart women, she keeps trim and stays slim." Ads justified judgments about women's weight in the name of patriotism, claiming that to be good citizens women must be fit and thin.[47]

The focus on women's weight did not abate after the war. With cultural attention focused on the boom in marriages during and after the war, advertisers used this pressure to encourage women to buy their foods. A 1946 ad showed a groom struggling to carry his heavy bride over the threshold and asked women, "Too tubby for your hubby?" suggesting that if a man could not carry you, perhaps he would not marry you. If women wanted their dreams to come true, they had "Better reduce the Ry-Krisp way!" A 1947 ad showed an overweight woman as a bridesmaid and asked, as she wistfully watched the bride and groom depart, "Fated not to be mated? . . . Alter your figure—it may be the first step to the altar!" Another ad had a full-figured woman hiding behind a plant watching a man and a thin woman kiss. The header confirmed, "When Jim likes 'em slim . . . Surprise the party who counts most by slimming down to youthful curves." The campaign, which earned Adams the 1941 Josephine Snapp national award for the best copy by a woman, insisted that men only liked thin, curvaceous women and that a woman's ultimate goal was to win the attention and commitment of a man.[48]

Ads creating and responding to these pressures did not just target adult women. The message that females should be concerned with their weight began with young girls. Women appeared time and again on the scales and little girls were no exception. A 1941 ad for Sparkies cereal featured a little girl of three or four checking her weight on a scale, while her older brother, perhaps six or seven, admired his bicep. While ads did not target young boys with diet messages, it was not uncommon to see girls perched on scales. Moreover, it grew more common, not less, as the century wore on. A 1966 ad featured a young girl standing on a scale; the ad asked, "What's a mother to do . . . about vitamins . . . with a teen-age daughter who's forever going on a diet?" The ad suggested serving Total cereal because it would ensure that her diet would be a healthy one, never questioning whether it was advisable for young girls to diet at all.[49]

Seventeen, with its young teen readership, devoted considerable attention to dieting concerns, featuring columns, articles, and advertising

Figure 19. Ads commonly featured girls and women on scales and eating diet foods. Boys and men generally appeared as physically fit athletes.

promoting and addressing teen concerns with their weight. The magazine commonly introduced party ideas, suggesting recipes and decorations for get-togethers, usually centering on ethnic or national themes. One idea they suggested, however, was unusual in its explicit attention to perceived differences between male and female eating habits. In a four-page spread called "Party Partnerships," the 1969 feature contrasted what boys could eat with what girls could eat, dividing all foods into "his" and "hers." The "Hearty Extras" were "especially for handsome he-men, while figure-conscious girls can fill up happily on the lower-calorie goodies." To help discerning eaters, it suggested displaying the caloric value of each dish, putting the hearty foods in a certain color dish and the foods for the "weak-willed" in another, or if the girls could not handle the temptation, even dividing the tables. One sample party plate for the "pickers" (i.e., the girls) added up to 405 calories, with one slice baked ham, two pickle wedges, mustard, coleslaw (only half a cup), one 7-inch breadstick, and a diet soda. The "packers" (i.e., the boys), however, could pile on 1210 calories, and their menu had larger helpings and such delectable treats as barbecue beans and spiced crab apples.[50]

Many food advertisers worried that girls would follow their mothers' example with regard to eating habits. The Institute for Motivational Research conducted a 1955 study for General Mills examining "Present and Future Psychological Trends in Cereals" and reported:

According to our findings, teen age girls, the future mothers are even more alienated than boys in this age group. Their resistance to dry cereals seems to be based mainly on three additional factors: Weight and calorie fears. Girls feel that cereals are too starchy and filling and might endanger their figures. . . . Ads and premiums are seen as talking to boys. Most budding teen-agers, however, are anxious to assert their femininity and tend to avoid associations which detract from the feminine impression she hopes to give. And finally, in many cases girls associate strongly with their mothers. Mother often doesn't eat dry cereal and thereby sets a bad example which the girl follows automatically.[51]

Cereal advertisers, then, had reason to be concerned that girls were not consuming their products. Ernest Dichter and his researchers also raised concerns for bread companies, alerting them to dieting women's aversion to bread. Dichter, in fact, encouraged bread companies to "combat *diet psychology*." In addition to suggesting bread's aroma and stressing taste appeal, they thought that bread ads should "show the housewife that bread is her *friendly* helper, not her enemy."

Looking for ways to address General Mills's marketing, sales, and advertising problems with one of its dessert products, D-Zerta, Dichter created a taxonomy of dieters in 1958. He placed dieters into the following categories: The Deprivational Eater, who denies food; the Compromise Dieter, who is a permissive dessert-eater but compulsive calorie counter; and the Fun Dieter, who expects "dieting without tears." Using this system, he suggested that the company target consumers with appeals to the idea of "pleasurable eating" and low calories. He specifically called on the company to

Give "Dietary Citizenship" to the teen-age girl. She is usually either a compromise or a fun dieter. She should be appealed to in family ads or in special ads in teen-age periodicals. It should be noted, however, that young girls are seldom deprivational dieters, and while they like to take themselves seriously, they also like to have fun—with desserts they can enjoy while counting calories.[52]

This rather tentative attempt to understand girls' attention to dieting grew more sophisticated during the latter part of the century. Psychiatrists, sociologists, and historians have examined the multitude of factors that led to a very high number of girls who had unhealthy body images and acted out their dissatisfaction through compulsive eating and anorexia in the late twentieth century. As more girls began to take dieting "seriously," advertisers also upped the ante, targeting ads with diet themes to teen-age girls.

One favorite image for advertisers was a woman with food provocatively held in front of her full lips. Like other diet foods, such as rice cakes, diet salad dressing ads also used a great deal of exposed flesh to demonstrate results. Ads for companies like Wish-Bone and Frenchette were filled with women in revealing bathing suits and leotards, demonstrating their lost pounds and attracting the viewer to the product and its promised outcome.[53]

Diet foods like Sego and Slim Fast, likewise, relied on images of thin, sexy women to sell their products. A notable feature of diet food ads, which appeared with increasing frequency starting in the 1960s, is the presence of adoring men, usually placed in intimate contact with women or depicted pursuing them. These ads held out the ideal and the promise, echoed in the earlier Ry-Krisp ads, that getting a man was the goal and that men would want to be with you if you were slim.[54]

Advertisers expanded on these subtle messages to include a more overt emphasis on sexiness. Diet foods were most likely to emphasize the triad between food, health, and sex. For example, yogurt ads used attractive, vivacious young women to sell their product. One ad from 1966 asked, "Why do teenagers with bikini figures eat yogurt?" The text promised, "It tastes good," but advertisers wanted viewers to take away several reasons why they should eat yogurt. The image suggested that if women ate the yogurt they could keep or achieve a thin figure. Further, the ad suggested that eating the yogurt would make women coy and playful. Another 1966 ad employed the words "slim" and "sexy," leaving nothing to chance. Again, advertisers used the text to emphasize the taste, but focused ads on women's sensuality.[55]

Diet salad dressing ads also promised women they would be thin and sexually attractive. The ads employed the salad dressing bottles as phallic symbols, with thin, glamorous women touching the bottleneck. In one ad for Wish-Bone salad dressing, the bottle pointed between a woman's open legs, which were splayed in the shape of a wishbone. Beyond sexual images, food ads also continued to use suggestive language to make connections between foods, women, and sexuality, with words such as sassy, spirited, uninhibited, and wild.[56]

By the 1980s, concern over weight had led to the tremendous success of countless companies, products, and magazines, all geared toward weight loss. Weight Watchers, which began in 1963, described not just

Figure 20. In the 1960s and 1970s, salad dressing companies often used bottles in sexually suggestive ways in their ads.

a group of people but also a line of frozen meals, a magazine devoted to the problem, and a self-help program, all designed to help people who actually wanted to do more than just watch their weight, they wanted it to disappear. Food advertisers did not need researchers to tell them this was the perfect market for their diet foods. Companies like Pillsbury and Swans Down published scores of small cookbooks with titles such as "Say Yes to Less Cookbook" and "Breakthrough Baking: Classic Cakes That Cut the Calories." The introduction to the Swans Down cookbook promised, "They are almost as easy to prepare as a cake mix—but they're grand, gorgeous, and indulgent without 'destroying' your diet . . . So have your cake and enjoy it, too! . . . without a trace of guilt." Advertisers wanted women to be concerned about eating, but assured them they could do so without consequences, as long as they ate their product.[57]

Advertisers particularly focused on countering the concern that diet products did not taste as good as regular foods. Aunt Jemima ran an ad campaign in the early 1980s featuring young women and girls slack-jawed in amazement that the syrup was "Lite." Girls and women holding aloft a bite of food repeatedly claimed, "It's too thick to be lite" and "It's thicker than my syrup." A 1983 ad assured women that Diet Delight canned fruit was for "Dieters with good taste."[58]

Companies such as Quaker Oats ran ads using humor and women's voices to sell their product. Targeting readers in traditional women's magazines and magazines devoted to dieters, like *Weight Watchers*, Quaker ran a campaign that exacerbated their fears (and certainly for some, their realities) that they had overeaten during the holidays. Over pictures of Christmas bread and cookies they placed quotations like, "I think these sizes must run small" and "The cleaners must have shrunk this." On the right was a picture of the rice cake package and the ad called the reader's bluff, with a reminder that each serving contained 50 calories and no excuses. Food advertisers at the end of the century still made the same claims about their products' ability to help people lose weight as they had at the outset.[59]

To combat the supposition that their diet products would not taste good, ads for SnackWell's cookies asserted the irreverent message that women liked their cookies better than sex (and by extension, men). In one such ad, a woman "making out with her lover on the beach" was "dreaming of cookies," instead of the man. The "male voiceover chuckled," " 'Passion. Desire. Devotion. Nah, it goes way beyond that.' " These sexual ads targeted women seeking to lose weight by suggesting that women who ate their cookies could command male attention, but then took the unusual step of asserting that their product was more valuable than a sexually attentive man. In fact, in one ad "Prince Charming in tight black pants who rode horseback through Central Park to a woman's New York brownstone" found himself turned into a toad when he tried to "snag one of her Devil Food Cookie Cakes." While the message seemed to affirm female sexuality and independence from men (as long as they were fulfilled by SnackWell's), the advertisements still made male attention the purported goal, even if it was to be rejected.[60]

One company in particular served as an important touchstone for the tensions between women, advertisers, and food. Kellogg's Special K ads, from their debut in 1955 through the 1960s and into the 1970s, focused on the cereal's health benefits. Most ads illustrated the breakfast meal with a glass of juice, a cup of coffee, and a bowl of Special K cereal with milk. They calculated that with one teaspoon of sugar this menu supplied only 240 calories. To attract the reader they used catchy phrases like, "We're watching your weight" and "We don't forget your figure. Don't forget ours." These ads did not feature any one person, male or female, eating. However, soon thereafter Kellogg's began to create ads that aggressively targeted women.[61]

Response to Kellogg's ads for its Special K cereal in the 1980s and 1990s was indicative of the frustrations some women felt toward advertisers and depictions of idealized body images. Print and television spots of thin women trying on a slinky black dress or tight jeans were evidently effective, but also alienated many female viewers, the "key target group" for Special K. Responding to criticism, Kellogg's drew on letters and focus groups to create a new campaign called "Reshape Your Attitude" that suggested that women should "Look Good on Your Own Terms." Advertisers still expected women to be concerned with how they looked, but ads temporarily suggested that a positive body image was what was most important.[62]

The Special K campaign, then, was unusual at the close of the century because it moved away from ads that objectified to those that focused on empowering girls and women to feel positively about their bodies. Even as they received praise for this new direction and some of their tongue-in-cheek ads, sales fell off. Other advertisers undoubtedly watched to see if the Kellogg's gimmick paid off. Given that there appeared to be no financial gain in presenting women positively, most advertisers continued the old course. Advertisers who employed sexuality and sensual women also came under criticism in the late twentieth century, but as with imagery connected with dieting, it appears these images will continue to be a constant of food advertising into the next century.[63]

"It's The One Thing a Man Never Turns Down"

Using portrayals of attractive, sensual women or sexual wording to sell products has been a long-standing practice. Accordingly, historians have analyzed advertisements that used these ploys, including those for clothing and make-up, as well as traditionally masculine products, such as automobiles, liquor, and air travel. While it was not one of the most obvious categories, food advertisers also employed sexuality to sell their products. In addition to hoping that these provocative ads would attract attention, advertisers were angling to ensure that women saw an association between their own sensuality and food, so that they would remain responsible for purchasing and preparing food. Particularly in the second half of the twentieth century, to keep pace with changing norms of behavior and shifting employment patterns for women, advertisers used more explicitly sexual images to convince women that their primary goal should be to please men. Ads threatened that if women did not use sexuality and food to please men, men's boredom and dissatisfaction would broadcast women's failure.[64]

According to historian Jackson Lears, "Sexual titillation was an established attention-getter from the earliest days of national advertising. Long before the turn of the century advertisements were serving up breasts and thighs."[65] Food advertising, however, tended not to be especially sexual in the first half of the twentieth century. As explored earlier, food advertisers have long used attractive women and men in their advertisements, eager to suggest that their foods would help consumers to be good looking and healthy. However, their images did in fact grow more sexually charged as the century progressed. Starting in the 1940s and 1950s, food advertisers began in earnest to promise women that they would be able to catch and keep men if they were pretty and sexy. They began to combine those visual promises of vitality and beauty with subtle sexual wording and imagery.

Food ads commonly used double-entendres to capitalize on the cultural tendency to liken women to foods. Unusual because of its early appearance, a 1938 Chicken of the Sea ad drew a clear link between its product and women, when it suggested, "Some like it HOT, Some like it COLD." Within the "O" in HOT was a dark-skinned woman from the tropics and within the "O" in COLD was an Eskimo woman. A 1947 Kraft Macaroni and Cheese ad exclaimed, "Make That 'One Hot Dish' in a hurry," above an illustration of a long-legged, incredibly thin woman carrying a steaming bowl of food. The ad suggested that women could make Kraft dinners quickly because they were easy to assemble. Moreover, the convenience of the food would give a woman plenty of

Figure 21. Food ads sometimes blurred the line between food and women, as in this 1938 ad that featured women and food as exotic desirables.

time to turn herself into an attractive "dish." Ads encouraged readers to make the connection between the appeal of women and food.[66]

Ads for Kellogg's Pep cereal appearing in the 1940s played on the word pep, asking readers, "How's your 'Pep Appeal'?" Clearly suggesting that Pep cereal could positively affect one's sex appeal, the ads starred male and female actors who did not convey enough "oomph" while being photographed or filmed. Sage older figures advised young characters, "None of us can have pep unless we get all our vitamins." After learning from an aunt that vitamins would help her boyfriend's pep, one woman remarked, "From now on, my handsome hero, you're going to be the most vitamized man in Suffolk county." This format allowed an older person to tout the scientific and sexual benefits of the cereal, leaving the younger person to proclaim it as the "most delicious cereal I ever tasted." Advertisers wanted consumers to believe that they could purchase sex appeal and that it was an essential trait for success on the stage of life. With coded language, they sent a clear message that Pep cereal would deliver.[67]

In the 1940s, ads began to posit that food in itself was good, but that food served by a woman was even better because it was sexually satisfying. In a 1946 Peanut Crunch Peanut Butter ad, for example, an older, full-figured woman sat on the lap of an older police chief while he ate a peanut butter sandwich. The text referred to two other police officers peering in the window, exclaiming, "5 minutes too late! The Chief also heard she has a jar of Peanut Crunch brand Peanut Butter!" The ad suggested that a woman's sexuality helped attract men, but that she should subordinate it to her primary role of preparing food for them.[68]

Advertisers frequently suggested that women use sex appeal to attain and maintain a husband. A 1947 Campbell's soup ad featured a man who walked in the door and asked his wife, who stood over the stove, "What's cookin', Good Lookin'?" She told the reader, "He's brought home his appetite" and confided that Campbell's soups are "a real lifesaver for us young-marrieds." The text and the image suggested that it was her ability and willingness to anticipate both his hunger for food and for sex that contributed to her achieving that most important goal for women: marriage.[69]

By the 1960s and 1970s, ads began to place an even greater emphasis on women's sexual powers. Food ads in this later period still suggested that women use sensuality to attract and please men. However, some ads became more sexually explicit. The ads overtly claimed that the advertised food would arouse and satisfy men, and that women would benefit from giving them pleasure. Food advertisers began to explicitly characterize women's eroticism as magic. They sought to boost women's confidence in their sexual agency by assuring them that they could control men's actions. Advertisers hoped that women, armed with the sorcery at their disposal, would get men to consume against their will and even convince them to eat unusual or foreign foods.[70]

Seeking to socialize women to both gender roles and buying habits early, food advertisers placed ads in various teen magazines. Even though they were targeting a younger female audience, food advertisers continued to appeal to female sexuality. The ads targeted girls as consumers, entreating them to both entice and please males with their cooking, with no attention to the girls' appetites for food—or sex. For example, a 1960s campaign featured attractive females and males holding Wonder Bread sandwiches. With bold headlines like "BOY TRAP" and "DATE BAIT," the ads recommended that girls seduce boys with Wonder Bread. In February 1967, this ad appeared in *Seventeen*:

Today a pretty girl knows how to succeed with boys without half trying. But let's face it. She's got a lot going for her—marvelous new cosmetics, smashing fashions, and Wonder Bread. *Wonder Bread?* Wonder Bread! Wonder's the newest, neatest, nicest way to trap a boy since . . . well . . . since apples . . . Just try tempting him with his favorite Wonder sandwich. He'll bite. And—ZAP! You've got him.[71]

Another ad in the campaign suggested that the attention of boys was not enough. It cautioned *Seventeen*'s young readers, "catching his eye is one thing; keeping it's another. Be a little sneaky. Remember, boys love to eat. . . . What a subtle, feline way to show you care." The ads affirmed that girls' fulfillment from food and sex should come from attracting and gratifying boys, rather than satisfying their own tastes and hunger.[72]

In addition to inculcating girls into traditional gender roles, advertisers had to contend with new ideas in a rapidly changing society. In a 1955 report, Dichter laid out his findings about women in American culture. Considering over 500 major studies over 24 years, he formulated three categories of women: the true housewife, the career woman, and the modern or "balanced" woman, who was a combination of the first two. Dichter counseled advertisers that the balanced woman was the "the woman of the future"; her psychological needs made her a perfect consumer of convenience foods. The balanced woman wanted not only to hold a job, but also to be a homemaker. He theorized that her desire to be all things meant she would take an interest in efficiency and credited this new woman with the self-confidence to "accept convenience products . . . without competing with them or worrying about their replacing her." Moreover, he believed that her investment in the home would lead her to seek innovative, imaginative ways to express her "femininity and individuality" in the kitchen.[73]

Dichter encouraged advertisers to abandon the rhetoric of traditional roles and embrace the "modern" woman. He saw that advertisers could accommodate the real changes taking place in society and capitalize on the burgeoning niche of balanced women. He also believed that this balanced woman would be the best food shopper because she would invest emotionally in the well-being of men and also have outside interests and pursuits necessitating convenience foods. As Dichter put it, "She can work, attend political meetings, join clubs, and in general participate in many outside activities. All this, and bake a cake, too!"[74]

In the 1960s and 1970s, drawing on Dichter's notion of the modern woman, various companies and the Rice Council of America began to advertise rice in an explicitly sexual way. They tied rice, cooking, and creativity together with women's sexual happiness. Motivational research helps explain why rice advertisers, in particular, used sexuality in their ads. The 1955 study, "The Sex of Rice," found that most people believed foods to be gendered. For example, Dichter found that those interviewed considered tea feminine, while most considered coffee masculine. Meat symbolized the most extreme masculinity, while cake was the most feminine of foods. Most respondents also considered rice a feminine food. Therefore, rice companies and ad agencies had to find a way to challenge the primacy of the potato, widely perceived to be masculine. They faced an interesting challenge because if, as they suggested, women's goal was to please men, and men wanted to eat potatoes, women would not buy rice. This was true even if women preferred the lighter, less filling rice because, according to the advertisers' rubric, they were supposed to subordinate their own tastes and preferences to men's. To capture a larger share of the market, rice advertisers used sexuality to convince women and men to eat the feminine rice instead of the masculine potato. Rice ads suggested that rice would lead to sex and emphasized women's sexual power and desires.[75]

Ads for Uncle Ben's rice in the 1960s featured recipes and photographs of cooked rice. It was the text of the ad, however, that was designed to arouse interest. The sexual language targeted married women who, in the words of the researchers, wanted to "satisfy and gratify" their husbands as well as themselves. One ad asked, "So he thinks the only thing that sends you is public transportation? And he only brings you practical presents on your birthday? Time to loosen him up a little. With this wild culinary happening." Another ad challenged women to liven up their sex lives with rice, suggesting, "If he thinks the vamp in you has slowed down to den mother and your go-go has gone-gone, shake him up a little. Show him what wild is all about." Clearly, the objective was still to intertwine cooking and pleasing men, but with these ads, there was a renewed emphasis on women's fear of losing men and her need to restore his flagging libido.[76]

Lipton advertised its Chicken Supreme as a one step, one pot, packaged dinner, ready in just twenty minutes. Their 1970 ad embraced women's desires, touting the sherry wine that came in every package, and concluding that women's efficiency would lead to sex, when they suggested, "don't end up in the kitchen. End up in his arms." Lipton capitalized on a woman's desire to be homemaker, career woman, and sexy partner by presenting a way to prepare a romantic meal that left her with more time to spend with her man. However, it was still up to women to do it all.[77]

By the late 1960s, advertisers for the Rice Council of America combined sexual innuendo and Dichter's admonition that they appeal to creativity, to design an ad campaign that linked women's ingenuity, rice, and sex. The half-page ads all featured attractive women, wide-eyed, with either a smile or an open mouth, some looking provocatively over their glasses or over their shoulder, and a bold one- or two-line attention grabber. The first line set up the sexual overture; the second line sold the rice. A series of these ads appeared in 1969 and 1970 in *Life* magazine. A coy woman in one ad challenged readers, "No man wants the same thing every night. Be creative with rice." Playing on sexual naiveté, another ad had a woman claiming, "The first time it kind of scared me. Now rice is the thing I do best." A third ad promised, "It's the one thing a man never turns down. A second helping of rice." The ad campaign used these titillating headers to draw the reader to their more mundane informational paragraphs about the many different ways to prepare rice. The ads concluded by appealing to women to write away for "Man-pleasing" rice recipes.[78]

Rice ads specifically, and food ads generally, continued to use sexual imagery and messages to sell their products throughout the late twentieth century. An April 1999 Uncle Ben's rice ad featured an attractive couple, with the woman suggestively feeding the man a forkful of rice. The text read, "Passion Lesson #13: From now on every night would be different . . . filled with endless variety." It concluded, "Stir up some passion with Uncle Ben's."[79]

Even into the twenty-first century, food advertisers embraced this approach. A 2001 Dannon La Crème ad featured a woman provocatively dressed up as a "French Maid" sitting on a man's lap, speaking to him in a false French accent, and spoon-feeding him yogurt. When presented with the historical trends laid out in this study, Belle Frank, Director of Planning at Young & Rubicam, disagreed that her ad "'perpetuates stereotypical gender roles' as they relate to food" and argued that "the spot actually shows a woman as a power player in a marriage." In spite of all of the changes in American society, food advertisers such as Young & Rubicam were still trying to convince women that they were responsible for feeding men and satisfying their desires. Beyond shopping and cooking for foods to appeal to men, advertisers suggested that for some products women also needed to sell the foods with their clothing and appearance, with some going so far as Dannon to cross over into the fantasy world of dress-up and explicit sexual double entendres.[80]

One subtle change in ads in this later period was the more common use of the vague word "man," instead of the more specific "husband." It did not take advertising researchers long to determine that, starting in the 1970s, a growing percentage of couples were living together without being married. Researchers also reported on these new households and found that the traditional division of household responsibilities was changing. They claimed that sex roles were "being blurred and even transposed." One of the most important changes for food companies was that men were doing more of the grocery shopping. Researchers

Figure 22. Rice advertisers in particular used sexually suggestive images and language to persuade women to cook rice for their meat-and-potatoes men.

Figure 23. Women cooking for and feeding men remained an ideal in food advertising throughout the century.

who interviewed male consumers reported that men claimed that they did not pay much attention to food commercials, were less likely to use convenience products, and were more practical about products and about shopping. Most unnerving to food manufacturers and advertisers was the finding that men's belief in their rational decision-making meant that they would break the brand loyalties of their wives.[81] Not surprisingly, advertisers decreased their emphasis on traditional roles, such as a normative marriage with wives cooking for husbands, to maintain the most important status quo: women feeding men.

Addressing cooking and shopping patterns that threatened to put them out of business late in the century, some companies, like those selling yeast, struggled to make ads that kept pace with the changing culture.

Using sexual language and imagery, ads in the 1970s began to ask questions like, "Baking from scratch is great . . . but what's in it for you?" The text answered, "All those happy faces . . . plus an affectionate hug and the satisfaction of baking a special gift." The imagery of a man and woman about to kiss suggested a strong sexual appreciation of homemade baked goods. Appearing in the staid *Farm Journal* in 1970, one ad claimed, "Baking Bread is Making Love and you can bake a lot of love with a little Red Star Yeast."[82]

Advertisers wanted women to make the consumer decisions because they believed they could more easily persuade women to buy namebrand products. They strategized that to hold on to women they had to convince them that in spite of their changing gender roles they still had to please men in the kitchen and the bedroom. Their general use of sexuality was consistent with a changing culture that was moving away from a more reserved past and embracing a more hedonistic ideal. Advertisers encouraged women to satisfy their own desires, but to subordinate their pleasures to those of men. [83]

To ensure women's loyalty as consumers, food advertisers continued to try to convince women that they had primary responsibility for the individual and collective health of their families. Ads held women liable for the ailments of their children and their husbands, but promised that the right convenience foods could help make their family members healthy. Men's health took on particular importance in food ads, as advertisers sought to convince women to please them with food. Advertisers for foods that helped people lose weight aggressively targeted women and girls throughout the century and pressured them that to please men they needed to acquire health and beauty. Closely related were ads that suggested that women should use sensuality to attract and please men. The next chapter explores the equally powerful pressures and expectations advertisers placed on mothers and their responsibility for their children's success.

Chapter 6

A Mother's Love: Children and Food Advertising

We've convinced the mothers of America that they're not good mothers if they don't serve Minute Maid.

—*Advertising executive to sociologist Michael Schudson,* Advertising, the Uneasy Persuasion

Children's dependence on adults for food is a reality of their existence. At the beginning of the twentieth century, before the advent of readily available convenience foods, women's breast milk was the primary food source for infants' survival. The early twentieth-century development of pasteurized milk products, however, meant that even parents of tiny infants could buy foods to sustain them. The development of such foods challenged the inevitability of women's responsibility for feeding their children. Advertisers played an important role in persuading Americans of the critical function mothers undertook in feeding their children. The expectation that mothers exclusively should nourish their children into adulthood continued almost unchallenged through to the end of the century. Rarely did copywriters include fathers in their appeals to choose foods that would nurture children.

"How to Grow Strong Children"

One of the most consistent food advertising messages directed at mothers concerned their children's health. As early as 1896, the advertising trade journal *Printers' Ink* announced, "The picture of a healthy, pretty child rivets the attention of most people, especially women. This fact is now generally recognized by advertisers, and the use of a multitude of child-faces as eye attractors is the result." Health and strength themes pervaded messages that promised that children would love the taste and texture of particular foods. While the approaches copywriters took did vary over time, the target was inevitably a mother. Ads that suggested fear ostensibly focused on children generally, but most often focused on a son. Because of the literary tendency, particularly early in the century, to use "he" to refer to a general "they," the language could be understood as intended to reflect all children. However, the images that accompanied the text throughout the century reinforced the primary emphasis placed on the health and strength of boys.[1]

Advertisers used pictures of chubby children to advertise the health benefits of their products for toddlers. The Campbell Soup Company, for example, ran a multitude of ads in the first third of the century promoting their soups' benefits by featuring drawings of plump children. The company icons, the Campbell Kids, were supposed to epitomize the outcome for children who ate their soups and assure mothers that Campbell's soups would help their children withstand disease.[2]

The Borden's Farm Products Company tried an unusual tactic in 1926 by targeting the middle, asking mothers, "Is your child Husky or Ailing or just In-between?" Believing that most children were "In-between," the company featured ads such as one with two boys playing baseball and text that suggested, "if yours are the in-between children—never actually laid up, yet not the active, energetic youngsters they should be . . . then you're one of the mothers we especially want to talk to."[3]

Still, most food advertisers chose more traditional tactics. Some featured drawings of idealized children who glowed with good health and asked readers to compare them to their own children. Promoting the positive physical outcomes for children who ate their foods, advertisers used testimonials from wealthy parents who relied on their products, as well as nameless clean-faced, tow-headed cherubs who exuded vitality to affirm their claims. An ad for Cream of Wheat appeared in *McCall's* in 1930 touting the health of two upper-class children and asserting that nothing was too good for their well-being. The ad claimed,

With the children, health laws are scrupulously observed. The dictates of famed child specialists are unfailingly enforced, especially in that all important matter of diet. For both children a special point was emphasized early in their lives. That was the habit of eating a hot, cooked cereal. A particular cereal advised by child specialists.[4]

A September 1932 ad for Shredded Wheat was more vague when it encouraged, "Mother keep that vacation glow in their cheeks." These ads usually showed children smiling broadly and eating the product.

Early ads started out promoting their products' benefits to young children, as in a 1905 ad for Ralston Health Food. It offered a dense narrative, characteristic of the time, about "How to Grow Strong Children" with the cereal. Other ads adopted similar approaches, touting babies and children who grew plump on their food and claiming that they liked the foods' taste. However, by 1911, ad writers, particularly those targeting mothers of infants and children to age six, also had introduced a foreboding tone.[5]

In the first third of the century, advertisers frequently employed scare tactics to intimidate women into buying their foods. Infant and child mortality had been significant problems in American history and continued to be a real and common possibility through 1920. While preventive measures and improvements in technology and medicine reduced the likelihood of death over time, particularly during the summer, and especially for urban mothers, this terrifying outcome loomed. Ads menacingly told mothers threatened with the possibility of their child dying that their only hope was to purchase the correct foods. Among the most sinister were those Nestlé's Food for babies. One 1911 ad started off benignly enough, claiming the food would "Help Your Baby Fight the Summer Heat." The first sentence of text, however, assumed a note of casual terror when it informed, "It isn't the heat, it is the food that kills our babies in the summer time—and alas, more of them die in these three summer months than in all the rest of the year together." Striking an empathetic tone, it then assured mothers, "With the help of Nestlé's Food the summer can be so comfortable for the baby and you will be free from anxiety."[6]

A few years later the threat was even more explicit in another Nestlé's Food ad titled, "The Dangerous Business of Being a Baby." Explaining that it was "Dangerous indeed when we see the tiny little bodies menaced by dirty dairies, by sick cows, by ignorance, by disease; and dangerous indeed when we know that one baby out of six—last year—died."[7] Nestlé's ads contrasted the threat of illness and death with the promise of cleanliness and health, assuring consumers that its milk was pure.

Not content just to target mothers of infants, advertisers also presented an ominous tone about children's health generally. Campbell's advertisements, for example, sometimes tried to frighten women into cooking with Campbell's soups. In the midst of the Depression, Campbell ran an ad with the headline "Play is just health out for a good time!" At first glance, it is an upbeat ad, with boys playing in the snow, building snowmen and forts and making snowballs. However, the text of the ad served to exacerbate mothers' fears for their children's future: "You want your child to be right out there in the thick of it, mingling with the rest of the children in normal, wholesome, healthful fun. It's the alert and able-bodied children who are the natural leaders in their little world, just as the strong prevail in later life." The Heinz Company also suggested imminent danger when they featured a young toddler with outstretched arms and warned, "PROTECT YOUR BABY with Foods you know are SAFE!"[8]

The Dangerous Business
of Being a Baby

DANGEROUS indeed when
we see the tiny little bodies
menaced by dirty dairies, by sick
cows, by ignorance, by disease;
and dangerous indeed when we
know that one baby out of six—last
year—died.

But the danger grows less—Doctors
and Scientists have learned much about
how to keep our babies; and now the
mothers of the nation have joined in the
movement for "Better Babies."

"Better Babies" means, first, healthier
mothers; second, mothers who know.

It means mothers who know that their Babies'
food is of most importance. Who know of the
dangers for little babies in cow's milk. Who
know that the Government Inspectors found
only eight Clean Dairies in every hundred, and
that in one State alone—under strict laws—there
are 200,000 infected cows. Who know that
even when cow's milk is pure it is too heavy in
curd for little babies. All milk contains curds.
But nature provided a light, fleecy curd for
babies, and never intended the heavy, tough curd
of cow's milk for such delicate little stomachs.

is nearer to mother's milk than any other diet
you can give your baby. In NESTLÉ'S the
curd of the milk is rendered soft and fleecy as
in mother's milk. The
best cow's milk is the
basis of NESTLÉ'S
FOOD—the milk from
clean, healthy cows, in
Sanitary Dairies, that are
carefully inspected.
Then to it are added
other food elements your
baby needs, and that
cow's milk does not
contain.

Send the Coupon for
a free trial package of
twelve feedings and our 72
page Book for Mothers.

Figure 24. Ads targeting mothers could be quite menacing, as with this 1914 Nestlé's Food ad, which reported, "one baby out of six–last year–died."

As in the above Campbell's ad, Social Darwinism was a common feature in ads during this period, striving to emphasize how women could affect their children's lives. As Edwin Black and others have demonstrated, eugenics took hold of the country's imagination in the first three decades of the century and undoubtedly fostered even more anxiety about children's ability to compete. In addition to health appeals, advertisers also prescribed mothers' duties, which included ensuring that their children would have the potential to succeed in a cruelly competitive economic environment. The warnings appeared in particular during the economic crisis of the 1930s. Whether or not children were gaining weight served as the focal point for ads that used scientific trappings, such as doctors and medical apparatus, to assert their claims. Teachers, coaches, and parents also gave testimonials to the foods' effectiveness, assuring mothers that with the right food purchases their children could be successful.[9]

Advertisers used grim statistics and omens to scare women into buying their foods. Cream of Wheat's campaign in the early 1930s was one of the most aggressive. Targeted at mothers of children aged one to six, headlines cautioned that children faced "GRAVE DANGERS!" during "The most hazardous period of childhood!" To spark women's action, ads encouraged mothers to "Guard your children, in every way, during this anxious time." They alerted them, "If your children are pale, nervous, listless or come in too tired from play; if little arms and legs have grown thin—take warning! You must build up their strength, their weight." Some ads argued that young children were "more susceptible to certain serious diseases now than a newborn baby is! Government records show that dangers grow thick about him—until these years from 1 to 6 become twice as hazardous as those that follow!" The suggested response to all of these threats was, of course, Cream of Wheat. Ads promised mothers that their cereal would "help you see them safely through it."[10] The ads deployed an abundance of exclamation points and photographs of vulnerable looking boys to suggest a need for mother's protection.

In addition to health benefits, advertisers during this period also promoted the economy of their products. Many advertisers, like Cream of Wheat, touted their value with claims that it only cost a "little more than ½ cent a serving." Others, however, cautioned women against taking financial short cuts with their children's food. A 1938 Heinz ad for Strained Foods warned, "Don't Bargain with Baby's Diet!" and pleaded with mothers to "Play safe by serving him foods of the same high quality you enjoy."[11]

The same Heinz ad also alluded to another fear advertisers hoped would resonate with mothers. Namely, they hoped that by promoting the ease of using their prepared foods, mothers would worry that they were not spending enough time with their children. Another Heinz ad featured a young boy shouting, " 'Come out of the kitchen mother!' " He went on to complain, "There's so much puttering around with pots and pans in our house, that I hardly *ever* get to see my mother! She should spend more time with me, and less in the kitchen. I'm growing now. Somebody has to teach me how to play and think and act."[12] Copywriters, then, wanted women to worry about their dual responsibility to their children: supply them with healthy, nutritious foods and be available to them as teachers and playmates.

During the 1940s and 1950s, alarmist tendencies decreased in most advertising, but Ovaltine ads stood out as some of the most consistently hysterical and exaggerated. While copywriters continued to blame children's health problems on mothers, fathers occasionally appeared to place the blame on mothers, too. A 1941 ad had a mother admitting, "I tell you Jimmy doesn't eat enough to keep a bird alive! Hasn't touched his vegetables again. No wonder he's so thin." The boy's father responded, "I don't want to be critical, Margaret, but it's high time you did something about it—before we have him sick on our hands." After the doctor suggested Ovaltine, the father reappeared and proclaimed that the boy was eating well and had already gained weight.[13]

More than just critics of their wives, men also appeared as menacing, impatient figures at the dinner table. A 1940 ad for Clapp's baby food had one father explaining, "He's our first baby, so naturally my wife and I got worried when he didn't seem to care about some of his vegetables. Sometimes we begged and pleaded, and sometimes we'd play games and try to sneak a spoonful in while he wasn't looking. One night I got annoyed and tried to force it down him." An ad for Ovaltine had a dad yelling at his son, "Young man, you'll either eat those vegetables and drink that milk or you'll go straight to bed."[14]

Historian Elaine Tyler May found that during the Cold War era the role of fathers took on particular importance, in part, at least, "to counteract the overabundance of maternal care. . . . The unhappy result would be 'sissies,' who were allegedly likely to become homosexuals." The popular media encouraged fathers to take a greater role in their children's lives. What this meant in terms of participation in actual child care undoubtedly varied from home to home, but magazines like *Woman's Home Companion* offered an illustrated guide. It included "photographs of dad in an apron, feeding his children, helping them make a box car, and teaching them about cars." Even less demanding was an *American Home* article, "Are you a Dud as a Dad?" that merely wanted dads to "Share your small son's hobbies, laugh at his jokes, lend a listening ear to his problems, the kinds of things a fellow wants to talk over with a man." Fathers of daughters presumably had no real need to be involved in their lives, given that they did not face the same dangers as sons who were too effeminate.[15]

In spite of men's occasional goading, the burden for caring for children's health continued to be women's responsibility. Moreover, during the 1950s advertisers began to assert that in addition to their child's current sickly condition being a liability, a "nervous underweight" boy would never become a man. One 1950 ad hissed disapprovingly at mothers, "Sissy . . . they called him." The aggressive Ovaltine campaign asked mothers, "How well do you *really* understand him?" They reminded readers, "The health of a child is largely in its mother's hands. His welfare depends upon how well she understands his needs." The drawings and photographs that dominated the ads featured boys who, in the words of the advertisers, appeared "frail and languid."[16] The mothers appeared in the background, over-wrought and concerned, appeased only by the knowledge that Ovaltine could help them and their sons.

Health concerns had always been a part of advertising to mothers. The J. Walter Thompson company understood as early as the 1920s that "the more authoritative and scientific a presentation to them on this subject is made, the better reading it will get" Ernest Dichter found in a 1954 study of Chex cereal that "the American consumer is fairly well educated nutritionally. She is generally aware of what constitutes a balanced diet." Toward the end of the century, ad writers capitalized on this knowledge by using even more specific, technical, scientific language to compel mothers to buy particular products. A 1992 ad for pork assured mothers, "Kids love the taste of today's pork. They don't care beans that it's good for them. But Moms appreciate the fact that today's pork is 31% leaner and 14% lower in calories than it was only 10 years ago. Yet it's packed with protein." An ad for Tyson's meats in 2000 in *Ebony* empathized with mothers, "You'd move mountains for him if you could. You give him quality chicken with no hormones and no steroids because you can. Tyson. It's what your family deserves."[17]

Two other trends also developed later in the century. First, advertisers promoted a mother's role, not just in nourishing but also in nurturing their children with food. While this notion did exist earlier in the century, it gained momentum when advertisers emphasized mother's ability to provide comfort from the literal and figurative cold outside world. Allusions to children's stomachs as burning stoves reflected the heat of their mother's love and the food's energy.[18]

The other significant development was advertising that suggested to mothers that in addition to creating a break for them, a father's participation in feeding might provide benefits to both child and father. Starting in the 1950s, fathers appeared as sporadic assistants, feeding infants and small toddlers. These advertisements suggested that feeding children was a temporary role for men, but later in the century ads took father-hood more seriously. Even though Gerber was only suggesting dad might help with one weekend feeding in 1970, their ads began to show fathers in more intimate proximity to their babies. By 1980, their ads had fathers kissing their children and proclaimed that "At Gerber, we're proud to help Dad have a part in Pat's feeding, because we know that feeding Pat can be a rewarding part of being Dad."[19] This transforma-tion in advertising, with fathers emerging from their previous role as in-visible outsiders, to a new one in which they found an emotional connection and fulfillment in their participation in feeding their chil-dren, was remarkable. It was a significant historical change in food ad-vertising, not only for the speed with which it happened, but really that it happened at all.

Still, men's participation in feeding children was limited. Rita Hub-bard analyzed the change in men's portrayals in her study of ads placed in three family magazines (*Children, Parenting,* and *Parents*) from July to December 1988. She found that of the 144 ads depicting children with parents, only 27 ads showed children with fathers. Hubbard found that most of these ads depicted fathers "engaged in behaviors considered tra-ditionally male, such as showing a boy how to use or install equipment. Further, whenever the child's gender could be determined, it was male." The food ads that differed from the traditional poses in Hubbard's study were an Oscar Mayer ad with a father and son excited about ba-con, and another ad with a father feeding an infant Gerber baby food.[20] As in this broader study, Hubbard found that fathers only appeared feeding very young children.

In part, it was possible for advertisers to promote men's participation in providing food for infants and small toddlers because it was consis-tent with the temporary, occasional way in which ads suggested men should participate in food preparation. Just as early airlines featured fe-male pilots to assure customers of the safety of airplane travel, food manufacturers used men in the kitchen to assure women that their products were truly easy to make.[21] After the burden of feeding very young children passed, however, advertisers rarely called on fathers to feed their children. The primary exceptions were fast food franchises, which presented their restaurants as fun outings for dads and their children.

Fast food advertisers faced a dilemma in attracting mothers to their es-tablishments. The unhealthy reputation of the traditional fare (hamburg-ers, french fries, fried chicken) made it difficult to attract women who had responsibility for their children's health. While women did appear in ads, they generally did so less often than men, most frequently as ro-mantic dates, sex objects, or grandmothers. Mothers did occasionally materialize, but they almost never ate the fast food advertised and rarely appeared alone with their children. Advertisers preferred to feature mothers peering into or approaching restaurants and usually involved them in a group or family setting.[22]

Fathers, however, made the perfect target and vastly outnumbered mothers in fast food ads. Perhaps that men were involved in their children's lives at all was assumed to be a victory for women; no advertisements expected fathers also to concern themselves with their children's health. Ads emphasized that a father was spending quality time with his child and that they both had fun. That it was an unusual event not only helped suggest it as a special time, it also offered mothers the reassurance that the child was only having one unhealthy meal and would soon resume eating under her watchful gaze.[23]

"Do Not Disappoint Your Own Children"

Responsibility for their children's education also fell to women. Advertisers suggested throughout the century that their foods were critical to academic success. Educational appeals promised that their products would make children smart, strong, and healthy. Most of these ads appeared in the fall, as they sought to persuade women to serve their products to children throughout the school year. Like most advertising concerning children, appeals to mothers about their sons predominated. Boys and girls appeared together, but if there was only one child, particularly in the first half of the century, it was usually a boy. Ads emphasized the importance of food to boys' physical and academic success, but did not make the same claims of significance for girls. Advertisers socialized parents to expect less from their daughters.[24]

In the first third of the century, when most children across the United States went home for a lunch break, ads encouraged mothers to plan daily breakfast and lunch menus that would spur on their children's academic and physical endurance. A September 1902 ad featured a grinning boy eating a bowl of cereal and suggested a strong parallel between the worlds of work and education. The copy proclaimed, "Whether you try for medals in class or in the athletic field,—whether you face the greater work and try for greater prizes,—your breakfast table is the daily starting point and Quaker Oats is your best fare. Work like a man, but don't be worked to death."[25]

Ads explicitly encouraged mothers to take responsibility for their children's educational performance by choosing the right convenience foods. A Campbell's soup ad appearing in October 1919, following the First World War, showed a female elementary school teacher pointing to Europe and the Soviet Union on a world map and stating that children "must grapple with new tasks, with harder problems. They have fresh worlds to conquer." With the emergence of communism as a threat, advertisers sought to situate their products as part of the offense and defense in contending with other nations. What many hoped was going to be a war to end all wars, instead revealed a changed world, rife with political and economic challenges. In addition to rivalry with European countries and the Soviet Union, the competition among native-borns and their antagonism with immigrants informed a number of ads in this period. A 1927 ad for Cream of Wheat set up the demands on children and mother's role in helping them when it allowed, "Ahead of him, so much to master . . . all alone! Yet only you can care for him in little things like this." In addition to the more benign message that their children were starting a school year with new and more difficult lessons, advertisers wanted to drive home the point that if their mothers wanted them to excel, they had best give them the advertised product. More than just asking mothers to shop for and prepare food, advertisers were asking women to see their role as nationally important, whereby their choices in the kitchen would shape not only their own children, but their community and their country.[26]

The warnings could be quite ominous, particularly against the backdrop of the eugenics movement that was sweeping the country. With the massive mobilization of troops for World War I, IQ testing was introduced on a large scale, and along with the growing professionalization of American society there was increasing pressure to compete, even, or perhaps especially, among children. A Grape Nuts ad claimed, "Statistics prove that much of the 'backwardness' of some children is due to faulty nourishment." A Postum Cereal ad asserted of the nation's first graders, "Half of the four million will fail this year. Will your child be among them?"[27]

While advertisers emphasized women's concern for their children's physical and mental needs, they also strove to ensure that mothers cared about their children's happiness. Ads suggested that meals had the potential to warm children's hearts, as well as their stomachs. A 1911 ad for Post Toasties cereal suggested that "The Memory Lingers" and a Rex Deviled Ham ad from the same year reminded mothers that it "makes a bright spot in the day for children." A Campbell's soup ad put it succinctly when it warned mothers, "Do not disappoint your own children."[28] Later, advertisers highlighted similar concerns. They claimed that children wanted to eat portable snacks and meals. At mid-century, advertisers began to suggest lunch box contents that would please children. Increasingly ads promoted cold cereals that mothers could buy and children could prepare themselves. At the end of the century, advertisers encouraged mothers' concern about children's angst and promised

Figure 25. With both language and imagery, ads more frequently promised health benefits for boys than for girls.

their products as the remedy for "Arithmetic. Braces. Cafeteria food. The class bully."[29]

Educational appeals allowed advertisers to build on mothers' anxieties about their children's health and zero in on their concern for their children's future. The importance of education to upward mobility in the United States was not lost on advertisers and they frequently took this tack in their appeals. Moreover, children's social success, in terms of popularity and fun in school, began to take on greater importance in food advertising starting in the 1940s. By the end of the century, this ideal predominated in ads.

Moreover, gender role expectations for children permeated all of these ads. Food advertisers throughout the century clearly delineated different roles for boys and girls and the men and women they would grow up to be.

"Say, I'll Make a Good Wife, Won't I?"

Companies frequently sponsored ads suggesting that their products would have different outcomes for girls than for boys. Take, for example, the contrast between two typical ads from the early century, both featuring Campbell Kids. The first, an ad for oxtail soup, depicted a boy wrestling an ox to the ground by the horns. The second showed a girl standing idly, with the doggerel, "My rosy cheeks, And winning looks, Are really due, To Campbell's cooks!"[30]

Contrasting ads from the same campaigns reveal a great deal about advertisers' views of gender differences. A 1957 campaign for Trix cereal, for example, had a mother pouring a bowl of cereal for her five-year-old daughter while the header proclaimed, "When a woman's five, she needs love—and a little applied psychology." Another ad in the campaign appeared with a similarly aged boy sitting, arms crossed, one leg crossed at the knee, with a defiant look on his face. The header for this ad, in sharp contrast to the one featuring a girl, asserted, "Rugged individualist—logic won't work but Trix will!"[31] Advertisers consistently suggested that girls were dependent and passive, while granting boys a startling degree of independence and individualism.

Even ads that featured girls and boys together suggested that foods would affect boys and girls differently. A 1933 ad for Campbell's vegetable soup provided a dramatic contrast of outcomes. It showcased a painting of an adoring girl standing next to a strong, tough-looking boy after a football game in which he has just played. The caption, "It's health that makes him a Hero!" focused attention on his strength, ignoring the girl in the picture. The boy looked out confidently at the viewer, while the girl looked at the boy. This was typical of most food ads throughout the century; while boys usually gazed directly at the reader, girls were more often the subject of the viewer's gaze. Moreover, food ads generally reinforced the ideal of females in supporting roles, not as actors in their own right.[32]

Girls did appear in food ads, but much less often than boys. Featured girls were almost always very young (under the age of ten, usually about age five). They typically had feminine hairstyles, such as braids, often adorned with ribbons, hats or bonnets, and barrettes. In keeping with the trend in portraying adult females, girls rarely appeared eating, and if they did, it was generally to take dainty bites of light foods, such as soup or salad. Much more common were smiling little girls dressed up in cute outfits, holding or observing the advertised food.[33]

Advertisers commonly used gendered language that described both their product and the featured girl. In a 1902 ad for Cream of Wheat, for example, the header proclaimed "Dainty and Wholesome," referring both to their cereal and to a girl holding a bundle of wheat. Food ads used language and imagery to contribute to the belief that girls were delicate. A 1960s ad for Kellogg's pictured a girl surrounded by tins of sugar and spice to allude to the nursery rhyme that affirmed that girls were "everything nice." The parallel ad for the Kellogg's campaign had a boy surrounded by frogs, snails, and a go-cart. Ads admonished women and girls to be mindful of their behavior, but never similarly controlled or castigated boys' behavior. Another ad featured a rhyme below a photograph of a little girl and observed, "There was a little girl / and she had a little curl / right in the middle of her forehead / when she was good she was very, very good . . ." The ad gave the familiar ending (and when she was bad she was horrid) a twist when it concluded, "and her mother gave her a big bowl of Kellogg's Corn Flakes." A 1970 ad by Riceland Rice reminded consumers, "Beef and Rice and other things nice; that's how good little girls make Hash Olé."[34]

Girls' "ladylike" behavior extended to their physical activities as well. One of the only physical activities girls did in ads was jump rope. Generally, girls did not appear in action. Exceptions to this pattern stand out for their rarity, as with girls who occasionally appeared running or sliding down a banister. Even in these rare instances, however, other imagery in the ads usually helped reinforce traditional gender ideals. For example, in a 1938 ad for Junket custard mix a girl of about seven appeared running headlong across the top of the page alongside the words "So strong and sturdy"; the other two girls in the ad appeared in domestic roles to prepare the custard.[35]

The value advertisers placed on girls' domestic activities is evident in two trends in food ads, both of which encouraged girls to be cooks and consumers. The first was the number of girls that appeared in ads feeding dolls or younger siblings, which advertisers likened to mothers feeding their children. Throughout the century, girls were supposed to learn how to feed children to prepare them for their female adult roles. Food companies like Purina referred to "Little cooks and big like Ralston Wheat Food" and had girls younger than five declaring their allegiance to brand name products.[36]

The other way in which advertisers assumed girls' inevitable involvement in the kitchen was the placement of girls engaged in cooking and in studying foods' qualities. Advertisers, promoting their foods' nutritious value, suggested that girls should understand and care about the importance of food content. The Wheat Flour Institute asserted that "Every teen-ager should *memorize* those flags," referring of course only to girls and the flags listing flour's properties (protein, iron, etc.). A woman's head, floating above the copy, announced, "Smart girls these days are well aware that the foods they eat have a great deal to do with their health and their dispositions, even their grades and their looks."[37]

While there is evidence that by the end of the nineteenth century girls had already moved away from learning to cook from their mothers, twentieth-century advertisers encouraged mothers to bring their daughters into the fold. Girls learned from advertisers and their mothers that heating up frozen and canned foods qualified as cooking. One pre-teen proclaimed, "Boy . . . can my mom cook! . . . and she's teaching me how to serve our favorite dish. Mom calls it Milady's Blintzes. It's so easy . . . Milady's Blintzes come already prepared. You just brown them on both sides and serve . . . She's a wonderful cook."[38] In encouraging mothers to pass on their sense of responsibility as caregivers to their daughters, advertisers also hoped young girls would be exposed to their products.

Advertisers focused on girls' role as cooks in training. The primary way girls functioned in food ads was as apprentices to their mothers. Conversely, boys almost never appeared as assistants, and were certainly not expected in image, words, or spirit to carry on their mother's work in the kitchen. Advertisers expected girls to see their ability to choose products to please others and to attract men as a key to their success as women.

One of the favorite mechanisms advertisers used to connect girls to their mothers was to dress them in similar costumes; most noticeably, the apron served this purpose. Standing side-by-side in the kitchen, young girls mimicked or assisted their mother's actions or sometimes listened intently to, or wrote down, instructions on what products to buy. Mother-daughter teams enabled advertisers to suggest products as family traditions, passed on from generation to generation. A 1917 ad assured women that they could offer a "Mother's gift—the lesson in thrift." Alongside a picture of a mother teaching a daughter to knead dough, it advised, "Teach your children thrift. In these days of rising costs home made bread represents the first principle in wise household economy." Things had not changed much thirty years later, when a 1945 ad featured a mother and daughter dressed identically, down to their beribboned hair style and matching aprons and blouses. As they stood over the stove, the mother counseled, "Remember, Betsy! That's the *very best—Swift's Premium.*" Inevitably, grandmothers also appeared as authorities training young girls. One 1966 ad had a teenage girl asking, "Like this?" to her grandmother as she kneaded dough. The tagline "and Pillsbury says it best" suggested the wisdom being passed on and the historic importance of using food to demonstrate affection.[39]

As in all other themes, the emphasis on pleasing men remained central. Pleasing husbands and fathers gave wives and daughters a shared goal that advertisers promised to help them meet. One girl of about ten, hair in braids and ribbons, wearing an apron, held forth a can of Derby Foods in a 1945 ad. She announced, "My house will have a pantry-full! Dad thinks I'm a born cook. . . . Mom knows it's Derby Foods. . . . Say,

I'll make a good wife, won't I?" Twenty-five years later, the message was still going strong. A 1970 Pillsbury ad encouraged girls to please their fathers by baking cinnamon rolls with a father crowing proudly, "There's a dough-ting daughter."[40]

Satisfying men extended beyond fathers, however, as advertisers encouraged girls to care about boys' desires, even at a tender age. A 1951 ad for Mor meats had a young boy dreaming lovingly of a Mor sandwich, while the girl pouted, hands on hips, that he was ignoring her. The ad offered girls and women a lesson in male priorities and preferences. Heinz ran several ads in *Seventeen* in a question-and-answer format that offered girls insights into pleasing boys with behavior and food. For example, one 1962 ad asked a girl whose reflection showed her brushing her hair, "How Do *You* Rate On A Date?" The first question asked, "Do you keep him waiting?" The answer cautioned, "Primp as long as you like, but not on *his* time, please." A 1967 ad featured two awkward teens at dinner and encouraged mothers, "Don't wait till Sally brings 'him' home. Serve your family Betty Crocker Noodles Romanoff tonight. Sally's pretty special all by herself." While seemingly granting positive praise to the girl, the emphasis on boys, dating, and romance undermined and understated her "special" qualities. Moreover, advertisers exerted pressure on girls to date boys, but no reciprocal pattern existed.[41]

More explicit were ads appearing in the late 1960s in *Seventeen* and *Mademoiselle*, in which teenage girls appeared as vixens trying to lure boys with Wonder Bread sandwich creations. Articles appearing in the same period reinforced this concern by casually introducing girls to boys and their food tastes in another format. One 1969 spread had a blurb on John Buchanan—"Most Intellectual." This eighteen-year-old Princeton freshman and presidential scholar liked a distinctive hamburger, "architecture, art, artichokes, dislikes 'too-smart' girls." Persuaded that this type of boy was attractive and a catch, the feature cautioned that if they wanted to attract a boy, girls had best know what kind of food he liked and be careful not to be "too-smart."[42]

Even young girls got the message. A 1970 ad summarized one girl's experience, "Boys used to kick sand in my face at the beach . . . then I sent for my beach ball and totebag. . . . Now the boys like me. They play with my beach ball all day. They might even talk to me one day soon." These messages continued through to the end of the century. In a May 2000 television commercial, three young girls, on separate occasions, brought the new boy in the neighborhood a dish of pudding. The ad suggested that girls should compete for the affections of boys, and Jell-O spokesperson Bill Cosby reminded girls and women that the "way to a man's heart is his stomach."[43] By setting the lowest possible standards for male behavior and suggesting that girls should still seek the approval of boys, advertisers counseled girls to accept a life devoted to pleasing boys, even with no clear rewards offered.

"Builds Men"

Boys, meanwhile, consistently appeared in food ads as physical, active, self-involved youngsters, and mothers were encouraged to be mindful of their well-being. Not only was their health on the line, their success on the field and in the classroom depended on their mother's shopping and cooking decisions. Advertisers encouraged mothers to see their sons as engrossed in their own worlds and never created ads that had boys caring for younger siblings or learning about food values.

Instead, advertisers presented the world of boys as one of high energy. Boys consistently appeared in garb denoting their sporting affiliations, usually appearing in outdoor settings, and frequently holding sports equipment. Boys also appeared in formal dress shirts, ties, and suits as if to suggest that they were miniature men.[44]

While boys did appear playing many different sports, including hockey, basketball, and soccer, they most commonly appeared in baseball and football regalia. Girls almost never appeared playing organized sports, but beginning in the 1920s, advertisers embraced the image of boys playing baseball and football to promote a range of foods, from soups to peanut butter, from bananas to margarine. Using the measure of a hit or a good run with the football, advertisers pressured mothers to provide their sons with these important, healthful foods as both necessity and reward.

Starting in the 1920s, the baseball theme continued consistently throughout the century. One 1922 ad promoted Campbell's soup with a male Campbell's Kid and the jingle, "I hit the ball with all my might, And sent it sailing out of sight! Hear the crowds just roar with glee—It's home and Campbell's now for me!" While most ads focused on boys getting the big hit, some advertisers used the tension of boys poised at the plate to highlight what could be lost or gained by eating the right foods. A 1947 Borden's Hemo drink ad used a photo of a boy hitting a long ball, with one onlooker shielding his eyes to see how far it would go. The company icon, Elsie the Cow, proclaimed, "They used to call him 'runty' . . . *Now* look at my Hemo Boy!"[45]

Focusing on baseball themes allowed advertisers to emphasize the amount of energy that boys expended and needed to have refueled with their meals. They reminded mothers, "Organized games and sports use up much of a child's energy" and promised boys that their foods would provide "more wham in your slam." While ads that focused on girls created beauty parallels between the products and girls, food ads that focused on boys, such as a 1953 Van Camp Pork and Beans ad, proclaimed that they were "Champion of the Bean League." Moreover, unlike ads focused on girls, companies such as Wheaties offered boys male sports heroes like Yogi Berra and Ted Williams.[46]

Ads with football themes also drew on boys' need for energy and suggested foods as a guarantee of and reward for their athletic success. As with baseball, ads used boys in action; uniforms, helmets, and the football itself suggested boys' athleticism. Cream of Wheat ran a campaign in the mid-1960s that offered images of boys caught up in the rough-and-tumble world of sports, and asked mothers, as in a 1966 ad with three boys on the ground tackling a football, "Right now . . . aren't you glad they had 'Cream of Wheat' for breakfast?"[47]

Advertisers used athletic competition and outdoor play to promote their foods' nutritional value to mothers with sons. They often made claims that their foods would help boys to become big and strong. For example, a 1970 Hostess ad featured a young boy clutching a football while eating a Twinkie. The ad announced "A major nutritional advance from Hostess. Snack Cakes with body-building vitamins and iron." A series of Wonder Bread ads also included a football themed ad with a young boy serving as the water boy to the football team dreaming, "Big enough to make the team. That's how big I want to be." The ad reminded mothers, "He'll never need Wonder Bread more than right now. The time to grow bigger and stronger is during the 'Wonder Years'—ages one through twelve—when a child reaches 90% of his adult height."[48]

While food ads never encouraged girls' growth, they consistently featured boys flexing their muscles and striving to get bigger. A 1937 Cream of Wheat ad had two boys showing off their muscles, seeking to emulate their boxing hero, with the title "The 'Champ'—he needs your help, mother!" The young girl with them stares in awe at one boy's "muscle," giving no sense that she might be an active or hungry child, too. JWT featured its Swift & Company Peanut Butter account as their "Campaign of the Week" in February 1950. Their newsletter explained their strategy:

Since peanut butter is bought chiefly for growing, school-age children, the big play is on the nutrition story, with such headlines as, "Here's the world's most POWERFUL sandwich filling!" This general statement is graphically illustrated for youthful readers by accounts of the amazing feats a 100 lb. boy can accomplish on the food energy in a single 2 oz. serving of Swift's Peanut Butter. (Run for 3½ miles; roller skate for 2½ hours; swim for 1400 yards; etc.)[49]

By their omission, advertisers apparently did not consider girls' actions a good example of a food's ability to provide power and energy. Advertisements that focused on strength, growth, and purpose also suggested another startling difference between the sexes; namely, that boys enjoyed eating. Indeed, ads frequently featured boys eating, sometimes messily and heartily.

Another disparity was that advertisers usually presented boys on a mission, as kids who had things to accomplish. Throughout the century, advertisers embraced the image of the cowboy to suggest that boys had serious, gun-toting business to attend to in their backyards. With its hats, kerchiefs, and weaponry, cowboy imagery allowed advertisers to proclaim, as in a 1915 ad, that their foods and boys were "Fortified inside as well as out. You can see this by his well-chosen bulwark of defense. His mother evidently is one of those sensible housewives."[50]

Soldier imagery also served a similar purpose, but appeared less often. Again, defending the country imbued boys and foods with patriotism and purpose. A 1944 ad, for example, in the midst of the Second World War featured a young boy wearing a soldier's helmet and exclaiming, "Give me Shredded Ralston *I've got a job to do!*" A 1961 ad had a young boy carrying home a box of Corn Flakes saluting back at the image of a Marine in his dress uniform underneath the words "Builds Men."[51]

Most ads featuring children focused on boys. Promotional items weighed heavily toward traditionally male interests and pursuits; frogmen, walkie-talkies, and weaponry covered cereal boxes and filled ads across the country. While advertisers did run ads with female images, most often highlighting girls' appearance, male images abounded in both abundance and range of experiences presented. The ads often incorporated boys and men, and included firefighters, police officers, bullfighters, and knights in shining armor.

Advertisers wanted mothers to see their children in distinctly gendered ways. It was imperative for the success of the industry, as they perceived it, for mothers to raise girls who would follow their example in the kitchen. Ads presented boys as heirs apparent to the service and doting that would be forever theirs as men.

"Born to Shop"

In addition to using children to appeal to mothers and shape gender roles, advertisers also valued children and adolescents as a consumer group. Not only did young people increasingly comprise a major market as consumers in their own right, but advertisers also believed that they were the future of consuming in the United States. In articles and reports they professed,

We also care a great deal about impressing the child for its own sake, because *the child of to-day is the buyer of to-morrow*. The years pass quickly and the seed that the advertiser sows to-day will produce a harvest for years to come. And it is easier to impress the child than it will be to impress the grown-up. The girls or boys of ten or seventeen have receptive, impressionable minds.[52]

They hoped that appeals to young people would not only ensure immediate sales, but also be an investment in enduring market viability. Later in the century, however, advertisers narrowed their target further. While food advertisers still targeted girls and boys in order to influence their mother's purchases, no longer would adolescent boys be considered long-term consumers. Instead, advertisers focused almost exclusively on girls and tried to inculcate gender role expectations that would foretell future consumption patterns. Beyond appealing to girls' preferences, advertisers also suggested that girls' consumerism should anticipate and accommodate boys' desires.

In the early twentieth century, advertisers hoped children would influence their mothers' purchases or make purchases for their mothers on a run to the market. However, they also considered both girls and boys as consumers and targeted them directly. In a 1911 article titled, "Catering to Children With an Eye on the Parents," W. P. Tuttle, who had been involved with the juvenile publication field, argued:

The child does not skip the advertising pages unless they fail to interest him. All pages, in fact, look alike to the child, and if the advertising section is made interesting to the child, he will pore over it with the same absorption that he does over the rest of the magazine . . . more or less true of them, also, until they get well along in their teens.[53]

In the early twentieth century, the advertising industry journal *Printers' Ink* carried a multitude of articles about targeting children, and advertisers quickly homed in on the idea of using children and children's fantasy. This would thus inform advertising decisions from the Campbell Kids to Joe Camel. A 1919 *Printers' Ink* article reflected that, "A comparison of old and recent issues of some of the leading magazines—general, women's and children's—shows a decided awakening to the value of the child appeal in merchandising for every conceivable kind of goods, whether or not the article itself has any real connection with the child." Moreover, it noted that the range of appeals ran "the whole gamut of merchandise with foods far in the lead."[54]

A 1920 campaign for National Oats illustrates the corporate decision to target children. The Advertising Manager for the National Oats Company laid out the company's rationale for changing their icon and slogan between 1918 and 1920. While their product had previously been advertised by a little girl with a basket and the slogan "You Can Taste the Difference," their new vision was to focus on active boys. They developed a new trademark, a robust young boy and a new slogan, "—makes kids husky." While the slogan sounds as though it refers to all children, the intention was to target boys as consumers. In early ads "a little girl was shown feeling the husky kid's muscle. In another advertisement the boy was swinging a little girl." Beyond the physical evidence, though, the company's vision included boys as consumers:

The company believes strongly in the purchasing influence of the boy. All boys love to be strong and athletic. When a mother tells her boy to go to the store and get a package of oatmeal, and on the way he passes a poster with a "—makes kids husky" boy, it will be the most natural thing in the world for him to ask for National Oats. He sees the advertisements in his own magazines and in those of his mother. He receives a vivid impression of physical superiority, and these early impressions are retained for years.[55]

Yet this focus on boys was short-lived. The evidence that boys shopped for food in large numbers throughout the century remained, but the expectation that boys would be making consumer decisions fell away. Perhaps due in part to changing shopping patterns with the widespread introduction and expansion of supermarkets in the 1930s and compounded by gender role anxieties stemming from the upheaval of the Great Depression, by the 1940s, food advertisers firmly turned their sights on teenage girls as the hope of the future of consumerism. Even when they included boys rhetorically as they talked about youths generally, they rarely included them in their consumer vision.

In addition to the consumer potential of young children, researchers consistently demonstrated the quality and depth of the teen consumer base. They documented their numbers and potential spending power in plentiful research studies in the second half of the century. While historians Paula Fass, Jackson Lears, and Jennifer Scanlon argued that teenagers were advertising targets as early as the 1920s, it was only after the Second World War that awareness of the category blossomed and advertisers pursued these budding adults and their wallets. According to historians Grace Palladino, Thomas Hine, and Samantha Yates, "teenagers," as a defined group, did not exist until the 1940s. With the dramatic social changes of the Great Depression setting the stage, the upheavals of the Second World War and the 1944 creation of *Seventeen* helped contribute to a generational shift in attitude, particularly with regard to the consumer behavior of young people.[56]

In 1946, the Opinion Research Corporation conducted a survey called "Life with Teena" for *Seventeen*. The second volume of the study focused on teenage girls' food shopping and cooking habits, with the express purpose of determining "The influence of teen-age girls on the eating and food buying habits of their families" and "brand awareness and brand preferences of teen-age girls with respect to various food categories." According to the report, the average teen-age girl was "taking a cooking course," "collects recipes and by the time she is fifteen owns her own cookbook as well," and was "dreaming of a home of her own and full-time job as a homemaker." Not only were these girls dreaming of caring for a family in the future, they were already working in their own families, "shopping for groceries at least three times a week," making their own breakfast and lunch, and helping make dinner about three times a week and occasionally making it all herself. The survey also ascertained that girls enjoyed throwing parties, and believed that food was central to their success with their peers.[57]

Encouraging advertisers to embrace this market, researchers touted benefits, in terms of both sales and brand loyalty. A 1958 *Printers' Ink* article, for example, showcased Vernon Stouffer, the frozen food king, and forecast that there would be almost 18.5 million potential homemakers between the ages of seventeen and twenty-one by 1970. Food advertisers were not blind to the purchasing potential of these teenage girls and young women. Indeed, for many producers of new food products and food types, such as frozen foods, these young consumers, not yet set in their ways, made ideal targets. Advertisers saw the teenage girl as *tabula rasa* whom they could convince to be more modern than their mothers.[58]

Food advertisers in the second half of the century targeted teens in such popular magazines as *Seventeen* and *American Girl. Seventeen* claimed to potential advertisers that their teenage readers were "branded for life," which shifted the language of branding from the product to the consumer. Its competitor, *American Girl*, sought to associate young readers with the adult women long presumed to be the consumers, with the explicit motto, "Selling to Women While They're Young." According to Ellen McCracken, *Seventeen* promoted a consumerist ideology, "reducing its readers to slogans such as 'Calculating consumer,' 'purchasing agent,' 'Born to shop.'" In 1962, editors at *Seventeen* lured advertisers with the news that most teenage girls were already responsible for some family shopping, in part because 66 percent of the subscribers had mothers who worked outside the home. With food advertising, cookbooks, and its monthly "Now You're Cooking" food section, *Seventeen* helped socialize "young women into their expected role in the kitchen." McCracken argued that *Seventeen* sent the message that "Meal preparation is as important as beauty and fashion concerns. . . . Correctly done, it will also attract 'boys' and allow teenage readers to integrate themselves into the residual unpaid household labor that much of contemporary society still expects women to perform."[59]

This emphasis on satisfying male expectations served as a consistent link between ads targeted to girls and to women. Researchers and advertisers believed that girls' immediate goal of attracting boys could motivate a purchase. Drawing on the findings of psychologists such as Dr. Norma Werner, who researched American youth for the Leo Burnett ad agency, advertisers believed they had a vulnerable market into which they could tap. Werner, for example, claimed that "the main goal of teenage girls is marriage, a female's principal source of status in our society." She noted further that pressures about the paramount importance of physical allure, "coupled with the physiological turmoil of adolescence, makes teen-agers tremendously insecure." Advertisers also hoped that marriage and childbirth would quickly transform these girls into women, from good consumers into more reliably great ones. While they clearly sought to capture teenagers' dollars, which the Rand research company consistently estimated in the tens of billions, they also knew that with the emphasis on marriage, young women were starting to plan for it earlier. Journalists Charles and Bonnie Remsberg noted in their article "Wooing the 'Dimply, Pimply,' " "Some 800,000 will become engaged this year. . . . Before they reach 20 half our young women will become housewives, the darlings of the merchants, and more female financiers will have their first child at 19 than at any other age." Teenage girls then, while part of a distinct subculture, also bridged the gap between youth and adult, making them an ideal market to reach.[60]

To further their goals, *Seventeen* editors published several etiquette and fashion guides, including, in 1964, *The Seventeen Cookbook: With a Complete Guide to Teen Party-Giving*. The book squarely placed responsibility for all party-giving on girls, suggesting more than fifty reasons to cook for friends. Several of the reasons revolved around a girl's boyfriend, including, "Your parents want to meet your best beau. You make the dinner; he'll make a hit" and "Your beau is going to Europe. Give him an International Dinner with food from the countries he's going to visit."[61] Unlike more traditional cookbooks, the recipes encouraged girls to make dishes with frozen fruits and vegetables, cake mixes, and countless other convenience foods.

Food manufacturers also sought to market their products directly to teens in their schools. Home economics classrooms provided an ideal forum for companies looking to impress their brand into young minds. In this setting, a primary authority figure, the teacher, relied on brand-name products to operate classes. Teachers lent credence to advertisers' claims and served as walking advertisements for the products. In the case of canned milk, for example, in 1958 the Evaporated Milk Association responded to the growing evidence that they "had ignored an increasingly influential consumer: The teen-ager." They began targeting teenage girls in home economics classes, starting with the Atlanta, Georgia, area. Beyond the more subtle method of providing their products for cooking classes, suggesting recipes, and supplying lesson plans, the Association also developed a plan with Mary Brooks, director of home economics for the Fulton County high school system. Together they created a curriculum that included "career-guidance benefits," so that each student

> would be working in a special field: teaching, dietetics, advertising, etc. That work would provide a deeper insight into the career possibilities in the assigned field. . . . For example, some students would undertake a teaching project. Using evaporated milk as the subject, they would plan and conduct teaching sessions for their classmates, thus gaining experience in teaching.[62]

While others sought to capitalize on this environment, food companies were ideally positioned to situate their products in the kitchen cabinets of "tomorrow's housewives."

Seeking to solidify their position as the guide to teen girls and integrate themselves into the home economics magazine field, *Seventeen* magazine decided to produce a complementary publication for teachers; from 1965 to 1969, they published *Seventeen-at-School,* which aimed to carry "advertising into high school home economics classrooms." The four main foci included fashion and fabrics, beauty and grooming, home furnishings, and food and nutrition. Wonderfully self-referential, the lesson plans were directly tied to features in the magazines, so that in February 1967 the regular magazine featured an article, "February Is Give-a-Boy-a-Party Month," while in the home-ec version girls learned "How to Set: A Modern, Man-Pleasing Table." The "Key Teaching Aids" also featured exclusive relationships with advertisers such as Nabisco, French's, and the Rice Council, who promised recipe booklets to teachers, either free or for a nominal fee. The promotions were often playful and tailored to student interests, like the October 1967 program, "Classrooms in Your Community: Supermarkets Help Teens Become Super-Shoppers." Themed " 'Super-Shop-Opoly," and with "the cooperation of supermarkets throughout the country," they aimed to help "teens learn the basic rules of the shopping game," and, not incidentally, shape part of the $60 million spent in supermarkets. For that month's classroom bulletin board, they recommended a *Seventeen* article on "Mood Foods" and particular advertisements for Coca-Cola, Kellogg's, and Wonder Bread. The school magazine also promoted the viability of these young women pursuing home economics careers with a monthly feature called "Homemaking educators in business." Spotlighting women like "Sally Watters, Director of the Continental Baking Company's Home Economics Department," these lectures on women's careers lent legitimacy and purpose to the pursuit of recipes that would be nutritious, economical, and pleasing, and, as in the case of Watters, suggested that the fit between women and home economics was a natural one.[63]

Even in areas where food would seemingly not have an appeal, such as beauty pageants, food advertisers sought brand recognition. For example, in 1964, amid advertisements from the more typical categories of cars (Lincoln-Mercury and Ford) and soft-drinks (Dr. Pepper), teen-age girls found themselves targets of Armour Meat Products advertising. As cosponsors of the pagaent, the Armour company wanted "'to familiarize teens with the Armour name, logotype, and quality so that when they become primary purchasers they will know Armour.'" Beyond broad brand recognition, the company had a specific concern. Their research demonstrated that the teen market was ignoring hot dogs and reflected that, "'After childhood, teens trade hot dogs for pizza, especially on dates, and don't return to franks until after marriage. Armour hopes to counter this trend and steer teenagers back to frankfurters.'"[64]

The power of the teen market is evident, not only in the emphasis placed on marketing directly to teens, but also in the effort to persuade mothers about teen preferences. In assessing the market, Ernest Dichter cited a 1955 study by the Home Testing Institute, which found that adolescents had significant "influence on food purchasing." In addition to 11.7 percent of packaged baked goods, family members aged ten to nineteen requested 16.7 percent of cookie mixes, 11.2 percent of the peanut butter, and 11.6 per cent of the vegetable soup. He noted that these figures are a low indicator of the influence of these teenagers, given that they "refer only to family purchases, leaving out of consideration the items the youngsters buy for themselves." By 1988, a teen survey by TRU found that these numbers had skyrocketed, with girls twelve to nineteen significantly influencing food product purchases such as soup (34.1 percent), cheese (48.7 percent), and cereal (58.0 percent). A Rand poll that same year found that girls aged thirteen to nineteen influenced 80 percent of the food purchased for their homes.[65]

While advertisers yearned to tap into this burgeoning market, there were reservations almost from the beginning. In 1956, the Institute for Motivational Research cautioned advertisers that, while they might hope to plant brand-name seeds in adolescents' heads, teenagers tend to be skeptical and "full of distrusts, ready to reject a positive claim at the first hint that it is exaggerated." The Institute went so far as to claim that "of all age groups this one will show the least brand loyalty, be the least bound by tradition, be the least willing to respond to a mere name, however prestigeful it may be."[66] Researchers argued that advertisers had to decide how and when to advertise to this market because the very qualities that made the group appealing also made it a risky gamble.

As much as they wanted to tap into it, advertisers seemed leery of the teen market. In a 1958 speech, Donald B. Armstrong, Jr., vice president of the McCann-Erickson advertising agency, cautioned that reaching this teen market was extraordinarily difficult. He noted that "a 13-year-old is more different from a 19-year-old than a person of 30 is from one of 50." He also warned that while the desire to cultivate an early relationship was tempting, it could also backfire; "If your brand was his favorite in his early teens, it is very likely to be put away with other childish things."[67]

Moreover, advertisers faced hostility from teens who suspected their tactics. Taking on young critics in an open forum, the chairman of Cunningham and Walsh ad agency, John P. Cunningham, was confronted with questions about advertisers' undue influence on political campaigns, subliminal projection, and motivational research. In 1960, he noted in a speech that "These young people come into our office regarding us as hidden persuaders, manipulators of the human mind and something a little malevolent in the free enterprise system."[68]

Beyond the advertising and food industries, *American Druggist* also propounded a cautionary tale in June 1965, as they recounted the findings of a study for the Brand Names Foundation. In addition to challenging the notion that teens were acting independently, with their findings that mothers were still shaping girls' purchasing decisions, they also reported that "Most significant of the conclusions reached in the study is that the brands rejected by the teen on her road to maturity tend to be excluded from future use regardless of merit. In fact, use of a brand at an early age tends to prevent its use later."[69] While the article acknowledged that most other studies have indicated girls' trendsetter identity, they stuck by their findings and questioned the strategy of limiting advertising to teens. In 1970, William S. Robinson of Quaker Oats observed that "we don't regard children as miniature adults, but as giant mysteries."[70]

Ernest Dichter also offered suggestions for reaching the youth market, challenging advertisers to break through their own ideas, even suggesting that they consider an "LSD philosophy." Embodying the times, Dichter called on advertisers to express the "soul" of a product and use psychedelic colors. By 1976, however, some advertisers believed that they had won over teens on their own terms. Considering his own teenage children and the teen market generally, Pat McGrath of the ad agency Case & McGrath reflected that, while cynical, teens still were susceptible. Encouraging advertisers not to give up on the market, the executive editor of *Product Management*, Barbara P. Johnson, suggested that McGrath's optimistic view was representative of successful marketers who "feel teens have become more predictable and understandable than in the past decade, and that teens can be sold by relating product benefits to the teen life."[71]

This hopefulness was supported by research findings in a 1986 Rand Youth Poll research study for *Seventeen*. Rand discovered that 30 percent of girls aged thirteen to nineteen shopped for food occasionally and nearly two-thirds shopped quite a bit. Even more important than these numbers, however, was the disclosure by 72 percent of those teens that advertising played a "Very Important" role in influencing their purchasing decisions. Another 19 percent considered advertising reasonably important. With only 9 percent of respondents stating that advertising was "Not Important," the culture seemed to have moved far beyond the cynicism and distrust evident earlier. Indeed, the reflections on why advertising played such a significant role read like an advertiser's dream. In the context of the acquisition culture of the 1980s, consumers enthusiastically reported that advertising gave them "Prestige (You like to buy something you've heard about)," "Advertising makes you aware of products' qualities," "Advertising gives impression product must be good," and "Creates excitement about product."[72]

Food advertisers, in particular, took teenage girls seriously as consumers. While researchers and social critics in the 1980s debated whether men were doing work in the home, few thought to consider whether children were doing any work. Food advertisers did begin to target teens even more directly and heavily, including the efforts by Kraft to tailor food ads to girls twelve to nineteen and General Foods' recognition that "kids have more and more influence over food purchases."[73]

As with so many markets, researchers continually rediscovered teens, particularly as they "re"-realized that mothers with teens were working outside the home in substantial numbers. While poor women and African American women had long been in the paid labor force, and white, middle-class women joined them in growing numbers during and after World War II, it was not until the 1970s that researchers and advertisers began to reflect on who might be shopping and cooking while mother was at work.

In 1974, for example, *Ad Age* reported that "nearly half of all women 18 years and over are now holding jobs, and half of that number are married and have children." They found that "Nearly 80% of the girls whose mothers work shop personally in food stores." Incidentally, it was the same percentage of girls whose mothers stayed home, but the researchers were excited about the daughters of working mothers because they "tended to shop more often and spend more money." They drew a distinction between the two groups of girls, even though the difference was only about five percentage points. Researchers discovered that, while teenage girls used convenience foods when they made dinner (on average three nights a week), including frozen foods and boxed mixes, they liked to cook and bake from scratch as well. This meant that a range of foods advertisers considered teenage girls a viable and important market. Indeed, increasingly they began to target even younger girls, finding that in 1988 "Youngsters not yet in their teens are shopping and cooking for the family." To lure food advertisers to their television station, Nickelodeon conducted a study with *USA Today* and Yankelovich researchers, and determined that "23% of kids six to 15 cook their own dinner some of the time, and 6% most of the time."[74]

While advertisers rarely addressed race explicitly, researchers did occasionally include race in their analysis. However, their findings did not persudae advertisers to capitalize on the striking evidence. For example, a 1989 survey of teens found that "Black teens are more likely than white teens to be the family's primary grocery shopper," by a dramatic split of 19 percent versus the national average of 8 percent.[75] Even with more than twice as many black teens as white ones doing the primary shopping, advertisers preferred to keep their sights on white, teenage girls. Advertisers, then, continued to ignore evidence and held firm to their long-standing beliefs about black consumers.

Still, even as they sought to appeal to white girls, their understanding of young female consumers was tentative at best, and time did not help unravel the mystery. A 1984 *Wall Street Journal* article headlined "Teen-Age Girls, Alas, Are Big Consumers But Poor Customers" concluded, "They are too unpredictable and fickle to count on." Just a few years later, however, in an article about teen influence for *Food & Beverage Marketing*, Phyllis Fine noted that a survey by Donnelly Marketing disclosed that one of the strengths of teenage girls as consumers was their "Strong brand loyalty." This may be because, according to Betsy Richardson of Reebok, while children "are notoriously fickle consumers," they are "less so for food . . . than for fashion." Still, contradictory research findings did not deter food advertisers set on shaping girls' shopping patterns. They hoped to mold girls who had taken "on an increased share of family grocery shopping as more of their mothers have gone off to work."[76]

In keeping with their attitudes toward women, while advertisers grudgingly respected girls' economic power, their overall opinion of these young consumers was decidedly disdainful. Researchers, manufacturers, and advertisers seemed to resent the girls' shopping patterns, charging, "It's like mass hysteria." Ellen Plusker, an advertising expert on teen-age marketing for JWT in the 1980s, surmised, as Dichter did nearly thirty years earlier, that "the reason teen-age girls are so mercurial is that they have only a fragile sense of self-identity. 'They are still trying to figure out who they are.' " Advertisers, then, believed they could rarely be certain of what appeals might work with this group.[77]

There was one appeal, however, that researchers and advertisers believed always worked with teenage girls: sex. One market research director claimed about sex in the mid-1980s, "It's the only constant thing you can sell these kids on." Appeals to sexuality dated to the earliest decades of the century.[78] Wrapped in overt promises of fun, beauty, and success in pleasing boys were covert allusions to sex appeal.

While Michael Schudson argued that "advertisements did not become markedly more sexual as time went on," food ads did. Early food ads generally embodied innocent appeals that were suggestive but not explicit. Ads told girls that consuming a food product could make all the difference in their popularity and featured parties that teenage girls planned, prepared, and hosted. They focused on girls' insecurity that the party would be successful and that everything—especially the food—would be perfect. Ads portrayed food as the centerpiece of young people's gatherings and tried to persuade girls that the food they chose could make or break their parties. The ads encouraged social gatherings, but placed emphasis on individual relationships, suggesting parties as opportunities to spend time with "that new fellow you've been dying to know better!"[79]

By the 1960s, however, these subtle messages gave way to overt sexual claims. While generally not as provocative as those for jeans, perfume, and make-up, food ads were surprisingly explicit in suggesting that girls could attract boys by offering the right foods. Serving the right kind of sandwich or hot dog, they said, made girls sexy.[80] These explicit ads persisted as sexually suggestive advertising became even more common across categories.

With a range of methods, copywriters tried to lure teenagers to shopping market aisles and fast food counters. By the end of the century, the number of girls shopping for and preparing food was phenomenal. During the mid-1980s, for example, 13 million teenage girls spent about $30 billion a year on food; the vast majority of girls aged 13 to 19 did at least some grocery shopping. In 1994, researchers found that in an average month more than 27 percent of teens did major food shopping. More than immediate gains, advertisers wanted to ensure long-term profits, in terms of both brand loyalty and gender loyalty. Food advertisers wanted the supermarket experience to be an integral part of girls' development.[81]

Food advertisers in the late twentieth century also realized that boys were shopping for groceries, but generally did not target them with ads. Two 1989 teen studies even found that boys shopped for food more than girls, with one in June finding that "of the 35% of teens shopping one or more times a week, the boys are shopping 8% more than the girls." A Youth Market Alert study found that when asked, "How often do teens do the grocery shopping for the family?" 5 percent of the young men were the primary shopper "most of the time" and another 24 percent shopped "occasionally" for their families. While 11 percent of the girls reported doing the family shopping "most of the time" and another 29 percent did it "occasionally," meaning that girls shopped 40 percent compared to boys' 29 percent. Advertisers apparently ignored the fact that 29 percent of boys were shopping for their families.[82] In contrast, the minimal differences between girls whose mothers stayed at home versus mothers who worked created a minor furor in the industry, as advertisers sought to target the bigger-spending daughters of working mothers. Still, even with evidence of significant shopping by boys, advertisers did not give any indication that they intended to pursue young male consumers. To persuade women of these ideals and of the value of their food products, advertisers used children's health, education, and general well-being to make their arguments. The power of food to shape their children's lives was a powerful, consistent message.

Epilogue

At the start of the twenty-first century, about 80 percent of mothers of school-age children brought home a paycheck, including more than half of mothers with children under the age of one. Still, as he brainstormed for a new ad campaign in 1988, Alan Waxenberg, publisher of *Good Housekeeping*, predicted that women in the 1990s were going to be "realists," focused on the family and home. He decided on a campaign focused on women's embrace of family. The first ad of the campaign featured a woman who had quit her job and moved to the suburbs to spend more time with her daughter. She claimed of her decision, "There's a renewal, a reaffirmation of values, a return to quality and quality of life."[1]

Food advertisers across the century had difficulty contending with the complexity of women's roles, and American society in general. Instead of broadening their scope to include men, or approaching the diverse market of women with a better reflection of their lives, food advertisers focused narrowly on women's role as caregiver. By denying the reality of men's participation in caregiving and housework, and shortchanging women's experiences, not just as paid workers, but also as women who liked to eat, who were athletic, and liked to be cared for by others, food advertisers did more than try to sell their products. They sought to shape an understanding of gender that left women with sole responsibility for feeding men and children, and equated that duty with love, citizenship, and womanhood.

Instead of recognizing that women, across the economic spectrum and regardless of race or ethnicity, faced a double shift of work, advertisers sought to hold on to their images of women in their roles as wives and mothers. Even while continuing the trend toward more vague characterizations of family structure that began appearing in the 1970s, magazines and food advertisers created ads for the traditional paradigm of women responsible for shopping for food and cooking. Though magazines and advertisers acknowledged and even targeted single mothers and women who worked outside the home, they predicated their acceptance on women's embrace of traditional family values and the expectation that women's primary focus be caring for her family.

The evidence researchers brought forth might have challenged their thinking, as they unveiled facts like men shopping and cooking. Instead, lacking any institutional memory, the advertising industry greeted each consumer study as a new revelation. By ignoring the old studies and distrusting the new ones, food advertisers often failed to grasp the patterns of consumption that the numbers suggested. They generally did not focus on the markets or trends that, time and again, suggested themselves in the data. Discounting the opportunities these studies portended only further entrenched industry conservatism. The advertising industry, controlled as it was largely by elite, white men, also largely shielded itself from other perspectives as well.

African Americans, for example, have had an extraordinarily difficult time breaking into the advertising business. While there was a brief period in the late 1960s and early 1970s when black ad firms found some success, the industry remained largely segregated and impenetrable at the end of the century. While African Americans held 3.5 percent of the Ph.D.s awarded in physics, they comprised only 2.9 percent of advertising hires; it was a tougher field to crack than medicine, law, and financial services. Moreover, it was not just employment but representation that suffered. Even in 1997, when African Americans comprised 12 percent of the U.S. population and 11.3 percent of all magazine readers, studies found that they comprised only about 3 percent of the people shown in reviewed ads.[2]

While women did make frequent appearances in advertisements, their role within the ad agency power structure was also limited. Historian Kathy Peiss found that even with increases in the number of career women after 1910, women still made up only 3 percent of the professionals in 1930. She noted that "Women were generally excluded from positions that required face-to-face interaction with manufacturers' representatives." One successful ad woman recalled that when she began working at J. Walter Thompson in the 1950s, company executives perceived women to be so weak and different that they devoted an entire floor of the agency as a hospital wing to administer to women's ailments and limited women executives to the Women's Department, segregated from the rest of the agency. At the end of the century, advertisers still balked at fully integrating women into their corporate structure. One of the most successful women in advertising, Charlotte Beers, found her career stalled at JWT because the company "was loath to have women in top posts."[3]

Food marketers' conservatism and patriarchal attitudes underlie their decision to target women solely for the responsibility to care for the children and the men in their lives. Perhaps in the early 1900s, when advertising and convenience food manufacturing were both fledgling industries, it made sense to address this de facto division of labor. However, as women entered the workforce in even greater numbers, spurred on by wars and recessions, and particularly after the rights movements of the 1960s and 1970s, advertisers held fast to their patriarchal ideal. As women and men have discussed, bantered, and fought over these issues in their own homes, so too have advertisers talked about other options. Across the country, across class and race lines, the breakdown of household responsibilities remains largely entrenched, with women responsible for the vast majority of the housework (and child care)—even if that means finding someone else to do it. A 1990 Virginia Slims Opinion Poll found that 70 percent of women responded that the single most important factor in helping them balance work and home "would be getting more help with housework from their husbands." Instead of capitalizing on women's call to share shopping and cooking, advertisers have consistently re-affirmed traditional gender roles.[4]

A survey of the American newsstand at the start of the twenty-first century reveals almost no food ads in men's magazines or even in those read by both women and men. Instead, food marketers continue to advertise to women in magazines catering only to women. Whether banking on tried and true strategies or testing out new ideas, food advertisers rarely strayed from their consistent goal—to keep women as their consumers. Few have questioned advertisers' insistence that only women could buy and prepare foods, but hopefully this study will challenge advertisers and consumers to consider the division of labor in American homes and the billions of dollars spent over the last century to solidify that gender role paradigm.

Periodical and Archive Sources
and Abbreviations

Abbreviations used in the notes follow the titles.

Magazines and Periodicals

Advertising Age
Adweek
American
American Demographics
American Druggist
American Girl
American Heritage
American Quarterly
American Studies International
Annals of the American Academy of Political and Social Sciences
Annual Review of Psychology
Atlantic Monthly
Back Stage
Better Homes and Gardens (*BHG*)
Black Enterprise
Business and Society Review
Californian
Camera Obscura
Centennial Review
Chain Store Age / Supermarkets
Christian Herald
Collier's
Columbia Journalism Review
Consumer Response
Dollars & Sense
Delineator
Ebony
Editor and Publisher

Entertainment Weekly
Ethnic and Regional Foodways
Family Circle (FC)
Farm and Ranch
Farm Journal
Food & Beverage Marketing
Food & Foodways: History & Culture of Human Nourishment
Food Business
Food Processing
Food Review
Fortune
Gastronomica—The Journal of Food and Culture
Gender and Society
Good Housekeeping (GH)
GQ
Harvard Business Review
Journal of Advertising
Journal of Advertising Research
Journal of American Culture: Focus on American Food and Foodways
Journal of the American Dietitic Association
Journal of American History
Journal of Black Studies
Journal of Communication
Journal of Consumer Research
Journal of Current Issues and Research in Advertising
Journal of Marketing
Journal for MultiMedia History
Journal of Popular Culture
Journal of Popular Film and Television
Journal of Retailing
Journal of Social History
Journalism History
Journalism and Mass Communications Quarterly
JWT News
Kansas Farmer
Ladies' Home Journal (LHJ)
Life
Look
Maclean's
Mademoiselle
Madison Avenue
Management Review
Marketing & Media Decisions
Marketing/Communications
Marketing Magazine
Marketing News
McCall's
Media/Scope
Men's Health
Missouri Ruralist
Monthly Labor Review

Motivations: Monthly Psychological Research Reports for Business
National 4-H News
National Geographic
Nebraska Farmer
New American
New England Homestead
New Woman
New York Times Magazine (NYTM)
New Yorker
Newsweek
Non-Foods Merchandising
Packaging and Design
Parade
Parents
People
Printers' Ink
Printers' Ink Monthly
Product Management
Product Marketing
Progressive Grocer
Reader's Digest (RD)
Reason
Redbook
Register of the Kentucky Historical Society
Sales and Marketing Management
Sales Management
Saturday Evening Post (SEP)
Seventeen
Seventeen-at-School
Smithsonian
Soap Opera Digest
Sociological Review
Sunset
Tide
Time
TV/Radio Age
U.S. News & World Report
Weight Watchers
Woman's Day (WD)
Western Folklore
Women's Home Companion (WHC)
Women's Studies

Newspapers

Advertising Daily
Atlanta Journal and Constitution
Chicago Sun-Times
Christian Science Monitor
Cleveland Plain Dealer

Los Angeles Times
Miami Herald
New York Times (NYT)
Philadelphia Inquirer
Philadelphia Weekly
Salt Lake Tribune
San Antonio Express News
USA Today
Wall Street Journal (WSJ)
Washington Post

Archival Collections

Campbell's Soup Company Archive, Archives Center, National Museum of American History, Smithsonian Institution, Washington, D.C. (Campbell Archive, D.C.)

Campbell's Soup Company Archive, Camden, N.J. (Campbell Archive, Camden).

Curtis Publishing Company, Special Collections, Van Pelt Library, University of Pennsylvania, Philadelphia. (Curtis Collection)

D'Arcy Masius Benton & Bowles Archives, John W. Hartman Center for Sales, Advertising & Marketing History, Rare Book, Manuscript, and Special Collections Library, Duke University, Durham, N.C. (DMB Archives)

DuPont de Nemours & Company, Hagley Museum and Library, Wilmington, Del. (Hagley)

Institute for Motivational Research, Peekskill, N.Y. (IMR)

J. Walter Thompson Advertising Company Archives, John W. Hartman Center for Sales, Advertising & Marketing History, Rare Book, Manuscript, and Special Collections Library, Duke University, Durham, N.C. (JWT Archives)

JWT Archives, Rena Bartos Papers, John W. Hartman Center for Sales, Advertising & Marketing History, Rare Book, Manuscript, and Special Collections Library, Duke University, Durham, N.C. (Bartos Papers)

Museum of Television and Radio, New York, N.Y.

Nicole DiBona Peterson Collection of Advertising Cookbooks, John W. Hartman Center for Sales, Advertising & Marketing History, Rare Book, Manuscript, and Special Collections Library, Duke University, Durham, N.C. (Peterson Collection)

Warshaw Collection of Business Americana, Archives Center, National Museum of American History, Smithsonian Institution, Washington, D.C. (Warshaw Collection)

Notes

Introduction

1. See for example, Vincent Vinikas, *Soft Soap, Hard Sell: American Hygiene in an Age of Advertisement* (Ames: Iowa State University Press, 1992); Kathy Peiss, *Hope in a Hope in a Jar: The Making of America's Beauty Culture* (New York: Metropolitan Books, 1998).

2. Ralph Hower, *The History of an Advertising Agency: N. W. Ayer & Son at Work, 1869–1949* (Cambridge, Mass.: Harvard University Press, 1939), 369; *Advertising in Women's Publications* (Philadelphia: Curtis, 1927); "Billions in the Pantry," *Time*, 9 June 1958; Alden C. Manchester, "The Food Marketing Revolution, 1950–1990," U.S. Department of Agriculture, *Agriculture Information Bulletin* 627, August 1991, 1; Theresa Y. Sun and Jane E. Allshouse, "Dramatic Growth in Mass Media Food Advertising in the 1980's," *Food Review* 16, 3 (September-December 1993): 3; Juliann Sivulka, *Soap, Sex, and Cigarettes: A Cultural History of American Advertising* (Belmont, Calif.: Wadsworth, 1998).

3. Catherine Mackenzie, "Changing Tastes in Food: In a Survey of Trends in the National Appetite Experts Discover That While Poundage Varies Little the Choice Swings Widely," *NYT*, 10 November 1935, SM21; Vergil D. Reed, "The Consumer Market in the American Economy," paper delivered before the Northeast Region Graduates of the Ford Merchandising School, Harwich, Massachusetts, 19 September 1955, Box 12, RG11, 12–13, JWT Archives—Company Publications, 1955–1958 Collection; *JWT News* 11, 43, 22 October 1956, Box 6, JWT Archives—JWT News Collection; " 'Revolution in the Kitchen': What It Means to the Family and to Industry," *U.S. News & World Report*, 15 February 1957, 56–57; Allen H. Center, "What You Find When You Look Inside Homes of the 19,000,000 'New Rich,' " History-Consumer Purchase Panel, 1943–1958, Box 4, reprinted from *Sales Management*, 15 March 1943, 2, JWT Archives—Information Center Records Collection; "Market Study of Consumer Preferences," *Printers' Ink*, 21 October 1955, 60–64; "R. T. French Report," Box 2, 1968, JWT Archives—Information Center Records Collection; Eva Jacobs and Stephanie Shipp, "How Family Spending Has Changed in the U.S.," *Monthly Labor Review*, March 1990, 20–27; Daniel Horowitz, *The Morality of Spending: Attitudes Toward the Consumer Society in America, 1875–1940* (1985; Chicago: Ivan R. Dee, 1992); Karal Ann Marling, *As Seen on TV: The Visual Culture of Everyday Life in the 1950s* (Cambridge, Mass.: Harvard University Press, 1994), 220; Harvey Levenstein, *Revolution at the Table: The Transformation of the American Diet* (Berkeley:

University of California Press, 2003), 33–34; *JWT News* 13, 4, (27 January 1958), Box 7, JWT Archives—JWT News Collection; Stanley Lebergott, *Pursuing Happiness: American Consumers in the Twentieth Century* (Princeton, N.J.: Princeton University Press, 1993), 76–77. Lebergott finds that American per capita spending grew 83 percent from 1900 to 1990. USDA researcher Alden C. Manchester found in 1991 that "The share of food expenditures away from home rose from 25 percent in 1954 to 46 percent in 1990" ("The Food Marketing Revolution, 1950–1990," 2). Daniel Horowitz found that "The greatest increases in expenditures—items for which spending more than doubled between 1939 and 1945–were for food, alcoholic beverages, women's clothing." He also pointed to one unanticipated outcome of rationing. Ironically, he noted, "because of the nature of the rationing program, lower income groups had to purchase more expensive food items such as fresh fish and vegetables." Horowitz, *The Anxieties of Affluence: Critiques of American Consumer Culture, 1939–1979* (Amherst: University of Massachusetts Press, 2004), 35.

4. *LHJ*, "Whatever Happened to Mealtime?" 1979, Hagley; Henry R. Bernstein, "Families Still Eat Together—'*LHJ*' Survey," *Advertising Age*, 21 May 1979, 52; Conde Nast survey in "But, the Family That Eats Together . . . ," *Consumer Briefs* 1 (2nd Quarter 1987), Domestic—Other, JWT Archives—JWT News Collection; Laura Shapiro, "Mmm, Mmm, Good," *Newsweek*, 25 September 1995.

5. Harvey Levenstein notes that "In 1960 Americans had spent twenty-six cents of every food dollar away from home; by 1981 thirty-eight cents of every dollar escaped the grocery trades." *Paradox of Plenty: A Social History of Eating in Modern America* (New York: Oxford University Press, 1993), 236.

6. Samantha Barbas, "Just like Home: 'Home Cooking' and the Domestication of the American Restaurant," *Gastronomica—The Journal of Food and Culture* 2, 4 (Fall 2002): 44.

7. Maureen Weiner Greenwald, "Mealtime over Time: Food Consumption and the Demographic Revolution in American Women's Lives, 1950–90," paper presented at the annual meeting of the Organization for American Historians, April 1994, 15–17.

8. Canned Food Alliance, " 'Suzy Homemaker' Still Alive and Well," 1998, in author's possession.

9. *LHJ*, January 1935, 29; *SEP*, 21 October 1950, inside cover; *LHJ*, July 1971, 105; *GH*, September 1971, 49.

10. Levenstein, *Paradox of Plenty*, 30–31; *LHJ*, August 1937, 35; *FC*, November 1972; *People*, 28 October 1996; *People*, 7 September 1998.

11. Jackson Lears, *Fables of Abundance: A Cultural History of Advertising in America* (New York: Basic Books, 1994); Stephen Fox, *The Mirror Makers: A History of American Advertising and Its Creators* (New York: William Morrow, 1984). Lears argued that advertisers' power in creating "knowledge" was considerable. He claimed that "rarely had the category of 'knowledge' been so obviously constructed by particular social groups with particular ideological agendas" as was the case with the elite white, Anglo-Saxon Protestant ad makers of the early twentieth century (220–21). Stephen Fox, while acknowledging its early power, argued in *The Mirror Makers* that by the 1920s advertising functioned more as a mirror than as a shaping force (272). While Fox's conclusions are generally true, his findings are not accurate with regard to food ads, particularly with regard to gender roles. He did not believe that advertisers had any "malevolent purpose" and blithely accepted that they were "an especially visible manifestation, good and bad, of the American way of life" (330). It is naïve, however, to

believe that advertisers spent billions of dollars and did not try to shape American life. Their promotion of consumerism, while not necessarily "malevolent," was a clear influence on society. Moreover, food advertising promoted strict gender roles that helped shape their consumer base and encouraged women's subservient roles. Historian David Potter more accurately captured the essence of twentieth-century food advertising when he observed that, "Advertising now compares with such long-standing institutions as the school and the church in magnitude of its social influence. It dominates the media, it has vast power in the shaping of popular standards, and it is really one of the very limited group of institutions which exercise social control" (*People of Plenty: Economic Abundance and the American Character* [Chicago: University of Chicago Press, 1954], 167). See also, Richard Ohmann, *Selling Culture: Magazines, Markets, and Class at the Turn of the Century* (London and New York: Verso, 1996), 116. This is not to say that advertisements did not have any connection to reality, but that they were, as advertising critic Erving Goffman asserted, "highly manipulated representations of recognizable scenes from 'real life'." Quoted in Judith Waters and George Ellis, "The Selling of Gender Identity," in *Advertising and Culture: Theoretical Perspectives*, ed. Mary Cross (Westport, Conn.: Praeger, 1996), 94–100.

12. Horowitz, *The Anxieties of Affluence*, 91, 109.

13. In particular, see Joanne Meyerowitz, "Beyond the Feminine Mystique: A Reassessment of Postwar Mass Culture, 1946–1958," in *Not June Cleaver: Women and Gender in Postwar America, 1945–1960*, ed. Joanne Meyerowitz (Philadelphia: Temple University Press, 1994).

14. J. A. C. Brown, *Techniques of Persuasion: From Propaganda to Brainwashing* (1963; Baltimore: Penguin, 1969), 178–80.

15. Batya Weinbaum and Amy Bridges, "The Other Side of the Paycheck," in *Capitalist Patriarchy and the Case for Socialist Feminism*, ed. Zillah R. Eisenstein (New York: Monthly Review Press, 1979). Nancy Walker described the ways advice to women about food was "deeply implicated in larger mid-century issues." This was true throughout the century, as well, as food preparation shaped women's centrality in their family's lives. *Shaping Our Mother's World* (Jackson: University Press of Mississippi, 2000), 177, 217.

16. Levenstein, *Paradox of Plenty*, 26–27.

17. Frederick quoted in Barbara B. Stern, "Literary Criticism and Consumer Research: Overview and Illustrative Analysis," *Journal of Consumer Research* 16, 3 (December 1989): 328; Levenstein, *Paradox of Plenty*, 18, 32. See also Janice Williams Rutherford, *Selling Mrs. Consumer: Christine Frederick & the Rise of Household Efficiency* (Athens: University of Georgia Press, 2003).

18. I examined four issues a year of *LHJ* (March, June, September, December), starting in 1902 and continuing every third year, ending with 1998. It also included dozens of issues outside the sample. See for example, Fox, *The Mirror Makers*, 173; Levenstein, *Paradox of Plenty*, 18, 210, 314 n 24. According to Levenstein, by the mid-1930s food was the largest advertiser in mass circulation magazines. Cigarettes, automobiles, and health and beauty products rounded out the top four for much of the century. *LHJ* had broad appeal across the country, in rural and urban markets. Its dominance was tempered somewhat as the century wore on, but it remained in the top ten of ad-revenue performers in 1989 and was still one of the most successful women's magazines heading into the twenty-first century.

19. "Summary of Magazine Advertising for April," *Printers' Ink*, April 1931, 139–40, 142 in Vinikas, *Soft Soap, Hard Sell*, 14–16; Ohmann, *Selling Culture*, 87–89;

LHJ, December 1959, 139; "Magazine Advertising and the Housewife: A Summary Statement," based on a memorandum prepared for the J. Walter Thompson Company, Chicago, by Social Research, Inc., October 1957, Vertical Files, Memorandum, 1955–1961, Box 1, JWT Archives—Information Center Records Collection. The J. Walter Thompson Company discovered that "women spend most of the money which turned the wheels of business, and that they could best be reached by magazines" (Vertical Files, Case Studies, Kohl, Howard, 1955–1961, Box 1, JWT Archives—Information Center Records Collection).

20. Jennifer Scanlon, *Inarticulate Longings: The Ladies' Home Journal, Gender, and the Promises of Consumer Culture* (New York: Routledge, 1995), 172, 199–200; Douglas B. Ward, "The Reader as Consumer: Curtis Publishing Company and Its Audience, 1910–1930, *Journalism History,* 22, 2 (Summer 1996): 47–48. As an example of JWT's early prowess, from 1910 to 1924 they did not launch on the market any product that failed (Scanlon, 200).

21. Betty Friedan, *The Feminine Mystique* (New York: Dell, 1963); Fox, *The Mirror Makers,* 183–86, 296; Ernest Dichter, *The Strategy of Desire* (Garden City, N.Y.: Doubleday, 1960); Rutherford, *Selling Mrs. Consumer,* 124; Daniel Horowitz, *Vance Packard and American Social Criticism* (Chapel Hill: University of North Carolina Press, 1994), 105–8, 181; Daniel Horowitz, "The Émigré as Celebrant of American Consumer Culture: George Katona and Ernest Dichter," in *Getting and Spending: European and American Consumer Societies in the Twentieth Century,* ed. Susan Strasser, Charles McGovern, and Matthias Judt, Publications of the German Historical Institute (Washington, D.C.: German Historical Institute and New York: Cambridge University Press, 1998); Jack Hitt, "Does the Smell of Coffee Brewing Remind You of Your Mother," *New York Times Magazine,* 7 May 2000, 71–74; Susan Strasser, *Satisfaction Guaranteed: The Making of the American Mass Market* (New York: Pantheon, 1989); Gerhart D. Wiebe, "A Briefing for Businessmen on Motivational Research," *Printers' Ink,* 17 September 1954, 33–34; "Ad Men View MR [Motivation Research]," *Printers' Ink,* 24 September 1954, 23–24; "Tide Panelists Evaluate MR," *Tide,* 11 July 1958, 49–50; Brown, *Techniques of Persuasion,* 176. Getting its start in the late 1930s, motivational research took off in the mid-1950s, and by 1963 was used "by more than two thirds of America's hundred largest advertisers." James Wands Riley, "Depth-Advertising," *Printers' Ink,* 22 September 1938, 11–13, 88–89. Ernest Dichter's work on motivational research led him to form several different companies, including the Institute for Research in Mass Motivations, the Institute for Motivational Research, and Motivations, Inc. Dichter's biographer, Daniel Horowitz, points to the financial success Dichter enjoyed for his work, noting that "In the late 1950s and early 1960s, Dichter's operation earned about $1 million in annual revenues, equal roughly to $6.5 million in 2004 dollars" (*Anxieties of Affluence,* 59). He also states explicitly what is evident in Dichter's case files, that "Throughout his career, Dichter had paid minimal attention to African Americans, focusing instead on the groups his clients targeted: white, mostly suburban, middle-class Americans" (63).

22. Leila J. Rupp, *Mobilizing Women for War: German and American Propaganda, 1939–1945* (Princeton, N.J.: Princeton University Press, 1978); Maureen Honey, *Creating Rosie the Riveter: Class, Gender, and Propaganda During World War II* (Amherst: University of Massachusetts Press, 1984); Jeffrey Steele, "Reduced to Images: American Indians in Nineteenth-Century Advertising" and Anne McClintock, "Soft-Soaping Empire: Commodity Racism and Imperial Advertising," both in *The Gender and Consumer Culture Reader,* ed. Jennifer Scanlon (New York: New York University Press, 2000).

23. *LHJ,* June 1921, 27; *Ebony,* April 2000, 51.

24. Thorstein Veblen, *The Theory of the Leisure Class: An Economic Study of Institutions* (1899; New York: Modern Library, 1934).

25. *Life,* 15 May 1970, 67.

Chapter 1. Advertisers and Their Paradigm: Women as Consumers

1. Pamela Walker Laird, *Advertising Progress: American Business and the Rise of Consumer Marketing* (Baltimore: Johns Hopkins University Press, 1998), 370. While researchers have critiqued the race, gender, and class of advertisers, largely left out of their analysis has been advertisers' sexual orientation. Stuart Elliott, "Advertising," *New York Times,* 30 June 1997, D12; Stuart Elliott, "Advertising," *New York Times,* 26 June 2000, C16.

2. Nancy Walker, *Shaping Our Mothers' World: American Women's Magazines* (Jackson: University Press of Mississippi, 2000), 37; Helen Damon-Moore, *Magazines for the Millions: Gender and Commerce in the* Ladies' Home Journal *and the* Saturday Evening Post, *1880–1910* (Albany: State University of New York Press, 1994); Douglas B. Ward, "The Reader as Consumer: Curtis Publishing Company and its Audience, 1910–1930," *Journalism History* 22, 2 (Summer 1996): 47–53.

3. Ward, "The Reader as Consumer," 52–53.

4. William B. Faber, "National Advertising Drive in Newspapers Is Based on Localized Appeals," *Printers' Ink,* 15 December 1938, 21–22; Robert E. Weems, Jr., *Desegregating the Dollar: African American Consumerism in the Twentieth Century* (New York: New York University Press, 1998), 26; Ronald Aslop, "Firms Still Struggle to Devise Best Approach to Black Buyers," *Wall Street Journal,* 25 October 1984, 1.

5. "Magazine Coverage of Native White Families," 19 January 1933, Reel 39, JWT Archives—Microfilm Collection; "Frequency of Visiting a Grocery Store," February 1941, JWT Archives.

6. The rural, farm market tried to persuade the industry that it deserved advertising dollars, but early twentieth-century advertisers focused their efforts on attracting urban women; as the century wore on, suburban markets grew increasingly significant.

7. "Men Are the Buyers," *Printers' Ink,* 25 November 1908, 2.

8. Albert Leffingwell, "The Practical Appeal in Advertising to Men," *JWT News,* adapted from *Printers' Ink,* January 1922, 14–17, JWT Archives—JWT News Collection; Kenon Breazeale, "In Spite of Women: *Esquire* Magazine and the Construction of the Male Consumer," *Signs* 20, 1 (Autumn 1994): 1–22; Susan Strasser, *Never Done: A History of American Housework* (New York: Pantheon Books, 1982), 242–62.

9. Jackson Lears, *Fables of Abundance: A Cultural History of Advertising in America* (New York: Basic Books, 1994), 209; Lears, "Some Version of Fantasy," in *Prospects: The Annual of American Cultural Studies* 9 (1984), 349–406.

10. Frances Maule, "The 'Woman Appeal'," *JWT News,* January 1924, 1–8, JWT Archives—JWT News Collection, 1–8; "I Spend Half My Life in the Kitchen," *J. Walter Thompson Newsletter,* January 1925, 9–14, JWT Archives—JWT News Collection.

11. Ibid.; "And They Say Women Don't Reason," *Printers' Ink,* 6 August 1925, 10–12; Bertha K. Landes, "A Woman—On Women," *Printers' Ink,* 7 July 1927, 156–60; H. C. North, "Advertising Technical Facts to Women, *Printers' Ink,* 14 July, 1927, 145–48.

12. Michael Schudson, *Advertising, the Uneasy Persuasion: Its Dubious Impact on American Society* (New York: Basic Books, 1984), 60–61.

13. Charles R. Wiers, "Handling of Inquiries from Women," *Printers' Ink*, 7 December 1911, 57–58. Belief in female intuition did not ever pass out of favor. Even at the end of the century, the belief that women and men were essentially different persisted in advertising. Even as late as 1997, Lori Moskowitz Lepler became president of the newly created Intuition Group, formed to concentrate on marketing to women. Mercedes M. Cardona, "Moskowitz Lepler Brings Women's Intuition to Ads," *Advertising Age* 68, 47, 24 November 1997, 36.

14. Marian Hertha Clarke, "A Little Light on that Dark Subject—Woman: Some of the Guide Posts Along the Road to Woman's Buying Instincts," *Printers' Ink*, 18 November 1926, 97–98, 100; Landes, "A Woman—On Women." See also Granville Toogood, "To the Ladies: The New Note in Advertising to Women," *Printers' Ink*, 15 December 1932, 27; Gilbert Burck, "What Makes Women Buy?" *Fortune*, August 1956, 94.

15. Tom Masson, "Advertising as a Buyer Views It," *Printers' Ink Monthly*, January 1928, 36–37, 97; Louis E. Bisch, "Psychiatry and Advertising: Why Copy Should Appeal to Human Emotions," *Printers' Ink*, 6 January 1938, 11–13, 72–77.

16. "The Wife as a Buyer," *Printers' Ink*, 21 September 1916, 33–35; "Women in Advertising," *Printers' Ink*, 19 September 1918, 8–9. Home economics maven Christine Frederick argued that women bought "87 per cent of raw and market foods," and suggested that "the only things men buy alone are 36 per cent of the newspapers, 24 per cent of the phonographs, and 20 per cent of the gas fixtures!" "Teach Women What Advertising Does," *Printers' Ink*, 10 June 1920, 177–81.

17. "The Wife as a Buyer," 26; Stuart Ewen, *Captains of Consciousness: Advertising and the Social Roots of the Consumer Culture* (New York: McGraw-Hill, 1976), 167; Jennifer Scanlon, *Inarticulate Longings: The* Ladies' Home Journal, *Gender, and the Promises of Consumer Culture* (New York: Routledge, 1995), 171; Anna E. Richardson, "The Woman Administrator in the Modern Home," *Annals of the American Academy of Political and Social Sciences* 143 (May 1929): 21–32; Benjamin R. Andrews, "The Home Woman as Buyer and Controller of Consumption," *Annals of the American Academy of Political and Social Sciences* 143 (May 1929): 48.

18. Louise Rice, "Page the Foodstuff Copy Writer," *Printers' Ink*, 20 May 1926, 185–90; Janet Paige, "'Mmm! That Smells Good!' vs. 'What a Fragrant Aroma!'" *Printers' Ink*, 29 July 1926, 41–44.

19. Clara Brown Lyman, "Advertisers Should Heed Signs of Times," *Printers' Ink*, 1 September 1938, 11–14; Upton Sinclair, *The Jungle* (1906; New York: New American Library, 1990).

20. Mabel Crews Ringland, "On Really Knowing the Consumer," *Printers' Ink*, 16 September 1937, 6–8, 100–106.

21. Ibid.; Clara Brown Lyman, "Women's Fight for Truth Now Brings Opportunity to the Advertiser," *Printers' Ink*, 5 January 1939, 64–66; "Consumer Has Her Day," *Printers' Ink*, 9 February 1939, 92–94; "Why Libby Made Its Labels Descriptive," *Printers' Ink*, 19 August 1937, 14–16, 86–90; Stephen Vaughn, "Morality and Entertainment: The Origins of the Motion Picture Production Code," *Journal of American History* 77, 1 (June 1990): 39–65.

22. Ringland, "On Really Knowing the Consumer," 6–7.

23. Margaret Dana, "Fear the Facts and Fool the Women," *Atlantic Monthly* (April 1936): 400.

24. Ibid.; Mabel Crews Ringland, "On Knowing the Consumer," *Printers' Ink*, 23

September 1937, 63–68; Mrs. Bert W. Henderson, "Mrs. Consumer," *Printers' Ink*, 16 June 1938, 65–68.

25. Ibid.; Albert E. Hasse, "Campbell Soup Advertising Program Expands," *Printers' Ink*, 17 December 1925, 10–12; Ringland, "On Really Knowing the Consumer." According to J. A. C. Brown's assessment of "Advertising and Industry," "Thus it is claimed that advertising cheapens goods by increasing the sale of an article which in turn lowers prices. . . . In fact, advertising may either raise or reduce prices." *Techniques of Persuasion: From Propaganda to Brainwashing* (1963; Baltimore: Penguin, 1969), 171.

26. C. B. Larrabee, "Consumer Groups Gain as Advertisers Beat Bushes for Witches," *Printers' Ink*, 24 November 1939, 11–12, 68–73; Alice Davis, "Friendly Consumers," *Printers' Ink*, 1 March 1940, 50–51; D. E. Robinson, "Advertisers Warned Against Flouting or Fighting Consumer Movement," *Printers' Ink*, 21 June 1940, 15–18.

27. L. D. H. Weld, "$5 Million Campaign Suggested to Educate Public About Advertising," *Printers' Ink*, 18 July 1941.

28. Henry Dorff, "The Woman's Market After the War," *Printers' Ink*, 17 December 1943, 20–21; Maureen Honey, *Creating Rosie the Riveter: Class, Gender, and Propaganda During World War II* (Amherst: University of Massachusetts Press, 1984).

29. Dorff, "The Woman's Market."

30. Ibid.; "Let Them Eat Cake!" *Printers' Ink*, 19 February 1943, 24, 28, 30; Burck, "What Makes Women Buy?" 93–94, 173–76, 179; Ernest Dichter, "Today's Woman as a Consumer," *Motivations: Monthly Psychological Research Reports for Business* (September 1956): 1–3, Institute for Motivational Research (IMR), Peekskill, New York.

31. Burck, "What Makes Women Buy?" 93–94, 173–76, 179.

32. Ibid., 173; Dichter, "Today's Woman as a Consumer," 1. Of course, these observations did not necessarily reflect the reality of women's lives. For example, Jennifer Scanlon noted that it was in the 1910s and 1920s that "the term 'superwoman' was coined to describe a woman who could juggle her overwhelming slate of commitments while concealing her exhaustion," in Samantha Barbas, "Just like Home: 'Home Cooking' and the Domestication of the American Restaurant," *Gastronomica–The Journal of Food and Culture*" 2, 4 (Fall 2002): 46.

33. Burck, "What Makes Women Buy?" 173.

34. Dichter, "Today's Woman as a Consumer," 1. Janice Williams Rutherford notes that Christine Frederick also laid out these categories in her book, *Selling Mrs. Consumer*, published in 1929. *Selling Mrs. Consumer: Christine Frederick & the Rise of Household Efficiency* (Athens: University of Georgia Press, 2003), 187.

35. Richard Pollay, *The Distorted Mirror: Reflections on the Unintended Consequences of Advertising* (Vancouver: History of Advertising Archives, University of British Columbia, 1984), 25. For example, even though Ernest Dichter observed that husbands and wives were forming democratic partnerships, with women taking on tasks previously considered " 'unladylike' " and, significantly, noting that "men do much more housework than ever before and are involved in discussions concerning food . . . formerly the privileged territories of women," he maintained his sole focus on women as consumers of food. "What Can Make People Buy in 1957?" *Sales Management*, 10 November 1956, 59, 64.

36. Harvey Levenstein, *Paradox of Plenty: A Social History of Eating in Modern America* (New York: Oxford University Press, 1993), 132–33.

37. *JWT News* 3, 20, 17 May 1948, 2, JWT Archives—JWT News Collection.

38. "Revolution in the Kitchen: What It Means to the Family and to Industry," *U.S. News & World Report*, 15 February 1957, 56, 63.

39. 11 August 1958 Memo, Stouffer's Corporate 1958–1959 Minutes, Box 31, JWT Archives—JWT Review Board Collection.

40. Brown, *Techniques of Persuasion*, 190; Alvin Shuster, "Consumers Held Led by Emotions," *New York Times*, 30 June 1961, 10. A 1964 industry response to a report by the President's National Commission on Food Marketing continued the scathing and dismissive tone of earlier consumer efforts. Connecting it to a history of "socialist doctrine," it charged that the report purported: "That private enterprise is the enemy of the people and must be curbed by politicians." W. Howard Chase, "How Can the Food Industry Answer That Damning Report?" *Printers' Ink*, 22 June 1964, 23–24, 26, 29.

41. John Crichton, "Consumer Protection: Do Women Want It?" *Printers' Ink*, 8 July 1966, 29–32.

42. *Progressive Grocer*, December 1969, 4; M. Venkatesan and Jean Losco, "Women in Magazine Ads: 1959–1971," *Journal of Advertising Research* 15, 5 (October 1975): 49–54.

43. Tina Grace Lichtenstein, "Feminists Demand 'Liberation' in *Ladies' Home Journal* Sit In," *New York Times*, 19 March 1970, 51; Mary D. O'Gorman, "Background Research for a Presentation on *The New American*," 27 March 1972, 19, 38, File 4/6, Box 20, JWT Archives—JWT Consumer Pamphlets Collection; Ellen Graham, "Advertisers Take Aim at a Neglected Market: The Working Woman," *Wall Street Journal*, 5 July 1977, 1A; Marilyn Hoffman, "Woman Buyers Gain New Clout," *Christian Science Monitor*, 16 January 1980, 15; Rena Bartos, "Beyond the Cookie Cutters," *Marketing & Media Decisions* (November 1981), JWT Archives—JWT Rena Bartos Collection; "America's New Elite: A Big-Spending Market Is Born: Two-Career Couples," *Time*, 21 August 1978, 56–57; Martha Smilgis, "Here Come the DINKs: Double-Income, No-Kids Couples Are the Latest Subset," *Time*, 20 April 1987, 75; Tina Santi, "The New Woman Is Here; How Do You Market to Her?" *Advertising Age*, 18 June 1979, 61.

44. "Consumer Watch," *Progressive Grocer*, August 1980, 31; Ralph Leezenbaum, "The New American Woman . . . and Marketing," *Marketing/Communication*, July 1970, 24. David Smallwood argued that black "Women in general spend more time and money on shopping trips than men, have less brand loyalty, plan shopping in advance more often and emphasize economy more than men." "A Case for Marketing to Black Women," *Dollars & Sense*, 9 August 1983, 120, Markets-Consumer—Ethnic-Black, Box 22, JWT Archives—JWT Marketing Vertical Files Collection.

45. Bernice Kanner, "Shop's Theory: It Takes a Woman to Sell One," *Advertising Age*, 21 July 1980, 68.

46. Carol Caldwell, "You Haven't Come a Long Way, Baby," *New York Times*, 10 June 1977, 58, Box 2, JWT Archives—Rena Bartos Collection.

47. Ibid.

48. Kanner, "Shop's Theory," 67–68; Mary Bralove, "Advertising World's Portrayal of Women Is Starting to Shift," *Wall Street Journal*, 18 October 1982. Joan Rothberg, executive vice-president, general manager of Ted Bates Advertising, acknowledged that "A high percentage of advertising has changed very little." Lori Kesler, "Behind the Wheel of a Quiet Revolution," *Advertising Age*, 26 July 1982, M-13. Reporter Bill Abrams found that television advertising also lagged behind, noting "many commercials seem little changed from 10 or 20 years ago." Bill Abrams, "TV Ads, Shows Struggle to Replace Bygone Images of Today's Mothers," *Wall Street Journal*, 5 October 1984, 35, 53.

49. Leezenbaum, "The New American Woman," 24.

50. Caldwell, "You Haven't Come a Long Way, Baby," 57–58. The campaign featured female flight attendants with broad smiles encouraging consumers to "Fly Me."

51. Leezenbaum, "The New American Woman," 24.

52. Caldwell, "You Haven't Come a Long Way, Baby," 62; Barbara Solomon, "The '90s Woman Makes Strides down Madison Avenue," *Management Review* 8, 3 (March 1992): 15. Lawrence Soley and Gary Kurzbard "found that some stereotypical female portrayals (e.g., overt sex-object roles) may actually have increased," in John B. Ford and Michael S. LaTour, "Differing Reaction to Female Role Portrayals in Advertising," *Journal of Advertising Research* (September/October 1993): 43–52. See also Lawrence Soley and Gary Kurzbard, "Sex in Advertising: A Comparison of 1964 and 1984 Magazine Advertisements," *Journal of Advertising* 15, 3 (1986): 46–64.

53. Betty Friedan, *The Feminine Mystique* (New York: Dell, 1963); Kesler, "Behind the Wheel of a Quiet Revolution," M-12; Irene Park, "Marketing Alternatives to Women," *Food & Beverage Marketing*, June 1987, 20.

54. *FC*, 13 December 1977, Box 15, JWT Archives—JWT Competitive Advertisements Collection. Erving Goffman's landmark study of advertisements was a significant force in shaping societal awareness of subtle tactics of the advertisers. *Gender Advertisements* (New York: Harper and Row, 1976).

55. Barbara Lippert, "You've Come a Short Way, Baby," *Adweek*, 15 March 1993, 21; Martha T. Moore, "Same Old Script? Critics: Sexism Still Thrives in Ads," *USA Today*, 22 March 1993; Ford and LaTour, "Differing Reaction to Female Role Portrayals"; Soley and Kurzbard, "Sex in Advertising," 54; Lynn J. Jaffe and Paul D. Berger, "The Effect of Modern Female Sex Role Portrayal on Advertising Effectiveness," *Journal of Advertising Research* 34, 4 (July/August 1994): 32–47; Sally Goll Beatty, "Women Dislike Their Reflection in Ads," *Wall Street Journal*, 19 December 1995; Solomon, "The '90s Woman Makes Strides," 15. Solomon, citing a lawsuit against the Stroh Brewing Company, further argued that advertisers may be forced to be more sensitive to women because of the potential connection between sexist advertising, more serious offenses within the company, and sexual harassment lawsuits.

56. Cyndee Miller, "Publisher Says Sexy Ads Are OK, But Sexist Ones Will Sink Sales," *Marketing News*, 23 November 1992, 8; Bob Garfield, "Chauvinist Pigskin: Super Bowl Advertisers Set the World Back 30 Years with Naked Appeals to Guys," *Advertising Age*, 1 February 1999.

57. Ford and LaTour, "Differing Reaction to Female Role Portrayals"; Jaffe, "The Effect of Modern Female Sex Role," 33–34.

Chapter 2. Love, Fear, and Freedom: Selling Traditional Gender Roles

1. James Wallen, "Emotion in Advertising Copy," *Printers' Ink*, 29 July 1920, 34; W. Livingston Larned, "Where Does Sentiment Belong in Advertising," *Printers' Ink*, 8 January 1920, 185–93; Edith Lewis, "The Emotional Quality in Advertisements," *J. Walter Thompson New Bulletin*, April 1923, 2, Box 1, JWT Archives—JWT News Collection; "Why the Shopper Buys (or Doesn't): Expert Says It's a Matter of Emotions," *NYT*, 13 June 1955, 31; June Owen, "Food Store Starts Riots in a Psyche," *NYT*, 9 November 1957, 34. As William Leach observed, "Women had to learn how to read through enticements and to assess the 'authenticity' of claims . . . the demands of 'spending money' and providing love were inextricably

intermingled in one place." *Land of Desire: Merchants, Power, and the Rise of a New American Culture* (New York: Vintage Books, 1993), 148. While not specifically focused on food, Bonnie Fox found that the theme of housework as a "labor of love" peaked between 1939 and 1940 when it reached 21 percent of advertising messages. In the other ads she studied between 1909 and 1980, the theme of love appeared between four and 14 percent of the time. Bonnie F. Fox, "Selling the Mechanized Household: 70 Years of Ads in *Ladies Home Journal*," *Gender & Society* 4, 1 (March 1990): 29.

2. Stephen Fox, *The Mirror Makers: A History of American Advertising and Its Creators* (New York: William Morrow, 1984), 84–85; Janice Williams Rutherford, *Selling Mrs. Consumer: Christine Frederick and the Rise of Household Efficiency* (Athens: University of Georgia Press, 2003), 124.

3. Ernest Dichter, *Motivations: Monthly Psychological Research Reports for Business* 2, 1 (March 1957), 3 (IMR).

4. Ernest Dichter, "Frosted Foods Need Emotional Defrosting," paper presented to Eastern Frosted Foods Association Meeting, 12 December 1962, 3, 8, IMR.

5. *LHJ*, June 1911, 32; *LHJ*, July 1947, 170; *LHJ*, January 1957, 21. Magazine and gender analyst Ellen Gruber Garvey argued that stories and advertisements drew the same parallels between women choosing between suitors and shopping wisely for products. *The Adman in the Parlor: Magazines and the Gendering of Consumer Culture, 1880s to 1910s* (New York: Oxford University Press, 1996), 157–65. Historian Susan Strasser argued that "By the 1930s . . . the most fundamental message of consumerism [was]: money *can* buy love." *Never Done: A History of American Housework* (New York: Pantheon, 1982, 253.

6. *LHJ*, September 1959, 37; *Parent's*, March 1960, Box 12.10, JWT Archives—Competitive Advertisements Collection; *Sunset*, November/December 1963, Box 8.1, JWT Archives—Competitive Advertisements Collection; *True Story*, November 1964, Standard Brands, Box 12, JWT Archives—Domestic Advertisements Collection.

7. *RD*, October 1968, 222D3; *Look*, 10 December 1968, M9; *LHJ*, July 1971, 120; *FC*, January 1971, 88. This Food Council ad was unusual because it featured a rare depiction of an African American family.

8. *King's Page*, December 1976, 4–5, Burger King, 1987, Box 1, JWT Archives—Domestic Advertisements Collection.

9. James Helmer, "Love on a Bun: How McDonald's Won the Burger Wars," *Journal of Popular Culture* 26 (Fall 1992): 85–95. The Nabisco Company for SnackWell's cookies also adopted this approach in the late 1990s. The senior business director for the product line, Terry Preskar, explained to a reporter for the *New York Times*, "Women don't necessarily just want a transaction. They want a relationship. That's the way we are in our lives. We wanted to build a relationship that would really drive deep loyalty to the brand, and build in a reason for the purchase that goes above and beyond the product. We want to stand for something." Constance L. Hays, "Snackwell's Tries to Forge Link Between Its Products and Mother-Daughter Relationships," *NYT*, 11 February 1999, C6. See also Robert Goldman, *Reading Ads Socially* (New York: Routledge, 1992), 85–105. This trend has continued into the twenty-first century, with McDonald's 2004–5 adoption of the slogan, "I'm Lovin' It." http://www.mcdonalds.com/

10. Ernest Dichter, "A Creative Memorandum on the Psychology of Soup," 2-12, prepared for Young & Rubicam,, April 1960, IMR; "Chicken Soup Really Is Good Medicine," *Cleveland Plain Dealer*, 4 November 2000, 1A.

11. Bob Garfield, "Campbell Warms Up Soupy Sentiment," *Advertising Age*, 69, no. 7, February 1998, 43.

12. Bob Garfield, "Kraft Tastefully Takes Spot at Family Table," *Advertising Age*, 69, 37, September 1998, 67. Jessamyn Neuhaus's analysis of meatloaf recipes suggests that this nostalgia does not even have to go back to "grandmothers," but in more recent history harkened back to foods that "mom" made, arguing in particular that 1980s recipes for meatloaf "revealed our continuing need to believe in Mom-cooked meals . . . and what could be more comforting than a home-cooked meal, made with love by Mom?" Jessamyn Neuhaus, "Is Meatloaf for Men?" in *Cooking Lessons: The Politics of Gender and Food*, ed. Sherrie A. Inness (Lanham, Md.: Rowman and Littlefield, 2001), 107.

13. Ernest Dichter, "Radio-TV Advertising of Fisher's Blend Flour," prepared for Pacific National Advertising Agency, Seattle, Washington, 15 October 1954, IMR; Dichter, "A Creative Memo on What Motivates Housewives to Buy Bakery Products Other Than Bread," prepared for Brooke, Smith, French & Dorrance, Detroit, January 1957, 27, IMR; Dichter, "Phase I: A Motivational Research Study of the Marketing, Sales and Advertising Problems of D-Zerta," submitted to General Foods, White Plains, New York, May 1958, IMR, 15; Dichter, "The Psychology of Identification: A Creative Memorandum on 'Grandma Keebler,'" 1, 8, submitted to Leo Burnett Company, Chicago, July 1968, IMR; Laura Shapiro, *Something from the Oven: Reinventing Dinner in 1950s America* (New York: Viking, 2004), 70, 253; *LHJ*, December 1965, 31; *FC*, December 1999, 145.

14. Daniel Miller, *A Theory of Shopping* (Ithaca, N.Y.: Cornell University Press, 1998), 12, 108, 138, 149–50; David Bell and Gill Valentine, *Consuming Geographies: We Are Where We Eat* (London: Routledge, 1997), 69–71, 75; Ruth Schwartz Cowan, "Two Washes in the Morning and a Bridge Party at Night: The American Housewife Between the Wars," *Women's Studies* 3 (1976): 147–72. Sociologists Francesca Cancian and Steven Gordon contended that as "love became feminized," "women remained responsible for the 'emotion work' of maintaining happy marriages." "Changing Emotion Norms in Marriage: Love and Anger in U.S. Women's Magazines Since 1900," *Gender & Society* 2, 3 (September 1988): 311.

15. Dichter, "Creative Memorandum on the Psychology of Soup," 12.

16. Dichter, "A Psychological Research Study on the Sales and Advertising Problems of Bisquick," submitted to Knox Reeves Advertising, Minneapolis, November 1952, IMR; Dichter, "A Creative Research Memo on the Psychology of a Woman on Food Shopping Day," 1–2, submitted to Fitzgerald Advertising Agency, New Orleans, September 1955, IMR.

17. Ellen McCracken, *Decoding Women's Magazines: From Mademoiselle to Ms.* (New York: St. Martin's, 1993); Irene Park, "Marketing Alternatives to Women," *Food & Beverage Marketing* (June 1987): 21; *WD*, 20 September 1977, Box 14.2, JWT Archives—Competitive Advertisements Collection; *WD*, 23 January 1979, Box 12.5, JWT Archives—Competitive Advertisements Collection; *LHJ*, December 1983, R2.

18. *GH*, December 1966, Food Misc., Box 20.32, JWT Archives—Competitive Advertisements Collection; *Life*, 7 October 1966, Food Miscellaneous, Box 21.23, JWT Archives—Competitive Advertisements Collection; *GH*, February 1970, Miscellaneous Sauces, Box 12.32, JWT Archives—Competitive Advertisements Collection; *LHJ*, September 1972, Box 16.18, JWT Archives—Competitive Advertisements Collection; *FC*, January 1971, 92; *FC*, January 1973, 11; *FC*, February 1971, 122; *Ebony*, November 1999, 103, 162; *Ebony*, February 2000, 96, 98.

19. *Farm Journal*, October 1970, 51.

20. *Sunset,* March 1972, Box 16.24, JWT Archives—Competitive Advertisements Collection; *LHJ,* June 1974, 112–13; *GH,* December 1974, Box 13.16, JWT Archives—Competitive Advertisements Collection; Oscar Mayer, 1977 File, Box 2, JWT Archives—Competitive Advertisements Collection.

21. *LHJ,* March 1986, 81; *Pillsbury's Best Cookbook,* 1988, 1980s-3, Peterson Collection; *LHJ,* December 1992, 37; *LHJ,* June 1995, 127; *FC,* 4 January 2000, 11.

22. *LHJ,* June 1921, 27; *Sunset,* August 1977, Box 15.37, JWT Archives—Competitive Advertisements Collection; *Ebony,* April 2000, 51.

23. Emphasis theirs. Jell-O, Box 7, Folder 20, Warshaw Collection.

24. *LHJ,* September 1941, 48; *Life,* 15 February 1943, 32; *LHJ,* June 1947, 85; *LHJ,* September 1947, 10; *GH,* January 1950, 23; *GH,* May 1950, 11; *LHJ,* February 1951, 149.

25. Ernest Dichter, "A Psychological Research Study on the Sales and Advertising Problems of Franco-American Spaghetti," submitted to Dancer-Fitzgerald-Sample, New York, October 1953, 14, IMR; Dichter, *Motivations,* 4.

26. *Life,* 11 October 1954, 148.

27. *BHG,* November 1965, Box 11.6, JWT Archives—Competitive Advertisements Collection; *GH,* December 1964, Standard Brands, Box 12, JWT Archives—Domestic Advertisements Collection.

28. *Farm Journal,* March 1971, Box 14.12, JWT Archives—Competitive Advertisements Collection.

29. *GH,* April 1965, Standard Brands, Box 13, JWT Archives—Domestic Advertisements Collection.

30. Ernest Dichter, "Why Men Marry Women Who Are Good Cooks," Cooking, File 2, n.d., IMR; *LHJ,* June 1946, 62; *LHJ,* January 1961, 2; *Seventeen,* January 1969, 100–101; *Seventeen,* February 1969, 170; *Seventeen,* April 1969, 203; *Seventeen,* August 1969, 341.

31. *LHJ,* March 1992, 84–85; *Soap Opera Digest,* 8 April 1997, 29.

32. Miller, *A Theory of Shopping,* 108–9, 149.

33. Barbara Olson, "Brand Loyalty and Consumption Patterns: The Lineage Factor," in *Contemporary Marketing and Consumer Behavior: An Anthropological Sourcebook,* ed. John F. Sherry, Jr. (Thousand Oaks, Calif.: Sage, 1995), 250–61.

34. Dichter and IMR, "A Psychological Research Study on the Sales & Advertising Problems of Betty Crocker Crustquick," 4, submitted to Knox Reeves Advertising, Minneapolis (n.d.), IMR.

35. *LHJ,* March 1902, 33; Warren Belasco, "Ethnic Fast Foods: The Corporate Melting Pot," *Food and Foodways* 2 (1987): 9.

36. *LHJ,* March 1923, 35; *LHJ,* June 1938, 39; *LHJ,* December 1964, 69.

37. *FC,* January 1957, 13. Soup was not the only product to be caught up in nostalgia; foods generally found themselves symbolic of and avenues to times past. Food writer Molly O'Neill assessed a sixty-year analysis of *Gourmet* magazine by food historian Anne Mendelson and found that "As if to balance the shifting class lines of the postwar era, food was romanticized primarily in nostalgic ways," which Mendelson characterized as "an intense fixation on the past'." "Food Porn," *Columbia Journalism Review,* September/October 2003.

38. *GH,* September 1971, 161.

39. Dichter, "A Creative Memorandum on the Psychology of Soup."

40. *LHJ,* March 1974, 91.

41. Carolyn Wyman, *I'm a Spam Fan: America's Best-Loved Foods* (Stamford, Conn.: Longmeadow Press, 1993), 16–18; *GH,* April 1966, 252.

42. Ernest Dichter, "A Psychological Research Study of the Effectiveness of

Current Packaged White Bread Advertising," 14, 17, c. 1955, IMR; *GH*, April 1966, 252; *Life*, 1 May 1970, 13; *FC*, April 1973, 199.

43. *FC*, October 1970, Gold Medal Flour, Box 12.6, JWT Archives—Domestic Advertisements Collection; *Parent's*, November 1970, Gold Medal Flour, Box 12.6, JWT Archives—Domestic Advertisements Collection; *FC*, November 1970, 97; *GH*, December 1970; *LHJ*, March 1971, 155; *FC*, April 1971, Box 14.13, JWT Archives—Competitive Advertisements Collection; *GH*, September 1971, 152–53; *Sunset*, October 1973, Box 14, JWT Archives—Competitive Advertisements Collection.

44. *Sunset*, October 1973; Dichter, "A Creative Memorandum on the Psychology of Soup," 21.

45. Jack Hitt, "Does the Smell of Coffee Brewing Remind You of Your Mother," *NYTM*, 7 May 2000, 71–74.

46. *LHJ*, December 1944, 73; *RD*, June 1973, 161; *BHG*, July 1973, Box 15.34, JWT Archives—Competitive Advertisements Collection; Kellogg's, Box 2, 1984, 1984, JWT Archives—Domestic Advertisements Collection. Writing about the effort to sell restaurants with the home ideal, Samantha Barbas noted that "At the core of 'home cooking' and 'home atmosphere' was cheerful and diligent female service. 'Deep down in every man's heart is a desire to have food handed to him by a woman,' reported a trade journal in 1928. . . .'Mature types' . . . conjured up nostalgic 'visions of Mother'." "Just like Home: 'Home Cooking' and the Domestication of the American Restaurant," *Gastronomica—The Journal of Food and Culture*" 2, 4 (Fall 2002): 48).

47. Mary Kitchen, Box 15.6, JWT Archives—Competitive Advertisements Collection; *Sunset*, November 1978, 197. Ernest Dichter encouraged the Keebler manufacturers to use "Grandma Keebler" to generate memories of "less complicated" times when "someone gave us a cookie, someone who had time." His clear implication is that the advertisers should use a grandmother figure to elicit memories of when women had time to make cookies for their loved ones ("Creative Memorandum on 'Grandma Keebler,' " 9).

48. *GH*, January 1950, 121; *Sunset*, November 1970, 198; *LHJ*, December 1986, 150; Susan Strasser, *Satisfaction Guaranteed: The Making of the American Mass Market* (New York: Pantheon, 1989), 118–21; Karal Ann Marling, *As Seen on TV: The Visual Culture of Everyday Life in the 1950s* (Cambridge, Mass.: Harvard University Press, 1994).

49. *People*, 26 July 1999, 100.

50. *LHJ*, June 1929, 53; *LHJ*, June 1940, 6; *Life*, 20 September 1954, 9; *New Yorker*, 26 December 1964, 9; *LHJ*, July 1971, 113.

51. *LHJ*, June 1929, 53; *LHJ*, June 1938, 56; *LHJ*, December 1941, 41; *FC*, 14 December 1999, 107.

52. James D. Norris, *Advertising and the Transformation of American Society, 1865–1920* (Westport, Conn: Greenwood Press, 1990); *LHJ*, June 1905, 34.

53. *LHJ*, December 1926, 33; Ruth Schwartz Cowan, *More Work for Mother: The Ironies of Household Technology from the Open Hearth to the Microwave* (New York: Basic Books, 1983); Roland Marchand, *Advertising the American Dream: Making Way for Modernity, 1920–1940* (Berkeley: University of California Press, 1985).

54. Ernest Dichter quoted in Gilbert Burck, "What Makes Women Buy?" *Fortune*, August 1956, 176. Laura Shapiro explores the Pillsbury campaign, the use of praise, and the significance of Betty Crocker (particularly her respect for women) in *Something from the Oven*, 39, 186.

55. *LHJ*, January 1960, 3.

56. *LHJ*, November 1926, 37; *LHJ*, December 1926, 33; *LHJ*, September 1929, 194; *LHJ*, December 1932, 97; *LHJ*, March 1936, 36; *GH*, December 1942, 130; Kellogg's, 1955, Box 1 of 2, JWT Archives—Competitive Advertisements Collection; Burck, "What Makes Women Buy?" 94, 173; *LHJ*, April 1961, 23; *FC*, February 1973, 97; *LHJ*, December 1986, 139; Nancy Walker, *Shaping Our Mothers' World: American Women's Magazines* (Jackson: University Press of Mississippi, 2000), 182–83.

57. Ernest Dichter, "A Psychological Research Study on the Effectiveness of Betty Crocker in Promoting General Mills Products," May 1953, 54, IMR; Dichter, "Today's Woman as a Consumer," 1–2, IMR (bold in original); Dichter, "Radio-TV Advertising of Fisher's Blend Flour;" Shapiro, *Something from the Oven*, 63–65, 75–76; *LHJ*, March 1977, 86; *LHJ*, September 1992, 220–21; *LHJ*, June 1995, 191.

58. *LHJ*, May 1946, 98; *Seventeen*, March 1958, 58.

59. *Seventeen*, January 1948, 19; Swift & Co, Box 2, c. 1950, JWT Archives—Domestic Advertisements Collection; *LHJ*, April 1960, 22–23; "Mom's Furlough Fixin's," Swift & Co, Box 1, c. 1943, JWT Archives—Domestic Advertisements Collection; *American*, October 1950, 11; *BHG*, December 1974, Standard Brands, Box 13, JWT Archives—Domestic Advertisements Collection; *GH*, March 1976, Standard Brands, Box 13, JWT Archives—Domestic Advertisements Collection; *GH*, December 1993, 203. The tree itself was simple. All it took was "just parsley sprigs or huckleberry leaves stapled by hand with #10 wire screen staples to a cone of Styrofoam. The base is a funnel from your kitchen." JWT, DA, Oscar Mayer, 1960, Trade, Multiple Product Promotions Folder, Box 1, Hartman Center.

60. *LHJ*, March 1965, 116; *GH*, February 1965, 196L; *LHJ*, July 1967, 57; *LHJ*, December 1986, 139; *Seventeen*, March 2000, 73; Jessamyn Neuhaus, "The Way to a Man's Heart: Gender Roles, Domestic Ideology, and Cookbooks in the 1950s," *Journal of Social History* 32, 3 (Spring 1999): 529–55; Elaine Tyler May, *Homeward Bound: American Families in the Cold War Era* (New York: Basic Books, 1988), 181–82.

61. Betty Friedan, *The Feminine Mystique* (New York: Dell, 1963). Thanks to historian Julie Berebitsky for her insights in this area.

62. "How to Polish Up Apple Sales by Answering Housewives' Questions," *Printers' Ink*, 18 December 1964, 35–36.

63. *LHJ*, February 1918, 29; *LHJ*, May 1927, 41; *LHJ*, November 1931, 31; *LHJ*, July 1935, 31; *LHJ*, June 1938, 52.

64. *LHJ*, 1 March 1911, 74; *WHC*, August 1934, 36; *LHJ*, July 1938, 5.

65. *GH*, February 1942, 9; *LHJ*, November 1947, 127; Scott Bruce, *Cereal Box Bonanza: The 1950s: Identification and Values* (Paducah, Ky.: Collector Books, 1995), 45.

66. While not unique in tone, the postwar era did see a large number of these ads and as Nancy Walker and others have noted, this period did see "women actively seeking help from a variety of authority figures." Walker also suggests that more than advice on tasks or purchases, one of the most important aspects of these ads was their role in dictating "how to be a woman" (*Shaping Our Mother's World*, 149–53).

67. *LHJ*, March 1941, 55; *Life*, 22 February 1943, 2. See Chapter 3 for analysis of food advertisements and social status. This trend existed even earlier. Tracey Deutsch notes that the A&P chain supermarket placed ads in the *Saturday Evening Post* in the 1920s promising that it stocked stores with "high-quality foods

with which to impress their husband's boss." Interestingly, Deutsch notes that the advertisements targeted men, reinforcing the notion that "their wives' difficulties with shopping were as challenging as the problems they encountered in the workplace." "Untangling Alliances: Social Tensions Surrounding Independent Grocery Stores and the Rise of Mass Retailing," in *Food Nations: Selling Taste in Consumer Societies*, ed. Warren Belasco and Philip Scranton (New York: Routledge, 2002), 167. Certainly, advertisers wanted to suggest that women's shopping and cooking could make or break their husbands' careers.

68. *LHJ*, January 1935; *LHJ*, June 1947, 215; *RD*, September 1955, 1.

69. Newspapers, 1982, Kraft, Box 10, JWT Archives—Domestic Advertisements Collection.

70. *LHJ*, September 1926, 65; *LHJ*, March 1929, 251; *LHJ*, November 1942, 37; *LHJ*, March 1956, 206; Stouffer's, August 11, 1958 Memo, Stouffer Corporate 1958–1959 Minutes, Box 31, JWT Archives—Review Board Review Meeting Collection. In notes concerning a review board meeting in 1959, members discussing possible advertising strategies noted "Stouffer's 'all woman' approach." See also Stouffer's, June 29, 1959 Memo, Stouffer Corporate 1958–1959 Minutes, Box 31, JWT Archives—Review Board Review Meeting Collection; *FC*, May 1972, Box 16.24, JWT Archives—Competitive Advertisements Collection.

71. *LHJ*, May 1928, 57; *LHJ*, July 1941, 2.

72. *LHJ*, September 1929, 105; *LHJ*, July 1941, 2; "The Self-Starter Breakfast, 60," newspaper advertisement 1653, Case File—Kellogg's, c. 1941, JWT Archives—Chicago Office Microfilm Collection; *Ebony*, September 1999, 9.

73. "The Current State of Live Trademarks, *Tide*, 22 March 1957, 26, 29–30. Karal Ann Marling reported that Dichter believed Betty Crocker's popularity "proved that Americans still hankered for individualism in an age of corporate monoliths" (*As Seen on TV*, 213).

74. Shapiro, *Something from the Oven*, 180; Dichter, "A Psychological Research Study on the Effectiveness of Betty Crocker," May 1953, 14–15; Catherine Manton, *Fed Up: Women and Food in America* (Westport, Conn.: Bergin and Garvey, 1999), 52–53; *GH*, December 1944, 218. Marling reported that in the 1950s "Ninety-seven percent of American women now recognized the Crocker name" and that "Dichter was a great admirer of Betty Crocker (*As Seen on TV*, 210).

75. Manton, *Fed Up*, 38–39, 54–56, 117–18, 132–34; Dichter, "A Psychological Research Study on the Effectiveness of Betty Crocker," 14–15. Advertisers had to be careful not to present infallible women. In a 1999 study for the Illuminations candle company, 51 percent of respondents reported that the *Martha Stewart Living* television show triggered stress, as compared to only 27 percent who found TV news stressful. Kay Harvey, "The Things That Trigger Stress: A Nationwide Survey Comes Up with Some Surprising Answers," *Philadelphia Inquirer*, 29 August 1999, G2. Author has possession of the original study.

76. William Meyers, *The Image Makers: Power and Persuasion on Madison Avenue* (New York: Times Books, 1984); Michelle Greene, "Still Cookin' Up a Storm: Betty Crocker 'Sweetalks' to a New Generation of Consumers," *Madison Avenue* 27, 3 (March 1985): 60; Marilyn Kern-Foxworth, *Aunt Jemima, Uncle Ben, and Rastus: Blacks in Advertising, Yesterday, Today, and Tomorrow* (Westport, Conn.: Praeger, 1994); Steven V. Roberts, "Betty, Meet Ashley, a '90s Woman," *U.S. News & World Report*, 1 April 1996, 10; K. Sue Jewell, *From Mammy to Miss America and Beyond: Cultural Images and the Shaping of U.S. Social Policy* (London: Routledge, 1993); M. M. Manring, *Slave in a Box: The Strange Career of Aunt Jemima* (Charlottesville: University Press of Virginia, 1998).

77. Barbara J. Phillips and Barbara Gyoerick, "The Cow, the Cook, and the Quaker: Fifty Years of Spokescharacter Advertising," *Journalism and Mass Communications Quarterly*," 76, 4 (Winter 1999): 713–28.

78. *LHJ*, June 1902, 31; *LHJ*, June 1919, 31; *LHJ*, March 1923, 149.

79. Jennifer Scanlon, *Inarticulate Longings: The Ladies' Home Journal, Gender, and the Promises of Consumer Culture* (New York: Routledge, 1995), 118, 224; Richard Ohmann, *Selling Culture: Magazines, Markets, and Class at the Turn of the Century* (New York: Verso, 1996), 80.

80. *LHJ*, June 1923, 165; *LHJ*, December 1932, 97; *New Yorker*, 28 September 1940, 31; *LHJ*, May 1953, 142. In addition to bridge, women in ads anxiously looked at their watches as they busied themselves with PTA meetings. See for example, *LHJ*, January 1953, 10; *LHJ*, December 1967, 105. Jennifer Scanlon argued that copywriters' class status led them to presume their experiences as the ideal, if not the norm (*Inarticulate Longings*, 191–92).

81. Dichter, "Today's Woman as a Consumer," 1–3.

82. Dichter, "A Motivational Research Study on the Personality of Duncan Hines as an Endorser of Cake Mix and Other Products," October 1955, 87–88, IMR; *LHJ*, September 1965, 91; *GH*, December 1966, 169; Uncle Ben's Food, 1970, Box 1, JWT Archives—Domestic Advertisements Collection; *GH*, November 1972, 155; *FC*, February 1973, 171; *BHG*, August 1974, 83; *BHG*, September 1974, 100; "Equality in Advertising: Selling Women, Selling Blacks," *Journal of Communication* (Autumn 1976): 167–68.

83. Swanson's, 1960, Box 12.15, JWT Archives—Competitive Advertisements Collection; *FC*, April 1973, 175; *LHJ*, March 1992, 181; Campbell's "Runner," CPRW4103, 1984, created by Backer & Spievogel, Warshaw Collection; *People*, 19 June 1999, 14; *People*, 17 January 2000, 13; Rena Bartos, *Marketing to Women Around the World* (Boston: Harvard Business School Press, 1989), 166; McCracken, *Decoding Women's Magazines*, 202. McCracken cites this ad from *Newsweek Woman*, November 1982, 90.

84. "Scarcity of Domestic Help Provides Opportunities for Advertisers," *Printers' Ink*, 6 December 1917, 17.

85. Ibid., 17–20; L. C. Devison, "Effect of Negro Migration on Advertiser's Markets," *Printers' Ink*, 1 August 1918, 24–28; Bertha K. Landes, "A Woman—On Women," *Printers' Ink*, July 7, 1927, 160. In 1933, the head of the Food Department at Lord & Thomas in Los Angeles acknowledged the cold realities of the Depression, but remained optimistic that it was still worthwhile to advertise because "incomes have largely been reduced, but the portion spent for food has probably been cut the least of any classification. People still must eat." Leigh Crosby, "Tests Women Apply When They Buy Things, *Printers' Ink Monthly*, May 1933, 1, 14–15, 49. Ads with servants continued to appear in the 1930s, including one for Libby's pineapple that appeared in 1934. Jim Heimann, ed., *All-American Ads of the 1930s* (Koln: Taschen, 2002), 565.

86. Pamela Walker Laird, *Advertising Progress: American Business and the Rise of Consumer Marketing* (Baltimore: Johns Hopkins University Press, 1998), 142; Campbell's Soup ad, *NG*, September 1914; Campbell's Soup ad, *NG*, June 1915.

87. Harvey Levenstein, *Paradox of Plenty: A Social History of Eating in Modern America* (New York: Oxford University Press, 1993), 108, 131; Jim Heimann, ed., *All-American Ads of the 1940s* (Koln: Taschen, 2002), 386–87; Walker, *Shaping Our Mothers' World*, 60, 104–5; C. P. Russell, "Advertising to Women by the Departmental Method," *Printers' Ink*, 27 May 1920, 17–18. A 1927 article claimed, "Women are today striving to run their homes as a business proposition, as a man

runs his factory, his store, or his office. They want and need to be informed, and informed truthfully, as to new improvements and new methods" (Landes, "A Woman—On Women," 159).

88. Levenstein, *Paradox of Plenty*, 105; Sinclair Lewis, "Woman Labor Is a Success!" *Printers' Ink*, 8 September 1967, 53–55; P. H. Erbes, Jr., "The Women Take Over, *Printers' Ink*, 15 August 1917, 53–55. *Printers' Ink* and other industry research journals commonly carried articles that either focused on women workers or considered their work in their analysis. See for example: John Allen Murphy, "Can Saleswomen Take the Place of Conscripted Salesmen," *Printers' Ink*, 16 August 1917, 25–32; Sinclair Lewis, "Training Women to Take Men's Positions," *Printers' Ink*, 4 July 1918, 3–6, 96; Erbes, "The Women Take Over," 9–11, 68–70; Ingrid C. Kildegaard, "Working Wives," *Journal of Advertising Research*, 3, 2 (1963): 44–47. Bruce Brown analyzed 521 advertisements that appeared between 1928 and 1972 and found that only five portrayed working wives (with four of those appearing during the Great Depression). *Images of Family Life in Magazine Advertising, 1920–1978* (New York: Praeger, 1981), 30.

89. *LHJ*, December 1908, 56; *LHJ*, December 1911, 88; Shredded Wheat ad (1912) in Daniel Delis Hill, *Advertising to the American Woman, 1900–1999* (Columbus: Ohio State University Press, 2002), 183; *LHJ*, June 1920, 33; Fleischmann's Yeast, "Colds Cost This Girl Her Job!," Spring 1932, Reel 49, JWT Archives—Microfilm Collection; *LHJ*, March 1938, 72; *LHJ*, September 1941, 77; *LHJ*, March 1944, 99; *SEP*, 17 March 1951, 92; *LHJ*, September 1989, 61.

90. *Life*, 18 January 1943, 38; *SEP*, 5 February 1944, 30; *SEP*, 26 February 1944, 58; *SEP*, 16 March 1944, 56; *JWT News*, 3, No. 20 (17 May 1948), JWT Archives—JWT News Collection.

91. Dichter, "Radio-TV Advertising of Fisher's Blend Flour." Dorothy Thompson in a 1952 article "The Employed Woman and Her Household" questioned why working women still had responsibility for housework, noting "Our society is still organized on the assumption that the conduct of the home is every woman's natural function, [but] no one has expected men to work from nine to five in an office and then come home and cook a dinner for four or five people; or get up hours before time to go to work to sweep, dust, make beds and prepare breakfast" (quoted in Walker, *Shaping Our Mothers' World*, 206).

92. James Wade, "The Seventies: A Marketing View," 1 February 1971; Standard Brands, Box 17, JWT Archives—Account Files Collection, 17; Andrew Hurley, "From Hash House to Family Restaurant: The Transformation of the Diner and Post-World War II Consumer Culture," *Journal of American History* (March 1997): 1294.

93. Wade, "The Seventies," 11, 16, 47–48, 140. A *Printers' Ink* article makes this point in the 1960s, reflecting on the market of working women: "How does having a job make a woman different from her housewife sister? Not much research has been done on this subject." This in spite of the fact that the same article reported that "Most women—80 per cent of them—work at some time during their lives, and to demonstrate that this means gainful employment beyond teenage baby sitting, women today have a work-life expectancy of 25 to 27 years, if they are married, 40 years if they are not . . . compared with the average work-life expectancy of men, which is 43 years." One of the earliest to analyze working women was an industry that stood to directly benefit from working women, the apparel industry, who found that even "though the working woman represents 36 per cent of the total female population, she is accountable for 50 per cent of all woman' apparel purchases" ("Executives' Guide to Marketing for 1965," n.d., 33).

94. Ralph Leezenbaum, "The New American Woman . . . and Marketing," *Marketing/Communication*, July 1970, 26–27.

95. Wade, "The Seventies," 15–20; Judith Waters and George Ellis, "The Selling of Gender Identity," in *Advertising and Culture: Theoretical Perspectives,* ed. Mary Cross (Westport, Conn.: Praeger, 1996), 93; Rena Bartos, "The Moving Target: The American Consumer: 1970–1990," Box 15, JWT Archives—J. Walter Thompson Publications Collection.

96. Campbell Marketing Research Department, "The Food World of Working Women and Dual-Earning Households," 8 August 1985, Campbell Soup Company Archive, Camden.

97. Stephanie Thompson, "Mobile Meals Gaining," *Advertising Age* 74, 25, 23 June 2003, 20.

98. *BHG*, August 1974, 83; *BHG*, September 1974, 100; *BHG*, February 2000, 186.

99. Catharine Beecher, *A Treatise on Domestic Economy, For the Use of Young Ladies at Home and at School* (New York: Harper, 1846); Charlotte Perkins Gilman, *Women and Economics* (New York: Harper and Row, 1966); Dolores Hayden, *The Grand Domestic Revolution: A History of Feminist Designs for American Homes, Neighborhoods, and Cities* (Cambridge, Mass.: MIT Press, 1981); Kathryn Kish Sklar, *Catharine Beecher: A Study in American Domesticity* (New Haven, Conn.: Yale University Press, 1973); Stuart Ewen, *Captains of Consciousness: Advertising and the Social Roots of the Consumer Culture* (New York: McGraw-Hill, 1976), 128; Laura Scott Holliday, "Kitchen Technologies: Promises and Alibis: 1944–1966," *Camera Obscura* 16, 47.2 (2001): 85; Harvey A. Levenstein, *Revolution at the Table: The Transformation of the American Diet* (New York: Oxford University Press, 1988), 68–69.

100. Alice Z. Cuneo, "Peas Fill Up the Pod," *Advertising Age* 71, 14, 3 April 2000, 52, 56.

101. Lears, "From Salvation to Self-Realization," 27; Norris, *Advertising and the Transformation of American Society,* 94; Ewen, *Captains of Consciousness,* 160; Scanlon, *Inarticulate Longings,* 4–5, 131–33; Garvey, *The Adman in the Parlor,* 157–59; *LHJ,* 1 April 1911, 48. Advertisers seemed uncertain about what feminism was going to mean for them early in the century. Writing about businesswoman Mrs. Charles B. Knox, widow of the founder of the Knox Gelatine Company, Bruce Bliven assured the reader that Mrs. Knox "is herself as far as possible from the type known as the 'aggressive feminist,' and which I for one am coming to believe exists only in the minds of the cartoonists" ("The Woman Advertiser and Manufacturer," *Printers' Ink,* 20 February 1919, 18). In an article reflecting on women as a group and their responses to advertisers, James H. Collins remarked that he had offended women "at a time when she was taking herself very seriously, demanding a vote and other privileges since secured." He warned that critiquing women would be to "Poke your stick into a nice fat yellow-jacket nest!" and explained that "Woman belongs to a party because she belongs to an oppressed race." Still, he couldn't help critiquing women, arguing that they were "naïve" and that "The vote hasn't made her any more at home in Man's systematic world" ("All About Women—for Advertisers Only," *Printers' Ink,* 18 February 1926, 3–8).

102. Ewen, *Captains of Consciousness,* 89–91; *LHJ,* June 1914, 77; *LHJ,* November 1920, 31; Campbell's Soup ad, *NG,* November 1922; Nancy Cott, *The Grounding of Modern Feminism* (New Haven, Conn.: Yale University Press, 1987), 171–74.

103. Ellen DuBois and Karen Kearns, *Votes for Women: A Seventy-Fifth Anniversary Album* (San Marino, Calif.: Huntington Library, 1995), 17; *Printers' Ink,* 21 November 1935, 8–9; Cott, *The Grounding of Modern Feminism,* 171–74; Scanlon,

Inarticulate Longings, 133; Robert Goldman, *Reading Ads Socially* (New York: Routledge, 1992), 85; Margaret Finnegan, *Selling Suffrage: Consumer Culture & Votes for Women* (New York: Columbia University Press, 1999), 128.

104. *New Yorker*, 26 October 1940, 31; Corn Flakes, 1960, Folder 12, Box 12, JWT Archives—Competitive Advertisements Collection.

105. Dichter, "A Motivational Research Study on the Personality of Duncan Hines"; Campbell's Soup ad, List "B" Ad, 17 February 1912, Campbell Soup Company Archive.

106. *LHJ*, March 1927, 37.

107. *LHJ*, January 1951, 77; *GH*, January 1970, 7; *GH*, February 1970, 57.

108. *LHJ*, July 1939, 35; *American*, January 1945, 97; *American*, April 1945, 67; *LHJ*, June 1950, 84; *LHJ*, December 1959, 101.

109. Ewen, *Captains of Consciousness*, 149, 168–69; *LHJ*, December 1957, 127; *LHJ*, September 1964, 42; *LHJ*, December 1974, 30; *LHJ*, December 1977, 28; *RD*, March 1982, 33; McCracken, *Decoding Women's Magazines*, 202; Thomas Frank, *The Conquest of Cool: Business Culture, Counterculture, and the Rise of Hip Consumerism* (Chicago: University of Chicago Press, 1997), 152–56; Ruth Rosen, *The World Split Open: How the Modern Women's Movement Changed America* (New York: Viking Penguin, 2000), 311–12.

110. Joanne Meyerowitz, "Beyond the Feminine Mystique: A Reassessment of Postwar Mass Culture, 1946–1958," in *Not June Cleaver: Women and Gender in Postwar America, 1945–1960*, ed. Joanne Meyerowitz (Philadelphia: Temple University Press, 1994). While Meyerowitz found that the nonfiction stories "expressed overt admiration for women whose individual striving moved them beyond the home," "supported women's wage work and urged greater participation in politics," these findings are not true of food advertising during this same period.

111. "Executives' Guide to Marketing for 1965," *Printers' Ink*, n.d., 33–36.

112. Leezenbaum, "The New American Woman," 22, 24.

113. "J. Walter Thompson Elects Vice President," *NYT*, 23 February 1968, 51; Anne Tolstoi Foster, "Ad Lib Takes Clue from Women," *NYT*, 28 November 1971, F13. Anne Tolstoi Wallach, a graduate of the Dalton School ('45) and Radcliffe College ('49), was "advised that the only way to get a job in the business world was to become a secretary. She found her first job at J. Walter Thompson as a typist, then through a copy-writer trainee program she was promoted to junior copywriter. Moving up through the ranks at other agencies, she came back to JWT as an editorial writer in 1959. A published author, she also was described as a "staunch feminist" and "composed some of the early copy for the National Organization for Women." Andree Brooks, "The Secretary: Still a Nowhere Woman," *NYT*, 11 October 1981, 31; Anne Tolstoi, "Story," *New Yorker*, 1 April 1950; http://www.dalton.org/alumni/books.html; AnneTolstoi Foster, JWT Archives—Personnel File Collection.

114. "A Report on Teen Trends," August 1976, Box 20, Teenage Pamphlets, 2 of 4, JWT Archives—Marketing Vertical File Collection; Leezenbaum, "The New American," 22–28.

115. "Middle America in the 1980s, September 1979, #480, Consumers: Pamphlets, File 2, Box 20, JWT Archives—Marketing Vertical File Collection. Back in 1970, Ralph Leezenbaum had predicted that working women and housewives would make fewer trips to the shopping center, but this woman was "more likely to be accompanied on shopping trips by her husband, and when he goes along, the evidence comes down on the side of higher purchases" ("The New American Woman," 27).

116. "Executives' Guide to Marketing for 1965," *Printers' Ink*, n.d., 39.

117. Ronald Alsop, "Firms Still Struggle to Devise Best Approach to Black Buyers," *Wall Street Journal*, 25 October 1984, 1.

118. Grace Lichtenstein, "Feminists Demand 'Liberation' in Ladies' Home Journal Sit-In," *NYT*, 19 March 1970, 51.

119. Sara Welles, "A Woman's View," *Printers' Ink*, 31 May 1963, 35.

120. In the fine tradition of Rena Bartos, Anne Tolstoi Wallach is convinced that the greatest mistake made by advertisers in the early twenty-first century is to ignore older consumers. She asserted that "The worst sin today, I think, is assuming that all consumers die by 38 and needn't be addressed at all, which is so silly." Email interview/correspondence, 30 June 2004, in author's possession. See also David Ogilvy, *Confessions of an Advertising Man* (New York: Ballantine, 1971), 84, with thanks to Jef Richards at the University of Texas, Austin.

121. Franchellie Cadwell, review of Caroline Bird and Sara Welles Briller, *Born Female: The High Cost of Keeping Women Down* (New York: David McKay, 1968), *Marketing/Communications*, September 1968, 70. Interestingly, Bird coauthored *Born Female* with Sara Welles Briller, who as Sara Welles was a columnist for *Printers' Ink* during the 1960s.

122. Midge Kovacs, "Women's Lib: Do's and Don'ts for Ad Men," *Marketing/Communications*, January 1971, 34–35.

123. Joanne Lipman, "Finally, Some Marketers Seem Ready to Give Bimbo Ads a Rest," *Wall Street Journal*, 31 January 1992, B2; "Libs Have Had Little Effect on Ads to Women," *Advertising Age* 14, 12, 19 March 1973, 44; Leslie Savan quoted in Nancy Walker, *Shaping Our Mothers' World*, 210–11. John B. Ford and Michael S. LaTour argue that the strongest critics of advertisers tended to be "women with higher levels of education, higher incomes and less tradition oriented." Pointing to the effects of feminist criticisms, they noted the potency of Jean Kilbourne's follow-up to her classic documentary, *Still Killing Us Softly*. In their research they found that "*mere exposure . . .* resulted in a significantly higher score on Arnott's Female Autonomy Inventory for those exposed as compared to a control group," *Journal of Current Issues and Research in Advertising* 18, 1 (Spring 1996): 81–94. See also John B. Ford, Michael S. LaTour, and Irvine Clarke, "A Prescriptive Essay Concerning Sex Role Portrayals in International Advertising Contexts," *American Business Review* 22, 1 (January 2004): 42–55, which suggests that while advertisers made some improvements in the 1980s, "studies in the 1990s indicated that women were still not happy with their portrayal in American advertisements" (43). Stuart Elliott explored whether the Anita Hill sexual harassment controversy "might accelerate changes that have taken place in advertising since the women's liberation movement gained strength two decades ago." Of those he interviewed, few were optimistic that the Clarence Thomas case or anything else was going to bring more change. Bob Garfield, advertising critic for *Advertising Age*, surmised, "'If 20 years of feminism and heightened awareness of sexual stereotypes have not influenced beer advertising, and they haven't, there's nothing that happened in the Thomas hearings that will make an iota of difference'," "A Possible Impact of Thomas Case," *NYT*, 15 October 1991, D20.

124. Lipman, "Finally, Some Marketers Seem Ready," B2. Indeed, in 1997 things were still so troubled that the Advertising Women of New York felt compelled to create The Good, the Bad, and the Ugly Awards. Of course, ever sensitive to their own employment status, Stuart Elliott noted that "The organization will probably disappoint luncheon-goers eager to watch Madison Avenue's women biting the hand that feeds them because the awards devote less attention

to the bad and the ugly than they do to the good. That was, Ms. Talcott said, because most ads submitted for consideration 'were not so egregious.' But Ms. Steedman said, 'But what was egregious was very egregious.'" *NYT*, 24 September 1997, D8.

125. Jill Hicks Ferguson, Peggy J. Kreshel, and Spencer F. Tinkham. "In the Pages of *Ms.*: Sex Role Portrayals of Women in Advertising," *Journal of Advertising*, 19, 1 (1990): 40–51.

Chapter 3. Women's Power to Make Us: Cooking Up a Family's Identity

1. Nancy Walker noted racism's decline generally, but also the continued characterization of nonwhites as "other." *Shaping Our Mothers' World: American Women's Magazines* (Jackson: University Press of Mississippi, 2000), xiv-xv.

2. Roland Marchand argued that advertising offered Americans a shared language, which helped to shape their shared perceptions and dreams. *Advertising the American Dream: Making Way for Modernity, 1920–1940* (Berkeley: University of California Press, 1985), x. Harvey Levenstein pointed to cultural anthropologists who discovered that "poor Americans were more often moved by considerations of status than by economy in choosing and preparing foods." *Paradox of Plenty: A Social History of Eating in Modern America* (New York: Oxford University Press, 1993), 70. For examples of the associations between food and identity, see Lee Rainwater, Richard P. Coleman, and Gerald Handel, *Workingman's Wife: Her Personality, World, and Life Style* (New York: Oceana 1959), 165, 173–74, 198–99; Terry Barr, "Eating Kosher, Staying Closer," *Journal of Popular Film and Television* 24, 3 (1996): 134–44; Susan Kalčik, "Symbolic Foodways in America: Symbol and the Performance of Identity," in *Ethnic and Regional Foodways in the United States: The Performance of Group Identity*, ed. Linda Keller Brown and Kay Mussell (Knoxville: University of Tennessee Press, 1984), 37–65. On the question of status, Mary Douglas and Baron Isherwood argued that "Food is the clearest example of a composite commodity." *The World of Goods* (New York: Basic Books, 1979), 96–97.

3. Levenstein, *Paradox of Plenty*; Donna Gabbaccia, *We Are What We Eat: Ethnic Food and the Making of Americans* (Cambridge, Mass.: Harvard University Press, 1998); Marilyn Halter, *Shopping for Identity: The Marketing of Ethnicity* (New York: Schocken Books, 2000), 106–12; Warren Belasco, "Ethnic Fast Foods: The Corporate Melting Pot," *Food and Foodways* 2 (1987): 9–11, 18–19. Judith Goode, Janet Theophano, and Karen Curtis argued that while some "research has assumed that ethnic or regional food habits are very conservative," other approaches contend that "the myth of closed ethnic eating communities is maintained only to extend mass products to all Americans," "A Framework for the Analysis of Continuity and Change in Shared Sociocultural Rules for Food Use: The Italian-American Pattern," in *Ethnic and Regional Foodways*, ed. Brown and Mussell, 68–69.

4. Raymond A. Bauer and Scott M. Cunningham, "The Negro Market," *Journal of Advertising Research* 10, 2 (April 1970): 7.

5. Long Range Planning, "The Negro American," 38, August 1966, Black Pamphlets, File 1 of 4, Box 22, JWT Archives—Marketing Vertical Files Collection; David Smallwood, "A Case for Marketing to Black Women," *Dollars & Sense*, 9 August 1983, 120; Robert E. Weems, Jr., *Desegregating the Dollar: African American Consumerism in the Twentieth Century* (New York: New York University Press, 1998),

22–26, 32–33. Even at the end of the century, researchers commented on the fact that African Americans remained "One of the most neglected groups in the marketing literature." Alan J. Bush, Rachel Smith, and Craig Martin, "The Influence of Consumer Socialization Variables on Attitudes Toward Advertising: A Comparison of African Americans and Caucasians," *Journal of Advertising* 28, 3 (Fall 1999): 13–25.

6. If they accidentally acquired data on an African American consumer, as through a questionnaire sent to subscribers of the *Ladies' Home Journal* through the mail, it was clearly not their intent (R. T. French Company, December 1937, Reel 338, JWT Archives—Microfilm Collection). Evidence of seeking out preferences and practices of African Americans does not appear to occur until the 1960s. John H. Johnson refuted the notion that businesses risked alienating whites by including blacks in advertisements when he cited a *Wall Street Journal* survey that reported that in a large number of desegregated businesses in the South business was better than ever, and Fred Harvey, president of Harvey's Department Store in Nashville, said, " 'The greatest surprise I ever had was the apparent 'so what' attitude of white customers'." John H. Johnson, "The New Negro Consumer: A Challenge, Responsibility and Opportunity," speech before New York Chapter of Public Relations Society of America, 18 September 1963, New York, Black Pamphlets, File 1 of 4, Box 22, JWT Archives—Marketing Vertical Files Collection. See also Theodore J. Gage, "RSVP: An Invitation to Buy," *Advertising Age*, 18 May 1981, S1.

7. "News of Food," *NYT*, 14 November 1949, 20; "The Changing Face of the Urban Markets," *Food Business*, reprinted from the July 1962 issue, 2–3, Black Pamphlets, File 1 of 4, Box 22, JWT Archives—Marketing Vertical Files Collection.

8. "Changing Face of Urban Markets"; "Probing the Negro Market: The Brand Loyalty Barrier," *Sales Management*, 1 March 1969, 4; "Spending by Nonwhites," *Business Week*, 23 February 1976; "Changing Minority Markets," U.S. Department of Commerce, April 1978, 6–7, 28–29, Black Pamphlets, File 2 of 4, Box 22, JWT Archives—Marketing Vertical Files Collection; Rielle Tack, "Numbers Don't Tell Minority Buying Power," *Advertising Age*, 16 April 1979, S22-S23; Richard L. Green, "Black Buying Patterns Are Revealing," *Advertising Age*, 16 April 1979, S34; Sheila Pharris and Levi Booker, "Black Consumer Market Grows," *Adweek*, 29 October 1979, 32; Gage, "RSVP: An Invitation to Buy," S1; "Tailoring Product Mix to the 'New Demographics,' " *Chain Store Age/Supermarkets*, August 1981, 75–76.

9. "News of Food," *NYT*, 20; "Negro Food and Entertainment Habits Make Negro Consumers Excellent Prospects for Planters Peanut Sales," c. 1962, Markets-Consumer-Ethnic-Black, Box 22, JWT Archives—Marketing Vertical Files Collection; Henry S. Clark, "Black *Is*," *Sales Management*, 15 September 1969, 64–68; Bauer and Cunningham, "The Negro Market," 9; B. Stuart Tolley and John J. Goett, "Reaction to Blacks in Newspaper Ads," *Journal of Advertising Research* 11, 2 (April 1971): 11–17. My relatively limited examination of African American magazines found few ads generally, compared to white women's magazines, and even when ads did appear almost none of them were for food. For example, no ads appeared in *Jet* in 1951 or 1952. *Ebony* did contain some general ads in the late 1940s, but almost no food ads. Interestingly, one of the few food companies to advertise in 1952 was for Planters Peanuts. Even when food ads did appear, as with a 1952 ad for Hunt's (*Ebony*, May 1952, 75), they did not always feature African Americans; companies took ads created for whites and placed them in the black media.

10. "Negro Food and Entertainment Habits," JWT Archives—Marketing Vertical Files Collection.

11. Henry Allen Bullock, "Consumer Motivations in Black and White—II," *Harvard Business Review* 39 (July/August 1961): 113; "The Changing Face of the Urban Markets," *Food Business*, 2–3; Bauer and Cunningham, "The Negro Market," 6–7; "Negro Food and Entertainment Habits," JWT Archives—Marketing Vertical Files Collection; "Business Highlights: The Black Customer," *Progressive Grocer*, January 1970, Black Pamphlets, File 2 of 4, Box 22, JWT Archives—Marketing Vertical Files Collection; Carl M. Larson and Hugh G. Wales, "Brand Preferences of Chicago Blacks, *Journal of Advertising Research* 13, 4 (August 1973): 18. A study by the Long Range Planning Service also argued that spending on food would have been higher "except for the fact that relatively large numbers of Negroes are employed in restaurants and hotels as domestic servants and consume food on the job that does not show up in the family budgets." Arguably this was less true in 1966 than it had been in decades past, and would be even less of a factor as the century wore on, perhaps increasing expenditures on food (Long Range Planning, "The Negro American," 38).

12. In a 1936 study of African American consumers, Paul E. Edwards found that "Constant and humiliating subordination has done something to the Negro. It has had a profound psychological effect upon him. It has affected his consumption characteristics—in fact his whole mode of living" (*Desegregating the Dollar*, 27, 42).

13. "The Changing Face of the Urban Markets"; Charles E. Van Tassel, "The Negro as a Consumer—What We Know and What We Need to Know," in *The Black Consumer: Dimensions of Behavior and Strategy*, ed. George Joyce and Norman A. P. Govoni (New York: Random House, 1971), 359–60.

14. "The Changing Face of the Urban Markets," 3–6; D. Parke Gibson, "'Creating Products for Negro Consumers,"' *Marketing Magazine*, 1 May 1969, 61–65; Walter Weiss, "Mass Media and Social Change," in *Attitudes, Conflict, and Social Change*, ed. Bert T. King and Elliott McGinnies (New York: Academic Press, 1972), 144–54; Pharris and Booker, "Black Consumer Market Grows"; Weems, *Desegregating the Dollar*, 50.

15. John H. Johnson, "The New Negro Consumer: A Challenge, Responsibility and Opportunity," speech to New York Chapter of Public Relations Society of America, 18 September 1963, New York, Black Pamphlets, File 1 of 4, Box 22, JWT Archives—Marketing Vertical Files Collection; Roy Wilkins, Executive Secretary NAACP, "Economic Impact of the Civil Rights Struggle," speech to the American Association of Advertising Agencies, November 1963, New York, Black Pamphlets, File 1 of 4, Box 22, JWT Archives—Marketing Vertical Files Collection; Long Range Planning, "The Negro American," 38.

16. "Do Advertisers Face a Negro Boycott?" *Printers' Ink*, 13 September 1963, 7; "Business Highlights," *Progressive Grocer*, January 1970; Larson and Wales, "Brand Preferences of Chicago Blacks, 20; "Survey Lists Brand Favorites Among Chicago Area Blacks," *Advertising Age* 45, 18, 6 May 1974, 10; Bennett W. Smith, "The Black Economic Giant Flexes Its Mighty Muscles," *Business & Society Review* 85, 53 (Spring 1974): 35–37; Weems, *Desegrating the Dollar*, 68–69. A 1981 *Black Enterprise* article on "Buying with a Conscience" traced the long history of boycotts, starting back in the 1920s, with Marcus Garvey's "buy black" campaign, but concluded that Jackson's efforts to pressure companies in the 1970s failed. Lynda M. Hill, "Buying with a Conscience" (October 1981): 75–76.

17. David C. Schmidt and Ivan L. Preston, "How NAACP Leaders View Integrated Advertising," *Journal of Advertising Research* 9, 3 (1969): 13–16; Ronald F. Bush, Paul J. Solomon, and Joseph F. Hair, Jr., "There Are More Blacks in TV Commercials," *Journal of Advertising Research* 17, 1 (February 1977): 21. In a look back at African Americans and advertising between 1946 and 1965, Harold H. Kassarijian noted that the appearance of African Americans was rare, with one study finding blacks in four ads out of 2,500 pages examined, and another noting that blacks had speaking roles in 0.65 percent of commercials studied. In his own analysis, he found only 546 separate different ads containing blacks in nearly 150,000 magazine pages. He concluded, "the ads that treat the Negro as an equal are so few that neither can the civil rights groups be acclaimed successful nor can the advertising industry take particular pride in their supposedly newly found social responsibility." "The Negro and American Advertising, 1946–1965," in *The Black Consumer*, ed. Joyce and Govoni, 319–41.

18. Rose DeNeve, "Packaging for the Inner City," *Packaging and Design* (1970): 24–27, 42–44, Markets-Consumer-Ethnic-Black, Box 22, JWT Archives—Marketing Vertical Files Collection; Kelvin A. Wall, "The Great Waste: Ignoring Blacks," *Marketing/Communication*, February 1970, 42–48; Marilyn Kern-Foxworth, *Aunt Jemima, Uncle Ben, and Rastus: Blacks in Advertising, Yesterday, Today, and Tomorrow* (Westport, Conn.: Praeger, 1994), 98.

19. Vernon E. Jordan, "Black-Aimed Advertising—Some Pluses, Some Minuses," *Advertising Age*, 16 April 1979, S29.

20. Walter Weiss, "Mass Media and Social Change," in *Attitudes, Conflict, and Social Change*, ed. Bert. T. King and Elliott McGinnies (New York: Academic Press, 1972): 152; James D. Culley and Rex Bennett, "Equality in Advertising: Selling Women, Selling Blacks," *Journal of Communication* (Autumn 1976): 168–73; "2% of Magazines Have Blacks; Same as in 1968," *Marketing News*, 22 August 1980, Markets-Consumer-Ethnic-Black, Box 22, JWT Archive-Marketing Vertical Files Collection.

21. Peter Cannellos, "Why Can't Blacks Talk to Whites?" *Back Stage Magazine Supplement*, 7M-9M, Markets-Consumer-Ethnic-Black, Box 22, JWT Archive-Marketing Vertical Files Collection; Mark Green, *Invisible People: The Depiction of Minorities in Magazine Ads and Catalogs* (New York: City of New York Department of Consumer Affairs, 1991); Mark Green, *Still Invisible: The Depiction of Minorities in Magazine Ads One Year After the Consumer Affairs Department Study, Invisible People* (New York: City of New York Department of Consumer Affairs, 1992).

22. Adrienne Ward, "What Role Do Ads Play in Racial Tension," *Advertising Age* 63, 32, 10 August 1992, 1. Reactions by industry insiders accurately reflected what the studies found to be true: "Minorities are 'grossly underrepresented' in advertisements appearing in the nation's most widely circulated magazines." M. Chinyelu, "No Color in Magazine Ads," *Black Enterprise* 22, 5 (December 1991): 11–12.

23. Fonda Marie Lloyd and Cassandra Hayes, "25 Years of Blacks in Advertising," *Black Enterprise* 25, 6 (January 1995): 91; John W. Templeton, "Ad Spending Slights Black Consumers," *Advertising Age* 68, 11, 17 March 1997, 28; Clifford Franklin, "The Need to Look Beyond Black History Month," *Advertising Age* 71, 9, 28 February 2000, 62.

24. Marjorie Whigham-Desir, "The Real Black Power," *Black Enterprise* 26, 12 (July 1996): 60–66.

25. Gracian Mack, "Blacks Pay More for Living Costs," *Black Enterprise* 25, 4 (November 1994): 65; Valerie Lynn Gray, "Going After Our Dollar," *Black Enterprise*

27, 12 (July 1997): 68–74; Monique R. Brown, "Supermarket Blackout," *Black Enterprise* 29, 12 (July 1999): 81.

26. Matthew S. Scott, "The Madison Ave. Initiative," *Black Enterprise* 29, 12 (July 1999): 95–100. Of course some food advertisers did target their ads to African Americans, led in their efforts by two convenience food companies, Campbell Soup and Kraft General Foods, and fast food corporations. See, for example, Gail Baker Woods's discussion of Kraft's Stove Top stuffing campaign in *Advertising and Marketing to the New Majority* (Belmont, Calif.: Wadsworth, 1995), 69–78. Racist attitudes certainly compelled many advertisers not to target African Americans. While many justified their action on the supposed racism of white consumers, whom they feared alienating, it is clear that many executives brought their own stereotypes and racism to the table. For example, "Sheila Gadsen reported in *Advertising Age* that a major car rental company told an ad executive that his company did not advertise to blacks because blacks rented cars only to steal the tires." Djata, "Madison Avenue Blindly Ignores the Black Consumer," *Business and Society Review* 60 (Winter 1987): 10.

27. "Do Negroes Feel Left Out by Ad Men, too?" *Printers' Ink*, 21 June 1963, 7, 11; "The Hispanic Market: An Untapped Resource," *Chain Store Age/Supermarkets*, June 1983, 41, Markets-Consumer-Ethnic-Spanish, File 1 of 2, Box 22, JWT Archives—Marketing Vertical Files Collection. The frustrating extent to which advertisers rediscovered the market was captured in a 1979 cartoon. A man (whose body was a dollar sign) says, "Aqui se habla espanol" ("Spanish is spoken here"). The men to his left proclaim him "An invisible giant," while those to his right acknowledge, "He's always been around" (*Advertising Age*, 16 April 1979, S1).

28. Richard P. Jones, "Spanish-Language Market in U.S. Now 8 Million," *Media/scope*, July 1967, 85–92, Markets-Consumer-Ethnic-Spanish, File 2 of 2, Box 22, JWT Archives—Marketing Vertical Files Collection; Jessica Sinha, "Ethnic Marketing: Is It Worth an Extra Effort?" *Product Marketing*, June 1977, 30; Howard Lucraft, "Ad Experts Disagree on Use of 'Hispanic,' Agree on Need to Market in Spanish," *Adweek (West)*, 30 March 1981, 54–56; Nariman K. Dhalla, "Background Information on the Spanish-American Market," prepared for the SPEG Committee, November 1971, 18, Markets-Consumer-Ethnic-Spanish, File 2 of 2, Box 22, JWT Archives—Marketing Vertical Files Collection; Joseph M. Aguayo, "Latinos: Los que importan son Ustedes," *Sales & Marketing Management*, 11 July 1977, 28; James P. Forkan, "Big, Booming—and Still Neglected," *Advertising Age*, Section 2, 16 April 1979, S1; David Astor, "The Hispanic Market: An In-Depth Profile," *Marketing Communications* 6, 7 (July 1981): 15–20; B. G. Yovovich, "Cultural Pride Galvanizes Heritages," *Advertising Age*, 15 February 1982, M9; Maurice A. Ferre, "Decade of the Hispanic," *Advertising Age*, 15 February 1982: M-16; "Habla sales?" *Progressive Grocer* 76, 11, November 1997, 10.

29. Dhalla, "Background Information on the Spanish-American Market," 18; Aguayo, "Latinos: los que importan son Ustedes," 28. Alan Rooks noted that Hispanic brand loyalty was aided by the "fact that American brands have been heavily advertised and promoted in Spanish-speaking countries for years, has created strong markets for individual products among Hispanic consumers even before they arrive in the U.S." ("The U.S. Hispanic Market: Huge and Growing Rapidly," 8); Marye C. Tharp, *Marketing and Consumer Identity in Multicultural America* (Thousand Oaks, Calif.: Sage, 2001), 129–32; John F. Sugg, "Miami's Latin Market Spans Two Continents," *Advertising Age*, 15 February 1982, M40.

30. Dhalla, "Background Information on the Spanish-American Market," 18, 24; Aguayo, "Latinos: los que importan son Ustedes," 27; Sinha, "Ethnic Marketing: Is It Worth an Extra Effort?" 30.

31. Aguayo, "Latinos: los que importan Son Ustedes," 23, 26–29; Mark Watanabe, "Hispanic Marketing: A Profile Grows to New Heights," *Advertising Age*, 6 April 1981, S-1; Jesus D. Aguirre, "View from the Inside: Agency Execs Look at Segments of the Market They Work With," *Advertising Age*, 6 April 1981, S-6; "Latins Prefer Big Mac's to Whoppers Says Miami Hamburger Survey Results," *Adweek (Southeast)*, 6 July 1981, 30. Sinha, "Ethnic Marketing: Is It Worth an Extra Effort?" 31; "The Hispanic Market: An Untapped Resource," *Chain Store Age/Supermarkets*, June 1983, 41; "Hispanics Found to Use More Cents-Off Coupons, "*Marketing & Media Decisions*, February 1982, Markets-Consumer-Ethnic-Spanish, File 1 of 2, Box 22, JWT Archives—Marketing Vertical Files Collection; Woods, *Advertising and Marketing to the New Majority*, 144–50. Occasionally a report revealed that Hispanic brand loyalty was overblown or mythical, but in the main, as with African Americans, it was largely believed to be true. See, for example, Gabrielle Guirl, "Study Reveals Hispanic Brand Loyalty Is a Myth," *Adweek (Southeast)*, 16 September 1985, 64. One caution, sounded by John Chervokas, was that it was possible "that the fierce loyalty of the Hispanic consumer isn't fierce loyalty at all, but fear . . . fearful of trying something new." He based this assertion on research findings he cited that found that Hispanics "have not lived in this country very long and have had fewer purchase opportunities, and Hispanics have less information about products. . . . Rarely does a Hispanic boast of having purchased a new product 'just to try something different." He did caution that these studies were of east coast Hispanics, and that westerners, both white and Hispanic were likely more adventurous. John Chervokas, "As Hispanic as Apple Pie," *Madison Avenue*, July 1985, 66.

32. Mike Psaltis, "Coupons, si . . . at last," *TV/Radio Age*, 14 December 1980, Markets-Consumer-Ethnic-Spanish, File 1 of 2, Box 22, JWT Archives—Marketing Vertical Files Collection; Luis Diaz-Albertini, "Brand-Loyal Hispanics Need Good Reason for Switching," *Advertising Age*, 16 April 1975, S22-S23; "Hispanics Found to Use More Cents-Off Coupons"; "Coupons Going Spanish," *Advertising Age*, 15 February 1982: M-21; "Upsacle Hispanics Use More Coupons," *Editor & Publisher*, 13 March 1982, Markets-Consumer-Ethnic-Spanish, File 1 of 2, Box 22, JWT Archives-Marketing Vertical Files Collection; Guirl, "Study Reveals Hispanic Brand Loyalty Is a Myth," 64. In 1977, for example, Sinha noted that "Mailing of coupons and samples to the inner city are almost nil" ("Ethnic Marketing: Is It Worth an Extra Effort?" 30).

33. Tharp, *Marketing and Consumer Identity in Multicultural America*, 162–63; Humberto Valencia, "Point of View: Avoiding Hispanic Market Blunders," *Journal of Advertising Research* 23, 6 (December 1983/January 1984): 19–22.

34. "KFC Adds Spice to Hispanic Family Dining with Launch of First National Spanish-Language Ad Campaign and Community Outreach Effort," 29 April 2002, http://www.kfc.com/about/pr.htm; Enrique J. Perez, "Food Companies Recognize Spanish Market Potential," *Advertising Age*, 16 April 1979, S31.

35. *LHJ*, June 1920, 95, 138; *LHJ*, March 1935, 71; *LHJ*, November 1947, 295; *LHJ*, June 1950, 145; Marchand, *Advertising the American Dream*, 193; Daniel Delis Hill, *Advertising to the American Woman, 1900–1999* (Columbus: Ohio State University Press, 2002), 280. Jeffrey Steele argued that advertisers used Native Americans in nineteenth-century advertising to convey a whole host of messages, including the more overt sexuality of Indian women, the static image of an exotic

other, and the "myth that American Indians were more closely attuned to the rhythms of nature." His findings certainly hold true, in this broad sense, throughout twentieth-century food advertising. "Reduced to Images: American Indians in Advertising," in *The Gender and Consumer Culture Reader*, ed. Jennifer Scanlon (New York: New York University Press, 2000), 109–28.

36. *LHJ*, September 1920, 99.

37. The Amaizo Cook Book, "Cookbook Collection, 1920s-2, Shortening, Peterson Collection.

38. Scott Bruce, *Cereal Box Bonanza: The 1950s: Identification and Values* (Paducah, Ky.: Collector Books, 1995), 35, 71. The fame of western heroes, such as the Lone Ranger and Roy Rogers, who increasingly appeared on television, contributed to the popularity of the game.

39. *Life*, 4 May 1962, Box 11.1, JWT Archives—Competitive Advertisements Collection; *Redbook*, October 1976, 88; George Dean, "Mazola Indian Represents Product Benefits of Corn," *Advertising Age*, 2 April 1979, S26; *FC*, 1 November 1999, 7; Terry H. Anderson, *The Movement and the Sixties: Protest in America from Greensboro to Wounded Knee* (New York: Oxford University Press, 1995); Minneapolis Department of Civil Rights, "The Indian Image in Advertising: A Special Report," 14 March 1969, Advertising-Targeted group-Ethnic, Bartos Papers; George Dean, "Mazola Indian Represents Product Benefits of Corn," *Advertising Age*, 16 April 1979, S26.

40. Sidney W. Mintz, "Eating American," in Mintz, *Tasting Food, Tasting Freedom: Excursions into Eating, Culture, and the Past* (Boston: Beacon Press, 1996); *LHJ*, June 1911, 68; *LHJ*, June 1914, 61; Towle's Log Cabin Syrup ad, *WHC*, September 1922, Misc. L, Box 1, JWT Archives—Domestic Advertisements Collection; *NG*, August 1925; *NG*, April 1927; *NG*, April 1928.

41. *LHJ*, March 1905, 45; Campbell's Soup ad, *NG*, December 1930; Oscar Mayer, 1984 and 1991, Box 4, JWT Archives—Domestic Advertisements Collection; *NG*, August 1925; *NG*, April 1927; *NG*, April 1928.

42. *LHJ*, December 1914, 57; *Printers' Ink*, 8 November 1934, 8–9; Daniel J. Boorstin, "How We Democratized the American Diet from Salt Fish to Frozen Berries" *Smithsonian* 4, 3 (1973): 26–35, adapted from Boorstin, *The Americans: The Democratic Experience* (New York: Random House, 1973); Harvey Levenstein, *Revolution at the Table: The Transformation of the American Diet* (Berkeley: University of California Press, 2003), 199.

43. *LHJ*, June 1917, back outside cover. For more examples, see: Campbell's ad, *NG*, June 1915; Campbell's ad, *NG*, November 1916. Another common symbol employed by advertisers to suggest the American, patriotic association was "Uncle Sam," in his top hat and long beard. See for example, *LHJ*, September 1941, 7, 124; *Redbook*, October 1976, 88.

44. *LHJ*, September 1917, 31; *LHJ*, June 1918, 33.

45. *WHC*, April 1943, 106; *SEP*, 16 October 1943, 6, 91; *SEP*, 8 January 1944, 48–49; *LHJ*, April 1944, 14, 53, 60, 124.

46. *GH*, September 1942, 9, 11; *Life*, 24 January 1943, 9; *LHJ*, June 1944, 89.

47. *SEP*, 12 February 1944, 87; *SEP*, 6 May 1944, 69. Touting grapefruit juice's fighting power, the Florida Citrus Commission challenged consumers in 1943, "Just ask a Jap what if feels like to be up against men who are fortified with '*Victory Vitamin C*'" (Heimann, ed., *All-American Ads of the 1940s*, 441, emphasis theirs).

48. *LHJ*, December 1944, 14.

49. T. Swann Harding, "'Food for Freedom,'" *Printers' Ink*, 2 January 1942, 19–20 (bold in original); Heimann, ed., *All-American Ads of the 1940s*, 373, 384.

50. Harding, "Food for Freedom"; Heimann, ed., *All-American Ads of the 1940s.* During World War II, Campbell's soup ads appearing in *LHJ* put forward messages acknowledging the work of people in the service as well as those on the homefront. One 1943 ad, for example, reminded readers, "Food fights for freedom: Produce all we are able, conserve and play fair. Support no black market, Be glad we can share!" A 1944 ad thanked high school students for helping pick the food crop that year (author's notes from reviewing Campbell's advertisements in all issues of *LHJ* from 1943 and 1944).

51. Ads of this kind did appear in the early decades of the century, but not as frequently as in the postwar period. *LHJ*, May 1939, 33; *LHJ*, April 1946, 53; *LHJ*, November 1946, 99.

52. Hasia S. Diner, *Hungering for America: Italian, Irish, and Jewish Foodways in the Age of Migration* (Cambridge, Mass.: Harvard University Press, 2001), 211–12.

53. Dhalla, "Background Information on the Spanish-American Market," 25, 35; Luis Diaz-Albertini, "Brand-Loyal Hispanics Need Good Reason for Switching," S22-S23; "The Hispanic Market: An Untapped Resource," *Chain Store Age/Supermarkets*, June 1983, 41.

54. Teri A. Zubizarreta, "Assimilation Far from Real in Hispanic Community," *Advertising Age*, 16 April 1979, S31.

55. "Study Shows Negro Food Habits Conform," n.d., Sidney Ralph Bernstein, Department Files, JWT Archives—Research Dept. Collection.

56. Historian Lori Bogle encouraged and enlightened my thinking on this aspect of women's power. Cultural analyst Josef Konvitz found that "The importance of diet to self-identity and community strength can be seen in the way that many religions and particularly Judaism have made diet into a means of spiritual sustenance and dietary differences into character building." "Identity, Self-Expression, and the American Cook," *Centennial Review* 19, 2 (1975): 85–95. See also Jean Soler, "The Semiotics of Food in the Bible," in *Food and Culture: A Reader*, ed. Carole Counihan and Penny Van Esterik (New York: Routledge, 1997), 55–66; Doris Witt, *Black Hunger: Food and the Politics of U.S. Identity* (New York: Oxford University Press, 1999). Witt's chapter, " 'Pork or Women': Purity and Danger in the Nation of Islam," 102–25, offers a nuanced understanding of this phenomenon.

57. Jenna Weissman Joselit, *The Wonders of America: Reinventing Jewish Culture, 1880–1950* (New York: Hill and Wang, 1994), 187–98; *Maclean's* 112, 48, 29 November 1999, 70–71; Standard Brands, 1962, Box 11, JWT Archives—Domestic Advertisements Collection. For example, in 1911 the American Association of Foreign-Language Newspapers, which represented 465 papers across the country and in Canada, ran an ad in *Printers' Ink* that stated, "Foreign-Speaking Americans Eat Better Food and Wear Better Clothes Than *Native* Americans Enjoying the Same Incomes. There Are Fourteen Million of Them" (15 June 1911, 30). In 1920 the "Big Four of Jewish journalism" ran an ad in *Printers' Ink* touting their influence in selling the Jewish consumer and the value of a consumer base that they claimed was loyal and of genuine quality (24 June 1920, 110–11). Localized food advertising certainly existed throughout the twentieth century, such as a Mother's Gefilte Fish ad in *NYT*, 13 September 1967, 16.2, JWT Archives—Competitive Advertisements Collection. Hasia Diner explored how advertisers sought out Jewish consumers in *Hungering for America*, noting that "By the 1910s such companies as Gold Medal Flour, Uneeda Biscuits, Quaker Oats, H. J. Heinz, Coca-Cola, and other giant producers of food, routinely advertised in the Yiddish press." She also recounted the story of Crisco (told first by Susan Strasser) and how Proctor and Gamble promoted its new product by gaining the

approval of an influential orthodox rabbi who endorsed it as "ritually pure." Their advertisements claimed, "'The Hebrew Race had been waiting for 4,000 years' for a solution to its shortening problems, and now, with the rabbi's blessing, it had Crisco" (211–12); Susan Strasser, *Satisfaction Guaranteed: The Making of the American Mass Market* (New York: Pantheon, 1989), 3–28.

58. *LHJ*, March 1910, 33; *LHJ*, June 1920, 81; *LHJ*, December 1929, 150; *LHJ*, October 1976, 124–25. This analysis focuses on Lent.

59. *LHJ*, March 1929, 39; *LHJ*, March 1930, 39; *LHJ*, April 1930, 39; *LHJ*, March 1942, 95; *LHJ*, March 1950, 157; *GH*, March 1966, 171; "Red and White Soup Recipe Advertising in *Catholic Church Bulletins*," 19 September 1984, No. 367, Folder 29, Box 3, Campbell Soup Company Archive, Archives Center, National Museum of American History, Smithsonian Institution.

60. *LHJ*, March 1941, 43; *LHJ*, March 1950, 141; *LHJ*, March 1953, 20.

61. *LHJ*, March 1950, 105; *LHJ*, March 1953, 157.

62. *LHJ*, March 1920, 57; Paul Messaris, *Visual Persuasion: The Role of Images in Advertising* (Thousand Oaks, Calif.: Sage, 1997), 225–36; Marchand, *Advertising the American Dream*, 194–202. While Roland Marchand argues that there was a shift from ads that held out the upper-class as an aspiration to those of the 1950s that suggested average Americans were upper class, consumers received a consistent message that they should consume products to reach or reflect a higher socioeconomic status. "Visions of Classlessness, Quests for Dominion: American Popular Culture, 1945–1960," in *Reshaping America: Society and Institutions*, ed. Robert H. Bremner and Gary W. Reichard (Columbus: Ohio State University Press, 1982), 169.

63. J. A. C. Brown, *Techniques of Persuasion: From Propaganda to Brainwashing* (1963; Baltimore: Penguin, 1969), 186. Marchand offers insights into advertisers' perceptions of the masses, noting "Most advertisers defined the market for their products as a relatively select audience of upper-class and upper-middle-class Americans" (xvii, *Advertising the American Dream*, 63). This was true for early avocado growers, according to Jeffrey Charles's essay, "Searching for Gold in Guacamole," in *Food Nations: Selling Taste in Consumer Societies*, ed. Warren Belasco and Philip Scranton (New York: Routledge, 2002), 143. See also Patricia Johnston, *Real Fantasies: Edward Steichen's Advertising Photography* (Berkeley: University of California Press, 1997), 50–55, 166–203.

64. "Garbage Dump Marks Long Ago Beginnings of Market Research," *Advertising Age*, 30 April 1980, 68; Charles Coolidge Parlin, "Dry Waste Survey Presentation" (post-1911), Box 98, Curtis Collections; *Helps for the Hostess* (Camden, N.J.: Joseph Campbell Company, c1916), Campbell Archive, Camden.

65. Henry Sherwood Youker, "Canned Soup" (1917), Box 50, Curtis Collection; Douglas Collins, *America's Favorite Food: The Story of Campbell Soup Company* (New York: Harry Abrams, 1994), 89–90.

66. Campbell's ad, 1912, Campbell Archive, Camden.

67. Marchand, *Advertising the American Dream*, 200–205.

68. *LHJ*, 1 December 1910, 32; *LHJ*, December 1926, 33.

69. *LHJ*, September 1926, 61; *RD*, May 1970, B3; *LHJ*, September 1980, 131; *LHJ*, September 1989, 177; Marchand, *Advertising the American Dream*, 217–22, 233–34, 290–95; Susan J. Matt, *Keeping Up with the Joneses: Envy in American Consumer Society, 1890–1930* (Philadelphia: University of Pennsylvania Press, 2003), 12, 44–50.

70. Ernest Dichter, "A Psychological Research Study of the Effectiveness of Current Packaged White Bread Advertising," c.1956, IMR.

71. *Helps for the Hostess*, 3–7; *LHJ*, March 1938, 37; Susan Williams, *Savory Suppers and Fashionable Feasts: Dining in Victorian America* (New York: Pantheon, 1985), 105–7; "Joan of Arc French Red Kidney Beans," Food Collection, Box 23, Warshaw Collection.

72. *LHJ*, June 1908, 47; *GH*, September 1971, 147; *New Yorker*, 19 October 1957.

73. *LHJ*, September 1905, 38; *LHJ*, June 1920, 144; *GH*, March 1940, 11; *LHJ*, March 1974, 99; *LHJ*, September 1980, 8. The Grey Poupon print and television ads allowed viewers to observe the wealthy in action and introduced the haughty, "Pardon me, would you have any Grey Poupon" into popular culture. Caroline Wyman, *I'm a Spam Fan: America's Best-Loved Foods* (Stamford, Conn.: Longmeadow Press, 1993), 117–18.

74. *GH*, May 1950, 162; *LHJ*, October 1967, 124; *LHJ*, September 1986, 157.

75. "The Fabulous Market for Food," *Fortune* (October 1953): 135–38; Dik Warren Twedt, "Consumer Psychology," *Annual Review of Psychology* 16 (1965): 269. The National Industrial Conference Board also reported in their 1969 statistical fact book, that expenditures for food at home (based on constant dollars from 1950) rose dramatically between 1950 and 1967. "Consumer Markets," 50–53, Markets: Consumer Pamphlets, 1 of 6, JWT Archives—Marketing Vertical File Collection.

76. Twedt, "Consumer Psychology," 271, 274; "Negro Food and Entertainment Habits," JWT Archives—Marketing Vertical Files Collection; "Business Highlights," *Progressive Grocer*, January 1970; "Probing the Negro Market," *Sales Management*, 44; Gibson, " 'Creating Products for Negro Consumers,' " 61–65; Bauer and Cunningham, "The Negro Market," 6–7; Donald E. Sexton, Jr., "Black Buyer Behavior," *Journal of Marketing* 36 (October 1972): 36–39; Henry Allen Bullock, "Consumer Motivations in Black and White—I," *Harvard Business Review* 39 (May/June 1961): 89–104; Henry Allen Bullock, "Consumer Motivations in Black and White—II," *Harvard Business Review* 39 (July/August 1961): 110–24; Alphonzia Wellington, "Traditional Brand Loyalty," *Advertising Age*, 18 May 1981, S2. While unusual, some researchers also recognized that there were differences among African Americans as well. One study analyzed perceptions of grocery stores, breaking down their comparisons along place (ghetto versus suburbs) and age (young vs. old), but leaving intact the assumption that the consumer was female. "Gerald E. Hills et al., "Black Consumer Perceptions of Food Store Attributes," *Journal of Marketing* 37 (April 1973): 47–57.

77. Wellington, "Traditional Brand Loyalty," S2.

78. Ed Meyer, "How to Promote to Black and Hispanic Consumers," *Advertising Age*, 16 April 1979, 54, 58; Wellington, "Traditional Brand Loyalty," S2; B. G. Yovovich, "Views on Coupons Changing," *Advertising Age*, 18 May 1981, S15; Roseann Caffaro, "430 Congregations Will Receive 'Black Shoppers Guide' Coupons," *Premium/Incentive Business*, October 1981; Lynn Engelhardt, "Blacks Favor Brands with Positive Image Advertising," *Adweek*, 3 May 1982, 46; Peter K. Tat and David Bejou, "Examining Black Consumer Motives for Coupon Usage," *Journal of Advertising Research* 34, 2 (March/April 1994): 29; Corliss L. Green, "Differential Responses to Retail Sales Promotion Among African American and Anglo-American Consumers," *Journal of Retailing* 71 (Spring 1995): 83–92.

79. "America's New Elite: A Big-Spending Market Is Born: Two-Career Couples," *Time*, 21 August 1978, 56–57; Maureen Dowd, "Advertising in the Post-Martini Age," *NYT*, 20 May 1986, B1; John J. Burnett and Alan J. Bush, "Profiling the Yuppies," *Journal of Advertising Research* 26, 2 (April 1986): 27; Belinda Hulin-Salkin, "Grocery Marketing: What Price Exposure?" *Advertising Age* 59, 42, 3

October 1988, S1; Martha Smilgis, "Here Come the DINKs: Double-Income, No-Kids Couples Are the Latest Subset," *Time*, 20 April 1987, 75; "A Luxury Supermarket Woos its Upscale Clients with a Yuppie Credo—You Are What You Eat!" *People Weekly* 32, 4 (11 December 1989): 135–36.

80. While Hispanic cooking was certainly a part of the American tradition in the Southwest, it is included in the section on ethnic foods, because early advertisements did not characterize the foods as American, but instead as "other." Creole cooking grew in national popularity in the late twentieth century, but its appeal was generally more limited. In part, its limited appeal makes sense given the foods' spiciness. Companies did not advertise their products on a national level, although the expression "Cajun" did find its way into advertising lexicon as a substitute for "spicy." See Waverly Root and Richard de Rochemont, "The Tepid Melting Pot" in *Eating in America: A History* (1976; Hopewell, N.J.: Ecco Press, 1995), 276–87. The market for Jewish foods also expanded late in the century, but national advertising was fairly limited for most kosher foods, bagels being the most common exception. William M. Freeman, "News of the Advertising and Marketing Fields," *NYT*, 9 October 1955, F10; "Minority Potential Big, But Still Unrealized," *Advertising Age* 50, 16 April 1979, S12; *LHJ*, September 1980, 118; *LHJ*, March 1995, 173; C. Paige Gutierrez, *Cajun Foodways* (Jackson: University Press of Mississippi, 1992). However, brand-name product advertisements in the Yiddish press found success. Marilyn Halter argued that "Jewish immigrants were more receptive than Italians or Germans to national advertising and participation in American consumer culture." She also noted that the late twentieth-century success of products with kosher certification was due to nonkosher customers. *Shopping for Identity: The Marketing of Ethnicity* (New York: Schocken Books, 2000), 35, 111–12.

81. "The Flavor of American Tradition: Corn Meal and Grits Recipes" (Quaker Oats Co.), 1960s-7, Peterson Collection; Root and DeRochemont, *Eating in America*, 84, 145. For example, the diet of Southern African Americans, with its basis in African traditions, was a largely regional phenomenon in the early twentieth century. Previously, most black migrants to the North had accommodated their diet to the foodstuffs and habits of their new surroundings. However, Tracy Poe found that the Great Migration created tension between local and migrating African Americans in Chicago. The local African American population prided itself on their moderately successful assimilation into the broader mainstream dietary culture, but the arriving Southern population were proud of and wanted to retain their diet. Some entrepreneurial migrating Southern African Americans found, like so many like-minded immigrants, that there was a market for familiar foods within their own communities. "Origins of Soul Food in Black Urban Identity: Chicago, 1915–1947," *American Studies International* 37, 1 (1999): 4–33.

82. *Ebony*, December 1999, 163; *Ebony*, June 2000, 132; "Eating like Soul Brothers," *Time*, 24 January 1969; Witt, *Black Hunger*, 79–135; "Yam & Okra Recipes" (B.F. Trappey's Sons, Inc.), 1970s-7, Peterson Collection; Psyche A. Williams-Forson, "'Suckin' the Chicken Bone Dry: African American Women, Fried Chicken, and the Power of a National Narrative," in *Cooking Lessons: The Politics of Gender and Food*, ed. Sherrie A. Inness (Lanham, Md.: Rowman and Littlefield, 2001), 177. The only advertisements I found showcasing African American cuisine appeared in the Black-themed magazines and were not especially plentiful. In addition to Black magazines, Black newspapers with national distribution also included some food ads. As with so many foods, the origins of "African American foods" are uncertain, particularly the extent to which foods are racial or regional.

It appears that throughout the century the poorest segments of the South ate similar foods, but as they were able, whites made subtle culinary choices to differentiate their identity from that of Blacks. See, for example, Joe Gray Taylor, *Eating, Drinking, and Visiting in the South: An Informal History* (Baton Rouge: Louisiana State University Press, 1982), 83–91. Some food companies did cater to the African American market, including Kentucky Fried Chicken (which responded to growing concern about fried foods by changing its name to KFC in 1991). The company believed that African Americans comprised 25 percent of their consumption in 1993. To boost their sales with this market they introduced the Neighborhood KFC program, which in addition to outfitting employees in "traditional African-oriented uniforms" and piping in music, featured "soul sides," including red beans and rice, sweet potato pie, and Mean Greens, a mixture of mustard, turnip, and collard greens. They also had a similar plan to target Hispanics. John P. Cortez, "KFC Stores Boast Flavor of Neighborhood," *Advertising Age*, 31 May 1993, 3.

83. "Minority Potential Big, But Still Unrealized," *Advertising Age*, S12; Michael Schudson, *Advertising, the Uneasy Persuasion: Its Dubious Impact on American Society* (New York: Basic Books, 1984), 119–20; Marchand, *Advertising the American Dream*, 192–93; Jennifer Scanlon, *Inarticulate Longings: The Ladies' Home Journal, Gender, and the Promises of Consumer Culture* (New York: Routledge, 1995), 4–5, 35, 221–24; Richard Ohmann, *Selling Culture: Magazines, Markets, and Class at the Turn of the Century* (New York: Verso, 1996), 255–66; Charlotte A. Pratt and Cornelius B. Pratt, "Nutrition Advertisements in Consumer Magazines: Health Implications for African Americans," *Journal of Black Studies* 26, 4 (March 1996): 504–23; Chester St. H. Mills and Rebecca A. Chaisson, "The Betrayal of the Media," in *Advertising and Culture: Theoretical Perspectives*, ed. Mary Cross (Westport, Conn.: Praeger, 1996), 113–24. A 1995 "Special Report" on Marketing to African Americans found that "Marketers are saying that, as the percentage of Hispanics, African Americans, and Asians grow, 'general' can't be typified by white anymore." While marketers might have suggested moving away from Whites as the standard, food advertising generally did not reflect that shift in mainstream print media at any time in the twentieth century. Adrienne Ward Fawcett, "Ethnic Shops See Shifting Definition of 'General' Ad Efforts," *Advertising Age*, 17 July 1995, S1-S3.

84. Fawcett, "Ethnic Shops,"; "White Swan Shortening," Box 23, Warshaw Collection; Campbell's Soup ad, *Christian Herald*, 23 September 1914, 885, depicted in Kern-Foxworth, *Aunt Jemima, Uncle Ben, and Rastus*, fig.14; G. A. Nichols, "Aunt Jemima Comes to Life," *Printers' Ink*, 18 March 1920, 17–20, 25–26; *LHJ*, September 1926, 87; *GH*, March 1940, 133; *LHJ*, May 1951, 253. M. M. Manring's analysis of Aunt Jemima explores how the flour company chose to promote the image of a slave woman. M. M. Manring, *Slave in a Box: The Strange Career of Aunt Jemima* (Charlottesville: University Press of Virginia, 1998). Aunt Jemima was not the only mammy to appear in advertising; they also appeared periodically in ads for companies including Hostess Cake and Kraft's Parkay margarine, as well as in a cookbook for Dixie Crystals Sugar. See for example, *LHJ*, September 1929, 125; *LHJ*, March 1942, 77; *Dixie Crystals Sugar*, 1950s-7, Peterson Collection; Ronnie Crocker, "Homage to Aunt Jemima Remains a Tricky Business," http://www.chron.com/content/chronicle/metropolitan/96/04/07/aunt-jemima.html.

85. *GH*, March 1940, 133; Manring, *Slave in a Box*, 149–83; Kern-Foxworth, *Aunt Jemima, Uncle Ben, and Rastus*, 82–107; Dichter, "A Psychological Research

Study on the Effectiveness of Betty Crocker in Promoting General Mills Products," May 1953, IMR, 121–22; K. Sue Jewell, *From Mammy to Miss America and Beyond: Cultural Images and the Shaping of U.S. Social Policy* (London: Routledge, 1993). One ad featured in an article about Aunt Jemima in 1916 had three panels showing white hands doing the cooking process, while the Aunt Jemima figure proclaimed, "I'se in Town Honey." Another had a white woman holding off another white woman, saying "'Never mind the milk—I'm using Aunt Jemima's,"' as if to say not only does it save you needing lots of different ingredients, but it also means you do not need extra help. Paul Findlay, "'Aunt Jemima' Back Among the Big Advertisers Again," *Printers' Ink*, 17 August 1916, 92, 95.

86. Rose DeNeve, "Packaging for the Inner City," *Packaging and Design*, 1970, 24–27, 42–44; Alphonzia Wellington, "Blacks and Hispanics: Power in Numbers and Market Concentration," *Dollars & Sense*, 9 August 1982, 134–42. Paul K. Edwards's 1932 book *The Southern Urban Negro as a Consumer* (New York: Prentice-Hall, 1932) "dealt with black consumer attitudes about advertisements that featured blacks in subservient or demeaning situations." Blacks of all classes in a variety of southern cities said things like "Illustration of Aunt Jemima utterly disgusts me"; "Not interested in picture of black mammy"; "Don't like exploitation of colored people. Whenever I see a picture such as this I am prejudiced against product." Weems, *Desegregating the Dollar*, 22–25.

87. Manring, *Slave in a Box*, 149–83; Kern-Foxworth, *Aunt Jemima, Uncle Ben, and Rastus*, 82–107; Jewell, *From Mammy to Miss America and Beyond*, 183–208; Quaker Oats, 1986, Box 10, JWT Archives—Domestic Advertisements Collection.

88. For the Uncle Ben corporate history, see Wyman, *I'm a Spam Fan*; *LHJ*, June 1992, 167; *LHJ*, September 1992, 198. While Uncle Ben's image was less controversial than Aunt Jemima's, for example, the company also perceived it as less critical to its product line. The company even removed his image for a period from the packages during the Civil Rights Movement and restored it later with much less prominence, although late in the century, he was back in a more central role. See, for example, Kern-Foxworth, *Aunt Jemima, Uncle Ben, and Rastus*, 98–100; Theodore J. Gage, "RSVP: An Invitation to Buy," *Advertising Age*, 16 May 1981, S1; *GH*, October 1997, 139. Aunt Jemima was not the only image to undergo "modernization." General Mills revamped Betty Crocker seven times since the original photo debuted in 1936, with five changes in just the past twenty years. See Steven V. Robert, "Betty, Meet Ashley, a '90s Woman," *U.S. News & World Report*, 1 April 1996, 10–11.

89. Department of Consumer Affairs, "The History of Cream of Wheat" (East Hanover, N.J.: Nabisco Brands, 1988); Helen Zailo, Consumer Representative of Nabisco Foods, to Katherine Parkin, describing history of Rastus, October 20, 1999, in author's possession.

90. Marisa Helms, "Cream of Wheat plant closes; leaves history behind," Minnesota Public Radio http://news.mpr.org/features/200202/14_helmsm_cream ofwheat.

91. David A. Hollinger, *From Melting Pot to Salad Bowl—Postethnic America: Beyond Multiculturalism* (New York: Basic Books, 1995); Peter Salins, "Assimilation, American Style," *Reason* 28, 9 (February 1997): 20–26; Alan M. Kraut, "Ethnic Foodways: The Significance of Food in the Designation of Cultural Boundaries Between Immigrant Groups in the U.S., 1840–1921," *Journal of American Culture: Focus on American Food and Foodways* 2, 3 (Fall 1979): 409–20; Judy Perkin and Stephanie F. McCann, "Food for Ethnic Americans: Is the Government Trying to

Turn the Melting Pot into a One-Dish Dinner?" *Ethnic and Regional Foodways,* ed. Brown and Mussell, 238–58.

92. Joseph R. Conlin, *Bacon, Beans, and Galantines: Food and Foodways on the Western Mining Frontier* (Reno: University of Nevada Press, 1986), 137–38, 186–94; Bryan R. Johnson, "Let's Eat Chinese Tonight," *American Heritag,* 38, 8 (December 1987): 98–107; Xiaolan Bao, "When Women Arrived: The Transformation of New York's Chinatown," in *Not June Cleaver: Women and Gender in Postwar America,* ed. Joanne Meyerowitz (Philadelphia: Temple University Press, 1994), 19–36; Gaye Tuchman and Harry Gene Levine, "New York Jews and Chinese Food: The Social Construction of an Ethnic Pattern," in *The Taste of American Place: A Reader on Regional and Ethnic Foods,* ed. Barbara G. Shortridge and James R. Shortridge (Lanham, Md.: Rowman and Littlefield, 1998), 163–84.

93. *LHJ,* September 1920, 89; *LHJ,* September 1929, 118; "The Art and Secrets of Chinese Cookery" (Detroit: La Choy Food Products, 1937); William Leach, *Land of Desire: Merchants, Power, and the Rise of a New American Culture* (New York: Vintage, 1993), 104–11, 325. A 1916 Kitchen Bouquet cookbook entitled *Savory Dishes* contained a recipe for "Chop Suey," 1910s-3, Peterson Collection.

94. *LHJ,* September 1929, 118, 121; *LHJ,* March 1938, 37.

95. *LHJ,* September 1929, 121.

96. *Printers' Ink,* 22 September 1932, 84; "The Art and Secrets of Chinese Cookery," 1–17; *LHJ,* March 1944, 156; La Choy Cookbook, 1949, 1940s-11, Peterson Collection; Shapiro, *Something from the Oven,* 29.

97. *LHJ,* January 1950, 4; *LHJ,* September 1950, 105; *SEP,* 17 March 1951, 68; *LHJ,* March 1959, 52.

98. Shapiro, *Something from the Oven,* 18–19; Levenstein, *Paradox of Plenty,* 87, 107, 122.

99. "Chun King—A New Mood in Food," *JWT News,* 37, 10 September 1956, 11, Box 6, JWT Archives—JWT News Collection; *RD,* September 1956, 18; *LHJ,* March 1959, 52.

100. 1963 Chun King ad, File 9.8, JWT Archives—Competitive Advertisements Collection.

101. *Life,* 17 January 1964, 13.

102. *Sunset,* October 1966.

103. Chun King, Box 14 and 26, JWT Archives—Review Board Records Collection. According to the JWT files, they began to track the growing popularity of Chinese food in about 1967. Two articles, one from *Ad Daily,* 15 April 1967, and the other from the *Salt Lake Tribune,* 16 April 1967, noted that "More Americans have a yen for Chinese food today," and commented on the growing ad dollars being put toward increasing their market share (R.J. Reynolds Co.: Chun King, Box 16, JWT Archives—Account Files Collection). John McDonough of the *Tribune* noted, "One out of every two families in America now eats Chinese food either at home or in a restaurant. Of those, 68 per cent eat it most often at home." He also reported that "Industry sources estimate the Chinese-American food market is growing at 15 per cent a year." *Madison Avenue Magazine,* October 1976, 24, featured an article that highlighted the advertising strategies of La Choy. With an ad claiming "LaChoy makes Chinese food as American as apple pie," the article noted that they were trying to reach housewives and increase the likelihood that young people would try their products.

104. Heimann, ed., *All-American Ads of the 1940s,* 799, 802; *McCall's,* May 1964, 155; *BHG,* July 1968; *LHJ,* June 1972; *LHJ,* March 1977, 113; *LHJ,* December 1980, PS6; *LHJ,* June 1983, 47; *LHJ,* March 1986, 147; *LHJ,* March 1989, 145; *LHJ,* March 1995, 149.

105. *Redbook,* December 1976, 150; Bernice Kanner, "'Shop's Theory:' It Takes a Woman to Sell One," *Advertising Age,* 21 July 1980, 68; *LHJ,* March 1983, 75; *RD,* September 1983, 174; *Reader's Digest,* December 1983, 42; *Weight Watchers,* March/April 1997, 125.

106. *LHJ,* September 1983, 122; *LHJ,* June 1992, 152; *LHJ,* September 1992, 210.

107. Udayan Gupta, "Look Out Burgers, Tacos Are on a Roll," *Advertising Age,* 21 November 1983, M18; Levenstein, *Paradox of Plenty,* 216–17. Jeffrey Charles considers consumer prejudice of Mexicans and its association with the avocado in his essay, "Searching for Gold in Guacamole," in *Food Nations,* 133, 142.

108. *LHJ,* June 1914, 61; *LHJ,* March 1917, 39. While Levenstein maintained that in addition to being a classic 'man's dish,' chili con carne was also "a traditional American (not Mexican) recipe, because of its call for garlic, food advertisers positioned it as a Mexican dish (in *Paradox of Plenty,* 269 n 89.

109. *SEP,* 5 February 1944, 87. Joseph R. Conlin found that Anglo western miners defined themselves against their Hispanic peers, and rejected their foods, even though they were less expensive. Conlin argues they did so for two primary reasons: they would not deign to eat the foods of a people they had conquered and they considered tortilla making to be women's work (*Bacon, Beans, and Galantines,* 183–86). See also Gage, "RSVP: An Invitation to Buy," S1.

110. *LHJ,* November 1947, 83; *LHJ,* January 1953, 122.

111. Gail Stern, "Ethnic Images in Advertising," Council of Better Business Bureau's Annual Forum Series (1985), 97–202, Ethnic Markets, Box 6, Bartos Papers; Alice E. Courtney and Thomas W. Whipple, *Sex Stereotyping in Advertising* (Lexington, Mass.: Heath and Company, 1983).

112. *Redbook,* October 1976, 159; *LHJ,* March 1980, 6; "Taco Bell Targets Mainstream America," *Marketing & Media Decisions,* June 1984, 66–69, 174.

113. *LHJ,* November 1947, 83; *Seventeen,* March 1966, 163; *LHJ,* June 1980, 64; *LHJ,* June 1986, 139; Elda Silva, "Head of Hispanic Group, Advertising Executive Differ on Taco Bell Dispute," *San Antonio Express-News,* 11 March 1998; Elaine Walker, "Taco Bell Drops the Chihuahua from Its Ads," *Miami Herald,* 20 July 2000; Bobby White, "Smiles Aside, Companies Walk Fine Line in Marketing to Blacks," *Atlanta Journal and Constitution,* 22 July 2001.

114. "Goya Foods Promotes to Anglo Buyers," *Advertising Age,* 16 April 1979, S30.

115. *LHJ,* March 1986, 156; *LHJ,* March 1986, 163; *LHJ,* December 1986, 8; Beatrice Foods, 1987, Box 1, JWT Archives—Domestic Advertisements Collection; *LHJ,* March 1989, 63; *GH,* December 1993, 147; *People,* 4 November 1996, 115; *New Woman,* March 1997, 70; *Weight Watchers,* March/April 1997, 15; "Manufacturer's Coupon," *Philadelphia Inquirer,* April 1998; Gabbaccia, *We Are What We Eat,* 219–21. In 1983, one manufacturer's rep noted, "A lot of the items in the Ortega, Tio Sancho and Old El Paso lines are probably more for Anglo tastes today than truly for people whose national origin is Spanish" ("The Hispanic Market: An Untapped Resource," *Chain Store Age/Supermarkets,* June 1983, 41).

116. Levenstein, "The American Response," 4–5; *McCall's,* May 1964, 155; *Redbook,* December 1976, 145; *GH,* October 1997, 123; *LHJ,* September 1920, 92. Olive oil, for example, had a vested interest in this approach, and Star Brand Olive Oil produced a cookbook in 1928 called *Pitanze Scelte Italiana,* 1920s-2, Peterson Collection.

117. *LHJ,* September 1926, 55; *LHJ,* September 1935, 46; *LHJ,* March 1941, 118; Levenstein, "The American Response," 12–15; Levenstein, *Paradox of Plenty,* 29–30. A 1926 assessment of the A.C. Krumm and Son Macaroni Company,

conducted by the J. Walter Thompson Company, reported "Macaroni is a foreign food, originated in Northern Germany. It can be sold to practically every nationality except Italians, who prefer the spaghetti made by their countrymen, and who buy bulk goods instead of packaged goods." A. C. Krumm and Son Macaroni Company Account History, 11 January 1926, JWT Archives—Domestic Advertisements Collection.

118. Of particular concern was stretching meat, which meshed perfectly with spaghetti dinners. *LHJ*, June 1932, 52; *LHJ*, September 1935, 46; *LHJ*, March 1941, 118; *LHJ*, June 1944, 89; *Woman's Day*, August 1972, 107; *LHJ*, October 1976, 128–129; Uncle' Ben's ad, 1979, JWT Archives—Domestic Advertisements Collection; Levenstein, "The American Response," 17–19; Levenstein, *Paradox of Plenty*, 122. Reflecting on the state of advertising generally, the president of Grey Advertising, Edward H. Meyer, noted that the styles of the 1960s were no longer suitable due to consumers' more serious attitudes, which he attributed to the state of the economy and the growing concern about the environment. While he alluded to the "broader social concerns," he did not mention the major changes the role women and African Americans wrought in the 1960s, nor did he mention that the United States was a country at war. "The Thinking Buyer," *NYT*, 4 April 1971, F13.

119. Hyphenated Italian-American in original. "Will Ads Prolong Italian Fad?" *Tide*, 22 June 1956, 44; "How to Stay on Top in the Freezer," *Printers' Ink*, 15 March 1963, 49–50; "Why Roman Put That Clock on TV," *Printers' Ink*, 19 July 1963, 36–39. In spite of Italian food's success in integrating into American culture, the records of a 1955 JWT meeting regarding their client Buitoni, concluded that they should "describe lasagna as well as illustrate the dish in the frozen food poster for this product, because a great many people are not acquainted with it . . . marinara sauce . . . name is undoubtedly unfamiliar to a large number of people." Buitoni, 7 June 1955, Box 6 of 34, JWT Archives—Review Board Records Collection.

120. Dichter, "A Psychological Research Study on the Sales and Advertising Problems of Franco-American Spaghetti," October, 1953, IMR, 9.

121. Ibid., 10.

122. Ibid., 25; *LHJ*, July 1971, 40; *LHJ*, July 1971, 95; *Time*, 13 December 1971; *Life*, 16 May 1955.

123. Dichter, "Study on Franco-American Spaghetti," IMR, 15; *LHJ*, March 1977, 153c; *LHJ*, September 1977, 174e.

124. 1960 Kraft ad, Box 12.7, JWT Archives—Domestic Advertisements Collection; *LHJ*, April 1961, 29; Heimann, ed., *All-American Ads of the 1940s*, 809; *LHJ*, September 1962, 91; 1963 Kraft ad, Box 8.47, JWT Archives—Domestic Advertisements Collection; *McCall's*, May 1964, 155; *LHJ*, March 1965, 43; *GH*, December 1966, 87; 1967 Chef Boy-Ar-Dee ad, Box 16.11, JWT Archives—Domestic Advertisements Collection; *LHJ*, October 1976, 124–25; *Let's "Cook Italian" with Hunt's Tomato Paste*, 1960s-8, JWT Archives—Peterson Collection. As with the Betty Crocker cakes that only needed water, so too the powdered Chef Boy-Ar-Dee spaghetti sauce that only needed water to become "glorious Italian-style sauce" went by the wayside.

125. Copper Kitchen Sauce Line, Box 14, JWT Archives—Review Board Records Collection.

126. *LHJ*, December 1953, 93; *Life*, 16 May 1955, 51; *Life*, 11 July 1955, 50; *LHJ*, March 1956, 36; *LHJ*, March 1977, S1.

127. *Look*, 21 February 1967; *RD*, January 1976, 19; *BHG*, September 1978, Box 16.38, JWT Archives—Competitive Advertisements Collection.

128. *GH*, February 1970, 3; James Wade, "The Seventies: A Marketing View" (1 February 1971), 17–18, Standard Brands, Box 17, JWT Archives—Account Files Collection; *LHJ*, December 1980, 64; *LHJ*, March 1983, 16; *LHJ*, September 1983, 141; *LHJ*, September 1983, 151; *LHJ*, March 1992, 65; *LHJ*, December 1992, 157; Warren J. Belasco, *Appetite for Change: How the CountercultureTook on the Food Industry, 1966–1988* (New York: Pantheon, 1989), 229–236. Food writer Molly O'Neill explored the influence of the International Olive Oil Council (IOOC) on American consumption of olive oil in the 1980s and 1990s. Between 1982 and 2003, olive oil imports rose from $8.4 million dollars worth to $64.3 million worth. Former director of the IOOC Fausto Luchetti contended that they " 'spent that money almost exclusively to influence the taste makers.' " O'Neill maintained that "Many in the persuasion business believe that for every dollar spent on food-related public relations three dollars would have to be spent on advertising to achieve the same results." Her assessment dealt not with advertisements, then, but instead considered the extent to which the council's promotion of the "Mediterranean mystique" might have led writers to embrace the oil. "Food Porn," *Columbia Journalism Review*, September/October 2003.

Chapter 4. Authority and Entitlement: Men in Food Shopping

1. Ernest Dichter, "Franco-American Spaghetti," IMR, 14; *GH*, June 1940, 7.
2. *LHJ*, September 1926, 55; *WHC*, September 1932, 54; *WHC*, October 1932, inside back cover; *LHJ*, May 1946, 166; *GH*, February 1978, Box 17.25, JWT Archives—Competitive Advertisements Collection.
3. Campbell's Soup ad, *NG*, January 1914; *LHJ*, June 1914, 42; "Mother-and-Child Pictures to Sell Cocoa," *Printers' Ink*, 8 July 1920, 49–50; *LHJ*, June 1932, 93; Campbell's Soup ad, *NG*, September 1932; *LHJ*, September 1935, 46; *American*, April 1935, 79; *American*, May 1935, 79; *LHJ*, March 1938, 93.
4. Campbell's Soup ad, List "B" Ad, 17 February 1912, Campbell Archive, Camden.
5. Ibid., *SEP*, 21 September 1912, Campbell Archive, Camden; *SEP*, 16 January 1943, 93.
6. Phyllis Palmer, *Domesticity and Dirt: Housewives and Domestic Servants in the United States, 1920–1945* (Philadelphia: Temple University Press, 1989), 7; *LHJ*, June 1920, 57; *LHJ*, September 1920, 61; *LHJ*, March 1938, 53.
7. Margaret Marsh, *Suburban Lives* (New Brunswick, N.J.: Rutgers University Press, 1990), xiv, 141.
8. Robert L. Griswold, *Fatherhood in America: A History* (New York: Basic Books, 1993), 117, 194, 226–27.
9. Ibid., 117, 194, 226–27.
10. *LHJ*, June 1913, 36; *LHJ*, January 1916, 48; *LHJ*, June 1932, 73; *LHJ*, December 1932, 82; *LHJ*, March 1941, 103.
11. *LHJ*, July 1910, 27; *LHJ*, March 1920, 33; *LHJ*, March 1929, 83; *Collier's*, 25 November 1933, 23; *Life*, 4 January 1943, 26.
12. *LHJ*, March 1929, 244.
13. *LHJ*, May 1915, 54; *LHJ*, June 1944, 49.
14. *LHJ*, December 1912, 30; Upton Sinclair, *The Jungle* (New York: Doubleday, 1906); *LHJ*, June 1914, 62; *LHJ*, December 1917, 31; *SEP*, July 1918, 21; *LHJ*, January 1919, 27; *LHJ*, February 1919, 33.

15. *LHJ*, December 1913, 59; *LHJ*, May 1920, 33; *LHJ*, May 1930, 39.

16. Cream of Wheat, 12 April 1926, Box 5, JWT Archives—Domestic Advertisements Collection; Marilyn Kern-Foxworth, *Aunt Jemima, Uncle Ben, and Rastus: Blacks in Advertising, Yesterday, Today, and Tomorrow* (Westport, Conn.: Praeger, 1994), 45–46; Jan Nederveen Pieterse, *White on Black: Images of Africa and Blacks in Western Popular Culture* (New Haven, Conn.: Yale University Press, 1992), 152–56; No. 88-5773 ad, 1902, Warshaw Collection.

17. *LHJ*, June 1902, 45; *LHJ*, September 1902, back page; *LHJ*, June 1908, 1; *LHJ*, September 1911, 1; *LHJ*, June 1914, 1; *LHJ*, September 1914, back page; *LHJ*, March 1932, 119; *LHJ*, December 1959, 8.

18. *LHJ*, March 1917, 58; *GH*, April 1999, back outside page; Carolyn Wyman, *I'm a Spam Fan: America's Best-Loved Foods* (Stamford, Conn.: Longmeadow Press, 1993), 68–69.

19. Wyman, *I'm a Spam Fan*, 80-81; Ernest Dichter, "A Motivational Research Study on the Personality of Duncan Hines as an Endorser of Cake Mix and Other Products," October 1955, 69, IMR; Emma S. Weigley, "Adventures in Good Eating: Duncan Hines of Kentucky," *Register of the Kentucky Historical Society* 91, 1 (Winter 1999): 27–41.

20. Dichter, "A Motivational Research Study on Duncan Hines," 32, 99–100.

21. *FC*, January 1973, 41; *BHG*, August 1974, 91.

22. *LHJ*, June 1950, 4; *LHJ*, June 1953, 133; *New Yorker*, 15 September 1962; Wyman, *I'm a Spam Fan*, 54–55; Stephen R. Fox, *The Mirror Makers: A History of American Advertising and Its Creators* (New York: William Morrow, 1984), 222.

23. Melvin Helitzer and Carl Heyel, "Youth Market: Are They Mini-Adults or Maxi-Mysteries?" *Marketing/Communications*, December 1970, 55–56.

24. In their study of Italian-American patterns of food use in Philadelphia, Judith Goode, Janet Theophano, and Karen Curtis found that "Husbands hold a particularly powerful place. Their preferences are most often the primary filters for decisions about basic menu structure." "A Framework for the Analysis of Continuity and Change in Shared Sociocultural Rules for Food Use: The Italian-American Pattern," in *Ethnic and Regional Foodways in the United States: The Performance of Group Identity*, ed Linda Keller Brown and Kay Mussell (Knoxville: University of Tennessee Press, 1984), 82.

25. "Mother-and Child Pictures to Sell Cocoa," *Printers' Ink*, 8 July 1920, 49–50; Kraft, *Look*, 10 April 1951, JWT Archives—Domestic Advertisements Collection; Chef Boy-Ar-Dee ad, 1955, JWT Archives—Competitive Advertisements Collection; Kellogg, 1959, JWT Archives—Domestic Advertisements Collection; *FC*, November 1969.

26. *Look*, 5 June 1951; *Look*, 28 August 1951; *LHJ*, December 1977, 86.

27. Newspaper ads, 1939, JWT Archives—Domestic Advertisements Collection.

28. *LHJ*, March 1932, 31.

29. *RD*, April 1957, 202.

30. *Life*, 1 July 1957, 72; *Life*, 16 March 1959, 51.

31. Dichter, "Frosted Foods Need Emotional Defrosting," paper presented to Eastern Frosted Foods Association Meeting, 1962, IMR.

32. *WD*, March 1966.

33. *WD*, May 1966.

34. *LHJ*, May 1966.

35. *Time*, 13 December 1971.

36. C. B. Larrabee, "Women Read Service Copy More Eagerly Than Hot War News," *Printers' Ink*, 2 August 1940, 14–15. A 1958 study, "Father's Influence on

Young Children's Food Preferences," found that, when mothers were "asked if there were any foods she did not serve or served infrequently because her husband did not like them," "Eighty-nine percent acknowledged that this was true." Marian S. Bryan and Miriam E. Lowenberg, *Journal of the American Dietetic Association* 34 (January 1958): 34.

37. *American,* June 1945, 61; *LHJ,* February 1950, 18; *LHJ,* December 1953, 93; *LHJ,* December 1971, 35; *Ebony,* November 1999, 7.

38. *LHJ,* September 1932, 48; *LHJ,* June 1935, 60; *West Virginia News,* 10 January 1957, JWT Archives—Competitive Advertisements Collection.

39. *LHJ,* March 1917, 39; *GH,* October 1944, 106.

40. *LHJ,* March 1935, 112; *WHC,* April 1943, 106; *LHJ,* March 1956, 124; *LHJ,* March 1968, 149; *LHJ,* March 1980, 125; Jessamyn Neuhaus, "The Way to a Man's Heart: Gender Roles, Domestic Ideology, and Cookbooks in the 1950s," *Journal of Social History* 32, 3 (Spring 1999): 538–40.

41. *LHJ,* March 1902, 33; *LHJ,* September 1932, 83; *LHJ,* January 1942, 77.

42. Aunt Jemima, 1917, JWT Archives—Domestic Advertisements Collection; *LHJ,* March 1941, 78; *LHJ,* July 1941, 44; Kellogg's, 1959, JWT Archives—Domestic Advertisements Collection; Campbell's Soup ad, 1945, Campbell Archive, Camden; *LHJ,* March 1992, 157.

43. *LHJ,* March 1947, 141. Several historians and sociologists (American and British) have recognized the historical connection between men's violence against women and food. See for example, Linda Gordon, *Heroes of Their Own Lives: The Politics and History of Family Violence, Boston 1880–1960* (New York: Penguin, 1988), 267–68, 285–88; Nickie Charles and Marion Kerr, *Women, Food, and Families* (Manchester: Manchester University Press, 1988); Rhian Ellis, "The Way to a Man's Heart: Food in the Violent Home," in *The Sociology of Food and Eating: Essays on the Sociological Significance of Food,* ed. Anne Murcott (Aldershot: Gower, 1983), 164–71; Lee Rainwater, Richard P. Coleman, and Gerald Handel, *Workingman's Wife: Her Personality, World, and Life Style* (New York: Oceana, 1959), 173–74.

44. *LHJ,* June 1938, 57; *LHJ,* December 1953, 18; *LHJ,* September 1956, 42. A feature called "One Adman's Opinion" proclaimed "Ad of the month," "appealing," and a "jewel" (*Tide,* 16 July 1955).

45. "French's Potatoes Copy Platform," 21 August 1961, Box 15, Meeting Minutes, 1960–1964, JWT Archives—Review Board Records Collection; R. T. French, "Potatoes," 12 February 1962, Box 15, Meeting Minutes, 1960-1964, JWT Archives—Review Board Records Collection; *LHJ,* March 1977, S1.

46. *LHJ,* December 1929, 79; *LHJ,* June 1935, 79; *LHJ,* April 1944, 45; *LHJ,* June 1947, 189; *LHJ,* January 1953, 20; *LHJ,* June 1962, 19; *LHJ,* September 1962, 93; *FC,* October 1973, 174–75.

47. *LHJ,* June 1929, 138; *LHJ,* February 1951, 96; *Life,* 8 November 1968, 39.

48. *Life,* 9 October 1970; *New Yorker,* 5 December 1970; *Life,* 11 December 1970; *LHJ,* June 1971, 96; *FC,* March 1972; "Man Pleasing Rice Recipes," Box 1970s-6, J Peterson Collection.

49. Jessamyn Neuhaus, "Is Meatloaf for Men?" in *Cooking Lessons: The Politics of Gender and Food,* ed. Sherrie A. Inness (Lanham, Md.: Rowman and Littlefield, 2001), 93–95; Catherine Mackenzie, "When a Man Cooks He Talks About It, Too," *NYT,* 2 January 1938, 110. See also Jessamyn Neuhaus, *Manly Meals and Mom's Home Cooking: Cookbooks and Gender in Modern America* (Baltimore: Johns Hopkins University Press, 2003). Harvey Levenstein noted that men's only culinary responsibility seemed to be to carve the meat women cooked. *Paradox of*

Plenty: A Social History of Eating in Modern America (New York: Oxford University Press, 1993), 104.

50. *St. Louis Post Dispatch*, 16 October 1956, Box 15.8, JWT Archives—Competitive Advertisements Collection; *New Yorker*, 14 September 1957.

51. Ernest Dichter, "Pancakes & Men," *Motivations: Monthly Psychological Research Reports for Business* 1, 12 (February 1957): 2, IMR.

52. Aunt Jemima, 1962, Quaker Oats, Box 6, JWT Archives—Domestic Advertisements Collection; Aunt Jemima, 1981, Quaker Oats, Box 9, JWT Archives—Domestic Advertisements Collection.

53. "Who Eats What, When—and Why," *Tide*, 13 June 1958, 29–30.

54. *LHJ*, May 1953, 10; *LHJ*, June 1956, 161; "Executives' Guide to Marketing for 1965," *Printers' Ink*, n.d., 36; *LHJ*, July 1971, 122; *People*, May 1999, insert from National Pork Producers Council; *People*, 21 June 1999, 101; Thomas Adler, "Making Pancakes on Sunday: The Male Cook in Family Tradition," *Western Folklore* 40, 1 (1981): 46–48; David Bell and Gill Valentine, *Consuming Geographies: We Are Where We Eat* (London: Routledge, 1997), 72–73; Neuhaus, "Is Meatloaf for Men?" 102.

55. Ernest Dichter, "The Great Barbecue and the TV Dinner," c. 1940, IMR.

56. Ibid.; *LHJ*, July 1941, 65; *LHJ*, May 1977, 137; Levenstein, *Paradox of Plenty*, 132; Barbecue Poll, *USA Today*, 10 August 1995, D1.

57. *LHJ*, February 1950, 88; *LHJ*, June 1950, 96; *Life*, 11 July 1955; *GH*, November 1978.

58. Fleischmann's Yeast ad 998, *New England Homestead*, 13 April 1957, JWT Archives—Domestic Advertisements Collection; Fleischmann's Yeast ad 150, *New England Homestead, The Farmer*, 19 October 1957, JWT Archives—Domestic Advertisements Collection,; Fleischmann's Yeast ad 154, *Kansas Farmer*, 19 October 1957, JWT Archives—Domestic Advertisements Collection; Fleischmann's Yeast ad 198, *Missouri Ruralist*, 25 January 1958, JWT Archives—Domestic Advertisements Collection.

59. Fleischmann's Yeast ad 994, *Nebraska Farmer*, 6 April 1957, JWT Archives—Domestic Advertisements Collection; Fleischmann's Yeast ad 200, *California Farmer*, 19 January 1958, JWT Archives—Domestic Advertisements Collection; Fleischmann's Yeast ad 212, *Farm & Ranch*, February 1958, JWT Archives—Domestic Advertisements Collection.

60. *FC*, November 1971, 124.

61. *GH*, November 1978; Pillsbury, 1976, Box 15.34, JWT Archives—Competitive Advertisements Collection.

62. *LHJ*, June 1950, 156; *LHJ*, August 1958, 59; *GH*, December 1967; *Sunset*, May 1970.

63. *This Week*, 16 November 1958, Box 16.9, JWT Archives—Competitive Advertisements Collection; *Parents*, March 1967; *WD*, March 1968; "Consumer Group Surveys TV Ads, Fault 19 of 23," *Washington Post*, 21 October 1980, C1.

64. "French's Mustard: Exploratory Thinking for 1963 Print Advertising," c. 1962, 1–11, Meeting Minutes 1960–1964, Box 15, JWT Archives—Review Board Records Collection; Adler, "Making Pancakes on Sunday," 47.

65. Adler, "Making Pancakes on Sunday, 47"; *LHJ*, September 1977, 47; Kraft, Light 'n' Lively, 1981, Box 10, JWT Archives—Domestic Advertisements Collection.

66. Betty Crocker, 1970, JWT Archives—Competitive Advertisements Collection. Advertisers surely heard claims that men were cooking, such as that made by Professors Mary Lou Roberts and Lawrence H. Wortzel: "The proportion of

husbands who prepare dinner for their families, while small, represents a market segment of significant size." "Husbands Who Prepare Dinner: A Test of Competing Theories of Marital Role Allocations," in *Advances in Consumer Research*, vol. 7, ed. Jerry C. Olson, *Proceedings of the Association for Consumer Research, Tenth Annual Conference, San Francisco, California, October 1979*, 669.

67. While capturing some of the rhetoric of the time, Harvey Levenstein slightly overstated the actual changes that occurred when he claimed about the late 1970s that, "Men were now expected to contribute to housework, and the old idea that home cooking was an exclusively female pursuit became passé. Husbands were no longer confined to the backyard barbecue ghetto, and the kitchen was no longer the mysterious female sanctum sanctorum, where displays of masculine competence were signs of effeminacy" (*Paradox of Plenty*, 226).

68. *WD*, February 1970; *FC*, 14 May 1991, 141. In the last quarter of the century, it became more acceptable and in some ways even fashionable for men to cook. While some men do assume this work on a daily basis, it more commonly occurs when it is a treat, a rare occasion, a specialized dish. Women are frequently expected to supply the ingredients, clean up, and watch and applaud. See for example, *GH*, September 1970, 42–43; "How Shopping at the Reading Terminal Market Works," *Philadelphia Weekly* 10 September 1997, 3.

69. Tracey Deutsch, "Untangling Alliances: Social Tensions Surrounding Independent Grocery Stores and the Rise of Mass Retailing," in *Food Nations: Selling Taste in Consumer Societies*, ed. Warren Belasco and Philip Scranton (New York: Routledge, 2002), 163; *Printers' Ink*, 18 January 1912, 94–95; *Printers' Ink*, July 1918, JWT Archives—Domestic Advertisements Collection.

70. Roland Marchand, *Advertising the American Dream: Making Way for Modernity, 1920–1940* (Berkeley: University of California Press, 1985), 66; *Printers' Ink Monthly*, July 1932, 7; *Printers' Ink Monthly*, August 1932, 5; *Printers' Ink Monthly*, January 1933, 10; *JWT News* 5, 16 January 1950, Box 5.2, JWT Archives—JWT News Collection; *JWT News* 5, 5 June 1950, Box 5.2, JWT Archives—JWT News Collection.

71. *JWT News* 7, 18 February 1952, Box 6.2, JWT Archives—JWT News Collection; Peggy Boomer, "Male Market: Big, Rich, But Tough," *Printers' Ink* 280, 20 July 1962, 22; Ernest Dichter, "Away from Momism . . . ," *Motivations: Monthly Psychological Research Reports for Business* 1, 8 (October 1956): 3–4, IMR; Neuhaus, "The Way to a Man's Heart," 555. In 1963, "According to a recent study of 2,000 supermarkets in the East, 25 per cent of today's cart pushers are men" "Executives' Guide to Marketing for 1965," *Printers' Ink*, n.d., 36.

72. Sara Welles, "A Woman's View," *Printers' Ink*, 3 April 1964, 51; "Executives' Guide to Marketing for 1965," 36.

73. "Executives' Guide," 36.

74. Ernest Dichter, "A Motivational Research Study of Luncheon Meats and Wieners," November 1968, 29, IMR.

75. Mary D. O'Gorman, "Background Research for a Presentation on *The New American*," March 27, 1972, 19, Consumer Pamphlets, File 4/6, Box 20, JWT Archives—Marketing Vertical File Collection; T. J. Wolfe, Senior Vice President, Sales and Marketing, Welch Foods Inc. to Mr. Ralph F. Lewis, Harvard Business Review, 9 May 1978, 1–2, Box 2, Collection 97–202, Bartos Papers.

76. Jo-Ann Zbytniewski, "The Men Who Man the Shopping Carts," *Progressive Grocer* (May 1979): 43–48, 49; Don German, "Men Buy Food and Men Cook, But Most Food Advertisers Are Ignoring Them," *Magazine Age* (March 1980): 46–50.

77. "Women's Libs Fume at 'Insulting' Ads; Ad Gals Are Unruffled," *Advertising Age*, 27 July 1970, 1; "The Role Men Play in Brand Selection of Food Products," 1979 Supermarket Survey, A Research Report from Newsweek, June 1979, Box 14, JWT Archives—Marketing Vertical File Collection; Zbytniewski, "The Men Who Man the Shopping Carts"; *Advertising Age*, 12 January 1981, 44; Alan Rooks, " "The U.S. Hispanic Market: Huge and Growing Rapidly," *Non-Foods Merchandising*, July 1983, 3, 8; Campbell Soup Company and *People Weekly*, "The Male Food Shopper: How Men are Changing Food Shopping in America," 1985, Marketing-Retail-Grocery-Supermarkets/III, Box 12, File 1 of 2, JWT Archives—Marketing Vertical File Collection; *Madison Avenue* 28 (February 1986): 88; *Marketing News* 22, 26 September 1988, 12; Dean D. Duxbury, "Teenage Food Survey," *Food Processing*, June 1989, 28–32; "What Are All Those Men Doing in Grocery Stores?" *Adweek*, 13 July 1992.

78. Don German, "What Kind of Man Reads *Good Housekeeping*," *Magazine Age*, March 1980, 50; Vince Steinman, "A Man, a Can, a Plan," *Men's Health* (June 2000),:96 and pullout.

79. *Marketing and Media Decision* 25 (March 1990): 32–36; *WSJ*, 22 February 1991, B1; Joanne Lipman, "Mr. Mom May Be a Force To Reckon With," *WSJ*, 3 October 1991, B6.

80. "The Shadow of a Man Stands Behind Every Woman Who Buys," *Printers' Ink Monthly*, July 1932, 7; "Review of Objectives for Stouffer's Frozen Food—Cooked Foods, 1959–1960," Stouffer's, c. 1959, JWT Archives—Review Board Records Collection. Responsive Database Services reported that Neilsen Marketing Research found in 1982 that men spent $96 billion a year on food in the United States, which represented more than a quarter of the total food market. Men accounted for "34.5% of edible grocery sales, 34% of dairy sales and 32.1 percent of frozen food sales." Responsive Database Servies, *Business and Industry* 1, 5, 1–3.

81. *LHJ*, March 1947, 156; *LHJ*, July 1947, 13; *LHJ*, April 1950, 181; *LHJ*, June 1950, 15; Del Monte, 1955, JWT Archives—Competitive Advertisements Collection. While not a food advertiser, *Redbook* magazine ran a series of ads in 1932 and 1933 with the slogan, "The Shadow of a Man Stands Behind Every Woman Who Buys." Each ad featured a woman making a purchasing decision, with the shadow of a man (evident by the hat) weighing in on her transaction. At that time a mainstream magazine, trying to reach both women and men, *Redbook* wanted to encourage advertisers to see their dual market as attractive. A January 1933 ad featured a fake product, "Ittsy Bitsies" crackers, and the woman remarked, " 'I think I'll take the other kind . . . My husband likes them better." The copy reminds the reader, "The shadow again. The shadow of a man standing behind the buying wife, influencing the choices she makes in everything from biscuits to refrigerators." *Printers' Ink Monthly*, 10, July 1932, 7; *Printers' Ink Monthly*, August 1932, 5.

82. *LHJ*, April 1950, 181. For a discussion of pipe smoking in advertisements, see Stuart Ewen, *Captains of Consciousness: Advertising and the Social Roots of Consumer Culture* (New York: McGraw-Hill, 1976), 154.

83. Jim Heimann, ed., *All-American Ads of the 1930s* (Koln: Taschen, 2002): 504; Del Monte, 1955, Box 4, JWT Archives—Competitive Advertisements Collection; *WHC*, October 1955, 54; *LHJ*, September 1962, 81; Del Monte, 1963, Box 8.37, JWT Archives—Competitive Advertisements Collection; *Life*, 8 November 1968, 39; E. I. DuPont de Nemours, *Packaging & People* 15.3, Hagley, Accession 2168, Box 1.8, 6–7. The cowboy consistently reappeared in food advertising. A *WSJ*

article appearing 5 July 1977 described a new approach by advertisers. The lead story, "Advertisers Take Aim at a Neglected Market: The Working Woman," reported on a new ad campaign, "'At first it was strange comin' home to the range, but I've got a working wife,' warbles the young husband on the Campbell's soup commercial. Declaring that 'the last thing she needs tonight is cookin', he proceeds to rustle up a soup-and-sandwich meal just in time for his wife's homecoming from the office" (1, 5). The lingo employed suggests that this husband was not a sissy or henpecked, but was a take-control cowboy who could heat up a can of soup with the best of 'em. For a discussion of the popularity of cowboy television programs and the masculinity of cowboys, see Steven D. Stark, *Glued to the Set: The 60 Television Shows and Events That Made Us Who We Are Today* (New York: Free Press, 1997), 62–68.

84. Post Cereal, 1957, Box 16.2, JWT Archives—Competitive Advertisements Collection; *LHJ*, January 1960, 74; Charlotte Montgomery, "The Woman's Viewpoint: Do Men in Markets Influence Food Buying?" *Tide*, 26 February 1955, 34.

Chapter 5. Health, Beauty, and Sexuality: A Woman's Responsibility

1. Michael Schudson, *Advertising, the Uneasy Persuasion: Its Dubious Impact on American Society* (New York: Basic Books, 1984), 162; "At Last Some News About Cancer You Can Live With," Kellogg's, 1984, Box 2, JWT Archives—Domestic Advertisements Collection; *LHJ*, March 1989, 166.

2. "Keep on the Sunny Side of Life: A New Way of Living" (Battle Creek, Mich.: Kellogg Company, 1933); Harvey Levenstein, *Revolution at the Table: The Transformation of the American Diet* (Berkeley: University of California Press, 2003), 33–34.

3. *LHJ*, March 1902, 42; *LHJ*, March 1942, 68; *LHJ*, 22 June 1942, 4; *LHJ*, September 1942, 171.

4. *Los Angeles Times*, 9 June 1955, JWT Archives—Competitive Advertisements Collection.

5. *RD*, January 1959, 167; *RD*, March 1959, 247; *RD*, March 1962, 54; *RD*, July 1965, 195; *RD*, January 1976, 41; *RD*, January 1982, 17; *RD*, February 1982, 166.

6. *LHJ*, March 1920, 74; *JWT News Letter* 61, January 1925, JWT Archives—News Letter Collection—Main Series; *LHJ*, September 1929, 86–87; *GH*, April 1933, 103; C. P. Russell, "Advertising in New Fields When the Initial Market Grows Smaller," *Printers' Ink*, 22 April 1920, 3–12; Roland Marchand, *Advertising the American Dream: Making Way for Modernity, 1920–1940* (Berkeley: University of California Press, 1985), 16–17.

7. Rima Apple, *Vitamania: Vitamins in American Culture* (New Brunswick, N.J.: Rutgers University Press, 1996); Catherine Manton, *Fed Up: Women and Food in America* (Westport, Conn.: Bergin and Garvey, 1999), 51–52; Levenstein, *Revolution at the Table*, 148–53; Harvey Levenstein, *Paradox of Plenty: A Social History of Eating in Modern America* (New York: Oxford University Press, 1993), 13; "Grape-Nuts Plan," 1923, Postum Cereal, Box 15, 1–4, JWT Archives—Account Files Collection; *JWT News Letter* 30, 5 June 1924, Box 2, JWT Archives—News Letter Collection.

8. *LHJ*, September 1902, 36.

9. *LHJ*, February 1916, 71; *LHJ*, March 1916, 89; *LHJ*, January 1939, 31; *LHJ*, January 1951, 61; Ernest Dichter, "Inter-Office Memo: Memo on Soup," 23 March 1960, 9, IMR, 9; "Chicken Soup Really Is Good Medicine," *Cleveland Plain*

Dealer, 4 November 2000, 1A; "Reinventing a Declining Campbell's Soup," 23 January 2003, http://www.iagresearch.com/ne_012903.jsp.

10. *LHJ*, December 1950, 209; *WHC*, November 1955, 68; *RD*, February 1960, 207; *RD*, March 1960, 166; *RD*, April 1960, 255; Competitive Advertisements, Box 12.10, 1960, JWT Archives—Competitive Advertisements Collection; *Good Housekeeping*, February, March, April 1961, Box 16, JWT Archives—Competitive Advertisements Collection.

11. Leigh Crosby, "Tests Women Apply When They Buy Things, *Printers' Ink Monthly*, May 1933, 1, 14–15, 49; Dichter, "Increasing the Sale of Ovaltine: Report of a Motivational Study," for Wander Company, Chicago, June 1957, 49–52, IMR.

12. James H. Collins, "Food Is No Longer Vittels—It Has Become Millinery," *Printers' Ink Monthly*, September 1927, 39; John Dough and Donald A. Laird, "The Health Appeal Is Being Overworked," *Printers' Ink Monthly*, June 1929, 38–39; "*Must* We Have Meals from the Medicine Chest," *Printers' Ink Monthly*, March 1934, 23–24; Luis Diaz-Albertini, "Brand-Loyal Hispanics Need Good Reason for Switching," *Advertising Age*, 16 April 1979, S22; Nancy Millman, "General Foods Raps Kellogg Ad," *Chicago Sun-Times*, 11 June 1985, 57.

13. James Wade, "The Seventies: A Marketing View," 1 February 1971, 16, JWT Archives—Account Files, Standard Brands Collection.

14. *LHJ*, January 1903, 49.

15. *LHJ*, June 1911, 44; *LHJ*, September 1926, 61.

16. Otto Klepner, *Advertising Procedure* (1925; New York: Garland, 1985), 67.

17. Fleischmann's Yeast, Spring 1932, Reel 49, JWT Archives—Microfilm Collection.

18. *GH*, April 1933, 161.

19. *LHJ*, June 1911, 70; *LHJ*, May 1950, 197.

20. *Delineator*, August 1931, 48; Kraft Miracle Whip, 1938 and 1945, JWT Archives—Competitive Advertisements Collection; *LHJ*, March 1941, 103; *LHJ*, June 1941, 7.

21. *LHJ*, October 1972; *Sunset*, October 1972, 145; *LHJ*, December 1974, 14–15. Competitive Advertisements, 1967, Box 16.2, JWT Archives—Competitive Advertisements Collection

22. *LHJ*, September 1941, 109; Sara Welles, "A Woman's View: That Male Waistline," *Printers' Ink*, 22 March 1963. 39; *GH*, March, May, July 1967, Box 16.2, JWT Archives—Competitive Advertisements Collection; *LHJ*, March 1977, 153d. For cultural pressure, see also Claudia H. Deutsch, "Photography Companies Try a New Approach," *NYT*, 20 July 2004.

23. *GH*, December 1942, 9; *GH*, September 1942, 9; *GH*, September 1942, 101; *LHJ*, November 1942, 107; Kraft, 1943, JWT Archives—Domestic Advertisements Collection; *SEP*, 30 January 1943, 44; *GH*, July 1944, 15; *LHJ*, December 1944, 59.

24. *RD*, May 1959, 222; Levenstein, *Paradox of Plenty*, 196, 199; Anastasia Toufexis, "Cookies the Heart Can Love," *Time*, 23 January 1989. See also Ralph Lee Smith, *The Health Hucksters* (New York: Thomas Crowell, 1960). Smith explored the 1957 discovery of cholesterol and advertisers' manipulation of it in his chapter "Advertising and Your Heart" (67–81).

25. *GH*, December 1966, 3; *GH*, July 1970, 3; *RD*, January 1976, 148.

26. *Sunset*, July 1978, 162; *BHG*, July 1978, Box 17.1, JWT Archives—Competitive Advertisements Collection; *LHJ*, March 1980, 172.

27. *LHJ*, March 1902, 2; *McCall's*, September 1924, 28; *LHJ*, June 1959, 78. Images of beauty consistently portrayed thin women, in spite of the occasional popularity of fuller figures. For a discussion of body type popularity, see historian

Lois Banner, *American Beauty* (Chicago: University of Chicago Press, 1983), 128–29, 151, 187, 203, 287–88. While acknowledging competing ideals, she asserted that thinness was the dominant ideal in the twentieth century. Jackson Lears also found that the turn-of-the-century drive for efficiency and personal control encouraged the embrace of a slim ideal body type. He claimed that in the nineteenth century doctors cautioned about the dangers of obesity and by the twentieth century "Fat became unfashionable." *Fables of Abundance: A Cultural History of Advertising in America* (New York: Basic Books, 1994), 165–69. Marchand asserted that "For the male copywriter or illustrator, the mirror served to epitomize women's supposedly unrivaled addiction to vanity; for a woman, it served as a reminder of an inescapable 'duty' beyond that of efficient homemaking—the duty 'to catch and hold the springtime of her beauty' " (*Advertising the American Dream*, 176–77).

28. *LHJ*, May 1908, 85; Kellogg Company, "Keep the Sunny Side of Life," 18–21; *Life*, 21 April 1961, 65; *Life*, 11 June 1965, 21; Richard Ohmann, *Selling Culture: Magazines, Markets, and Class at the Turn of the Century* (New York: Verso, 1996), 202.

29. *LHJ*, September 1921, 27; *LHJ*, September 1941, 33. Store displays and cereal boxes frequently employed this type of advertising. Scott Bruce, *Cereal Box Bonanza: The 1950s: Identification and Values* (Paducah, Ky.: Collector Books, 1995) provides plentiful examples of this phenomenon.

30. *LHJ*, December 1911, 91.

31. *LHJ*, March 1926, 65; *Delineator*, August 1931, 56; *LHJ*, April 1950, 128; *Seventeen*, October 1958, 102; *NYTM*, 25 June 1978, Box 16.32, JWT Archives—Competitive Advertisements Collection; Vincent Vinikas, *Soft Soap, Hard Sell: American Hygiene in an Age of Advertisement* (Ames: Iowa State University Press, 1992), 33–42.

32. *LHJ*, July 1941, 105; Joan Jacobs Brumberg, *The Body Project: An Intimate History of American Girls* (New York: Random House, 1997). Marchand explained the early attention to young girls' beauty, "If a woman's life was to be simply a never-ending 'Beauty Contest,' it only made sense to train for the competition early" (*Advertising the American Dream*, 178–79).

33. *LHJ*, July 1947, 6; *LHJ*, September 1947, 179; *LHJ*, November 1947, 144; Brumberg, *Body Project*, 99, 125–27.

34. *LHJ*, March 1932, 44; Kellogg, "Keep on the Sunny Side."

35. Brumberg, *Body Project*, 59–94; Russell, "Advertising in New Fields," 8–12; Fleischmann's Yeast, Spring 1932, Reel 49, JWT Archives—Microfilm Collection; *LHJ*, December 1935, 48.

36. Kathy Peiss, *Hope in a Jar: The Making of America's Beauty Culture* (New York: Metropolitan Books, 1998), 245; *GH*, December 1944, 79.

37. *LHJ*, November 1947, 247.

38. *Life*, 8 June 1942, 56; *GH*, October 1944, 136; *LHJ*, November 1947, 10; *LHJ*, April 1957, 23.

39. *LHJ*, May 1946, 7; *LHJ*, July 1947, 98; Brumberg, *Body Project*, 108–18.

40. *LHJ*, March 1959, 133; *LHJ*, December 1970, 89; *LHJ*, March 1977, 113; Carolyn Wyman, *I'm a Spam Fan: America's Best Loved Foods* (Stamford, Conn.: Longmeadow Press, 1993), 133–34.

41. Stephanie Thompson, "Marketers Feed into Needs with Female-Targeted Lines," *Advertising Age* 71, 45, 30 October 2000, 16–17; Marianne Sullivan, "Food Marketers Pitch 'Strong Women' Products," *Women's enews*, 19 February 2005.

42. Levenstein, *Paradox of Plenty*, viii, 9–11, 36, 134–36, 239–44; Jesse Berrett,

"Feeding the Organization Man: Diet and Masculinity in Postwar America," *Journal of Social History* 30, 4 (Summer 1997): 810.

43. *JWT News*, 2, 35, 1 September 1947, JWT Archives—JWT News Collection; *LHJ*, February 1950, 117; *RD*, September 1955, 14; *RD*, December 1955, 9; Nickie Charles and Marion Kerr, "Food for Feminist Thought," *Sociological Review* 34, 3 (August 1986): 537–72; "The 'Better for You' Market Can Be Better Than You Think," *Consumer Response*, April 1983, 1–6, JWT Archives—Information Center Records Collection. Advertisers were particularly interested in reaching women as consumers for their diet products. The role of the visual media in shaping the relationship between food and women's bodies underwent intense scrutiny in the late twentieth century. Concerned especially with women's unhealthy attitudes and actions toward food, historians, sociologists, anthropologists, and medical doctors studied and wrote about the personal, social, and cultural factors that helped shape women's eating patterns. One of the first to call attention to representations of women in advertising was sociologist Erving Goffman. His *Gender Advertisements* (1976; New York: Harper Colophon, 1979) remains a classic for his original, insightful analysis of gendered images found in advertisements. Goffman's critique of the messages bombarding society challenged their inevitability, both in form and in content, and provided a framework to make sense of them. Building on Goffman's observations, fellow sociologist Diane Barthel examined gender and advertising in the late 1980s in her book, *Putting on Appearances: Gender and Advertising* (Philadelphia: Temple University Press, 1988). She was critical of advertising, not for existing per se, but because, "taken as a whole (it) comprises a 'privileged discourse.' What is wrong is not its presence, but rather the increasingly felt absence of any competing set of cultural messages and values." She argued that in spite of new ideas being entertained by society, especially those drawn from the feminist movement, advertisers continued to manipulate women's low self-esteem and falsely promised food products as the means to achieve beauty, power, and success (186, 139–50).

44. *LHJ*, March 1932, 88.

45. Kellogg's, "Keep the Sunny Side of Life," 25–31.

46. *LHJ*, October 1940, 63; *LHJ*, December 1940, 145; *LHJ*, June 1941, 145; *WHC*, November 1946. In a history of the Gardner Advertising Agency, Beatrice Adams reflected on the cultural phenomenon Ry-Krisp became, with people publicly chastising overweight people with the "Someone ought to tell her about Ry-Krisp" line, as during a 1940 Christmas parade when a cowgirl appeared and an onlooker shouted it out to her. *Let's Not Mince Any Bones: An Admittedly Unorthodox History of Gardner Advertising Company's First Sixty-Five Years* (n.p..: Western Publishing Company, 1972), 86–87.

47. *LHJ*, April 1943, 48.

48. *LHJ*, May 1946, 191; *LHJ*, June 1946, 184; *LHJ*, March 1947, 251; *LHJ*, June 1947, 192; *LHJ*, July 1947, 155; "Ry-Krisp," 1951, 1950s-9, Peterson Collection; "Women in Advertising," *Printers' Ink*, 14 June 1963, 316–19.

49. *LHJ*, July 1941, 95; *LHJ*, March 1950, 185; *JWT News* 9, 1 February 1954, JWT Archives—JWT News Collection; *RD*, September 1955, 14; *Seventeen*, October 1958, 128; *GH*, January 1966, 43; *RD*, March 1966; Oscar Mayer, 1986, Box 4, JWT Archives—Competitive Advertisements Collection. For a thoughtful analysis of women's relationship with food, see philosopher Susan Bordo's work, including "Hunger as Ideology," in *The Consumer Society Reader*, ed. Juliet B. Schor and Douglas B. Holt (New York: New Press, 2000) and *Unbearable Weight: Feminism, Western Culture, and the Body* (Berkeley: University of California Press, 1993).

50. Competitive Advertisements, 1966, Box 20.32, JWT Archives—Competitive Advertisements Collection; *Seventeen*, January 1967, April 1967, July 1968, Box 16.1, JWT Archives—Competitive Advertisements Collection; *Seventeen*, April 1969, 192–95. To sell their products, advertisers frequently suggested a dichotomy between what women and men ate. See, for example, Burger King, 1983, Box 1, JWT Archives—Domestic Advertisements Collection,; *LHJ*, June 1992, 71.

51. Ernest Dichter, "A Motivational Research Study on Present and Future Psychological Trends in Cereals," for General Mills, October 1955, IMR; *LHJ*, March 1986, 171; *LHJ*, September 1986, 135; Dichter, "A Psychological Research Study of the Effectiveness of Current Packaged White Bread Advertising," A Cooperative Study by the Staff of the IMR, c. 1955, 24, IMR; *LHJ*, October 1967, 145; *LHJ*, September 1968, 126j; *RD*, May 1970, A5; *LHJ*, March 1983, R-6. The Roman Meal Bread Company made their product into a diet staple and published a 1956 cookbook called "Diet Plan" that featured a woman dressed only in a brief towel atop a scale (1950s-9, JWT Archives - Nicole DiBona Peterson Collection).

52. Ernest Dichter, "Tentative Blueprint for Action: A Proposed New Goal—De-Zerta Model 1959: A Super-Jello," May 1958, 1–3, IMR; Dichter, "Phase I: A Motivational Research Study of the Marketing, Sales, and Advertising Problems of D-Zerta," for General Foods, May 1958, 10–17, IMR; *RD*, April 1970, 194c; Charles and Kerr, "Food for Feminist Thought," 537–72. One example of cereal manufacturers' efforts to combat a negative association appeared in a March 1997 issue of *Mademoiselle*, targeted to young women. Titled, "The Good Fast Food," the article (106) examined the nutritious qualities of cereal and assured women, "cereal isn't fattening."

53. *LHJ*, July 1964, 18; *LHJ*, March 1965, 61; *GH*, January 1966, 43; *RD*, April 1970, 178; *RD*, July 1970, 28; *LHJ*, March 1983, 124, R-6; Quaker Oats, 1986, 1987, and 1988–89, Box 10, JWT Archives—Domestic Advertisements Collection.

54. *LHJ*, July 1964, 69; *LHJ*, June 1965, 49; *LHJ*, July 1971, 60; *LHJ*, July 1971, 71; *BHG*, July 1974, 78; *BHG*, September 1974, 72.

55. Dannon Yogurt, 1966, Box 20.32, JWT Archives—Competitive Advertisements Collection.

56. *McCall's*, May 1964, 25; *LHJ*, July 1964, 18; *LHJ*, September 1964, 70–71; *LHJ*, March 1965, 61; *LHJ*, July 1967, 24; *GH*, December 1969, Box 17, JWT Archives—Competitive Advertisements Collection; *RD*, April 1970, 178; *RD*, May 1970, 187; *RD*, June 1970, 47; *RD*, July 1970, 28; *LHJ*, July 1971, 107.

57. Louis Calta, "New Magazine Aims to Help the Overweight," *NYT*, 18 January 1968, B36; *Say Yes to Less Cookbook*, 1980s-7, JWT Archives—Nicole DiBona Peterson Collection; *Swans Down Breakthrough Baking: Classic Cakes That Cut the Calories*, 1980s-3, Peterson Collection.

58. *RD*, February 1981, Quaker Oats, Box 9, JWT Archives—Domestic Advertisements Collection; Aunt Jemima, Quaker Oats, 1982, Box 9, JWT Archives—Domestic Advertisements Collection; *RD*, March 1983, 164; *LHJ*, March 1983, 143; *LHJ*, December 1983, 135; Oscar Mayer, 1988, Box 4, JWT Archives—Domestic Advertisements Collection; *LHJ*, September 1992, 225; *LHJ*, June 1995, 73, 161.

59. *LHJ*, January 1982, 176; *Weight Watchers*, January/February 1997, 108, 110, 112; *Weight Watchers*, March/April 1997, 23, 123, 125.

60. Vanessa O'Connell, "Nabisco Portrays Cookies as Boost to Women's Sense of Self-Esteem," *Wall Street Journal*, 10 July 1988, 1.

61. *LHJ*, January 1961, 27; *LHJ*, September 1968, 63; *LHJ*, August 1970, 101; *LHJ*, March 1983, 5.

62. Kellogg's, 1983, Box 2, JWT Archives—Domestic Advertisements Collection; *LHJ*, March 1986, 13; David Goodman, "Special K Drops Thin Models for Health Theme," *Marketing News* 32, 5, 2 March 1998, 8; Vanessa O'Connell, "Nabisco Portrays Cookies as Boost to Women's Sense of Self-Esteem," *WSJ*, 10 July 1988, B2; Melanie Wells, "Special K Ads Liked, But Sales Down," *USA Today*, 2 November 1998, 12B.

63. *LHJ*, January 1961, 27; *LHJ*, September 1968, 63; *LHJ*, August 1970, 101. In the early twenty-first century, Special K introduced "Kay" in its on-line advertising. An animated woman who guided women in their "get-fit journey," she assured women that she was their friend and spouted supportive sayings, like "I believe in you." Trying to capitalize on the success of the online version of Weight Watchers, Kellogg's used a svelte animated model to send its positive message to women, thereby accomplishing two goals—reinforcing its products' role in weight loss and supporting women's self-esteem (http://www.specialk.com/brand/sk_kay/kay.shtml).

64. *LHJ*, September 1920, 67; Libby's, Miscellaneous L, 1970, Box 1, JWT Archives—Domestic Advertisements Collection; *LHJ*, December 1980, 155. See, for example, Peiss, *Hope in a Jar*; Vinikas, *Soft Soap, Hard Sell*; Paul Messaris, *Visual Persuasion: The Role of Images in Advertising* (Thousand Oaks, Calif.: Sage, 1997), 48; Roland Barthes, "Toward a Psychosociology of Contemporary Food Consumption," in *Food and Culture: A Reader*, ed. Carole Counihan and Penny Van Esterik (New York: Routledge, 1997), 24–25. Historian Jennifer Scanlon argued that "What has turned into one of the major controversies in advertising—women as sex objects—was developed by a woman who most likely saw the recognition of women's sexuality as a step forward in an advertising world that had primarily portrayed women as asexual wives and mothers. *Inarticulate Longings: The Ladies' Home Journal, Gender, and the Promises of Consumer Culture* (New York: Routledge, 1995), 176. See also Thomas W. Whipple, "The Existence and Effectiveness of Sexual Content in Advertising," in *Advertising and Popular Culture: Studies in Variety and Versatility*, ed. Sammy R. Danna (Bowling Green, Ohio: Bowling Green State University Press, 1992), 134–40; Alice E. Courtney and Thomas W. Whipple, *Sex Stereotyping in Advertising* (Lexington, Mass.: Lexington Books, 1983), 104–5.

65. Jackson Lears quoted in Schudson, *Advertising, The Uneasy Persuasion*, 55–60.

66. *LHJ*, March 1938, 5, 120; Kraft ad, 1947, in author's possession; *LHJ*, January 1950, 93; Scott Bruce, *Cereal Box Bonanza: The 1950s: Identification and Values* (Paducah, Ky.: Collector Books, 1995), 30, 63; *LHJ*, May 1950, 194; Information Center Records, Box 1, JWT Archives—Information Center Records Collection; *GH*, December 1969, Box 17.16, JWT Archives—Competitive Advertisements Collection; *FC*, September 1973, 155; Warren J. Belasco, *Appetite for Change: How the Counterculture Took on the Food Industry, 1966–1988* (New York: Pantheon, 1989), 156; *Parade Magazine*, 1 February 1998, 8.

67. *American*, July 1940, 97; *American*, August 1940, 95; *American*, September 1940, 69; *LHJ*, September 1944, 57.

68. *LHJ*, May 1946, 187.

69. *LHJ*, December 1947, 71; *Seventeen*, September 1958, 165.

70. *Seventeen*, November 1958, 117; *NYTM*, 24 December 1961, Box 15.20, JWT Archives—Competitive Advertisements Collection; *GH*, October 1964, 43; *Seventeen*, April 1969, 202; *McCall's*, May 1970, Box 12.40, JWT Archives - Competitive Advertisements Collection.

71. *Seventeen*, February 1967, 177.

72. Competitive Advertisements, 1966, Box 22.1, JWT Archives—Competitive Advertisements Collection; *Seventeen,* March 1967, 171; *Seventeen,* May 1967, 185; *Seventeen,* February 1969, 170; *Seventeen,* April 1969, 202; *Seventeen,* August 1969, 341.

73. Ernest Dichter, "The Psychology of the Modern Woman in Relation to Cooking and Homemaking," for Young and Rubicam and General Foods Corporation, 5 May 1952, IMR; Dichter, "The Modern Woman," October 1955, IMR; Dichter, "Memorandum on the Changing Role of the American Woman," for Lever Brothers Company, February 1964, IMR.

74. Dichter, "Memorandum." This brings to mind the memorable campaign for Enjoli perfume, which set the standard for modern women: "I can bring home the bacon, fry it up in the pan, and never, ever let you forget you're a man." Marianne Sullivan, "Food Marketers Pitch 'Strong Women' Products," Women's enews, January 5, 2004 (http://www.womensenews.org/article.cfm/dyn/aid/1664/context/archive).

75. "The Sexy Sell," *Newsweek,* 29 April 1968, 58; Ernest Dichter, "Creative Research Memo on the Sex of Rice," for Leo Burnett Co., IMR; "The Sex and Character of Food," *Motivations: The Monthly Newsletter of Psychological Research for Business* 1, 2 (April 1956): 4, IMR; "Sexy Approach Aims to Sell More Rice, Baby," *Advertising Age,* 29 September 1969, 52; "Rice: Low-Calorie Menus and Recipes, Box 1970s-6, Peterson Collection; James R. Shortridge and Barbara G. Shortridge, "Patterns of American Rice Consumption 1955 and 1980," in *The Taste of American Place: A Reader on Regional and Ethnic Foods,* ed. Barbara G. Shortridge and James R. Shortridge (Lanham, Md.: Rowman and Littlefield, 1998), 95. In contrast to this sexualized appeal, the Southern Rice Growers Association put out a cookbook in the 1910s titled *How to Cook Rice,* 1910s-3, Peterson Collection.

76. *FC,* November 1966; *FC,* December 1966.

77. *Sunset,* February 1970; *RD,* April 1970, 145.

78. "Sexy Approach Aims to Sell More Rice, Baby," *Advertising Age,* 29 September 1969, 52; *Life,* 30 1970, 19; *Life,* 3 April 1970, 51; *Life,* 24 April 1970, 22; *Life,* 15 May 1970, 67; *Life,* 17 July 1970, 36; *LHJ,* October 1970, 143; *Life,* November 1970, 60R; *Life,* December 1970, 108; *FC,* January 1972, 124; *Seventeen,* February 1973, Box 16.18, JWT Archives—Competitive Advertisements Collection.

79. *GH,* April 1999, back page.

80. *LHJ,* September 1980, S15; *LHJ,* March 1983, 124; *LHJ,* June 1989, 163; *LHJ,* March 1992, 76–77, 137; *LHJ,* June 1992, 35; *LHJ,* September 1992, 59; Christopher Cooper, "Uncle Ben's New Ad Campaign Seeks to Steam Up the TV Screen," *WSJ,* 28 August 1998, B5; *GH,* April 1999, back page; *LHJ,* April 2001, 55; email from Belle Frank to Katherine Parkin, 1 August 2002; Abigail Klingbeil, "Groupe DANONE's The Dannon Co. tries to regain Yogurt King title," Journal News.com, http://www.nyjournalnews.com/newsroom/012703/d0127danone.html.

81. Harvey Levenstein reports in *Paradox of Plenty* that a March 1977 Labor Department survey found that "the concept of a family in which 'the husband is the only breadwinner and the wife is a homemaker out of the labor force and there are children' now applied to only seven out of every hundred households" (232–33).

82. *Farm Journal,* October 1970, 51, Box 12.14, JWT Archives—Competitive Advertisements Collection; *GH,* November 1970, Box 12.15, JWT Archives—Competitive Advertisements Collection; Courtney and Whipple, *Sex Stereotyping in Advertising.*

83. *JWT Trends*, 19 January 1976, JWT Archives—JWT Trends Collection; *Motivations: Monthly Psychological Research Reports for Business*, 1, 8 (October 1956): 3–4, IMR; Michael Lev, "Bomb Factory's Specialty: Trendy Pizza with Hint of Sex," *NYT*, 12 July 1991, D16.

Chapter 6. A Mother's Love: Children and Food Advertising

1. Frank Presbrey, *The History and Development of Advertising* (New York: Greenwood Press, 1968), 387, *JWT News*, 15, 7.3, 13 February 1950, Box 5, JWT Archives—JWT News Collection.

2. *LHJ*, December 1917, 31; *LHJ*, April 1921, 27; *SEP*, 11 April 1931, 29; *LHJ*, November 1931, 31; *LHJ*, March 1942, 100.

3. John Allen Murphy, "How to Frame an Appeal for Mr. and Mrs. Average," *Printers' Ink*, 29 April 1926, 41–44.

4. *McCall's*, March 1930; *LHJ*, September 1932, 92.

5. *LHJ*, March 1902, 37; *LHJ*, March 1905, 47; *LHJ*, September 1905, 31; *LHJ*, November 1905, 64; *LHJ*, September 1908, 42; *LHJ*, December 1911, 72; *LHJ*, March 1932, 72; *LHJ*, March 1935, 97; *Life*, 9 June 1942, 45.

6. *LHJ*, September 1911, 64.

7. *LHJ*, March 1914, 54.

8. *LHJ*, March 1914, 71; *McCall's*, September 1924, 43; *LHJ*, February 1932, 25; Jim Heimann, ed., *All-American Ads of the 1930s* (Koln,: Taschen, 2002), 510. Reinforcing their advertisers' message and the need to turn to their periodical, a 1918 *Today's Housewife* ad claimed, "In 1907, 144 babies of every 1000 died in New York City. In 1917, only 88 babies of every 1000 died. New York City now has the lowest infant death rate of any large city. This unparalleled achievement is due to Dr. S. Josephine Baker, Chief of the Bureau of Child Hygiene. . . . Her monthly department in our Homemakers Bureau is *another reason* why over 600,000 women carefully read *Today's Housewife*" (*Printers' Ink*, 5 December 1918, 93). While the alarmist element declined after the Great Depression, children's health continued to be a theme in food ads throughout the century.

9. *LHJ*, March 1929, 160; *LHJ*, March 1932, 103; *LHJ*, June 1932, 81; *WHC*, July 1932, 64; *WHC*, September 1932, 61; *GH*, April 1933, 110; *WHC*, August 1934, inside cover, 43, 53, back page; *LHJ*, December 1935, 92; *LHJ*, June 1938, back cover; *American*, July 1940, 69; *LHJ*, January 1942, 67. For the history of eugenics in the United States, see Edwin Black, *War Against the Weak: Eugenics and America's Campaign to Create a Master Race* (New York: Four Walls Eight Windows, 2003).

10. *Delineator*, August 1931, 3, 59; *LHJ*, March 1932, 119; *WHC*, July 1932, 69; *LHJ*, September 1932, 51; 1933 Cream of Wheat ads, Misc. C, Box 1, JWT Archives—Domestic Advertisements Collection.

11. 1933 Cream of Wheat ads; *LHJ*, June 1920, 83; *LHJ*, September 1920, 50; *LHJ*, March 1938, 86; *LHJ*, March 1941, 74.

12. Emphasis theirs. *LHJ*, September 1935, 90; Stuart Ewen, *Captains of Consciousness: Advertising and the Social Roots of the Consumer Culture* (New York: McGraw-Hill, 1976), 173.

13. *LHJ*, March 1941, 105.

14. *American*, September 1940, 67; *LHJ*, March 1942, 43.

15. Elaine Tyler May, *Homeward Bound: American Families in the Cold War Era* (New York: Basic Books, 1988), 146–48. All these examples appear in *Homeward Bound*.

16. Emphasis theirs. *LHJ*, February 1950, 87; *LHJ*, March 1950, 129; *LHJ*, May 1950, 113; Harvey Levenstein, *Paradox of Plenty: A Social History of Eating in Modern America* (New York: Oxford University Press, 1993), 153; Catherine Manton, *Fed Up: Women and Food in America* (Westport: Conn.: Bergin & Garvey, 1999), 51–52.

17. Cream of Wheat, Box 5, 12 April 1926, JWT Archives—JWT Account Files Collection; Ernest Dichter, "The Comparative Effectiveness of a Rice and Wheat Chex Advertisement," submitted to Ralston Purina Company, June 1954, IMR; *LHJ*, September 1992, 207; *Ebony*, May 2000, 118.

18. *GH*, February 1966, 185; *LHJ*, February 1997, 131.

19. *This Week*, 10 November 1957, Box 16.9, JWT Archives—Competitive Advertisements Collection; Campbell's ad, *Parents*, March 1967, JWT Archives—Competitive Advertisements Collection; *GH*, February 1970, 36; *GH*, March 1970, 46; *GH*, April 1970, 83; *WD*, November 1970, Box 13.37, JWT Archives—Competitive Advertisements Collection; Gerber, Box 1, 1980, JWT Archives—Domestic Advertisements Collection.

20. Rita C. Hubbard, "Male Parent Images in Advertising," in *Advertising and Popular Culture: Studies in Variety and Versatility*, ed. Sammy R. Danna (Bowling Green, Oh.: Bowling Green State University Popular Press, 1992), 141–45.

21. Joseph C. Corn, "Making Flying 'Thinkable': Women Pilots and the Selling of Aviation, 1927–1940," *American Quarterly* 31, 4 (Autumn 1979): 556–71.

22. Hardees, 1978, DMB Archives; Burger King, 1976–1981, JWT Archives—Domestic Advertisements Collection; McDonald's, AT88:099, AT88:097, AT32270, AT88104, AT88:102, AT88:114, Museum of Television and Radio, New York; *People*, 3 April 2000, 165; *Ebony*, May 2000, 107.

23. *BHG*, August 1977, Oscar Mayer, Box 2, JWT Archives—Domestic Advertisements Collection; *Ebony*, May 1980, Burger King, 1976–1981, JWT Archives—Domestic Advertisements Collection; *Ebony*, March 1981, Burger King, 1976–1981, JWT Archives—Domestic Advertisements Collection.

24. *McCall's*, September 1924, 38; Cream of Wheat, Misc. C, 1927, Box 1, JWT Archives—Domestic Advertisements Collection; Kellogg's, 1959, JWT Archives—Domestic Advertisements Collection; *FC*, April 1970, Box 13.18, JWT Archives—Competitive Advertisements Collection; Ewen, *Captains of Consciousness*, 144–45.

25. *LHJ*, September 1902, 29; *LHJ*, October 1910, 27; *LHJ*, June 1911, 42; *Delineator*, August 1931, 43.

26. *LHJ*, October 1919, 35; Cream of Wheat, Misc. C, 1927, Box 1, JWT Archives—Domestic Advertisements Collection, y.

27. *LHJ*, 15 May 1911, 1; *LHJ*, September 1911, 85; *LHJ*, September 1916, 33; *LHJ*, February 1920, 33; *LHJ*, October 1920, 33; "Half of the Four Million" in author's possession, n.d.; *LHJ*, September 1923, 63; Cream of Wheat, Misc. C, 1925, Box 1, JWT Archives—Domestic Advertisements Collection; *LHJ*, March 1926, inside cover; *SEP*, 19 September 1937, 126; *LHJ*, July 1938, 31; Black, *War Against the Weak*; T. J. Jackson Lears, *No Place of Grace: Antimodernism and the Transformation of American Culture, 1880–1920* (Chicago: University of Chicago Press, 1981), 30; Edward M. Coffman, *The War to End All Wars: The American Military Experience in World War I* (1968; Lexington: University Press of Kentucky, 1986), 59–61.

28. *LHJ*, June 1911, 42; *LHJ*, September 1911, 84.

29. *LHJ*, October 1946, 57; *LHJ*, September 1948, 73; *LHJ*, September 1950, 69; *Life*, 20 September 1954, inside cover; *LHJ*, September 1992, 127; *GH*, December 1993, 225; *GH*, October 1997, 133.

30. *LHJ*, April 1917, 29; *LHJ*, June 1917, 31.

31. *GH*, July 1957; *Look*, 9 July 1957.

32. *LHJ*, September 1920, 162; *LHJ*, November 1933, 33; *LHJ*, April 1935, 39.

33. *LHJ*, June 1917, 31; *Life*, 20 September 1954, 159; *GH*, February 1966, 167; *LHJ*, September 1971, 180; *LHJ*, March 1989, 183; *Ebony*, August 1999, 24; *People*, 4 September 2000, 14.

34. *LHJ*, September 1902, back page; *LHJ*, September 1917, 40; *LHJ*, December 1947; *RD*, December 1955, 193; Kellogg's, c. 1960s, Box 8.52, JWT Archives—Competitive Advertisements Collection; *GH*, March 1970, SE246a; Daniel Delis Hill, *Advertising to the American Woman, 1900–1999* (Columbus: Ohio State University Press, 2002), 280–81.

35. *LHJ*, March 1938, 71; *LHJ*, December 1944, 122; *LHJ*, July 1947, 73; *GH*, August 1966, 115.

36. *LHJ*, September 1917, 35; *LHJ*, December 1917, 55, 87; *SEP*, 28 April 1945, Swift & Co., Box 1, JWT Archives—Domestic Advertisements Collection; *LHJ*, January 1961, 9. Miriam Formanek-Brunell found that playing with dolls was not always girls' primary activity. Very popular in the nineteenth century, in the first two decades of the twentieth century it declined significantly. In fact, she found that one 1918 survey reported that playing with dolls had dropped to eighth place in popularity. *Made to Play House: Dolls and the Commercialization of American Girlhood, 1830–1930* (New Haven, Conn.: Yale University Press, 1993), 165–68.

37. Emphasis theirs. *LHJ*, March 1950, 185; *FC*, November 1972, 53; *GH*, October 1997, 141.

38. *NYTM*, 5 February 1956, 64. Historian Helen Damon-Moore discovered that by the late nineteenth century women's magazines had already stepped in to help facilitate food preparation because there was already a decline in the number of girls learning these tasks at home at their mother's elbow. Noted in Nancy Walker, *Shaping Our Mothers' World: American Women's Magazines* (Jackson: University Press of Mississippi, 2000), 23.

39. *LHJ*, September 1917, 38; *LHJ*, September 1917, 43; *Parents*, June 1945; *Life*, 25 February 1966; *LHJ*, December 1977.

40. *McCall's*, September 1924, 30; *American*, October 1945, 73; *GH*, October 1970.

41. *LHJ*, September 1926, 145; *LHJ*, May 1951, 152; *Seventeen*, October 1962, 142; *Seventeen*, November 1962, 162; *Seventeen*, January 1963, 6; *LHJ*, 1967.

42. *Seventeen*, March 1967, 171; *Seventeen*, May 1967, 185; *Seventeen*, January 1969, 100–101; *Seventeen*, February 1969, 170; *Seventeen*, April 1969, 203; *Seventeen*, August 1969, 341.

43. *FC*, August 1970, 23; Jell-O pudding commercial, F/X Channel, 8 May 2000. This Jell-O ad, produced by Young & Rubicam, was awarded a "bad" award by the Advertising Women of New York Good, the Bad, and the Ugly Awards in 2000, which were sponsored in part by *Maxim* magazine. Explaining their decision to embrace a men's magazine with a "reputation as the leader of the 'beer and babes' category," spokesperson Cindy Gallop claimed, "It has an enormous sense of humor." Stuart Elliott, "Advertising," *NYT*, 25 September 2000, C19.

44. *LHJ*, September 1926, 64; *GH*, June 1940, 7, 135; *LHJ*, June 1950, 96; *Life*, 27 July 1962, 83; *FC*, January 1973, 41; *LHJ*, March 1983, 141.

45. *LHJ*, August 1922, 25; *LHJ*, June 1947, 193; *Parents*, July 1966.

46. *LHJ*, June 1926, 137; *LHJ*, September 1926, 64; *LHJ*, September 1947, 73; Swift & Co., Box 2, JWT Archives—Domestic Advertisements Collection; *LHJ*, September 1953, 173; Scott Bruce, *Cereal Box Bonanza: The 1950s: Identification*

and Values (Paducah, Ky.: Collector Books, 1995), 60, 173; *Life*, 13 April 1962; *Life*, 11 May 1962; *GH*, June 1966, 150, 201; *GH*, December 1966, 3; *LHJ*, December 1970, 33; *LHJ*, May 1977, 138.

47. *Life*, 1 June 1959; *RD*, March 1960, 166; *GH*, September 1966, 141; *Parents*, October 1966.

48. *Parents*, October 1966; *LHJ*, November 1933, 33; *GH*, December 1944, 122; *LHJ*, October 1951, 73; Bruce, *Cereal Box Bonanza*, 158; *Life*, 7 May 1965; *Life*, 11 June 1965; *Life*, 10 September 1965; *LHJ*, November 1966; *LHJ*, October 1970, 133;

49. Jim Heimann, ed., *All-American Ads of the 1930s* (Koln: Taschen, 2002), 524–25; *LHJ*, January 1943, 63; *JWT News*, 13 February 1950, 3, 15(7), Box 5, JWT Archives—JWT News Collection, Duke University; *LHJ*, March 1953, 142; *LHJ*, September 1977, 61; *LHJ*, March 1980, R1.

50. *LHJ*, March 1915, 57; *LHJ*, March 1953, 122; *LHJ*, July 1971, 49; *LHJ*, December 1980, 144d.

51. Emphasis theirs. *LHJ*, September 1944, 150; *GH*, December 1944, 13; *Look*, 10 April 1951, Kraft, JWT Archives—Domestic Advertisements Collection; *LHJ*, March 1953, 122; *LHJ*, May 1953, 144; Bruce, *Cereal Box Bonanza*, 139; Kellogg's, 1960, JWT Archives—Domestic Advertisements Collection; *Life*, June 1961, Kellogg's, Box 16, JWT Archives—Competitive Advertisements Collection; *LHJ*, July 1971, 49; *LHJ*, December 1980, 144d.

52. *Printers' Ink*, 7 September 1911, 42. Emphasis theirs.

53. *Printers' Ink*, 7 September 1911, 40.

54. Paul Findlay, "'Aunt Jemima' Back Among the Big Advertisers Again," *Printers' Ink*, 17 August 1916, 96; *Printers' Ink*, 19 June 1919, 93; "Who Is Going to Tell Her?" (d for George Batten Company) (Advertising), *Printers' Ink*, 5 May 1921, 49–52; Margaret A. Bartlett, "A Mother Tells of the Advertising That Appeals to Her Children," *Printers' Ink*, 17 November 1922, 129–32. For coloring books as entry into children's subconscious, see Carleton Dyer, "Sugar-Coated Sales Capsules for Toddling Tots," *Printers' Ink*, 26 May, 1927, 134–41 and "My-T-Fine for the Children," activity book, n.d. (company began 1918). Advertisers commonly used fairy tale imagery and cartoonish characters to target children. A 1921 *Printers' Ink* article details the Chapin-Sacks Corporation's use of "Mother Goose" and "Alice in Wonderland" to promote their Velvet Kind Ice Cream, 18 August 1921, 33–34, 36. See also Jell-O's campaigns in the 1920s and 1950s that employed children's nursery rhymes to promote products. The debate over children's sophistication raged as the century wore on, with Martin Helitzer, president of Helitzer, Waring & Wayne, noting that "Children today see so much advertising that they have developed a high degree of sophistication and have grown as hostile to hard sell ads as their parents." Eugene Gilbert also argued that "children even in the 5-to-7 age range exhibit a high degree of sophistication. 'Our studies indicate that a child can be easily as skeptical as its parent when it comes to advertising'." Peter Bart, "Advertising: A Case of Who's Boss at Home," *NYT*, 29 July 1963, 29. Reformers sought to limit the amount and kinds of advertising permitted during children's programming, but consistently faced opposition and stonewalling. In 1974 the *NYT* reported that even a 'moderate' young TV "viewer sees "more than 25,000 commercials a year." One influential reformer, Robert B. Choate, Chairman of the Council on Children, Media, and Merchandising, argued before a Senate Commerce Committee in 1974 that "in motivational research houses across the country, children are being used in laboratory situations to formulate, analyze, polish, compare, and act in advertisements

designed to make other children salesmen in the home." Robert Berkvist, "Can TV Keep Giving Kids the Business?" *NYT*, 12 May 1974, 105.

55. *Printers' Ink*, 9 September 1920, 57–58, 60. This is not to suggest that advertisers generally stopped valuing teenage boys as consumers. Eugene Gilbert, for example, did extensive research on boys' buying habits. However, the focus of food advertisers, in spite of the evidence that boys did shop and cook, shifted almost entirely to teenage girls. For evidence of advertisers' attention to male consumers, see for example, "Monthly Poll Set of Buying Habits for Younger Men," *NYT*, 2 January 1960, 19; Myron Kandel, "Teen-Ager Courted as a Big Consumer," *NYT* 20 May 1962, F1; Barbara P. Johnson, "The New Youth Market: Fewer Teens . . . More Dollars," *Product Management* (June 1976): 29, Markets-Consumer-Teenage, 1 of 2, Box 20, JWT Archives—Marketing Vertical File Collection; "Teens Big Grocery Shoppers and Fast Food Lovers," *Arizona Grocer*, March 1984, Markets-Consumer-Teenage, 1 of 2, Box 20, JWT Archives—Marketing Vertical File Collection.

56. Paula S. Fass and Mary Ann Mason, *Childhood in America* (New York: New York University Press, 2000); Thomas Hine, *The Rise and Fall of the American Teenager* (New York: Bard Books, 1999); Steven Mintz and Susan Kellogg, *Domestic Revolutions: A Social History of American Family Life* (New York: Free Press, 1988); Lears, "Some Version of Fantasy," 390; Jennifer Scanlon, *Inarticulate Longings: The Ladies' Home Journal, Gender, and the Promises of Consumer Culture* (New York: Routledge, 1995), 46; Grace Palladino, *Teenagers: An American History* (New York: Basic Books, 1996); Samantha Yates, "Girls With Influence: Selling Consumerism to Teenage Girls, 1930–1960" (Ph.D. dissertation, University of California, Davis, 2001); Mark Clements Research, "Food Survey 1978" for *American Girl*, Box 20, JWT Archives—Marketing Vertical File Collection.

57. *Life With Teena, A Seventeen Magazine Survey of Teen-Age Girls and Their Mothers Conducted and Compiled June-August, 1946*, vol. 2 (Princeton, N.J.: Opinion Research Corporation, 1947), Estelle Ellis Collection, Box 18, Folder 3, Smithsonian Institution. As Elaine Tyler May considers in *Homeward Bound*, 119, and Beth Bailey notes in *From Front Porch to Back Seat: Courtship in Twentieth-Century America* (Baltimore: Johns Hopkins University Press, 1988), 49, the postwar period accelerated the early practice of "play marriages," with Bailey noting that as early as twelve young people embraced this ideal. While sexuality was largely the focus of both studies, it follows that girls would similarly mimic homemaking skills and begin to prepare for their married lives, coming up faster than ever before.

58. "Like Salmon to the Sea," *Printers' Ink*, 12 March 1948, 80–81; "Youth Market Held Neglected," *NYT*, 15 February 1951, 47; Eugene Gilbert, *Advertising and Marketing to Young People* (Pleasantville, N.Y.: Printers' Ink Books, 1957); "Cleveland's Ambitious Vernon Stouffer: Putting the Heat on Frozen Foods," *Printers' Ink* 21, November 1958, 51–53; Joan Cook, "Teen-Age Fashions Represent a Major Business Today," *NYT*, 6 July 1959, 30; Patricia Sellers, "The ABC's of Marketing to Kids," *Fortune*, 8 May 1989, Seventeen Magazine File, Box 4, Bartos Papers; Palladino, *Teenagers*, 109–11.

59. *Printers' Ink*, 2, April 1943, 43; Mary McCabe English, "How to Stay *Seventeen* and Keep Growing," *Advertising Age*, 2 August 1982, M27-M28; *The Seventeen Cookbook: With a Complete Guide to Teen Party-giving* (New York: Macmillan, 1964); Ellen McCracken, *Decoding Women's Magazines from Mademoiselle to Ms.* (New York: St. Martin's, 1993), 143–47; Philip H. Dougherty, "Advertising: Forming Habits at Seventeen," *NYT*, 25 October 1979, D19. Other girls' magazines, such as *American Girl*, also sought out food advertisers by producing studies documenting their

readers' food habits. See, for example, Mark Clements Research, "Food Survey 1978" for *American Girl*, Box 20, JWT Archives—Marketing Vertical File Collection. According to Palladino, "Since *Seventeen* published at least three food columns a month, grocery executives had good reason to appeal to teenage customers" (*Teenagers*, 107). Susan J. Douglas's study of postwar era girls' culture also contended that advertisers stood to profit from the distinct market segmentation of teenage girls. Noted in Walker, *Shaping Our Mothers' World*, 23.

60. Werner cited in Charles and Bonnie Remsberg, "Wooing the 'Dimply, Pimply,'" *NYT*, 5 June 1966, 291. The Remsbergs reported that in 1966 Rand forecasters estimated that by 1970 teenage spending would reach $30 billion. In 1979 *WSJ* reported that in 1978 teenage spending had reached a record $32.2 billion, 24 May 1979, Teenagers, File 1 of 2, Box 20, JWT Archives—Marketing Vertical File Collection.

61. *The Seventeen Cookbook*, 268–69, back cover. This was not just the strategy of teen magazines, as *McCall's* in 1959 featured an article by Dorothy Chaun Lee called "It's a Date," that suggested teenage girls invite Dreamboat over for dinner: "A girl with an eye on a guy should show off her skill at the stove." Jessamyn Neuhaus, "Is Meatloaf for Men?" in *Cooking Lessons: The Politics of Gender and Food*, ed. Sherrie A. Inness (Lanham, Md.: Rowman and Littlefield, 2001), 103.

62. "Milk Canners Aim Marketing at Teen-agers," *Printers' Ink*, 21 November 1958, 58–59; Levenstein, *Paradox of Plenty*, 15–16; *Printers' Ink Monthly*, November 1932, 41; Penelope Orth, "Teenager: What Kind of Consumer?" *Printers' Ink*, 20 September 1963, 67–71.

63. "Seventeen-at-School Key Teaching Aids," *Seventeen-at-School*, October 1965, 10–11; "How to Set a Modern, Man-Pleasing Table," *Seventeen-at-School*, February 1967, 10–11; "Homemaking Educator in Business: Sally Watters of the Continental Baking Company," *Seventeen-at-School*, February 1966, 9; "Homemaking Educator in Business: At the J. Walter Thompson Company, San Francisco," *Seventeen-at-School*, September 1967, 9; "Classrooms in Your Community: Supermarkets Help Teens Become Super-Shoppers," *Seventeen-at-School*, October 1967, 1–8; Laura Shapiro, *Something from the Oven*, 80.

64. "Reaching the Rich Teenage Market," *Printers' Ink*, 16 October 1964, 31–32.

65. Ernest Dichter, "What's the Age of Your Customer: Part 3," IMR; Charlotte Montgomery, "The Woman's Viewpoint," *Tide*, 12 March 1955, 34; *National 4-H News*, June 1963, Standard Brands, Box 12, JWT Archives—Domestic Advertisements Collection, Duke University; *National 4-H News*, October 1964, Standard Brands, Box 12, JWT Archives—Domestic Advertisements Collection; English, "How to Stay *Seventeen* and Keep Growing," M27; Youth Research Institute, "1988 Rand Youth Poll," Teens, Box 6, 9–17, Bartos Papers; Fall 1988 TRU Survey, Teens, Box 6, 17–41, Bartos Papers.

66. Dichter, "What's the Age of Your Customer: Part 3."

67. Ad Aide Warns on Teen Buying," *NYT*, 2 May 1958, 33.

68. Robert Alden, "Advertising: Youthful Critics Confronted," *NYT*, 30 November 1960, 60.

69. "'Mother Influences Much Teen Buying,'" *American Druggist*, 7 June 1965, 67.

70. Quoted in Melvin Helitzer and Carl Heyel, "'Your Market' Are They Mini-adults or Maxi-mysteries?" *Marketing/Communications*, December 1970, 54.

71. Ernest Dichter, *Motivating Human Behavior* (New York: McGraw-Hill, 1971), 87–101; Barbara P. Johnson, "The New Youth Market: Fewer Teens . . . More Dollars," *Product Management* (June 1976): 29.

72. Rand Youth Poll, 1986, Teenage Pamphlets, File 3 of 4, Box 20, JWT Archives—Marketing Vertical File Collection.

73. Ellen Graham, "Children's Hour: As Kids Gain Power of Purse, Marketing Takes Aim at Them," *NYT*, 19 January 1988, 1.

74. Mary D. O'Gorman, "Background Research for a Presentation on *The New American*," 27 March 1972, 19, Consumer Pamphlets, File 4 of 6, Box 20, JWT Archives—Marketing Vertical File Collection; "Working Mom's Daughter Is Researchers' Newest Find," *Ad Age*, 25 February 1974, Teens, File 1 of 2, Box 20, JWT Archives—Marketing Vertical File Collection; "Teen Girls Spend $17 Billion on Food," *Supermarketing*, January 1978, Teens, File 1 of 2, Box 20, JWT Archives—Marketing Vertical File Collection; *American Girl* Food Survey, 1978, Conducted by Mark Clements Research, Teenage Pamphlets, File 3 of 4, Box 20, JWT Archives—Marketing Vertical File Collection; Ellen Graham, "Children's Hour: As Kids Gain Power of Purse, Marketing Takes Aim at Them: Double-Career Parents Yield Many Spending Decisions to Tykes 'Born to Shop'—Far Beyond Toys and Candy," *WSJ*, 19 January 1988, 1.

75. "The Truth About Teens: Facts Behind Twenty Common Myths," *Youth Markets Alert*, July 1989, 3, Teenage Pamphlets, Folder 3 of 4, Box 20, JWT Archives—Marketing Vertical File Collection.

76. Fleischmann's Yeast, 1979, Standard Brands, Box 13, JWT Archives—Domestic Advertisements Collection; John Koten, "Teen-Age Girls, Alas, Are Big Consumers, But Poor Customers," *WSJ*, 9 November 1984, 1, 24; Phyllis Fine, "The Teen Market: A $70 B Opportunity," *Food and Beverage Marketing*, April 1987, 22, 24; Graham, "Children's Hour," 1; Trish Hall, "Teen-Agers Invade the Kitchen; Not Even Shopping Is Safe," *WSJ*, 20 April 1988, Teens, Box 6, Bartos Papers; Oscar Mayer, 1989, c; Sellers, "The ABC's of Marketing to Kids"; Dean Duxbury, "Teenage Food Survey: More Teens Shop for Family, Spend Food $$$," *Food Processing* (June 1989): 28–32.

77. Koten, "Teen-Age Girls, 1, 24.

78. Ibid.; Schudson, *Advertising, The Uneasy Persuasion*, 54. Writing about the early decades of *LHJ*, Scanlon found that "While the *Journal* was perhaps never as blatant on the subject of romance as were best-selling novels, the appeal to the sexual imagination of young women formed an aspect of the magazine that permeated not only the fiction, but also the advertisements, and, occasionally, the advice" (*Inarticulate Longings*, 29). In an article on "Insulting" ads, Don Grant quoted Lucy Komisar, a free lance writer and a National Organization of Women national vice president, as saying, "Advertisers trade in sex as if it were listed on the stock exchange." "Women's Libs Fume at 'Insulting' Ads; Ad Gals Are Unruffled," *Advertising Age*, 27 July 1970, 28.

79. Ibid.; Schudson, *Advertising, The Uneasy Persuasion*, 54–60; *LHJ*, March 1935, 112; *Life*, 8 June 1942, 4; *Seventeen*, September 1947; *American Girl*, November 1947; *Seventeen*, January 1948.

80. Oscar Mayer, Box 2, 1978, JWT Archives—Domestic Advertisements Collection; 1966 ads, Box 22.1, JWT Archives—Domestic Advertisements Collection; *Seventeen*, February 1967, 177; *Seventeen*, March 1967, 171; *Seventeen*, May 1967, 185; *Seventeen*, February 1969, 170; *Seventeen*, April 1969, 202; *Seventeen*, August 1969, 341. Arguably, advertisers also targeted younger children in this way as well. A 1987 article on targeting teens and the growing awareness of the tween market gave the example of a television commercial targeted at tweens, which featured "a young girl talking to an imaginary older boy. She informs him that, while he may not notice her now, she's drinking milk and will grow up to be someone special." Fine, "The Teen Market: A $70 B Opportunity," 22, 24.

81. Renee Blakkan, "To Know 'What's Cooking,' Ask a Teen Ager," *Advertising Age*, 54, 32, 1 August 1983, M1-M2; Koten, "Teen-Age Girls," 1, 24; Hall, "Teen-Agers Invade the Kitchen"; Sellers, "The ABC's of Marketing to Kids"; "If Both Parents Are Breadwinners, Teenagers Often Are the Bread Buyers," *Marketing News* 21, 4 (13 February 1987): 5; Selina S. Guber, "The Teenage Mind," *American Demographics* 9, 8 (August 1987): 42–44; Duxbury, "Teenage Food Survey," 29; Marjorie Wold, "Are Kids Really Shopping Your Store?" *Progressive Grocer* 70, 5, May 1991, 197–98; Leah Rickard, "Teens Taking on More Family Shopping," *Advertising Age* 65, 38, 12 September 1994, 44.

82. Duxbury, "Teenage Food Survey," 29 ; "The Truth About Teens: Facts Behind Twenty Common Myths," *Youth Markets Alert*, July 1989, 3, Teenage pamphlets, File 3 of 4, Box 20, JWT Archives—Marketing Vertical File Collection.

Epilogue

1. Kathleen Deveny, "Grappling with Women's Evolving Roles," *WSJ*, 5 September 1990, B1; Philip H. Dougherty, "Advertising; Social Analysis from Good Housekeeping," *NYT*, 11 August 1988, D18; http://www.aflcio.org/yourjobeconomy/women/factsaboutworkingwomen.cfm?RenderForPrint=1. Undoubtedly contributing to the industry's conservatism, most of the industry's decision-makers operated from a position of relative wealth, and their elevated economic class shaped their experiences with things like luxury foods and domestic servants. Strong economic standing also allowed most advertisers to live in sophisticated urban settings or posh suburban ones, literally putting them at a remove from the middle-class consumers with whom they sought to communicate. See for example, Nancy Walker, *Shaping Our Mothers' World: American Women's Magazines* (Jackson: University Press of Mississippi, 2000), x-xi.

2. Reva Korda, "The New Ethnic Creatives: Look Where the Longing Is," *Marketing/Communications*, March 1971, 29; Peter Cannellos, "Why Can't Blacks Talk to Whites," *Back Stage Magazine* Supplement, 9 March 1984, 7M-9M; Fonda Marie Lloyd and Cassandra Hayes, "25 Years of Blacks in Advertising," *Black Enterprise* 25, 6 (January 1995): 91–92; Stuart Elliott, "Caroline Jones, 59, Founder of Black-Run Ad Companies," *NYT*, 8 July 2001, 28; John W. Templeton, "Ad Spending Slights Black Consumers," *Advertising Age*, 68, 11, 17 March 1997, 28; Ellen Byron, "Founder of UniWorld Prospers by Serving Underserved Market," *WSJ*, 3 March 2004, 1. Admittedly, American society generally only began openly to accept homosexuality in the last quarter of the century, but it is consistent with their general conservatism that instead of reflecting the societal changes taking place in the country, advertisers have been reluctant to employ, acknowledge, or target homosexuals, particularly in public roles. The industry maintained, just as they did with women in positions of influence, that clients were too conservative to have homosexual executives handle their accounts. *NYT* advertising columnist Stuart Elliott noted in 2000 that, "An informal survey finds don't ask, don't tell is still observed on Madison Avenue." Stuart Elliott, "Advertising," *NYT*, 30 June 1997, D12; Stuart Elliott, "Advertising," *NYT*, 26 June 2000, C16; http://www.commercialcloset.org/cgi-bin/iowa/portrayals.html?record=326).

3. Jennifer Scanlon, *Inarticulate Longings: The Ladies' Home Journal, Gender, and the Promises of Consumer Culture* (New York: Routledge, 1995); email correspondence, Anne Wallach to author, 30 June 2004; Kathy Peiss, "American Women and the Making of Modern Consumer Culture," *Journal for MultiMedia History* 1, 1 (Fall 1998); Stuart Elliott, "From One Woman to Another, Ogilvy & Mather Is

Making History," *NYT*, 9 September 1996, D7; Stuart Elliott, "Advertising," *NYT*, 9 March 1999, C8.

4. Lynn J. Jaffe and Paul D. Berger, "The Effect of Modern Female Sex Role Portrayal on Advertising Effectiveness," *Journal of Advertising Research* 34, 4 (July/August 1994): 33. As Arlie Hochschild demonstrated in her landmark study, *The Second Shift*, in addition to working outside the home, almost all women continued to be responsible for unpaid housework, such as shopping, cooking, and cleaning (New York: Avon Books, 1989). In 1985, according to John P. Robinson and Geoffrey Godbey, women still put in an average of nearly twice as many hours a week than the men (30.9 versus 15.7 hours) doing childcare, housework, or shopping. Indeed, in 1985 women still did at least 40 percent more of the shopping in America than men, much as in 1965. Moreover, researchers found that the 16 hours men put into housework in 1985 remained the same effort they made at the end of the twentieth century.[4] Reinforcing these trends, food advertisers consistently chose to pitch ads to women exclusively. See for example, Jody Heymann, *The Widening Gap: Why America's Working Families Are in Jeopardy and What Can Be Done About It* (New York: Basic Books, 2000), 99–105; John P. Robinson and Geoffrey Godbey, *Time for Life: The Surprising Ways Americans Use Their Time* (University Park: Pennsylvania State University Press, 1997), 97-10; *Hochschild, The Time Bind: When Work Becomes Home and Home Becomes Work* (New York: Metropolitan Books, 1997); "U.S. Husbands Are Doing More Housework While Wives Are Doing Less," University of Michigan, http://www.umich.edu/~newsinfo/Releases/2002/Mar02/r031202a.html.

Index

Acknowledgments

I am grateful to have the opportunity to thank publicly the many people and institutions who have helped me write this book. It has been a rewarding process, enriched by sharing it with others.

From the beginning, I benefited from the sage advice of Margaret Marsh, who has always modeled her professionalism and kindness, and been a tremendous advisor to me. I am grateful to Kathy Peiss, Allen F. Davis, and Herbert Ershkowitz for their thoughtful comments on my work. I would like to thank Temple University and its History Department for its support of my work with assistantships and grants.

I was also fortunate to gain financial support at the Rare Book, Manuscript, and Special Collections Library at Duke University in Durham, North Carolina, where Ellen Gartrell and Jacqueline Reid both served as knowledgeable guides to their collections. And Hedy Dichter kindly opened up her home in Peekskill, New York, which holds the archive of her late husband, Ernest Dichter.

Entrusting this book to Robert Lockhart at the University of Pennsylvania Press has been one of the best decisions I have ever made. Thoughtful, respectful, and supportive, he, along with Eleanor Goldberg and Alison Anderson, have made the production experience a pleasurable one. The responses of Jennifer Scanlon and my other anonymous reader improved this book immeasurably, and I deeply appreciate their suggestions and support for the book.

At Monmouth University I have found wonderful colleagues, and I am grateful to the members of the History and Anthropology Department, especially Brian Greenberg, Rich Veit, Fred McKitrick, Karen Schmelzkopf, Julius Adekunle, Ken Campbell, Matthew O'Brien, Maureen Dorment, Susan Douglass, Frank Dooley, Kathy Smith-Wenning, Bill Mitchell, Mustafa Aksakal, Stan Greenberg, Tom Pearson, and Chris DeRosa. My undergraduate and graduate students, too, have been wonderful supporters. In particular, I would like to thank Lindsay Currie,

Gina Isaacs, and Andrea Pierce. Jim Reme, the university photographer, assembled pictures for the book, and Linda "No Problem" Silverstein placed the world at my fingertips, acquiring hundreds of studies, magazines, and books. This work was supported, in part, by a grant-in-aid-for-creativity award from Monmouth University.

To my dear friends who helped make this book possible, I am so grateful. Robin Levine, Celia Feinstein, Lillian Pelios, George Katsikas, Alexandra Friedrich, Shelia Thomas Northington, your kindnesses have been so appreciated. Special thanks go to wonderful friends who also read the manuscript: Arlene Eskilson, Samantha Yates Francois, Yvette Lane, and Frank Hoeber. Julie Berebitsky, your sharp insights and deep love and knowledge strengthened this work and made my life and this book better. Nancy Banks, you have been there for me for the last twenty years as my best friend, and it would take another book to explain all the ways that you are important to me; I am so grateful.

My mother, Marilyn Parkin, along with my brother, Ernest Parkin, has been a terrific supporter. Mom, your bravery and strength have always inspired me. Joe and Esther DeRosa have been incredible in-laws and grandparents. Along with Ben and Jon DeRosa and Amelia Etrie, your help and support has been so generous—thank you. My amazing daughters Vivian and Quinn have filled each day with love and laughter, I love you both so much. Finally, my husband, Chris DeRosa. You have given me such a beautiful life. Not many people are fortunate enough to find the person of their dreams and then get to share every aspect of their lives with them, raising children, writing books, teaching at the same university, and pursuing a social, political, and intellectual life filled with such fine friends. With you, I am that lucky and all that we have imagined has come true. Thank you for believing in me and this book.